D1645050

FATHER FABER

FREDERICK WILLIAM FABER
About 1840

FATHER FABER

by

RONALD CHAPMAN

LONDON

BURNS & OATES

MADE AND PRINTED IN GREAT BRITAIN BY
HAZELL WATSON AND VINEY LTD
AYLESBURY AND SLOUGH FOR
BURNS AND OATES LIMITED
28 ASHLEY PLACE, LONDON, S.W.I

Nihil obstat: Andreas Moore, L.C.L., Censor deputatus; Imprimatur: E. Morrogh Bernard,
Vicarius Generalis, Westmonasterii: die iv Octobris MCMLX. The Nihil obstat and
Imprimatur are a declaration that a book or pamphlet is considered to be free from
doctrinal or moral error. It is not implied that those who have granted the Nihil obstat
and Imprimatur agree with the contents, opinions or statements expressed

FOR
V.J.M.

CONTENTS

ILLUSTRATIONS

PREFACE

I AM deeply grateful to the Superior and Fathers of the London Oratory for handing over to me all the material about Faber in their archives. I must apologize for the time they have had to wait for the book, but the delay was not due to idleness. The Superior and Fathers of the Birmingham Oratory have kindly allowed me to examine and to quote from their archives. I am very grateful to Father Dessain for his hospitality. Father V. J. Matthews has inspired, encouraged and helped me from start to finish. I wish I knew how to thank him. My father-in-law, Mr E. I. Watkin, has painstakingly read each chapter as it was written and made numerous extremely helpful criticisms. I am very grateful to Miss Helen Palmer for invaluable help in rearranging and shortening the MS., to Mrs Magdalen Goffin, and to Father P. Bushell for preventing several blunders.

The opinions expressed are my own. They do not represent the views of the London or Birmingham Fathers either individually or collectively. Faber was in his life a controversial figure. Now after a hundred years he remains so, especially in his relations with that great man John Henry Newman. My object has been, so far as it is possible, to arrive at the truth by letting the documents speak for themselves. Inevitably the book contains controversial matter but I hope it will not be difficult to separate fact from opinion. In this way I hope the book may be a contribution to that most neglected subject, the post-Reformation Church in England. It may also be useful in the study of Newman.

I wish also to thank for their kindness in helping me Father Vincent Blehl, S. J., Mr Paul Brydson, Miss N. I. Clay, Miss Helen Darbishire, Sir Geoffrey Faber, Mr T. H. Faber, Mr Ronald Jenkinson, Rev. G. G. Lane, Mr J. B. Oldham, Sir Richard Proby, Bt., Mr E. V. Quinn, Mr F. G. Roberts, Mrs D. B. Seckersen, Mr Bruce Thompson and Miss A. L. Wyatt.

NOTES

I have given chapter and verse for every quotation but the references have been reduced to a minimum and relegated to the end of the book. The references contain dates sometimes not in the text. The Bibliography will make the references intelligible. The index sometimes contains information not in the text.

ACKNOWLEDGMENTS

I wish to thank the following publishers for permission to quote excerpts from various books:

Robert Hale Ltd.: *Durham*, by Sir T. Eden.

William Blackwood & Sons: *Lord John Manners and his Friends*, by C. Whibley.

J. M. Dent & Sons: *H. C. Robinson on Books and their Writers*, ed. by E. J. Morley; *Essays and Addresses on the Philosophy of Religion*, by F. von Hügel.

Oxford University Press: *Correspondence of H. C. Robinson with the Wordsworth Circle*, ed. by E. H. Morley; *Letters of William and Dorothy Wordsworth, the Later Years*, ed. by E. De Selincourt.

Longmans, Green & Co.: B. Ward: *The Sequel to Catholic Emancipation*; W. Ward: *Life of J. H. Cardinal Newman*, 4th ed.; *W. G. Ward and the Catholic Revival* (reissue).

CHAPTER I

BEGINNINGS

FREDERICK WILLIAM FABER was born on the 28th June 1814, in the vicarage of his grandfather at Calverley, Yorkshire. The Fabers were a rising but not distinguished family. Distinction was to come later. They were self-reliant, self-confident, capable, moderately well-to-do; Yorkshiremen to the core. The vicar of Calverley, who had graduated from St John's, Cambridge, as 14th Wrangler in 1753, was the son of a Leeds business man.

As became a family rising in the social scale there was a family story, concerned with the vicar of Calverley's second wife, which was at once romantic, an inspiration and socially satisfying. It also accorded well with the commercial backcloth against which the family found itself. This is the story as it appears in the family Bible:

At the revocation of the Edict of Nantes in the year 1685, M. de Dibon was arrested by order of Louis XIV, and on his firm refusal to abandon the religion of his ancestors, his whole property was confiscated, and he himself thrown into prison.

Before the arrival of the dragoons at his residence, he had time sufficient to bury this, his family Bible, within a chest in his garden. Here he left it, in hopes of some day recovering what he esteemed his best treasure.

While in confinement he was frequently tortured by the application of fire to wreaths of straw which were fastened round his legs: but through the grace of God, he was enabled to persevere in making a good confession. This particular torture was specially resorted to in consequence of his being a sufferer from the gout.

He at length effected his escape; but ere he quitted his native land for ever, he had the resolution to re-visit the estate of his forefathers, now no longer his, for the purpose of recovering his Bible. This he accomplished; and with the word of God in his hand, an impoverished exile, he finally reached England in the reign of William III of glorious memory.[1]

Henri de Dibon's grand-daughter married the vicar of Snape and her daughter married the vicar of Calverley, and was Frederick William's grandmother. Religion and religious controversy surrounded Frederick William from the beginning.

There was not, therefore, much French blood in Frederick Faber and to describe the Faber family as of Huguenot origin is an exaggeration.[2] Nevertheless the Huguenot story played an important part in the family *ethos*. The Fabers prospered from the time of the vicar of Calverley's marriage and a young Faber was expected to show himself, in the words of the family Bible, "the faithful descendant of a faithful ancestry". *Faith of our fathers*, written later in such unlikely circumstances, was surely an echo of the Huguenot story.

The vicarage at Calverley had been the scene of the birth of another Faber forty-one years before. This was Frederick's uncle, George Stanley Faber, the redoubtable theologian and pamphleteer. His outlook may be gauged by the titles of some of his works: *A Dissertation on the Prophecies relative to the Great Period of 1,200 years, the Papal and Mohamedan Apostasies, the reign of Antichrist and the Restoration of the Jews*, 2 vols., 1807; *Remarks on the Fifth Apocalyptic Vial and the Restoration of the Imperial Government of France*, 1815; *The Difficulties of Romanism*, 1826; *The Testimony of Antiquity against the peculiarities of the Latin Church*, 1828; *The Sacred Calendar of Prophecy, or A dissertation on the Prophecies of the Grand Period of Seven Times, and of its second moiety, or the latter three times and a half*, 3 vols., 1828. There is an enormous list. He never gained much preferment but was very widely read, his books on prophecy being the most popular. "When he had once ventured upon an elucidation of prophecy according to his fixed canons", the *Gentleman's Magazine* remarked, "he was never swayed towards a varied interpretation under the immediate presence of events apparently irreconcilable with his first deliberate impression".[3]

It might be supposed that such a man so much occupied with

prophecy was a crank. Stanley Faber was nothing of the sort. In turn Oxford don, vicar and finally master of Sherburn hospital, Durham, he was capable and successful. He greatly influenced his brothers and their children. He was downright and honest, irritable but pious. He was much loved by his intimate friends, whom he entertained with racy stories in his native dialect. Conservative, independent to a fault, a good churchman, he hated anything that savoured of Rome. He was never tempted to set foot outside England. Like his nephew, he was a man of extraordinary energy. Although not strong and often nervous he never got up later than 6.0 a.m. winter and summer. As he said of himself, he was a noun substantive not a noun adjective, by which he meant he needed nothing to lean against. He is said to have been moderate in his controversial papers, but one sentence, apparently exceptional, is almost worthy of Dr Johnson. "We have been wont to esteem the well polished sword the appropriate weapon of the gentleman; but the Bishop inclines to prefer the obtuseness of a bludgeon, or the deformity of the tomahawk."[4] George Stanley Faber was also a writer of hymns.

Nothing much is known of Frederick William's other uncles except their dates. One seems to have married an heiress, another to have become a doctor. Nor is there much to be discovered of his father Thomas Henry, the third son of the vicar of Calverley. He married Betty Atkinson of Bradford and was thirty-five at the time of Frederick William's birth. It is not known what work he was doing at this time and it is a little mysterious why Frederick William was born in his grandfather's vicarage. In the December following Frederick's birth he was appointed secretary to Dr Barrington, Bishop of Durham, who was already George Stanley's friend and patron. The family moved to Bishop Auckland, an attractive market town where the bishop had a second residence, eleven miles from Durham. In the meantime Frederick had been baptized some six weeks after his birth, a delay of which the future Tractarian would certainly have disapproved. The parish church of Calverley was dedicated to St Wilfrid, a not very attractive saint, but one whom Frederick was greatly to admire.

Thomas Henry Faber's family at the time of its removal to
Bishop Auckland consisted of three boys: Thomas Henry junior,
now aged twelve, Francis Atkinson, known in the family as Frank,
aged nine, and Charles Edward, aged seven. The gap between
Frederick and his brothers was therefore wide and was caused
by a family disaster common enough at the time. The two
children who came between him and Charles Edward both died
on the same day in 1813. His mother felt that Frederick had been
given to her as an exchange for this loss. Her love for Frederick
was thus especially strong. It was increased, too, by the loss of
another child who followed him. The final child, Ellen, seems
to have been born in 1816. Frederick's position was that of an
elder rather than a younger child. His nearest brother was seven
years older than himself and his only sister was probably two
years younger.

His brothers being at school, Frederick was largely left to himself in the nursery with only his young sister as a companion.
There seems to be little doubt that he was spoilt. Ardent, candid,
good-looking, from his earliest years he attracted and amused.
His mother adored him. The self-confidence induced by the ad-
miring family circle was to lead him into, and out of, many
situations which a less confident man would have avoided. The
exaggerations of speech and writing so characteristic of the grown
man date from these years in the nursery. It pleased him as a
little boy, as it did later, to talk big. Perhaps it was to impress his
sister, perhaps it was an obscure desire to emulate his brothers
already out in the world.

I remember [his brother wrote] when he was still quite a
child, a friend desiring to hear him read, and putting a passage
into his hand which contained some hard words. The boy made
no attempt to spell them, neither did he avoid them in any
way, but charged the difficulty with the resolution of a fox-
hunter, making, as may be supposed, strange work with the
sesquipedalian words in question. His auditor closed the book
laughing heartily and told him he was the most *intrepid* reader
he had ever listened to . . .

He was overheard, as he expatiated to his sister on the great superiority of the masculine sex; and after laying down his argument in general, he proceeded to enforce it in particular. "For example," he said, "if you were the Queen of England, I should still be greater than you, because I am *a man* and you are only a woman."[5]

The world outside the nursery window was a strangely romantic place for the impressionable boy. The domain of Bishop Auckland intersected by the Gaunless was a place of great beauty. The scene was dominated by the Bishop of Durham—a bishop who was also Count Palatine. "When the bishops of Durham went to prayers at the Cathedral," wrote the Rev. George Ornsby,

> their progress thither from the Castle, as also their return, was a matter of some state and ceremony. The [writer] well remembers seeing Bishop van Mildert, the last Count Palatine, walking in procession from the Castle to the Cathedral. His mace-bearer went first. Then followed his secretary [this was probably Frederick's father], in full dress, hat in hand, immediately preceding the bishop who was attended by a chaplain on either hand in full canonicals. The train of the Prince Bishop was borne by his gentlemen, and four footmen in purple liveries brought up the rear. All were bareheaded except the bishop.

Sir Walter Scott describes the scene when he dined in the great hall of Durham Castle as the guest of the bishop. "The bright moon," he wrote in his diary,

> streaming in through the old Gothic windows contrasted strangely with the artificial lights within; spears, banners, and armour were intermixed with the pictures of old bishops, and the whole had a singular mixture of baronial pomp and the more chastened dignity of prelacy. The conduct of our reverend entertainer suited the character remarkably well. Amid the welcome of a Count Palatine he did not for an instant forget the gravity of the church dignitary ... I ought not to forget that the singers of the choir attended at dinner, and sang the anthem, *Non Nobis, Domine*.[6]

But it was a sunset glory, a dying splendour. The flood of industrialism, unbelief and liberalism was rapidly rising. Secure and solid though it seemed to the eyes of the little self-confident boy it was threatened and undermined. Very soon Durham Castle was to be a university and the bishops no longer Counts Palatine. Soon there would be more Dissenters and Roman Catholics than members of the Established Church. Thomas Henry's family belonged and yet did not belong to this old order. Thomas Henry came from a clerical family and was a dependant of the bishop—yet he was a layman. His position was unusual, equivocal. It is not perhaps those who fully belong to the old ways who most regret the passing of time and the concomitant ruins. It is those on the fringe of a society who feel these things the most. They feel with peculiar intensity because the destruction of the old order is to them not merely a loss but the disappointment of who knows what aspirations as well. Such was the position of Thomas Henry's family and such we know to have been the sentiments of the precocious boy.

Only a glimpse of the boy's world survives.

... The side window of the drawing room at Auckland, looking out upon the Bishop's gateway, and wherein stood an old stained table, the drawer of which specially pertained to me. Here I played the geographic game with my mother for hours; there I studied a fat duodecimo in red sheep entitled The Wonders of the World where the wall of China and the leaning tower of Pisa made an ineffaceable impression upon me...[7]

Faber went for a short time to the Grammar School at Bishop Auckland. He was then sent to the house of a clergyman, John Gibson, at Kirkby Stephen. Here the scenery of the Lake District really did, without exaggeration, make an ineffaceable impression upon him. His poetry was to be filled with descriptions of the Lakes, as were also his spiritual works. In a rather ludicrous passage in Bethlehem he attempts to paint a picture of Heaven— inevitably it is the Lakes. There was little discipline and he wandered, for the most part alone, among the hills and lakes at will, his rambles, we are told, "sometimes extending over two or three days".[8] Already, like his uncle George Stanley, he was a noun substantive.

But these wanderings were not simply communings with nature. He visited all the ruins he could find—halls, castles and abbeys. His imagination re-peopled them. As he was to write later:[9]

The abbeys and chantries were haunted by church-music, while the lesser cells in the secluded pastoral vales heard once more the nightly aspirations of wakeful prayer, and Cistercian shepherds could scarcely be distinguished, in their white habits, from the sheep they tended as they moved across the fells high up above their moorland granges.

Faber, however, was always more than a Lakeland dreamer. He was also more than a man caught up in the romantic vision of the ancient Church. Behind the dreams and the vision there was always present to him the reality of God. Faber felt, even as a boy, and to an unusual extent, the presence of God. Every circumstance of his life, however apparently trivial, was the work of the hidden but keenly felt hand of God. There was no situation, no time or place in which God was not actively present. He was to write that it was an event in a man's life when he made the discovery of God's personal love of himself. But Faber seems to have been aware of God's love from the start. "Surely", he was to write,

God cannot have been to others as he has been to us; they cannot have had such boyhoods, such minute, secret buildings up of mind and soul; we have a feeling that about our own lives there has all along been a marked purpose, a divine speciality.[10]

Among his hymns, poetically of little merit, there is one, *The God of my Childhood,* which portrays the inner life of the boy.

O God! who wert my childhood's love,
My boyhood's pure delight,
A presence felt the livelong day,
A welcome fear at night . . .

They bade me call Thee Father, Lord!
　　Sweet was the freedom deemed,
And yet more like a mother's ways
　　Thy quiet mercies seemed.

At school Thou wert a kindly face
　　Which I could almost see;
But home and holyday appeared
　　Somehow more full of Thee.

I could not sleep unless Thy Hand
　　Were underneath my head,
That I might kiss it, if I lay
　　Wakeful upon my bed.

And quite alone I never felt,
　　I knew that Thou wert near,
A silence tingling in the room,
　　A strangely pleasant fear.

And to home-Sundays long since past
　　How fondly memory clings;
For then my mother told of Thee
　　Such sweet, such wondrous things . . .

I know I used to lie awake
　　And tremble at the shape
Of my own thoughts, yet did not wish
　　Thy terrors to escape.

I had no secrets as a child,
　　Yet never spoke of Thee;
The nights we spent together, Lord!
　　Were only known to me.

I lived two lives, which seemed distinct,
　　Yet which did intertwine:
One was my mother's—it is gone—
　　The other, Lord! was Thine.

I never wandered from Thee, Lord!
　　But sinned before Thy Face;
Yet now, on looking back, my sins
　　Seem all beset with grace.

The poem, which for its artlessness, if for nothing else, must surely be taken as a true picture, needs explanation. Where did the boy learn this communing with God? A religious family background is not explanation enough. Were the bounce and exaggeration of the precocious child somehow connected with this confidence in God? Or was it the other way about? Was Faber a born noun substantive to whom confidence in God came naturally, almost inevitably? Sir Geoffrey Faber has seen in Newman's belief in providence a rationalized egotism caused by some (unexplained) psychological maladjustment. The same charge of egotism could also be levelled against F. W. Faber. Belief in a special providence can always be made to seem egocentric. But what in Faber's case was the maladjustment? He was surrounded by love, admiration and security. His behaviour as a boy was the antithesis of neurotic. Psychology in fact provides no answer. The physical basis of his personality which made him restless, ardent, impulsive and imaginative also offers no explanation. Such a temperament is more often than not individualistic to the point of atheism. Perhaps it is sufficient to say that he was a born mystic. John Bowden may have had something of the same idea when he said Faber's was "a life which from first to last had been *religious*". If Faber had not found God in Christianity and the Church he would have found Him in nature and pantheism. To some, thinking of St John of the Cross or St Teresa, mystic will seem too strong a word for Faber. But can he adequately be described by any other term? For Faber was a visionary in the best meaning of the word. His intuition of God's love was a personal experience, or series of experiences, from his earliest childhood. His biography is simply and solely a response to this vision. It could, indeed, be said that every man's biography is such a response. But whereas with the majority of men this response is indistinct and blurred, in Faber's case all is on the contrary relatively clear.

He left Kirkby Stephen in 1825 and was sent early the next year to Shrewsbury School. For some reason, perhaps on account of an unexpected vacancy, he was then sent, in Midsummer 1827, to Mills's house at Harrow—the year that Dr Arnold was elected headmaster of Rugby. Life at Harrow must have been harsher and more brutal than the happy years he had spent in the Lake District. But in both places there was an almost breathtaking amount of freedom. There were, it is true, all the abuses that go with freedom. It was remotely possible to be roasted alive by some terrifying bully, there were unpleasant initiation ceremonies and there was some blanket tossing. Flogging was severe, but the system of prefectorial espionage, associated with Dr Arnold's name, was still embryonic. In Faber's day a boy at Harrow was treated like a man. It was possible to go to London on frequent jaunts, to make home-made fireworks, to be interested in coins or botany and not to care a fig for sport. At nights after lock-up there were forbidden games of Jack-o'-lantern in which a boy with a lantern would lead his pursuers through mud, hedges and ponds. A boy would sometimes be asked to have a glass of wine or to dine with the headmaster. Harrow, like other public schools at this date, was going through a period of decline. Discipline was slack. The curriculum was entirely classical. A boy's life was dominated by Greek and Latin. Everything depended on his ability to write elegant verses.

Obviously in such a world a boy could be very happy or very unhappy. Trollope as a day-boy at Harrow about this time was hopelessly miserable. Nothing much is known of Faber as a schoolboy, but it is probable that he was happy. Slight and girlish though he may have appeared the mettle beneath the exterior must have become quickly known. A boy with a flair for leadership would not have been bullied. His natural linguistic dexterity made the scholastic side of his life easy. However, he neglected the classics as much as he could and avidly read English literature. In consequence he did not do himself justice in spite of the fact that he was considered to be without intellectual rival in the school. He rode and swam very well but seems to have been a little aloof. Already he had poetic ambitions, a Romantic disposition. The lack of discipline also made him self-willed.

He had plenty of friends. He spent a holiday with Benjamin Brodie, whose father was a well-known surgeon. He annoyed the famous doctor by calculating how much time he would save in his life by signing his name, Frederic, without the "K". Young Brodie was to become a distinguished chemist and it was probably from him or from his family that Faber acquired a knowledge of science. This was to be a lifelong interest, to colour and broaden his theology. He went for another holiday in the Lake District with John Merivale, son of John Herman Merivale the minor poet and friend of Byron. The elder Merivale had married the daughter of Dr Drury and was therefore well known at Harrow. Throughout his life Faber had the knack of getting to know distinguished people. Another holiday was spent with John Norton in the Highlands. John Norton was a good cricketer who played twice against Eton at Lord's. It does not seem to have mattered that Faber was utterly indifferent to all games.

In the middle of his school career a heavy blow fell. His mother, who for some years had been in bad health, died. He wrote very little about this calamity but it is possible to reconstruct what happened. He was deeply loved by his mother, almost to the point of idolatry, and loved her deeply in return. His security and self-confidence, the possibility of happiness even, seemed to fall to dust with her death. It was as if the sun had ceased to shine. Grief cannot be described but its intensity can be gauged by its effects. In Faber's case his mother's death coincided with a religious crisis which undoubtedly influenced him to the day of his death.

The famous Dr George Butler was headmaster at Faber's entry but must have remained a remote figure to the young boy. He was succeeded by Dr Charles Longley in 1829—the year when Faber lost his mother at the age of 15—a man with a fine head, prematurely bald, conscientious, impressive, gentlemanly, later to be Archbishop of Canterbury. Faber turned to him for consolation. Influenced no doubt by the poetry he had been reading and in particular by Byron, a hero at Harrow, the romantic boy had become sceptical. The blow was bound either to destroy his faith, in spite of his religious intuitions, or to deepen it. In the event it was a very close thing. Faber saw the issue with the terrible clarity of youth. Either Christianity was true or it was false. If it was true then his whole life must be devoted to God. If it was false ... who knows what tearing of the soul even the contemplation of the possibility entailed? It was like approaching the brink of a chasm. Faber had the courage to scrutinize the possibility before finally turning away. It is strange that a man like Dr Longley, not much of a thinker nor much given to confidences, should have helped, but Faber gives his word for it. He never forgot his headmaster's gentle kindness. Perhaps a cleverer man might have argued and the boy might have found confidence in his own counter arguments. It was due to Dr Longley that his faith in the goodness of God was restored.

It is noticeable, however, that when the crisis passed Faber turned to John Cunningham, the Evangelical vicar of Harrow. Cunningham had been curate to John Venn, vicar of Clapham, around whose parish had formed the so-called Clapham sect, a nickname coined by Sidney Smith. Among the better known members of the group were William Wilberforce, the saintly philanthropist, and Zachary Macaulay, the historian's father. The sect, though small in numbers, through the social position of its members, many of whom were interrelated by marriage, exercised an enormous influence. Their basic conviction was a strong sense of moral responsibility and the belief that religion must bear fruit in good works. Among the good works was the struggle for the abolition of the slave trade, the extension of missionary enterprise, the foundation of the British and Foreign Bible Society, the extension of Sunday schools, the Society for Bettering the Conditions and Increasing the Comforts of the Poor. To our minds coloured by the dislike of Dickens and Trollope the sect does not appear attractive. It combines all the features of "Victorianism" used in a pejorative sense. It may have been self-righteous and it was certainly condescending but it represented a real movement away from the spiritual stagnation of eighteenth-century Anglicanism. Its leader, William Wilberforce, at all events, stood for something great and good.

Cunningham made an immense impression on Faber. He was a handsome man with a good presence. But Thomas Adolphus Trollope found him "*too* suave and *too* soft, carrying with it a certain suspicion of insincerity".[11] Frances Trollope, who is said to have portrayed him in the *Vicar of Wrexhill*, thought him a toadying hypocrite not above kissing a pretty parishioner if the occasion allowed. Cunningham certainly was the enemy of the Drurys, the Trollopes's allies, and they maintained among other things that he was the son of a London hatter. The truth seems to be that neither the Trollopes nor the Drurys could stomach his religion. He was now forty-nine, at the height of his powers, and had been vicar of Harrow for eighteen years. The position entailed being unofficial chaplain to the school which as yet possessed no chapel of its own.

Kind-hearted, conscientious, perhaps a little too plausible, he was also a well-known author. *The Velvet Cushion*, his most celebrated book, passed through many editions in a few months. It is easy to understand its success. It is a charming history of the Church of England told as a sort of fairy-tale. The velvet cushion in the pulpit of a remote Westmorland church is found by its pious incumbent to contain a manuscript telling the cushion's adventures. The book breathes the simple piety of the Evengeli-cals at its best. It is neither narrow nor rigid. It is deplored that the Puritans did not go "abroad among the glories of nature". The ideal clergyman, who resembles the Vicar of Wakefield, thought "God eager to save all his creatures. 'Look at the most signal ex-amples of divine vengeance,' he used to say, 'and love will always be seen sheathing or tempering the sword of justice.'" The book is dedicated to the Church of England, "trusting that it may serve to remind your enemies of some of your excel-lencies".

His sermons have some unexpected resemblances to Faber's own spiritual works written thirty years later. "The besetting sin" closely resembles chapter seven of *Growth in Holiness*, "The ruling passion". Cunningham's "The Christian not a ser-vant but a son" is also paralleled in Faber's *Bethlehem* where the realization of our sonship of God is regarded as the ultimate devotion. If these resemblances show nothing else they at least prove how much of an Evangelical Faber remained to the end. They certainly show how central much of Evangelicalism is to Christianity.

There was, however, one work of Cunningham's which Faber

was not to take to heart. *Cautions to Continental Travellers*, published in 1818, when at the end of the French wars Englishmen were again travelling widely, is a warning against Popery. It was, in Faber's case, to be prophetic. "Pious minds", Cunningham wrote,

> of more susceptibility than strength, and the slaves of impressions rather than the simple and sober scholars of Christ, can scarcely fail, for a time at least, to have their attention arrested and their affections interested by some of the solemnity of the Roman Church. A celebrated living German poet is said to have embraced Popery from having seen a funeral procession issue at midnight from a church, followed by a picturesque train of monks with torches, whose dim lustre flashed across their wan countenances and solemnly lighted up the ancient edifice which towered above them and whose chaunt seemed nothing less than the requiem of angels to the soul of the dead. Others have looked themselves into Popery at the solemnity of the Papal benediction at Rome; when the Pontiff appears, as it were, suspended in air, and pronounces his blessing on the universe, and, at the firing of cannon, the whole of the innumerable multitude collected before him prostrate themselves as one man in his awful presence. Others, of a timid cast of mind, are perhaps frightened out of Protestantism into Popery by the solemn bodings of some smooth solemn priest, who with an air of infallibility denounces everlasting ruin upon every soul which is not within the pale of the Roman Church. If such instances of apostacy from a pure to a corrupt faith are rare, I myself have known cases sufficient to convince me that the danger is not by any means chimerical.[12]

Cunningham strengthened Faber's faith, gave it direction. Faber is said to have often been the only boy at Sunday Communion. Cunningham reinforced the religion Faber had learnt at home or had perhaps picked up from his uncle and gave it an Evangelical colour. This Evangelicalism was marked by a deep moral earnestness, a love of the Church of England as the purest well of Christianity, and a tender love of Jesus. It was stamped throughout with an anti-Catholic attitude. With much that was good Faber undoubtedly picked up from the Evangelicals some unpleasant mannerisms apparent even in *All for Jesus*. Cunningham also stood for much that Faber admired and wished to emulate. He was a gentleman (or appeared to be so in spite of the Drurys) and influential, a clergyman and an author of distinction. He was even a poet.

There were already two important strands in Faber's life, lying uneasily together—religion and literature. Before he left Harrow, he already had the ambition to become a poet. But there was always religion—the great moral imperative. At the back of the Evangelical mind there lurked the fear that nothing was valuable unless it was of positive use to religion. There were no indifferent actions, or such as there unfortunately were, could be tolerated only because they would not be eliminated. It was a sad dilemma for a poet—unless there could be a poetry of religion. It became Faber's ambition to be a religious poet. In 1832, having duly become a monitor, Faber matriculated at Oxford. At Oxford if he was not to become a poet he was at least to be known for his poetry.

CHAPTER II

OXFORD UNDERGRADUATE

IN the Winter of 1832 Faber sat for a scholarship at Balliol. He was unsuccessful but the college offered rooms at once and he came into residence at the beginning of Hilary term (Spring) 1833.[1] In the meantime there was another desolating blow. His father died and the old home at Bishop Auckland was broken up. From now on his eldest brother, Thomas Henry, took his father's place. Thomas Henry junior was at this time only thirty-one but already was making something of a name for himself as a lawyer in Stockton-on-Tees. George Stanley had been incumbent of the place and no doubt helped his nephew. It seems that Thomas Henry senior had no money to leave his family. The young lawyer therefore shouldered the burden of educating his young brother and sister. The other children, Frank and Charles, were old enough to fend for themselves though Frank made Stockton-on-Tees his home for some years. As time went on Frank took over many of the duties of father to his younger brother.

His father's death pressed on Faber as he said "with the dead weight of desolation". But he was young, clever, graceful. He was eighteen. Life lay before him like a summer's day. He was always charming, versatile, amusing—never more so than at this time. He soon made his mark. Roundell Palmer, a man somewhat older than himself, describes him as

> extremely prepossessing, of good height, slender figure, fair complexion, bright blue eyes, well-formed features, almost feminine grace. The attraction of his looks and manners and our agreement in poetical tastes (particularly in appreciation of Coleridge and Wordsworth) soon made us friends, and our affection for each other became not only strong but passionate. There is a place for passion, even in friendship; it was so among the Greeks; and the love of Jonathan for David was "wonderful, passing the love of women". Evening after evening in

Frederic Faber's rooms, we spent together in reading and comparing our impressions of our favourite poets ... His usual flow of spirits was great; and in conversation he was positive, sometimes paradoxical. There was in his mental nature an element of waywardness and inconstancy ... It manifested itself sometimes in a rapid change of opinion, from one extreme to another; and at other times (though this never happened to myself) in his relations to particular persons. The key to this was doubtless in some law of sympathy, which, whenever it drew him towards those from whom he differed, repelled him from others with whom he had agreed. But those sympathies which depend upon the beauty and mystery of nature were always active within him.[2]

Jack (John Brande) Morris was probably his earliest Oxford friend. He was the son of Dr John Morris, D.D., who had been taught by George Stanley Faber and now kept a boarding school at Brentford. Faber may first have become friendly with Tom Morris, the younger brother, who was more nearly his contemporary. Jack, an undergraduate at Balliol, slightly older than Faber, was to remain a firm friend throughout life. Credulous, eccentric in appearance and manner, as deeply learned as he was devout, he strongly influenced Faber. Faber was also a strong influence on Morris. They wrote to each other constantly. Most of what we know of Faber's early life is through these letters which Morris preserved with scrupulous fidelity.

Faber was still a very ordinary undergraduate, clever indeed, as many undergraduates are, or as his enemies called him, "flashy", but fundamentally a schoolboy. His first terms were spent in a whirl of activity making friends. To his chagrin he found that his ability and especially his knowledge which he had thought unrivalled were inferior to those of many contemporaries. At the beginning of the Long Vacation he travelled home by way of Harrow, no doubt to call on Mr Cunningham. "To show my wonderful skill and sagacity in horses," he wrote to Morris,

I rode the wrong hack from Harrow and left the man at the livery stables in London to make the best he could of the dilemma. I then embarked forthwith on the James Watt steam

packet and the next morning had done with the Thames and
was on the broad bosom of the beautiful German Ocean. With
lovely weather and calm seas we sailed on and I was gradually
becoming exhilarated by some fresh breezes, an *aliquod ignotum*
to me after a *séjour* in London, till Thursday evening. On
Friday morning I awoke and commenced dressing: the Ocean
was clad in a dense fog and the wreaths of mist were hanging
like impalpable veils over the heaving billows, as if the Nereids
were modest and were concealing their *toilettes* from our rude
gaze. I, poor soul, thought we were far on the bosom of the
sea from the white cliffs of Albion; but alas! it was not so. I was
preparing to perform ablutions when crash crash went the
vessel on a rock, and over on her side fell the good gallant ship.
Fear being an emotion unknown to me, a great fund of amusement presented itself. Half a dozen cabin doors flew open and
females in *déshabille* with clasped hands and tearful eyes rushed
frantic out: they in their ignorance thought they were lost, and
I in apathy had before me a representation of what a real wreck
is, and thus had an opportunity for indulging my favourite
propensity of observing human nature among mankind themselves. I was soon on deck; when the fog cleared up we were
not fifty yards from the perpendicular cliffs of Yorkshire:
to make brief work—we all got ashore—the sea was as calm as
glass, we were delayed fourteen hours and then got off.[3]

After this mishap the vacation was spent dully enough. Stockton-
on-Tees was neither smart nor intellectual nor romantic. It was
in fact tediously the reverse. Faber helped his sister with her education and tried to make new friends. In the evenings there was a
social circle and he read aloud the life of Cranmer. It was all
very bourgeois and uninteresting. He longed to be back at
Oxford.

Oxford, indeed, at this time was a fascinating place. A religious
whirlwind was in process of formation. For the moment there
were four main groups—all, to some extent, to be swept away
in the path of the gathering storm. The dominant school, tradition-
ally Oxonian, was the High Church party, "High and Dry" as
it was called. It was Tory, political, for the rights of the Establishment, untouched, perhaps untouchable, by fervent religious

feeling. The next group were the Evangelicals. Sermons, commit-
tees, good works, sudden conversions were their stock-in-trade.
The appeal was to the heart and not to the head. The Oxford
Evangelicals were dowdy and dull. The smart and the clever
did not know the Oxford Evangelicals. Then there was a middle-
of-the-road party associated with the names of D'Oyley and
Mant, whose ideal was "the sober piety of the Church of England".
Simeon the Evangelical described this party "as moderate men
who love God moderately and their neighbours moderately
and hate sin moderately and desire Heaven and fear Hell moderately". Finally there was the school of such men as Whately,
Hampden and Arnold which is more difficult to define. It was to
grow into the Broad Church party but at this time was less coherent. Its tendency was liberal and rationalistic, to bring Christianity into line with modern thought, to diminish, as far as
possible, the supernatural. To its enemies the tenets of this
party were little better than scepticism. Newman's reaction
against Whately, whom he had much admired, played a large
part in the formation of his mind.

The Tractarian movement cut across all four groups. It defended
the rights of the Church with all the vigour of a two-bottle
parson but its religious fervour was at least equal to that of the
Evangelicals. "The sober piety of the Church of England" was
no negligible element in its make up. And who dare say how
much, particularly in the case of those Tractarians who became
Catholics, it owed to the scepticism of Whately's school? The
origin of the Movement was fear. Something, someone, was
needed to face the triple-headed enemy—Liberalism, Dissent
and Rome. Otherwise in the raw Utilitarian age that was dawning
the whole fabric of the Church might collapse and be swept
away. Men turned from the horrors of Revolutionary France
and the uncertain present to the security of the past—to a time
when the Church spoke with certainty, when she was great and
glorious. The Romantic Movement and especially the novels of
Scott made a virtue of nostalgia. What the Church had been,
could she not be again? There was a new interest in the Fathers,
in the history of the liturgy, in liturgical functions. Catholic

Emancipation, the Reform Bill and the suppression of ten Irish bishoprics seemed to be deliberate blows aimed at the heart of religion.

Faber returned to Oxford for the Michaelmas term in October 1833. But in the meantime a great deal had happened. Hurrell Froude, who combined wonderfully in one person the Toryism, the brilliant sceptical thought and the deep piety of the Movement, had come home—unhappily far gone in consumption. Newman was back, his mind filled with the certainty that he was an instrument of God. No prophet ever returned to his people with a greater sense of mission than he did to Oxford in 1833. Keble had preached his Assize sermon on National Apostacy, the Hadleigh conference had taken place, the first of the tracts had been published—all this before Faber's return.

Faber was soon in the thick of it, enjoying Oxford life with uninhibited vigour. The whirligig of ideas stimulated him. He worried about the presidency of the Union, he took a prominent part in debates, he argued and laid down the law with Palmer and Morris. He sat up late with his friends, drinking porter, eating sausages, reading Wordsworth. All the time he was writing poetry with easy fluency. The poems were shown round and he had quite a reputation. Then he became active on the *Oxford University Magazine* which was intended but did not turn out to be a rival to the *Edinburgh Review*. He threw himself into the work with incredible energy[4] and got to know a large circle of potential writers, many gratifyingly older than himself.

He immediately fell under Newman's sway by attending the services in St Mary's. His emotional nature thrilled to the marvellous silver voice, so quiet, so effective. But as yet his ideas were a jumble. The liberalism of Arnold was almost as captivating as the new Tractarian views. In fact a hundred different opinions seemed plausible.

"I am almost a Whig now," he wrote at this time,

liberality is taking my pericranium by storm—several of the counterscarps are demolished—it has been a severer siege than Platea. Transubstantiation has been bothering me: not that I lean to it but *I have seen no refutation of it!* How can it be absurd and contradictory to the evidence of our senses when they cannot by any means take cognisance of the unknown being, substance, which alone is held up as the subject of this conversion?[5]

But four days later he was writing:

I am only a liberal Conservative. I am no Transubstantiationist—it is unwarranted by Scripture.[6]

Oxford had gone to his head like champagne. But it was not long before his conscience became uneasy. He looked back on his conduct with disgust. Had he behaved himself as became a future clergyman? He had long seen that no other vocation could satisfy him. "I became", he confided to Morris during his second Long Vacation (1834),

the prey of intellectual ambition—the veriest slave of literary vanity. This brought numerous evils in its train. To support a reputation far above my talents (which however was not sought nor earned by dishonest means, but forced upon me) I was obliged to ruin my health by robbing myself of almost all my natural rest: this necessitated non-attendance upon morning chapel: and here was the *fons* and *origo* of all my evils ... It is a positive fact, that upon leaving Oxford for the Long Vacation I did not bring down one single volume relating directly or indirectly to religion, save a Prayer Book![7]

To rectify this state of affairs he began reading seriously and determined to get through the New Testament four times during the course of the Vacation. He had begun a little treatise on the nature of Christian charity. He wrote to his friends pressing on them various religious publications. His letters took on a more pronounced Evangelical tone. There may also have been something a little priggish in his behaviour. It is known that he was by no means universally popular. He was accused of being affected and condescending, of being unable to stand chaff, and of being "a tuft hunter". All these accusations were made against Mr Cunningham and against the Evangelicals generally.

My dear Jack, I begin another letter to you because I am now never happy unless I am thinking, talking and writing respecting things eternal. One therefore of my greatest pleasures consists in writing to you. If the faith of the good king David—the most cheerful of saints and most melodious of poets—felt renovated and refreshed by going up into the house of God with his familiar friend how much more should the degenerate Christians of these lukewarm days rejoice in it!

Literature was tame and dull in comparison with religion.

It is like one of Tom Moore's melodies after an Handelian chorus, at once ludicrous and disgusting from its inferiority.

He hoped that his quarrel with a friend would clear up in spite of a cold letter and that "identity of opinion on religious subjects may be a bond of fellowship to us once more". He asked Morris to find out "the views on religious subjects" of his old friend Fitzgerald.[8] It was always difficult to remain Faber's friend unless there was an "identity of opinion on religious subjects".

As an Evangelical, as he now considered himself, and as an avid reader of Evangelical books Faber expected a dramatic conversion. He certainly made the most of the difference between his present mood and that earlier giddy period of light-hearted abandon. "It somewhat disheartens me", he confessed, however,

to see the maturity of faith and the spiritual perfection to which many good men arrive so early. They seem to be made Christians all at once. Their conversion appears to have been almost miraculous; and the process as palpable as the scales falling from the blind man's eyes. It is true that I have often had hours of ecstatic enthusiastic devotion but the fever has soon subsided, and my feelings have flowed on calmly and soberly in their accustomed channels. Yet I have had none of those miraculous heart-awakenings—none of those *visible* interferences of the Spirit to pluck me as a brand from the burning. However, I suppose the power of religion acts in ten thousand different ways . . .

Whatever doubts he may have had on the subject of Evangelical conversion he was now Evangelical enough to draw back from the new opinions in Oxford. He wrote to Morris:

I suspect and mistrust that sort of religion in which *apostolicity—establishment—episcopacy* . . . are terms in more frequent usage than *depravity, atonement, justification*, etc.: in which the Church is defined to be a body corporate as opposed to Dissent; and not a mystical union and incorporation of its members with Christ and with each other, as opposed to the carnal world . . . I think that we best serve our venerable Church not always by lauding her ordinances, but by practising in their primitive purity, her truly Scriptural doctrines. This is a most neglected truism . . .[9]

Morris, however, was not satisfied by this dogmatic statement of the Peculiars' case. "Peculiar" was the Tractarian nickname for Evangelical. He felt indeed that Faber was tainted by Calvinism and quoted a letter which Faber had written to his friend Fitzgerald. "You recollect", Faber replied,

the irrational precipitation with which I rush to a conclusion in political and literary matters, and you recollect also the pertinacious obstinacy with which I adhere to a conclusion once formed, and it was natural that you should imagine I had been doing the same thing in matters of religion. Now I took care to guard most earnestly against this idea in my letter to Fitz. I said there, as I repeat here, that I met with several passages, and the whole tenor of several epistles, which I should have said *decidedly* favoured the Calvinistic tenets: but I recollected the great authorities against them. I bore in my mind my own ignorance and incapability to decide, so *I did violence to my judgment* . . . I appealed to commentators: for the most part they were in favour of the Calvinistic interpretation and where they were not so they seemed at a loss to explain the passages in any unconstrained manner. The result of my enquiry is simply this that I, like my uncle, disavow all Arminianism and all Calvinism . . . I uphold in the fullest and the most latitudinarian manner the tenets of universal toleration, and the supremacy of private judgment. But surely this is only the freedom and liberty of the Gospel.[10]

Morris, however, was no fool. Faber might emotionally rely on Evangelicalism in times of stress, but in the long run would he ever respect it with his intellect? Would he even be able to swallow it *socially*? An Evangelicalism so deeply coloured by Calvinism as to be Evangelicalism no longer—that, indeed Morris saw, was a possible choice for Faber. There was in fact from this time a Calvinistic bias in his thought, so much so that John Bowden supposed that he had been brought up a Calvinist.

When Faber returned to Balliol in October for the Michaelmas term of 1834 he called on young Arthur Penrhyn Stanley, who had just arrived from Rugby. Stanley in his letters home classified the undergraduates into five groups—the disreputable; the idle and respectable; those who read much but are not over-gentlemanly; the literary but dull men; and then the highest class, "men who are both clever and gentlemanly". Faber was put without qualification into the highest group. Faber and he soon became friendly and went for many walks round Oxford. Stanley may have been thinking of Faber when he wrote that his friends

> dogmatise very much. When they are together this is softened down, so as to be amusing and lively, but when I am alone with them, I find it tedious and unsatisfactory, and when to this is added constant exaggeration, which is also only amusing in general society, the matter is worse still.

But Stanley was a Whig and an ardent admirer of Dr Arnold. He found much in the Oxford of these early Tractarian years irksome. He describes a freshman who quoted "the Articles as Scripture, the Church as infallible" stopping suddenly in his walk with a look of horror on his face. "I did not know that such a thing was tolerated in Oxford," pointing to a notice on the wall. I imagined it to be "something dreadful"; it was an innocent *To the chapel.* "Oh!" said I, "you mean the Dissenting chapel?" "Yes, how could it have been built here? I wonder they did not pull it down long ago." He was thunderstruck when Roundell explained the doctrine of Apostolical succession but he found some people to agree with, "Ward and Faber, chiefly".

Ward, "a huge moon-faced man", was at this time a great admirer of Dr Arnold and it seems that Faber, in spite of his Calvinistic vacation, was an admirer also. Stanley and Faber talked of Southey, Wordsworth and Henry Taylor's† *Philip van Artevelde* in each other's rooms. They discussed the bearing of Geology on the Book of Genesis. They attended Keble's lecture on poetry. They were closely linked over a motion brought forward at the Oxford Union for closing the Union on Sundays. "The Sunday men", Stanley wrote,

> behaved as nobly and as quietly as their adversaries did shamelessly and turbulently; that ——— made a clever but degraded speech against, Massie a fine speech for, it; that it was carried by eighty-four against eighty, never to be repealed; that in vengeance the windows of Capes‡ and Faber were smashed at half after twelve that night, and Faber nearly killed by a bottle thrown at him through the window.[11]

But the friendship between Stanley and Faber, though it continued, was not destined to ripen further. Stanley wrote home that he liked Faber but he added significantly "in spite of all drawbacks". What these drawbacks were it is not possible to say. Perhaps the difference in their temperaments made itself felt. Or it may be that Stanley did not like the fervent Evangelical religion of the group round Faber. It is doubtful if he would have sympathized with the prayer meetings Faber was now holding. Faber was also organizing what he called "aggressive efforts in favour of religion".

At the end of the year Faber was elected a scholar of University College and migrated there from Balliol. The change does not seem to have made much difference to his life. He began to work harder and regretted the modern literature he had read at Harrow in preference to the classics. But he still spoke at the debates in the Union, was still devoted to Wordsworth, still wrote for the *Oxford University Magazine* and above all still searched for religious truth. His opinions were beginning to settle. Mr Cunningham and the Evangelicals still seemed in the right. He had thought

† Sir Henry Taylor (1800–86), poet and civil servant. He is now as well known for his work at the Colonial Office as for his poetry.

‡ John Moore Capes (b.1813), future editor of the *Rambler*. At this time an undergraduate at Balliol.

out his position with some care as he was writing an article on the Church.

I have been thinking a great deal on the merits and tendency of Newmanism, and I have become more than ever convinced of its falsehood. There is in the human mind at all times a strong tendency to mysticism; and when you add to this natural propension the accidents of depth of thought, peculiar line of study, and a somewhat monastic seclusion, I do not wonder that Newman's mind has become deeply tinctured by that mystical allegorizing spirit of Origen and the school of Alexandria. I can answer from personal experience for the manner in which it captivates a mind which is in the least imaginative. But there is a cause beyond this. Newman felt himself thrown into complete opposition to Whately and that school which embodies the modern notions on religion; and was thus led to take up a more decisive position, to define and systematize floating ideas and theories, and proselytize with greater vehemence than he otherwise would have done. He who hung his dripping garments and votive tablet to the ocean god had no doubt a keener sense of the perils of the sea than anyone else: and this perhaps leads me to regard with deep sorrow the spread of this amiable devotional mysticism in Oxford. It must inevitably, as it does legitimately, lead to that distinction between the *religio philosophi* and the *superstitio populi* which was the main earthly cause of the tremendous downfall of the huge fabric of paganism. No such consequences can of course ensue in Christianity; but a very serious blow may be given to the Church by bodies of young men going out to be parish priests, believing that there are inner doctrines which *it is as well* not to reveal to the vulgar, mysteries—I am using Newman's own words which are his peculiar treasure, *thoughts which it is scarcely right to enlarge upon in a mixed congregation.*

Am I chimerical in anticipating quite as much danger from the mysticisms of Newman as from the rationalities of Whately? It is not in my case, as you well know, that "he jests at scars who never felt a wound". I can most sincerely say, that after having been an unprejudiced acolyth of Newman's, an attentive reader of his works, a diligent attender at his church—I found the impressive simplicities of the Bible irksome to me:

all its quiet consolations were knocked away from under me, and vague, bodiless Platonic reveries were the food my soul craved for. Observe, I *know* that this is not the case with Newman himself: I believe him to be an eminently pious, humble-minded Christian: but I think he has sat at the feet of the early contemplative philosophers with an unscriptural humility—that he has imbibed their notions—and that his followers are likely to become a sort of Christian Essenes. Of course it would be preposterous in me to charge upon Newman what was probably in a great measure my own fault; but still I think I may argue that the tendency of his system is bad: whether it is that uncongenial minds misunderstand it, or wayward fancies pervert it, I think it is bad: and I look upon its onward course with fear and with distrust. What makes me fear most is that I have seen Newman himself *growing* in his opinions! I have seen indistinct visions become distinct embodiments: I have seen the conclusion of one proposition become the premise of the next, through a long series: all this is still going on—to my eyes more like the blind march of error than the steady uniformity of truth—and I know not when it will stop.[12]

He spoke with all the gravity of youth.

Faber may have been no Tractarian, but he felt with keen excitement the perils through which the Church of England was passing. When he spoke of these perils he talked the language of the most agitated of the Tractarians. "And how can a Christian be tranquil", he wrote on 5th August 1835,

when he contemplates the career of the English Nation since the year 1827 [1829?]. It was then that the legislature ceased to be a Christian body and by consequence the state to be a Christian state. Since then not a year has rolled over our heads in which some act has not emanated from the legislature tending with nervous anxiety and laborious sedulity to abolish all those glorious characteristics which held us up to the nations of Europe as *par excellence—the Christian state!* As to Church matters, scarcely a vote has passed the House of Commons which has not been an insult to God, and, so far as *they could* make it a deathblow to his religion ... It has been the object of modern legislators to wipe away, as if it were a bar sinister in the proud escutcheon of the British Empire every mark of connection with the religion of the lowly Son of God. They have offered a premium to all kinds of laxity of creed: they have violated the universal code of justice and trampled upon the commonest rights of property, in depriving God (for why should we not state the matter boldly) of the pittance which more primitive and I presume barbarous piety had in its benighted liberality bestowed upon His Levites. They have wrenched the scriptures from the hands of the Irish peasantry, famishing and crying aloud for the bread of life . . .[13]

He was now reading very hard and pushed himself almost beyond endurance. He had already determined to attempt the Newdigate Prize for a poem on *The Knights of St. John*. The writing of the poem was therefore added to his classical studies which were burden enough owing to his neglect at Harrow. Many of his letters written during the Long Vacation of 1835 survive. He was now a dyed-in-the-wool Evangelical and his religion tormented him. Was it right to spend so much time on the classics? Why was there not a specifically Christian education? He found Butler's *Analogy* "the greatest work of *Pagan* Wisdom". What did it have to do with his own vibrant contact with Jesus? What did it have to do with the declaration—that "the blood of Christ cleanseth from all sin"? He remembered a remark made at Harrow: "I cannot tell why it is, but that Faber fascinates everybody." He determined to lay this talent at the feet of His Redeemer, as he put it. But what storms of spiritual pride could he not expect as a consequence? The truth was he had a calling to a higher vocation and was unhappy.

Often when I am in companies where religion is not named, where earth and the things of earth are dominant, the soft still accents of the voice of Christ fall with meek power upon my ear. "Rise up, my love, my fair one, and *come away*." And yet I do not sufficiently come forth from the world, and take my stand manfully beneath the banners of my Lord.

When he returned to Oxford for the Michaelmas term, 1835, he still felt he was not a sufficient witness to the truth. On 10th October he dined with Cardwell of Balliol, and a wearisome evening it was to me. He was all kindness: but the idle words, the frivolous conversation, the open and coarse satire on the *Evangelicals*! I refrained even from good words, but it was a pain and grief to me: so I retired from the party before 8 o'clock and sought for rest to my troubled spirit in prayer and the dear, dear Bible.

He was nervous about the approaching final examinations.

I begin now to be very nervous about the backward state of my preparations, and what is most provoking of all, just now when I want to begin to read, an absolute fervour of [poetic] inspiration has carried away my spirit, like the wind in its tempestuous strength and I am up far away in regions beyond Oxford honours, gathering the gold fruitage of sunny thoughts and glorious imaginings. However it *shall* be pent up, if it *will*, and that is all I can say. Oh! bitterly, bitterly do I rue the day when I first put pen to paper, or rather the sandpaper of fancy to the rusty swords of the Knights Hospitallers of St. John of Jerusalem.

By November, however, he was more hopeful and his religious opinions were undergoing a subtle change.

I never studied [Herbert] as a poet till quite lately, and I regret my never having done so. You will when you read him agree with me that he takes a first rank among the poets of our land. His individuality will prevent his ever being generally popular: for to read him and appreciate him you must be a thinking-mind, a quiet-thinking-mind, a religious-quiet-thinking-mind, a *dutiful-Church-of-England-religious-quiet-thinking-mind* . . . I cannot describe to you my delight when late at night I close my classics, and resign myself to the quiet influences of George Herbert; the fret of weariness melts down into the tranquil stillness of devotion and my spirit is sent with a gentle impulse to tend its flock of quiet thoughts . . . I feel that under the blessing of God the study of Herbert has imparted to me more real, more felt humility and meekness than ever I had before: and is I trust successfully effecting the restoration of my mind's equilibrium, destroyed by my recoil from Newman's theology and Platonism.[14]

Dr Morris, Jack's father, sent warnings that he would be ill unless he gave himself some rest. But it was useless, as it was useless all his life. Brilliance, power of fascination and a ready pen are all very well, but he now had to expose himself in the eyes of the world. Finals were on top of him. His sensitive emotional nature shied away from the merciless test he must undergo. What if it were *proved* that he was second rate or worse? He had alarming depressions and almost as alarming times of exaltation. His Evangelical faith seemed particularly liable to cause these emotional fluctuations. On Christmas Day, which he spent in Oxford, he became so ill that he was forced to leave for a fortnight. Besides the fear of the examination he was also battling with the feeling that Evangelicalism was not sufficient. He became more zealous about the prerogatives of the Church, read Bishop Andrewes and even quoted Wiseman in a letter. Everything was ready for a change of opinion.

It came after hearing a sermon by Pusey on Septuagesima Sunday 1836 and appeared to the Evangelical young men round him totally unexpected, even capricious. In reality the climate of his mind had been changing for some months. Only a week after the sermon he was explaining to Palmer why he could no longer consider himself an Evangelical.

I had seemed to many of my friends to be much advanced, for a young man, in spirituality of heart. But alas! I had laid nothing by. It was the natural result of that system that nothing should be laid by. I had been as a child walking across a room, helping itself by every chair and table: in a word, I had lived upon the religious excitements of the passing day, and I had yet to learn that a *de die in diem* Christianity will not bring a man peace at the last . . .

I see that the Evangelical system feeds the heart at the expense of the head; and as man is constituted, what can be more perilous? I see that it tends to make religion a series of frames of feeling, that with spiritual cowardice it flies from forms for fear of formality; that it makes an unnatural union between the ideas of good works and legality, so as to infuse into the whole man and his life's blood the subtle baleful venom of Antinomianism; that it looks at truth only on one side.

Unfortunately it was not as simple as he thought. His intellect rejected Evangelicalism, but could his heart accept the Anglicanism of Pusey and Keble? That was to be the question for years to come. The "sober piety of the Church of England" never meant much to Faber. But there was another powerful factor. His nostalgia for the past—especially the Church of the past—had much to do with his acceptance of Tractarianism and his consequent severance from the Evangelicals. *The Last Palatine*, a poem on the death of the last prince bishop of Durham, and one of the best he wrote, displays well-regulated but very deep feelings:

> Hath not a sacred lamp gone out today
> With ominous extinction? Can ye fill,
> Wild men! the hallowed vases that ye spill,
> And light our darkened shrines with purer ray?
> O where shall trust and love have fitting scope?
> Our children will cry out for very dearth
> Of grandeur, fortified upon the earth
> As refuges for faith and holy hope.
>
> The cloud of music hushed still loads the air;
> The herald breaks the wand while he proclaims
> The sainted Palatine's puissant names:
> Yon kingless throne is now for ever bare!
> This is a gesture, whereby we may solve
> The temper of the age; upon this day,
> And in St. Cuthbert's shrine, the times display
> The secret hinge on which they now revolve.

In spite of the change of opinion there was not a little of the Evangelical still in his diction. And emotionally he remained an Evangelical to the end. But he had already taken up with what was central to the early Tractarians and which Jack Morris also was to preach in and out of season—fasting. "I would fain turn away", he wrote,

as far as may be from this hubbub and perturbation, and listen to my God, who calls me up into the mount to be with Him. And it is good for me to be there. After Moses had fasted, the

Lord God passed with gracious proclamation before him; after Elias fasted, the Almighty chose that season for coming to His servant in the still small voice; after the Lord of all creatures had Himself fasted, then was the time for angels to minister. Surely God's view of fasting must be different from man's; for greatly has He blessed me in it. And with fond eyes I turn to the primitive church, and sit at the feet of her apostles, bishops and doctors, studying that system of penitential discipline which this self-indulgent age derides; and I doubt not that I shall find, as they have left on record that they found, that the "girdle of celibacy and the lamp of watching" stood them in good stead in times of trial.[15]

It is not surprising that after these wrestlings of the spirit he was in no state to sit for his finals. He put off the examination from the Easter term till November and went for a holiday in the North. His health was badly shaken but he wrote with undiminished vigour from Stockton to Jack about the storm clouds that were gathering in Oxford. The chair of divinity had fallen vacant and the Tractarians, in alliance with many Evangelicals, were opposing Dr Hampden's appointment. Hampden was considered unorthodox on account of some enigmatic passages in his Bampton lectures. Pusey played an important part and Faber wrote of him with all the awe of a new convert.

When I think of the calm and tranquil piety, the unruffled quietness, the affectionate sobermindedness, the lowliness, the Christlike meekness of his character, and then view him full of the old Isaiahlike majesty of uncompromising zeal—very zealous for the Lord of Hosts—it speaks more than volumes to my heart of the advantage of silent days and nights of prayer, of fasting and of alms deeds.[16]

Meanwhile he had been awarded the Newdigate Prize for his poem and returned to Oxford for the recitation. On the 9th June he wrote:

Newman is delivering lectures against the Church of Rome. I have just come from a magnificent one on Peter's prerogative. He admits the text in its full literal completeness, and shows that it makes not one iota for the jurisdiction of the Bishop of Rome.[17]

On 15th June he recited his poem in the Sheldonian.

Palmer, who remained a moderate High Churchman all his life, began to fear the vehemence of Faber's new religious opinions. He wrote to say that his friend was far too bitter against the Evangelicals whose opinions he had so lately been holding. But Faber wrote back more emphatically than ever.

> I hold [the Evangelicals] to be *fundamentally* wrong. Wrong in doctrine of Faith above all, because wrong in their doctrine of the Sacraments . . .[18]

The Long Vacation of 1836 ended on an ominous note. "Palmer thinks", he wrote to Morris, "I have barely time to do what I ought to do before my exam."[19]

But even when back at Oxford in October Faber hardly mentioned his books to Morris. But he did eagerly enquire about Pusey's and Newman's scheme for editing the Fathers. Morris mentioned Faber's name to Pusey as a possible translator. In the meantime in spite of "being completely engaged with my reading" he was able to read and write out for Morris's benefit a long extract from Wiseman's lectures.

> I read these lectures—and I could only say, we walk by faith and not by sight. And oh! when he talks of our theory and our rites and our liturgy which we use not—"I cannot but look upon [the Church of England] as I should upon one whom God's hand hath touched, in whom the light of reason is darkened, though the feelings of the heart have not been seared; who presses to her bosom and cherishes there the empty locket which once contained the image of all she loved on earth and continues to rock the cradle of her departed child!"[20]

On 18th November he wrote to Palmer:

> You will be sorry to hear that I have had a sorry *viva voce*. It was a province in which I was far too nervous ever to shine, and the knowledge that I *needed* a good one added to my confusion . . . I cannot think that if I *needed* (which I surely did) a

viva voce to redeem past mistakes, I can possibly succeed. However it cannot be helped.[21]

On 30th November the results were out. There was some doubt as to how to place Faber but he was eventually given a Second. Frank, already a fellow of Magdalen, was extremely dejected. "For three days", Faber wrote to Morris,

> ill in body as well as mind, I had a grievous struggle. Many were the hard thoughts of my dear Lord which were suggested to me; but by His help I conquered: and the conflict ended in such a mortification of all proud thoughts and vain opinions of myself that I was left in a calmness and evenness of spirit, more refreshing to me than I can express.

But he had not drained the cup. The next day he wrote:

> The Fellowship Election [to University College] is over, and I have had a fresh disappointment, but I am still cheerful. *Fiat voluntas Dei:* and He will take charge for me of "the things of tomorrow". On Saturday I set off for Germany ... My dear Jack, I am this day moving all my books out of my dear old rooms: you who love Oxford so much can enter into my feelings ...[22]

The German holiday was an absolute necessity for Faber in his nervous depressed condition. He stayed with English friends and had Frank as a companion for excursions. But he was forced to stay in bed for a week. When he did get out he was immediately impressed by what he saw of the Catholic Church—peasant girls with baskets of fruit on their heads stepping into the churches to say their prayers, the week-day services well attended. The change acted like a tonic. He was already planning the reading he considered necessary for his ordination and examining Pusey's plan for the Library of the Fathers. With his usual surprising resilience he was back in Oxford before the end of January, indefatigable, unconquered. He took Palmer severely to task in a vigorous letter for telling him "to stick to Pusey" as if Newman was a danger.

> This is only one instance of what I think the pervading tone of your letter—a quiet assumption of a man in the right over a

man in the wrong. Again: what are these uncharitable dashes under Pusey's name? Are they not to imply censure of Newman? Is it impossible to praise one saint of God, but you must aim darts at another?[23]

Palmer was now living a new life in London among lawyers and men of the world. The two friends were almost quarrelling. Faber turned to his other friend, Morris:

The Fellowship exam. at Univ[ersity College] begins tomorrow morning, and the election takes place on Saturday. I have two competitors, I understand. [One of these was Mark Pattison] . . . Pusey commenced his lectures yesterday with Noah: and I really was so carried away by the majesty of his interpretations that I could scarcely conceive him uninspired. It seemed as if a live coal from the altar had been placed upon his lips.[24]

The new vigour and optimism produced by the holiday was a prelude to a change of the tide.

On Saturday night, my dear Jack, I was elected Fellow of Univ. . . . I seem as it were landed in a harbour where I would be, hemmed in on all sides by such means of grace, as are not ordinarily to be found elsewhere: and God grant that my growth may be proportionable. Hitherto I have been foolish and thoughtless and over self-indulgent: I have now but one wish—to employ my whole life in doing [the] little good to Christ and His Church which my dear Master has rendered me capable of doing in my generation.[25]

He failed to get the Chancellor's Prize or the Ellerton Theological Prize, but his position as a fellow of his college was now assured. Faber had in his grasp what he had long wanted—a position of influence at a critical time. Unfortunately the future was not to turn out as he expected.

Chapter III

DON, POET, CLERGYMAN

FABER used to say that "a man has many biographies moving in parallel lines". It was anyway true of himself and never more true than in these next years. One life was spent at Oxford, a fellow of his college and a clergyman caught up in the Oxford Movement. Then there was the other brilliant, social Faber of the Long Vacations in the Lake District, a preacher, a poet and a friend of Wordsworth.

Faber was not a success as an Oxford don. As it happens there is only one account of him as a fellow and that is poisoned by malice. Here is Faber as seen by a hostile eye.

In due time Frederick Faber became a Fellow of University; then private tutor (vulgarly called "Coach") for some time; then college tutor. Still he was not a success, in any sort. His position made the condescending attitude more graceful, and he was just the man to adorn it. His parties were singularly agreeable and his conversation very fascinating, at all events for a day or two; but the conversation had an unhappy knack of revolving continually round the axis of himself and his doings. His memory was so imaginative that people used to amuse themselves with the ever-varying versions of the same Long Vacation story, and ungodly undergraduates occasionally whispered "Gammon" as they came away. The tutoring also was not of the most effective sort. It was a common joke that everybody went through a "break-fasting" term, a "coaching" term and a "cutting" term. This last was an unsavoury commentary and was not redeemed by the glimpses to which the pupils had been admitted of stained-glass newly imported into the old college windows and the scout's hole metamorphosed into an oratory—to the great perturbation of that legitimate functionary. It was remarked also that his attendance in chapel was by no means so exemplary as his sonnet to that place of worship seemed to indicate. Altogether there was a sort of refined self-indulgence about him of which Oxford is singularly intolerant ... He preached ladylike sermons and wrote loves of tracts about the "ancient things of the Church of England", abused Rome in the most picturesque English and prayed with unfeigned—if, perhaps stilted—gravity "May God have mercy upon her".[1]

It was easy to underestimate Faber. (It was possible also to do the reverse.) But behind the flashy façade that could be made to appear so silly and emotional there was a strong logical mind. Rather disconcertingly there was, too, a will of iron. He was singularly detached in his judgments of his own conduct. Faber feared his own emotional nature almost as much as his critic disliked it. He learnt never to be ruled by it. It must be admitted, however, that there was much that was adolescent in his Oxford years. He had succeeded early and he found it intolerably hard to grow up.

He received deacon's orders from Dr Longley, now Bishop of Ripon, in the cathedral on 6th August 1837, and priest's orders from Bishop Bagot at Oxford on 26th May 1839. After the ordination Faber read the absolution for the first time "with a trembling voice" in college chapel at 4 o'clock that afternoon. It was a pleasant summer evening and by way of celebration Frank hired a gig. They drove over Magdalen Bridge past the tower and the stream. There was "a sort of golden haze over Cowley Marsh" which was not however as golden as the hopes Faber had for the future. They drove to Nettlebed where they slept the night. He was to remember it all years later. But the search for religious truth went on. He was moving to the Romeward wing of the Movement. He had now met Newman as well as Pusey. Newman, however, repulsed him. Newman always disliked flashiness and brilliance—except in Hurrell Froude. He may also have regarded Faber as still more than half an Evangelical—which was true enough.

In Holy Week 1837 he was reading Newman's *Prophetical Office of the Church*. The object of Newman's work was to discover a tenable *rationale* for his beliefs after a careful consideration of the principal Anglican divines of the seventeenth century. Newman felt that Hampden had committed himself in his Bamp-

ton lectures but that the Tractarians for all their high principles
and talk against Hampden had not done so. The book was a
presentation of the Via Media theory of the Church of England
and the relationship of that Church with Rome. The Anglican
Church reminded Faber as he read the book of the valley of dry
bones—"but the full resurrection into unity is not yet: and shall
it ever be? God only knows!" A few days later, however, he was
less despondent in a letter to Morris.

> I think you will be delighted with Newman's Lecture. It
> supplied me with what I had long wanted—clear and positive
> statements of Anglican principles. It has been too long the
> fashion for the doctors and teachers of Anglicanism to evolve
> their principles in the way of negation of Roman principles.[2]

The threat of a Royal Commission on the universities, however,
was exciting him in April. The party of Utility was unsleeping in
its hostility, or so it seemed to him. How could a few Tractarians
halt the march of economic progress and Liberalism?

> It almost brings the tears to my eyes to think that we are at
> last to be disturbed in these abodes of religious peace and joy ..
> With much prayer and much fasting and in extreme self-abase-
> ment I trust many college fellows are already prepared to meet
> the blow.[3]

Nothing, however, as even he saw, was more unlikely.
In June he wrote:

> I am quite sick of all Reformers. I have been studying that
> mournful history for Ordination Exam. and it has ruffled my
> spirit more than it ought. "It is the Lord—let Him do what
> seemeth Him good." Oh that there were a history of the
> Reformation written in the same spirit with that one glorious
> paragraph about Zwingli in Pusey's Baptism. What an addition
> it would be to the literature of the nation.

He hoped for a history of the Church written by various
writers. He had been assigned the translation of the works of
St Optatus in Pusey's Library of the Fathers. His mind had naturally turned to the Donatist dispute and the African Church.

Both in its rise and fall it seems to stand apart, as it does in its geographical position. Its history is most eventful: in close ecclesiastical relation with Rome, yet ever protesting against the claims of her prelates, just as we were and are; brought by the schism of Donatus into a state of things strangely resembling our own in Ireland: two Bishops on every throne, two Presbyters in every Presbytery: standing with the unthoughtful in the same disadvantageous position as regards argument, the Donatists trapping unwary Catholics by urging at all events it is *safer* to come to us, the Catholics do not rebaptize us nay they even admit our orders, just as Rome argues now.[4]

The parallel was not very exact as Newman was to notice later. But Faber's mind, at once logical and imaginative, was probing ahead of his leader. It was dangerous to make comparisons. A few days later he was writing on the sacraments and ended: "How frightened one is when one gets near Rome."[5] Faber was never the man to keep his mouth shut and it was not long before the redoubtable George Stanley heard of his nephew's opinions. He wrote to Faber at great length. But by now uncle and nephew spoke a different language. They could not influence each other.

By the middle of 1838 Faber had begun to realize that he could never be happy at Oxford.

This, my dear Jack, leads me to a point I feel sadly and deeply about. I am perfectly well aware that my character and temperament are peculiarly liable to misapprehension: and consequently Oxford is not the place for me. It is one mass of cruel misunderstandings from top to bottom. As soon as ever an opportunity of leaving it compatible with my not leaving my College to its hurt I shall depart. Human nature, say what you will, in spite of abundantly profuse gifts and graces of the place, is of more dwindled stature there than elsewhere. Good men are less there than in any other place. Men think about nothing but men—talk about nothing but men—meddle with nothing but men—as if Pope's miserable jargon were the standing canon of the University ... Oxford ... is unfresh and, spite of the glories of it, dear to me as my own soul, I shall hasten from it for that soul's sake as soon as ever I can do so Christianly. I loathe the *ethos* of a great part of it—I loathe it for its own foulness' sake and also because it has not left myself untainted.[6]

The truth was Faber could not get on easily with those who disagreed with him. There had at any rate to be a modicum of agreement. That was often lacking in a Common Room. He was easily wounded by repeated gossip or criticism in the form of a joke. Personal feelings run deep in a community of men without a common purpose—never more so than at this time of religious crisis.

Faber was isolated and unhappy. An Evangelical by temperament and a Tractarian by principle he upheld both sides of his religion with tremendous poetic exaggeration. He disconcerted Tractarians, puzzled Evangelicals and disgusted High Churchmen. Liberals and Sceptics thought of him as a joke. Was not the whole thing a self-indulgent romance by a none too adult minor poet? It was only very much later and to everyone's great surprise that there was seen to be much more to it after all.

He was desperately looking round for a private tutorship which would get him out of Oxford and at the same time allow him to retain his Fellowship. In the Summer of 1839 he made a trip to the Continent with R. W. Church, the rising young fellow of Oriel. They met Arthur Stanley, Faber's old Balliol companion, on board the Ostend boat. The three Oxford men then travelled by canal "in a sort of oblong chaise drawn by two horses"— Stanley describes it—as far as Bruges. There they saw a procession with the bishop carrying the Host under a gilded canopy. They took a moonlight walk along the ramparts before setting out for Ghent. They enjoyed the sights of Ghent and cracked endless jokes at Stanley's expense on account of the landlady's open affection for that charming and unpractical man. Here Stanley left for Bonn while Faber and Church travelled on to Cologne.[7]

Faber described his reactions at some length to Morris.

I determined, and so did Church, to conform to the Catholic ritual here. We both of us got Mechlin Breviaries at Mechlin, and go to church pretty regularly every day to say the Hours, and we say the rest of the Hours as the priests do in carriages or inns or anywhere. Also I have been tutorised in the Breviary by a very *nice* priest, a simple hearted, pious fellow, with little knowledge of theology.

But it all will not do. The careless irreverence, the noise, the going in and out, the spitting of the priests on the Altar steps, the distressing and, may I use the word, indecent representations of our B. Lord—I cannot get over them ... In England at choral service there is the lonely organ and the little boys in white, filling the Psalms with life and meaning and sending them up like Church incense into Heaven ... Here the organ is drowned with innumerable fiddles, there is a leader of the band in a box as at the opera, and instead of the boys in white a row of meretricious looking females, talking, nodding and looking about in the intervals. As to the psalms of David, they are smothered ... There is no quietness, no being able to hide oneself in its penitent services. The offices performed are like the Churches, hot with incense, smelling of wax candles, and glaring with paint, and dazzling with tin offerings hung on the limbs of images. Up to today I have lived just as a Belgian Catholic would have lived. This afternoon however I was quite sick and weary, home Church sick; and I cannot describe to you the wonderful pleasure of retiring to my own bedroom to say the Evening Prayer out of the Prayer Book. I could almost have cried ...[8]

Nevertheless Faber was ill at ease. He had second and third thoughts. Already by 1841 he lay in that unhappy limbo between Canterbury and Rome—intellectually distrusting the one, emotionally distrusting the other. Might not Anglicanism change? Might it not be something other than it appeared to be? Faber's quick logical mind tested every possibility, trying to find a satisfying synthesis. He built up theories and rearranged history with the assiduity of a beaver—but it would not do. At the end he was as perplexed as ever. The extent of the *malaise* in Anglicanism as a whole can be gauged by R. W. Church's behaviour. Church was no Tractarian fanatic and yet on the Continent he behaved as if he were a Catholic priest. Consciously or unconsciously he was testing Catholicism. He was no exception.

England was nearer conversion than she knew. For the first time since the Reformation Englishmen were trying to judge the Catholic Church without prejudice. Serious Protestants were ashamed of their national churches erected by princes for convenience and not for the love of God. They were looking for Catholicity. Unhappily for a variety of reasons, pure and impure, rational and irrational, they did not find what they wanted in the Catholic Church. Protestant and Catholic no longer spoke the same language. There were a thousand cultural barriers. As it turned out the Protestants groped their way to a Catholicity outside Catholicism. They fitted their churches within the idea of a universal Church whose Catholicity could not be denied. An unkind historian might say they mistook comprehensiveness for Catholicity—or at least put up with it.

"Very well," Faber wrote at the end of an enormously long letter to Morris,

> now what does all this show? Why so much, that Anglicanism is a thing in training, in tendency, in aspiration, incomplete —a real view, YET NEVER HITHERTO REALISED. And things in tendency have many *désagrémens* which they will forgo in their complete state ... We make neither head nor tail of the present Church. Western Christendom lies at our feet, and we scamper over it every summer by hundreds. But we forget it is that awful, old thing, Western Christendom ... English travellers say, What can we do? We are excommunicate. Would it not be something if they *felt* that excommunication on their minds as they travelled?[9]

This was very, very far from the state of mind Mr Cunningham had advocated for travellers on the Continent.

But there was another life, far happier, to be lived in the Vacations. It was a life cut off from Oxford by the mountains he loved.

He first took a cottage in the Lakes in 1837 and he was there regularly till 1842. Faber had been a devoted "Wordsworthian", as he called himself, from Harrow days. Wordsworth is often loosely referred to as a pantheist and it comes as a surprise that he was almost worshipped by many Tractarians. It was not simply that Wordsworth grew more Christian as he grew older. There was in the Tractarians a streak of mysticism as well as Romanticism. Morris and Faber shared a common attitude to nature. To them it was a special revelation of God. The theme recurs again and again in Faber's spiritual works as one of his deepest convictions. Morris's whole attitude to life was coloured by this view. His poem *Nature a parable* is an exposition of his belief. The Tractarians and Faber in particular were unfamiliar with the conception of Nature as being "red in tooth and claw". They would not have approved of a man who went for a stroll "among the beauties of Nature" instead of going to Church on Sunday, but they would have understood him. They would not have thought of him as being necessarily a pantheist.

"There seems", Faber wrote from his newly rented cottage almost overlooking Wordsworth's house,

> to be somewhat sacramental in nature, adapting itself to all moods and tempers of mind: and this is another reason why I *feel* Berkeleyism must be true. We *have* come to the heavenly city—and we *are* with God: and Spirit lives with and acts on spirit *directly* and *immediately*. Persons would think that mountains were too solid, everlasting-looking things for that theory: those who said so never could have seen one. Could you but see them as I see them daily: dim in the silver mist of morning—fast asleep in the thin blue haze of sunny noon—outlined coldly, greenly, liquidly in the still evening—reflected in the unsteady lake or steady as it may be—shrouded in the purple gloom of such awful storms as we had on Saturday, with the live thunder leaping and crashing among the crags—or *felt* to be nigh when for the dark driving mists they cannot be seen, though within 100 yards of my window you could not but feel that of all things a mountain was the most unreal of natural forms: and that the everlasting hills like the gorgeous retinue of clouds that cluster round the deathbed of the sun were but majestic phantasmagoria put before us for high moral purposes.[10]

"People often talk of types," he wrote later,

> analogies and the like as if they were put before us to represent certain realities. I am inclined to think that this is not going far

enough. It seems to me that types are the *necessary consequences*, so to speak, of their antitypes: and not a dispensation of adumbrations raised up side by side with their realities. It seems to me that an abstract does more for its concrete than *imply* it merely. A type may not be separable from, it may be *part* of its antitype, a part substantial or hypostatical. Thus the relation of the typical characters of the Old Testament to their antitype may be I hardly dare say what. Thus all good men are types of the Best of *Men*: and therefore part of their Antitype, i.e. *members* of Christ. This brings us at once into the doctrine of the Church Visible; through the Communion of Saints into the doctrine of the Church Invisible, and back again to the Most Blessed Eucharist. It is difficult to discipline one's mind: but there are times when I have connected the Bread of Life with Bishop Berkeley's system, and I have felt myself overcome with the magnificent conclusions flowing out of that connection. But perhaps it is best to shrink back . . . If the mind will go quietly feeding among all the quiet Sacraments of external Nature what may not be disclosed to it? . . . It may be then that external Nature may be the necessary consequence of internal nature: earth part of heaven.

That the dispensation of sights and sounds is by angels I cannot doubt: whence but for them those thrills and sensible contacts when the soul rubs against something else in her solitary communings with external things—the recollection of which makes me thrill even now. Only the *dull* heart requires mountains and great things to shock it into a consciousness of all this . . .[11]

He had begun preaching in Ambleside church after the reception of deacon's orders. He was an immediate success, though, as he complained to Newman, he was misunderstood. But Newman praised his efforts and that was always enough for Faber. "My congregation here," he wrote enthusiastically to Morris,

is a most important one. There are very few poor people, and as I am not able to follow it [preaching] up with visiting and the like I am less jealous of my sermons being hard. Twenty-one Cantabs and three Oxonians, many candidates for Holy

Orders, with about thirty or forty educated gentry, ignorant but well inclined to the Church are most important auditors; and the interest they take one hopes will bring good along with it. I pray God it may be so: but as He pleases. I thought before I was ordained that I would not at first preach the doctrine of the Church too often: but I find there is no such doctrine: it is only a way of viewing all doctrines, so now I am fearless. What I have said of Baptism has been much noticed . . .[12]

One of his sermons taken down in a notebook at the time survives. The text was Ezekiel 14.14.

Then in the Ark, that glorious type of the Church of Christ, did the lion and the lamb lie down in peace, and the door was closed. "The Lord shut him in." Earth is full of wonders; yet none so wonderful as the perversity, the wickedness of man. Christ has been lifted up and we will not be drawn unto Him. God took us at our Baptism and placed us safe within the Ark and yet we will not be shut in. We will go in and out. We will divide our time and our affections between the Church and the World . . . Let us take heed the waters rise not on the earth and prevail greatly and cut off our retreat to the Ark which we have left so wantonly to gather fading flowers in fields far from our prison house, for so we thought (the Ark), looked so fair and green, and to be warmed with those false suns that shine uncertainly and are for ever setting. Christ came the last to his own bridal feast and the doors are closed for ever and there are no more sacraments wherewith to open them.[13]

Faber found himself introducing Tractarianism into the Lakes and beyond. In 1836 he had made a number of aristocratic friends, some years younger than himself, in Cambridge and had greatly influenced them. "The twenty-one Cantabs" mentioned in Faber's letter certainly included some of these friends. They were remarkable men. The best known was Lord John Manners. Faber's influence on the one side and Disraeli's on the other produced *Young England*. Disraeli never met Faber but an idealized portrait of Faber as seen through Manners's eye is given in Aubrey St Lys, the clergyman in *Sybil*. Manners was a great believer in "all old things"—in James II, the Stuarts, the Jacobites, Carlism. He was a Romantic High Churchman and was to try later on to start an Anglican sisterhood of mercy.

"The most salient feature of the happy two years I spent at Cambridge," Manners wrote in a fragment of autobiography,

> was the Long Vacation of 1838, which in company with New-port, now Lord Bradford, I spent at his father's charming cot-tage, St. Catherine's, above Windermere, reading with John Morse Heath. It was here I first fell in with Frederick Faber,[14] and heard him preach in Ambleside Church. The magic of his voice and the charm of his society and conversation were irresistible. I at least found them so and his influence over me was great . . .[15]

Three other Cambridge friends were reading at Keswick. Henry Goulburn, son of the politician, headed this party. He was a brilliant young man destined to die young. He seems to have been the least influenced by Faber. Then there was Thomas Whyte-head, already a fellow of St John's, Cambridge, also to die young, but at this time ardent, poetic, a convert from Evangelicalism to High Church views. Whytehead had walked down the Duddon with a friend taking Wordsworth's sonnets on the river as his guide. Above all there was George Smythe, Lord Strangford's son, to whom Faber had become almost passionately devoted. He is described as

> the most brilliant talker I ever heard, eloquent, imaginative, and paradoxical, and in consequence, although his appearance was unattractive, small and dingy, he exercised a fascination over women which was quite remarkable. It was a bad day for everyone of those who listened to the voice of the charmer, for he was as remorseless as he was capricious, and rolled in the mud and destroyed the reputation of the woman he had been adoring the day before . . . He was selfish and heartless but a most delightful fascinating companion.[16]

Faber and Smythe went for long walks in the mountains. Faber wrote his friend a sonnet.

Oh, by the love which unto thee I bear—
By the tall trees and streams and everything
In the white-clouded sky or woodland air,
Whether of sight or sound, that here may bring
The glorious freshness of the grassy spring—
Fain would I warn thee, for too well I know
Be what thou wilt thou must be dear to me;
And lo! thou art in utter bondage now
Whence I would have thy manly spirit free.
Among the hills we two did never mar
The moss about the springs, but learnt to spare
Pale flowers which rude hands would not leave to grow:
And—dearest! if thou wert so gentle there—
Thy soul hath better flowers—Oh! be as guiltless now!

"Now I really do think," Faber continued the letter which contained the poem,

I really do think, Mr. George—you have had in prose and verse
more warnings than any other Christen [*sic*] man ever had.
Yet doubtless you will receive and read this in bed, some fine
Chapelless morning—Friday for example.[17]

Smythe who had very considerable literary gifts in prose
replied:

Dear Master—I do love thee with a love
Which has with fond endeavour built a throne
In my heart's holiest place. Come sit thereon
And rule with thy sweet power, and reign above
All my thoughts, feelings, they to thee will prove
Loyal and loving vassals, for they burn
With a most passionate fire and ever yearn
And cleave to thee as ne'er before they clove,
Dearest, to others. Oh, for some strong spell
To give me back my childish heart, to shrine
Treasures I love too dearly and too well
To mar by contact with this life of mine.
Yet am I full of fears. Alas—beware
For knowing me, is ever knowing care![18]

Smythe knew himself. After the failure of his maiden speech in the House of Commons he wrote to his father:

What a position! I might have recovered myself but this is not an heroic age and I took to drinking as an opiate and an anodyne.[19]

A friend wrote of him:

He died young, worn out by dissipation, brandy and water, and a delicate chest.[20]

Frank, Faber's brother, suggested that the epithets used in this poetry-making between friends were unhealthy. He was probably thinking of a verse in a poem to Smythe:

> We pulled each other's hair about,
>   Peeped in each other's eyes,
> And spoke the first light silly words
>   That to our lips did rise.[21]

or

> Ah, dearest!—wouldst thou know how much
>   My aching heart in thee doth live?
> One look of thy blue eye—one touch
>   Of thy dear hand last night could give
> Fresh hopes to shine amid my fears,
> And thoughts that shed themselves in tears.[22]

And "A dream of blue eyes", also about Smythe, is not the sort of poem usually written by one man to another.

But Faber replied without any feelings of shame.

Strong expressions towards male friends are matters of taste. I feel what they express to *men*: I never did to a born woman. Brodie [his Harrow friend] thinks a revival of chivalry in male friendships a characteristic of the rising generation, and a hopeful one.[23]

As Sir Geoffrey Faber implied long ago in *Oxford Apostles* there was undoubtedly a homosexual element in Faber's early friendships. There is the background of the adoring mother suddenly lost. There are the typical highly idealized relationships, the talk of celibacy and so on. But Faber's manhood, as has been said before, was delayed. He was at this time still an adolescent. The conventions of the age, too, must be taken into account. The ideal woman of the time, simpering over a teapot, was no companion for a serious man. She was intellectually too much his inferior. Is there to be no strong affection without immorality? It must also be remembered that Faber always wrote in superlatives. Much of what he says, for instance about Whytehead in *Memorials of a Happy Time*, may be taken with a pinch of salt. He was, moreover, almost equally bewitched by Manners, who was Smythe's best friend. He longed for the affection and love of home life which had been denied him since his mother's death. His whole nature was poured out in his friendships. In consequence they were apt to become too intimate, too intense.

> I have been too long without a home,
>   And yearned too much for one;
> And scanty are the deeds of faith
>   My lonely heart hath done:
> For many a night my weary bed
>   Hath felt the weak tears run.
>
> Cold armour of ambitious dreams
>   I bade my soul to wear,
> And to false friendship's wildfire sweet
>   Have laid my spirit bare;
> And some few times pure heavenly thoughts
>   Awhile have lighted there.[24]

But when all is said and done is there very much to it all? Faber came of good, steady, middle-class stock, clergymen, merchants and men of business. Is it to be wondered at that his head was turned by the affection, almost the adoration, of a brilliant aristocratic boy? Smythe and Manners seemed the embodiment of all his highest standards. When he realized that Smythe would not or could not live decently he is heard of no more.

If the friendship of these years was the "wildfire" he thought it

(and he was probably right) it was, all the same, "wildfire sweet".
In many ways it was the happiest time of his life.

Faber brought with him (in 1838) from Oxford the romance
of the Movement, which its leaders believed, was re-awaken-
ing our lethargic England, and became henceforth a kind of
missionary, whose duty it was to inspire the sister university of
Cambridge with new ideas . . . No better place could have
been found for his influence to work in than the Lakes . . .
Wordsworth, good humoured in spite of sciatica, alarmed the
Cambridge men by his "venerable appearance" and entertained
them amiably to tea. If Christopher North [John Wilson of
Blackwoods] "the Admiral of the Lakes" was absent, Hamil-
ton, the once famous author of *Cyril Thornton* was at Elleray.
Thomas Arnold who was hard by at Fox Howe, seemed the
one element of discord. "An ugly clever-looking man, something like Lord Aberdeen", he is described by John Manners
. . . But it was Faber who overshadowed the poets and dons
and friends alike.[25]

"We have now virtually pledged ourselves", Manners wrote
in his Journal on 4th August 1838, "to attempt to restore what?
I hardly know—but still it is a glorious attempt, and he is
really well qualified to take the lead in it, but what rebuffs,
sneers and opposition must we expect; however, I think a
change is working for the better, and all, or nearly all, the
enthusiasm of the young spirits of Britain is with us."[26]

The friendship was heightened to a sort of reciprocal hero-
worship. If Faber was set by John Manners and Smythe upon
a pedestal of theological infallibility, they were to him the
burnished mirrors of knighthood. They exchanged ardent
letters . . .

Faber gave one Bridges a commission to paint Lord John's
portrait "standing in an old brown coat with St. John's Vale in
the background half-length", and when it was finished, he
looked at the picture, till, in his own words "I have begun to
worship it and worship him." On either side the influence was
open and acknowledged. Faber confessed to John Manners, in
a long letter of autobiography, that he had never known
quietness—not an hour—since he first met Smythe. "As I told
him last summer," he writes,

"Thou hast broken down
All mine old images, and didst uncrown
The glorious things that reigned in this my heart,
Because thou art more glorious."

He kept a watchful eye upon John Manners' spiritual welfare, and was content to be guided by him in the affairs of the world. "I always go wrong upon politics," he says, "I will give them up now. You shall be my Pope in politics. If you ever gain one tithe of the power over my intellect which you have over my heart, Hildebrand himself might envy you."[27]

The friendship continued outside the Lakes. "Now next Sunday being Epiphany", Faber wrote from Oxford on 31st December 1838,

Newman preaches twice before the University. How grim the heads will look! He will probably never do it again as long as he lives. It is a mere chance; and I am engaged out to meet him that day, and you shall go and we shall have him to ourselves afterwards. Write and say whether you will keep your Epiphany "in Oxford" as the phrase of chronicler's is about Kings of old.[28]

Manners came from Cambridge and nearly lost his degree by going. They dined with a friend. Newman made rabbits on the wall and when the friend snubbed him he fell asleep in his chair.

Afterwards Manners and Faber drifted slowly apart but their mutual friend A. J. Beresford Hope kept them in touch till "the going out of the '45".†

† Faber wrote from his deathbed to Manners a letter of goodbye. The portrait was sent to (James Alexander) Beresford Hope (1810–87), the politician and High Churchman, in 1845.

CHAPTER IV

THE LAKES AND THE CONTINENT

IN the Vacation of 1840 Faber obtained the post he wanted. He became tutor to the eldest son of Mr Benson Harrison at Green Bank, Ambleside. Mr Harrison was partner in the old foundry of Harrison Ainslie & Co., a rich man and a J.P. But he had interesting literary connections which were no doubt attractive to Faber. He had married as his second wife Dorothy Wordsworth, a cousin of the poet, who had been brought up with Wordsworth's own children at Rydal Bank. The connection with the poet was therefore very close. There may also have been a family connection between the Fabers and the Harrisons. The family was large, five boys and a girl, ranging from sixteen to eight, and Faber was expected not only to coach Matthew the eldest but also to assist Parson Dawes of Ambleside as his curate. Parson Dawes was growing infirm and was greatly worried by the success of Dissenting ministers in his parish. It seems that Faber kept on his cottage, for he erected the first cross seen in Ambleside since the Reformation in his garden. But in the winters he may have lived with the Harrisons at Green Bank. It was in every way a satisfactory post, the more so because the Harrisons were great churchgoers and patrons of the Church. Faber became devoted to Mrs Harrison, who mothered and fussed over him.

But almost immediately there was a difficulty. In his collection of poems called *The Cherwell Water-lily* which he published about this time there was one entitled *First Love*. Part of it has already been quoted. It ended:

> Thou art too young for me to tell
>   My hidden love to thee;
> And, till fit season, it must burn
>   In darkest privacy;
> For years must pass and fortunes change
>   Till such season be.

Young as thou art, hadst thou but seen
　This withered heart before,
And poured thy love, as o'er some plant
　Thou dost fresh water pour,
And watch the fragrance and the hue
　Grow into it once more—

Thou wouldst, mayhap, have felt within
　Thy first and sweetest strife
And marvelled much at the new taste
　And power it gave to life;
And so less like a dream had been
　My first dream of a wife.

The Wren was on the same theme.

I will not blame thee, Friar Wren,
Because among stout-hearted men
　Some truant monks there be;
And, if you could their names collect,
I rather more than half suspect
　That I should not be free.

Erewhile I dreamed of cloistered cells
Of gloomy courts and matin bells,
　And painted windows rare;
But common life's less real gleams
Shone warm on my monastic dreams
　And melted them to air.

My captive heart is altered now;
And, had I but one little bough
　Of yon green alder tree,
I would not live too long alone
Or languish there for want of one
　To share the nest with me!

These effusions seemed to the wits in Oxford to point to
one thing—the marriage of the poetical clergyman. What else?
The idea was greeted with sniggers. The Puseyites were always
talking of celibacy—but could they stick it? Faber's friends became

alarmed, especially poor Morris, to whom the idea was most repugnant. Newman's advice was asked but his answer was inconclusive and donnish.

Faber seems to have toyed with the idea of falling in love with Dora Harrison, to whom these poems were addressed. She was about twelve or thirteen, but it is doubtful if he ever thought the marriage a serious possibility. In any case the girl was not asked, nor were her parents consulted. Dora represented to Faber domesticity, the family circle—all the happiness which had been destroyed by his mother's death. She grew to be a woman of great sweetness of character and strong personality, but she does not seem to have been much of a beauty. And, as it turned out, by the time she had reached and grown beyond puberty, Faber no longer felt himself free to marry.

Nevertheless it was not altogether pleasant to have rumours floating around which might injure his position with the Harrisons. He wrote to Morris:

> You know my views on this subject; you may remember our talk in the Christ Church meadow about living alone, and moral as distinguished from physical continence. My present state is just this. I am not even in love as most people would count love; and I very seldom turn my thoughts that way. I honour the celibate [life] so highly and regard it as so eminently the fittest way of life for a priest, that if Christ would graciously enable me to learn to live alone, I should prefer much even with great self denials, to live a virgin life, and to die a virgin, as God has kept me so hitherto. But I am under no vow, and distrust myself too much to make one. Secondly I think my marrying more likely at some time or other than I used to think it; from the great unhappiness I had at Oxford, and the difficulty I felt in pressing my life into that mould. My health suffered from it. I carried on the struggle with hope. I have now less hope; but I have by no means abandoned the contest. I hope to live a single life; but I shall not be surprised if I marry. People who have not been deprived of a home and all home thoughts, as I have, in early boyhood, who are not sick with pent-up domestic wishes, and have not had "the vents of sweet mortal feeling closed with cold earth from the grave", having

expended part of their nature, are ill fitted to judge the trials of men left in early orphanhood, with hot feelings glowing in them unexpended still.[1]

Next day he felt so dissatisfied that he wrote again. But his friend was no nearer to knowing what was likely to happen. "*At present*", he wrote,

I have not put Holy Matrimony away from me; though I scarce think of it once a month. As I said before, I am not going to be married, and I have no prospect of marriage; and the report has as much foundation as one which should make me elect Archbishop of York.[2]

Three months later he wrote:

I never felt so strongly determined by God's grace to "make a venture of a lonely life" as J. H. N[ewman] says, as I do now.[3]

Faber was capable of, and often felt, deep affection. His nature was warm, sensitive, responsive. There are born bachelors incapable of love either through a deficiency in their natures or because of an unconscious egotism. Faber was not such a person. He was intensely preoccupied by the people around him, men or women. He had great difficulty in mastering his sexual feelings. But it seems likely that he could not, just as Newman could not, have ever given himself wholly to another being. The most intimate recesses of the souls of such men are reserved for God. Sensuality seemed to him a violation—and·who would dare say, with the sequel in mind, that it would not have been so?

This side of his mind, unnoticed by the gossips, is obscurely expressed in *Birthday thoughts at the grave of Bishop Ken*, 1839.

If in the years of my most wandering youth
Some few untended plants have learned to flower,
Thine was the mercy, Lord! and Thine the power
That sowed and kept alive the seeds of Truth.
Father and earthly mother, I have none,
Sweet bride nor marriage home, nor children here.
No looks of love—but Thine, my Saviour dear!
And my young heart bears ill to live alone.

So to the wild and weedy grave I come
Of this meek man of heart, who bore the Cross
Hid in a lordly crosier, to his home,
And for Thy love did count all else but loss.
Long as my life may be, reach me like him
To follow Thee by pathways lone and dim.
Better they should be lonely—better far
The world should all be dark; so through the night
And with fresh tears to multiply the light,
Mine eyes might see Thy pale and single star.
Yet, Lord! 'tis hard when evening shadows come
To have no sight or sound of earthly cheer;
Still were my faith but strong, Thou wouldst be near,
And I in my pure thoughts might find a home:
And memory might hear her dead loves breathe
Soft as the songs of some shy hidden bird
From the low fields or woodlands nightly heard,
That evening spell which Ken did once bequeath.—
O shame on me to fear the Cross should press
Too hard in chaste and thoughtful loneliness!

But these difficulties were thrown into the shade by Mr Harrison's consent to a continental tour. It was exactly what Faber needed. He needed to get away from his humiliations at Oxford, to see his religious problems in a wider setting, above all he needed a change. He had preached too much, written too much poetry, helped too many young men in their religious troubles. And of course he eagerly looked forward to testing again with a maturer mind "that awful, old thing, Western Christendom".

What young Harrison gained from his travels is not known or recorded. But Faber filled huge journals with copious memoranda from which he compiled a heavy volume called *Sights and Thoughts in Foreign Churches and among Foreign People*. He was prepared to produce a second volume but changed his mind and wrote a poem called *The Styrian Lake* based on the sight of a pilgrimage in the Tyrol. The prose work is still worth reading, for Faber had a flair for description. But apart from this the book stands as a memorial to that time before 1845 when Tractarian clergymen "used to distinguish themselves by making extraordinarily low bows to priests, and genuflecting, even in public places, to everyone who looked the least like a bishop". This unkind commentary by Oakeley (Faber's examiner when he failed to get his first) continues:

> In the Churches they were always in a state of prostration, or of ecstasy. Everything and everybody was charming; and such a contrast to England! Catholics might have their faults like other people, but even their faults were better than Protestant virtues. There was always a redeeming point even in their greatest misdemeanours; their acts of insobriety were far less offensive than those of Englishmen, and evidences of their Catholicity might be traced in their very oaths.[4]

Faber was too occupied with the religious schism in his mind to write merely a book of travel. It is full of history, ideas and theories upon religion. A strange imaginary character from the Middle Ages is introduced who voices Faber's Catholic aspirations. The book thus manages to reproduce the dialogue, the tension in the young clergyman's heart. It was a simple device but extraordinarily effective, especially as the meaning of the stranger's remarks becomes dramatically plainer and plainer as the book proceeds. It also gives the book a coherent form, and a variety of interest, that it would otherwise have lacked.

"The traveller in the Middle Ages rose with religious men", Faber began,

> beneath whose roof he had found shelter for the night; with them he sought, first of all, the house, oftentimes the Altar of God, and joined in the matin service of the Western Church . . .

It was very different now, Faber lamented, and indeed they visited the tombs of Voltaire and Rousseau in Paris. "Of the crowds who daily see these tombs," he commented,

> how few remember that these two men are still alive, and in a place, a waiting place, where perchance, they now see— Merciful Heavens! the very thought is horrible—the continual generation of sin and misery and unchaste disbelief by their own works.

There is a fascinating description of Avignon, anecdotes about the Avignon popes, the story of Petrarch's love for Laura. It significantly ends with a dialogue on celibacy between Faber and the stranger from the Middle Ages. The stranger insists on the virtues of celibacy. "Believe me, you will convince nobody", Faber says petulantly. "The words which I have used I have pondered, was his reply, and he returned into the city. I repeated the expression after him. 'The words which I have used I have pondered.' I remained sitting on the beach with a very vacant mind and amused myself, almost unconsciously, with throwing pebbles into the Mediterranean."[5]

The tutor and his charge travelled into Italy.

Genoa was plunged in one entire tumult of holiday [for the Annunciation]. All the shops were shut; but booths of fruit and every kind of eatables crowded the streets. Lent seemed forgotten. The churches were thronged by men well dressed and women almost gorgeously apparelled. Bells ringing, chiming, and playing tunes without intermission all day. Genoa was a chaos of bells. All sounds of labour were hushed; the steamboats were stopped in the middle of their voyages and every street was filled with heaps, or rather stacks of flowers, wherewith to honour the images and altars of the Blessed Virgin.

At the Certosa of Pavia Faber pointed out with enthusiasm to his pupil "work in very precious materials in more than one place where it could scarcely be seen by any human eye". This always appealed to Faber as it appealed to all the Tractarians from Hurrell Froude onwards. "We would as soon throw ourselves from our own steeples", Faber commented, "as do anything elaborate or costly or beautiful where it would never meet the eyes of men."

Outside, the stranger reappeared and they talked of Rome which Faber had decided not to visit.

. . . And, continued I, not heeding his interruption, if the day of Rome's penitence comes not, then England is as it were the limit of the old continent, whence Catholic teaching and Catholic form may pass over to the last harvest-field of the Cross. "What," said he angrily, "does not the majesty of Rome, that awful Church, so overawe your spirit as to prevent you talking with such curious ingenuity of Rome's penitence? . . . Rome is not as other Churches. She is not a common city: she has no common chair . . . Oh Rome! the city of my times, the place of our glad and lowly pilgrimages, how changed thou art in many things, but still thou art Rome, and hast Rome's prerogative,—a tremendous power to ban or bless."

At Milan they visited the tomb of St Charles Borromeo.

The longer we remained in the Cathedral, the more its glory and magnificence, and coloured gloom, took possession of our spirits. It is an oppressive thing to be a priest in the city of St Ambrose and St Charles Borromeo, and yet a stranger; a gazer,—a mere English looker-on,—a tourist, where one should be upon one's knees at home, and in that divine temple a legitimate worshipper. But where rests the blame?

Venice was not beyond Faber's descriptive powers.

One by one rose steeple, tower and dome, street and marble palace. They rose to our eyes slowly as from the weedy deeps; and then they and their images wavered and floated, like a dream upon the pale sunny sea.

So the journey went on across Europe, the scenes of travel a backcloth to the inner religious debate. From Venice they visited Greece.

Faber had had high expectations of the Orthodox Church which seemed to many Tractarians to stand where they wished the Church of England to be. But he was soon disillusioned in Greece.

We are entering the low vine-clad convent which is to be our home for the night, and the priest is descending from the small chapel on the hill, where he has been saying the afternoon prayers, and the little boy who makes the responses is with him. He leads a happy life, yon old priest. From sunrise to sunset, except at prayer time, he smokes a cherry-stick pipe, and is happy. He threatens the cattle with evil eye, and the people with anathema, and kids are brought to him and he is fed, and paid and feared, and the cherry-stick pipe never goes out, and he sits under the shade of the convent fig-tree, and he

gazes on Marathon always. The green lizard on the wall beside
the tank is not happier than the long-bearded convent priest.
But what if more be required of the one than of the other?
Then it is not so well.

"Alas!" Faber wrote home to Morris,

I can learn little good of the poor forlorn Greek Church. It is,
excepting the Russian branch of which I know nothing, in a
very sad state. . . . Depend upon it, Jack, cast about as we will,
if we want foreign Catholic sympathies we must find them as
they will let us in our Latin mother.[6]

They had an uncomfortable time in Greece. Faber fell ill with
"an inflammation of the bowels followed by a prickly rash . . .
and a slight *coup de soleil*". By the time they reached Constantinople
he was in no condition to go on to Jerusalem as they had hoped.
They reluctantly decided to turn homewards.

In the Tyrol Faber was present at a pilgrimage which greatly
impressed him. Four of the pilgrims had died on the way but the
scene in the church was magnificent. Faith really seemed to have
overcome death. "When the organ burst forth", he wrote in his
journal,

and about three thousand voices raised the hymn to the
Virgin, I thought the roof of the church would have been lifted
up. I never heard such a volume of musical, really musical
sound before. Then the grand mass began, and the incense
floated all round. It was a bewildering sight. I thought how
faith ran in my own country in thin and scattered rivulets,
and I looked with envious surprise at this huge wave which the
Austrian capital had flung upon this green platform of Styrian
highland—a wave of pure, hearty, earnest faith.[7]

On his return Faber worked up his journal into a book and
dedicated it to "William Wordsworth Esq., in affectionate remembrance of much personal kindness, and many thoughtful conversations on the rites, prerogatives, and doctrines of Holy
Church"—a dedication which Crabb Robinson thought un-
scrupulous. But then Faber had always been a Wordsworthian
and he wanted to annex Wordsworth's name to the Tractarian

Movement. Wordsworth may or may not have read the book
but there is no evidence that he made any objection.

Faber ended the volume with an outspoken allegory.

After midnight I fell asleep, and dreamed again. Methought
I was with the mysterious stranger, on a bright sunny bank
of velvet turf, a little brook murmuring near and a copse
hard by, full of meadow-sweet, the odour of which filled all
the air. Everything around spoke the voluptuous langour of
midsummer. The Stranger asked me to explain all the doctrines
and customs of my Church. So I took a sheet of vellum, and
I wrote them all out in columns, in a fair hand, from the calen-
dars and rubrics of the Service Books. He was much pleased
with it, and said it was very beautiful and good. Then he
proposed we should walk up the stream some little way. So
I hid the vellum among the meadow-sweet, and we walked
together up the stream. But a heavy shower of rain came on,
and we took shelter in a cave which was in the face of a rock,
all clasped with ivy, bindweed, and eglantine. When the sun
shone again we returned to our bank, and I looked for the vellum, and the rain had washed all the characters away. Upon
this the Stranger said I had deceived him; that if what I had
written were true, no rain would have washed it away; and he
would not believe me when I said it was true, but he was very
angry. However he said he would judge for himself. So we
rose up, and went a long way for many weeks till we came to
Canterbury on Advent Sunday. From thence we went all
over the land throughout the parishes, and the Stranger took
strict note of all he saw and heard. At length we came to the
banks of the Tweed. The Stranger would not cross over, but
he lifted up his hands, and blessed the land on the other side.
So we turned back again toward the south; and on Ascension-
day we were in a forlorn and desolate chancel belonging to a
spacious church. It was a dreary, unadorned place, for the
beauty was lavished on the nave rather than the chancel; and
over the altar, a very mournful symbol, were seven empty
white-washed niches. The Stranger regarded them with indignation, but did not speak. When we came out of the church,
he turned to me and said in a solemn voice, somewhat tremu-
lous from deep emotion. "You have led me through a land of

closed churches and hushed bells, of unlighted altars and un-stoled priests: Is England beneath an interdict?"[8]

Back in England Faber tried to settle down at Ambleside. But the Tractarian Movement had entered stormy water. While Faber was still on the Continent Tract 90 was published. New-man's purpose was to show that the 39 Articles were capable of a Catholic interpretation. With a lack of foresight amounting to blindness, of which pious men alone seem capable, he pub-lished the Tract without any forebodings. Was it not intended to keep the Romeward wing of the movement inside the Church of England? The heads of houses and the bishop soon made it plain that they intended to use the Tract for exactly the opposite purpose—to drive the more advanced Tractarians into the Catho-lic Church. Faber seems to have been equally blind:

> I shall be sorry if [*Sights and Thoughts in Foreign Churches*] disquiets anyone's mind as it was written for one particular class of men who are verging Romewards and whom I have aided in staying.[9]

It is difficult to see in what way the book would have aided any-one in staying in the Church of England. Faber and his fellow Tractarians were at this time hopelessly out of touch with ordinary churchgoers. They behaved as if they did not understand the implications of what they said. And of course Protestants were not slow to accuse Faber of duplicity. Soon after his return he was described as

> very good looking with eyes of fine blue, set in deeply hol-lowed sockets, an aquiline nose, and a general expression wild—imaginative—unsettled.[10]

His mind indeed was in a muddle. "Though I think orthodoxy most important," he wrote confusingly to Morris about the Hampden controversy,

> yet I think charity to unproved or unpronounced suspected persons would be in St Paul's view more important than a faith which would remove mountains . . .[11]

At this time his aim seems to have been restricted to an attempt to push the Articles to their very utmost Catholic limits. He apparently accepted the corollary that Anglicanism could also be stretched in other directions. It was a moment of Liberalism and later he bitterly repented of it. But it was a time of great uncertainty.

He was very unsettled. The thought that the Roman Church might be the true Catholic fold hung like a shadow over his spirit. If it were so, what should he do? From his earliest boyhood his one ambition had been to be a clergyman. He loved England and the English countryside with an almost passionate warmth. He wanted to serve England. What if his conscience made him relinquish his vocation, become a layman? Anything further was unthinkable. But at least he had the consolation of his poetry.

His poetry is, as read today, competent, dextrous, melodious but damned throughout by slovenliness and prolixity. Here and there are memorable lines, there are often memorable phrases. But the unerring judgment of time has cast it all into oblivion. Now there is none to read it without a yawn. But at the time it was written there was a poetical vacuum. Wordsworth was growing in fame, but his greatest poetry had long since been written. Byron and Shelley, long dead, were also growing popular. Keats was still viewed with some disparagement. Faber himself quotes *The Ode to a Grecian Urn* with the remark that Keats's

real merits false principles of taste and a singularly feeble dominion over his mother-tongue have perhaps too much overshadowed.[12]

Tennyson was unknown. Sir Henry Taylor's frigid *Philip van Artevelde* was considered great art. Keble's poetry was eagerly read. At such a time of transition and critical uncertainty Faber was taken seriously enough. If the Oxford movement could produce the *Lyra apostolica* and *The Christian Year* could it not also create something more? Was it not likely that this great stirring of conscience would produce a poetry that would rival the work of Crashaw, Vaughan and Herbert? Was it conceivable that it would produce no art?

The truth, as we know it now, is that the Oxford Movement produced no poetry, no painting, no architecture. It did indeed produce the greatest prose writer of the 19th century, a rival, if not a superior to Dryden. But there is no poetry even to compare with Wesley's hymns, the architecture is second-hand, the painting non-existent. There was, it is true, a late weak flowering in the hot-house atmosphere of the Pre-Raphaelite Brotherhood. But even that was evanescent. The Brotherhood may have been the last genuine artistic movement in England but it lacked directness and reality. The lyric poetry of Christina Rossetti, the paintings of Holman Hunt, the architecture of Street—that was the late, final artistic achievement when the aims of the Movement had been mixed, diluted and changed by a multitude of other influences. In itself the Movement was artistically dead. Looking back we find it strange, and it was considered strange at the time, for the Tractarians were no Philistines. They were intensely interested in the arts. Many of them scribbled or sketched. But there was a fatal malady somewhere. Tractarian art was second-hand, derived. It could produce nothing. Whether Evangelicalism which played so much greater a part in the Movement than is generally allowed blighted such art as there was; or whether, more charitably, it may be supposed that strong religious feeling may best be expressed in other ways than art; or whether the Movement was too short, too broken, too torn by controversy to be creative; or whether the fact of its deliberate reaction against the Liberal and Utilitarian stream of the time rendered it sterile—however it may be explained, the fact speaks for itself—the Movement contained innumerable amateurs of art but no creators. And this was not expected. It was considered that one of the poetical clergymen in the Movement would become—what Tennyson and Browning were to be. Was it not likely that Whytehead or Faber might become the poet of the Movement?

That was the hope. *The Cherwell Water-lily* might reasonably be compared to *Poems by Two Brothers* but scarcely to anything better. There is much natural description which Faber did so well in prose. The sonnet sequences are remarkable for their ease and clarity. But there is little intensity, too much facility, no compression. And behind the free-flowing verses—what was there? Except in the few instances quoted there is no sight of the Faber manifest in the letters—a man of strong feelings struggling for truth as if with a giant, for ever falling and for ever rising again. The Faber of the poems is altogether a different person, effeminate, sweet, cultivated, with charming ways and high religious aspirations. His poetry was not half of the man. From his letters it is known how deeply he was hurt during the period of his fellowship at Oxford. Yet his poetry would lead any reader to suppose that he had not felt very much. His poem *Unkind Judging* perhaps pinpoints the faults of his poetry and Tractarian verse as a whole. Instead of expressing what he felt he expresses what he ought to feel—which is unhappily a very different thing.

> To be thought ill of, worse than we deserve,
> To have hard speeches said, cold looks displayed
> By those who should have cheered us when we swerve—
> Is one of Heaven's best lots, and may be made
> A treasure ere we know it, a lone field
> Which to hot hearts may bitter blessings yield.
> Either we learn from our past sins to shrink,
> When their full guilt is kept before our eye,
> And, thinking of ourselves as others think,
> We so are gainers in humility:—
> Or the harsh judgments are a gloomy screen,
> Fencing our altered lives from praise and glare;
> And plants that grow in shades retain their green,
> While unmeet sternness kindly chills the air.

In the mind of a true poet an experience of this kind grows, fed by some inner food, till it becomes a new thing, a creation. In Faber's case the experience is not transformed, it is truncated, consciously spiritualized. The bite of true poetry, the ache and anger of true feeling are lacking.

Faber had an immense sense of fun and amusement but was devoid of critical detachment. He was for ever putting himself in a ludicrous light. His poems are full of blunders of taste—irritating blunders which he was to perpetrate to the end of his

life. In one poem he takes a poor girl to task who is upset by
the rain which has spoilt her picnic:

> Angels are round thee and Heaven's above
> And thy soul is alive within;
> Shall a rainy day and a cloudy sky
> Make a Christian soul to sin?

Another unwary female fails to please:

> But she sang light songs at a solemn time
> And the spell was gone forever;
> And who shall say 'twas a trivial thing
> That delicate chain to sever.

An Anglican bishop, annoyed by the Tractarian habit of head-
ing letters with the Saint's day—St Wilfrid's Day, etc.—headed
his "Washing Day". The title of one of Faber's poems makes the
reader sympathize with the bishop. "Birthday Thoughts. June 28,
1838. A.S. The Feast of St Irenaeus. The Vigil of St Peter. The
Coronation of Queen Victoria."

But on his return home from the Continent after illness at
Constantinople and another illness in England Faber changed. A
shadow had fallen, youth had gone. Manners complained that he
no longer felt the impulse of those old dreams. Faber replied as if
an impenetrable barrier lay between them.

> I mourn not as thou mournest, o'er the fate
> Of our own summer year of thirty eight.
> It came and went within us like a breeze,
> Chiming among our thoughts as in the trees.
> It stirred us, as a breeze may stir the lake,
> And thou art gazing yet on its bright wake.
> A glory is no glory, if it last;
> Thou art entranced, young dreamer! in the past.

Faber was conscious of a ripening and deepening of his spirit.
He wanted quietness as if to brace himself for the future. He tried
to explain it to Manners.

Time was when from within myself I drew
My powers and thoughts and instincts: all I knew
Was but the self-sprung harvest of my heart,
And the whole outward world was cast apart;
I was a worldless man, a thing detached,
A wandering cloud, a being all unmatched
With outward destiny; but now my power
Is from the world imported every hour.
The pains I suffer, and the tears I see,
Men's passions, chance-encountered, and the child's glee
And moral contradictions and green leaves,
And skies and streams,—from these my spirit weaves
Her web, and every day that passes by
Both add some little to the tapestry:
For moral wisdom is a growing thing
Whene'er it rises from an outward spring.[13]

Faber was shedding something of the preciousness of his youth. He no longer wanted to appear so poetical, almost he no longer wanted to be a poet, and in the event his poetic powers increased. He wished above all to master himself. He seems to have had an obscure desire to suffer. He recalled in his poetry again and again the loss of his mother. He remembered walks by the sea with her, angry words he had spoken to her, and he passionately wished she was with him again. She would have counselled him what to do. What if it was his duty to throw religious perplexity aside, be content to stay where he was, to be a Wordsworthian poet among the lakes and mountains? And yet . . .

Meanwhile staying with the Benson Harrisons he assisted Parson Dawes. An old custom, the renewing of the rushes in the church had been revived and a hymn written for the occasion. As the rushes were, of course, no longer needed for the floor the custom was a conscious archaism. The children came in a procession through Ambleside with garlands of rushes which were used to decorate the church. To Faber it was the revival of an old, more spiritual England that had died at the Reformation. He remembered the pilgrimage in the Tyrol. If it could not be quite that, it was something near it. His sermons for this feast were long remembered.

It was as a "poet-priest, habited in a blouse with a broad-brimmed straw hat"[14] that he was regarded in the Lakes—as much one as the other. Wordsworth was impressed with him and Faber undoubtedly influenced the old man. The poet wrote a sonnet on the rush-bearing ceremony which with its reference to Laud and Hooker must have been inspired by Faber. Wordsworth spoke of Faber as having, more than any other man known to him, a sympathy with Nature, like his own.[15] Faber's influence was so great that some people feared that the poet might become a full-blooded Tractarian—if not worse.

Henry Crabb Robinson, lawyer, Protestant, correspondent of *The Times* and the friend of many famous men confided to his diary:

> 1841. Dec. 27th. We had a dinner party: Mr. and Mrs. Robinson, Mr. and Mrs. Harrison, and Mr. Faber. This ultra-Puseyite High Churchman, whom I had taken a dislike to, pleased me today very much. He has been a long journey with Mr. Harrison's son to Constantinople and has written a book about the state of religion in the countries he passed through. He is a lively narrator and a very spirited talker. His prejudices are strong, or should I rather say his opinions are *one-sided* and *violent*? He speaks with abhorrence of French Protestants and says Huguenots were always a factious and worthless set. Their representative Henry IV. Like him ready to change their religion (manifestly false, why did they not?). He speaks with equal contempt of religion in Prussia and of the Prussian government. The King wishes to establish a Church without rights and entirely dependent on the State. Faber is one of those who would make the Church independent. In nothing do I so much dissent from him as in his admission that he thinks the true Church ought to be supported by pains and penalties. He is not friendly to Romanism, says Lingard's *History* is one consistent *lie* throughout. He says Wiseman is not an honest man and has been convicted of false quotations. Yet with my utter dissent from much that Faber said, his manner pleased me and I should like to see him again.[16]

Faber fascinated the liberal journalist as much as his theological views disgusted him. "I meant a few days ago", he was writing the next year,

> to send a civil message to your friend Mr. Faber. The book
> [*Sights and Thoughts in Foreign Churches*] has matters that will
> justify many a civil word. . . . But it has also detestable doc-
> trines—the only damnable heresies I know. There is on p. 421
> a vindication of putting to death for heresy coupled with
> something like Mr. W's [Wordsworth's] philosophy of capital
> punishment; or which the world will consider as such—And
> perhaps as the produce of their *thoughtful conversations* together.[17]

In another letter he explains the views of Wordsworth's circle.

> The *Church* as you are aware is now much more than *Religion*
> the subject of general interest—And the *Puseyites* are the body
> who are now pushing the claim of *Church Authority* to a
> revolting excess. The poet [Wordsworth] is a *high* Churchman
> but luckily does not go all lengths with the Oxford school—
> He praises the *reformers* (for they assume to be such) for inspiring
> the age with deeper reverence for antiquity. And a more
> special conformity with ritual observances—As well as a
> warmer piety—But he goes no further—Nevertheless he is
> claimed by them as *their* poet. And they have published a selec-
> tion from his works with a dishonest preface from which one
> might infer he went all lengths with them—This great question
> forms our *Champs de Mars*—which *we* of the liberal party
> occupy to a sad disadvantage. Last year we had with us an
> admirable and most excellent man *Dr. Arnold*—but whom the
> poet was on doctrinal points forced to oppose, tho' he was
> warmly attached to him—Instead of him we have this year a
> sad fanatic of an opposite character—I doubt whether I have
> mentioned him on any former occasion—This is *Faber* the
> Author of a strange book lately published Sights etc., in foreign
> lands. He is a flaming zealot for the new doctrines. And like
> Froud[e] does not conceal his predilection for the Church—
> in Rome—(not *of* Rome yet) and his dislike to Protestantism.
> In his book of travels he puts into the mouth of a visionary
> character, a doctrine which in his own person he indirectly
> assents to, or at least does not contradict—that whenever the

Church declares anyone a *heretic*, the State violates its duty, if it hesitates in putting him to death!!! This is going the whole hog with a witness—This Faber is an agreeable man. All the young ladies are in love with him. And he has high spirits, conversational talent and great facility in writing both polemics and poetry. He and I spar together on all occasions and have never yet betrayed ill humour tho' we have exchanged pretty hard knocks. . . . You are aware that here I am considered as a sort of Advocatus Diaboli.[18]

"He is certain he will never go over to Rome", Robinson wrote sardonically in his diary,

> though he rather regrets not having been born in that communion. He believes both the Roman and the Anglican Churches to be portions of the Catholic Church. On my objecting to the manifold corruptions of the Romish Church he admitted these, but held they did not invalidate its authority. They are trials of the faith of the believer. This same idea of the trial of faith he applied to other difficulties, and to the seeming irrationality of certain orthodox doctrines. A revelation ought to have difficulties. It is one of the signs of its Divine origin that it seems incredible to the natural man. On this topic, I confessed that I agreed with him so far as obvious mysteries are concerned . . . but I could not extend this to those pretended revelations which are repugnant to my moral sense. Did I find, for instance, in the Scriptures, the eternal damnation of infants, this would, in spite of all evidence in their favour, make me reject the Scriptures: that is I would imagine any falsification or corruption of the text, rather than believe they contained a doctrine which blasphemed against God. To this, he declared, that were even this doctrine in the Scriptures (but the contrary of which is there), he would believe it, because what God affirms must be true, however repugnant. I conceded the last position but observed that it begged the question to say the Scriptures must, even in that case, be believed to be true. And as to the Scriptures Faber's own notions should lead him to agree to this; for one of the most remarkable parts of his system is his placing the Church above the Scriptures. . . . Mr. Faber declared that, without the Church, the Scriptures would not suffice to convince him—he should

be an unbeliever; and he declared Bibliolatry to be the *worst of idolatries* . . .[19]

And so the theological discussions went on and were all duly committed to his diary.

He did, in fact, in emphatic terms, assert the Real Presence and that the Sacraments could only be validly administered by the clergy legitimately appointed by Episcopal ordination, in Apostolic succession. . . . Nothing could be more agreeable than his manner, and he impressed me strongly with his amiability, his candour, and his ability. But I could agree with very little indeed.[20]

"I have had a very pleasant chat with Mr Faber", he wrote to a friend,

who, in spite of everything in his book, protests that he can never by any possibility become a member of the Church of Rome. He takes credit for having rescued a considerable number of persons standing on the brink of the precipice from tumbling down. But to introduce Popery into the Church of England is, I think, a much greater evil than joining the Church of Rome.[21]

Wordsworth told Robinson that Faber had considerable poetic talent. In theological matters the old man deferred to the clergyman. Faber persuaded him to place a cedar cross made by Morris in his bedroom where, he said, "the good old man's pleased eye rests on it first thing when he wakes". Robinson went for a walk with the two men.

Their conversation I was not competent altogether to follow, but certainly Wordsworth's tone was that of deference towards his younger and more consistent friend. . . . Wordsworth denied Transubstantiation on grounds on which, says Faber, "I should deny the Trinity". Faber objected to the sonnet on Alexander III putting his foot on the neck of the Emperor and says it is founded on a flagrant falsehood. . . . Wordsworth declared in strong terms his disbelief of eternal punishment which Faber did not attempt to defend.[22]

Wordsworth gave his final opinion of Faber some years later when Faber had written a very long poem in blank verse called *Sir Lancelot*.

It is however too obvious that he is in the habit of using strong expressions, so that what he says must be taken with some qualification. This practice in so very pious, good and able a man is deeply to be regretted. Mary says to me, tell him of it, but if it be a specific fact, say of numbers or quantity in respect to which his accounts at different times have varied, it is surely an awkward thing to mention that to a gentleman. And if diversity of statements concerns vague and indefinite matters one does not see how one can fasten the charge upon the speaker so as to produce any effect.

I have told him what I thought of his poem, as far as I have read it. It is a mine of description, and valuable thought and feeling: but too minute and diffusive and disproportioned: and in the workmanship very defective. The Poem was begun too soon and carried on too rapidly before he had attained sufficient experience in the art of writing and this he candidly and readily admits. Some of his friends wish and urge him to continue writing verse. I had a long conversation with him upon this subject yesterday, in which he gave me such an account of himself that I could not concur with those advisers in their opinion. A man like him cannot serve two Masters ... No man can write verses that will live in the hearts of his fellow creatures but through an overpowering impulse in his own mind, involving him often times in labour that he cannot dismiss or escape from, though his duty to himself and others may require it.[23]

In the summer of 1842 he was working on *Sir Lancelot* at a terrific pace. The object of the poem was

to show how to one in ascetic living nature is a kind of Church. Sir Lancelot is a Knight of the XIIIth century supposed to be excommunicated under very peculiar circumstances.[24]

The idea that lay behind the poem was the peculiar solution to which, since his return from the Continent, he was fumbling. Like Sir Lancelot he felt himself excommunicated. He had lost faith in the Church of England. Was it possible that he might do without a Church at all and substitute Nature for it? Wordsworth seemed to have done so, and who could say that he was wrong? Nature in itself as a manifestation of God was a sort of sacrament. Perhaps he would be able to do more good as a poet than in any other way. Morris had published a poem similar to *Sir Lancelot* on much the same theme and it gave Faber confidence. And yet it is doubtful if this bizarre solution could ever have satisfied him. It was, in fact, more of a temptation than a solution. There was nothing he would have liked better than to be able to spend the rest of his life as a "poet-priest" in the Lakes. But would his conscience allow it? Would his intellect allow it?

Then the issue was taken out of his hands. University College offered him the living of Elton in Huntingdonshire. At first he refused and then with a feeling of fatalism he accepted. The rickety structure on which he had built his life in the Lakes was kicked away from under him. "I have today made up my mind", he wrote to Morris,

> to accept Elton when it is formally offered. I really trust that in the heart of the prayer and fasting of this Ember week I have been enabled to put aside my own will in the matter: yet I would speak diffidently about it as knowing my wilfulness. This living hovered about my head in the spring like a bird uncertain where to light. That was an admonition. Again I positively refused it, consulting my own wilfulness, ten days ago: then the Master *forced* the consideration of it upon me again. And, as Pusey says somewhere, "events not of our own seeking are mostly God's ordering"; and Mr. Wordsworth thinks the Providence so obvious that he should not dare to refuse, were it his own case. Further, I feel that my chief rock of offence is the subduing of the priest to the poet,[25] and I have felt more strongly this Advent than ever, that I have very sinfully permitted the man of letters to overlay the priest . . . There was something of officious alacrity and pertinacious zeal in the way the Master and Twiss (I believe) threw the matter back upon me which was not agreeable to my vanity. . . . Further, the only *pure* pleasure which has perhaps aided my decision was at having the opportunity afforded me of clearing

myself of debt. .... But now comes what makes me tremble, the solitude of that lone place. I do assure you, my dear Jack, that I am perfectly fancy-free! ... I do believe, my dear Jack, that I am judging right in this matter. I feel so happy and so open I know not why, or how, that I think I must be doing right: and Oh! how slight a sacrifice is parting with this "sweet mountain-land", and all the Wordsworths and my dear friends for a man of such sins as mine. My books are gone [he had to sell them to settle a debt], now my mountains go. God be praised. O pray for me that buried in that village I may endeavour to live an apostolical life in Church, parsonage, and cottages.[26]

Once he had fully braced himself for the sacrifice a new draught of life flooded into him. He visited Elton itself which he found far less dreadful than expected. Then came an annoying hitch and all seemed off. He spent his time writing to friends defending *Sir Lancelot* against charges of pantheism. Finally there was a visit to old George Stanley at Sherburn.

Harry was very nervous about it, but Uncle was very affectionate and except a sly poke in the ribs from time to time kept clear of the detested Tractarianism and boasted he was a "stiff backed Protestant." O, thought I, how nicely the Protestant *ethos* is all packed up in that epithet.[27]

On Sunday 2nd April 1843 Faber read himself in at Elton. He was very affected by the warmth of his reception by the village. And then, with that strange inconsequence which was part of his charm, he set off the very next day for the Continent. His intention was to learn from the Catholic Church how he should carry out his duties as parish priest of Elton. Much had changed in his mind since his visit to Belgium with Church, much, indeed, since his tour with Matthew Harrison. He was now armed with letters of introduction from Dr Wiseman to Cardinal Acton and Dr Grant at Rome. The journey was no longer a tour. He considered it a pilgrimage.[28]

CHAPTER V

A PILGRIMAGE

HE was accompanied on his pilgrimage by another pupil and the journey was chronicled in long letters home to his brother Frank. Faber had an immense capacity for enjoyment. Throughout his life he found it impossible to believe that anyone could wish not to be alive. In spite of headaches and minor complaints his letters bubble over with pleasure. "It was a picture of plenty," he wrote of Provence,

> of beautiful plenty—vine, olive, corn, fig, mulberry, rose, orange, lemon, jujube, walnut, cherry, and I know not what, and all with fine dappled mountains to the north; and on the south, scarcely ever absent from the eye, the glittering indigo of the Mediterranean.

He found the road from Nice to Genoa

> not to be described, the beauty of it is so exquisite ... Now you are among orange-gardens, now in woods of pinaster, and by cliffs with giant aloes sticking out of the rifts; add to this the sensual pleasure of alternating between slow ascents and rattling descents, the childish thrill of joy at there being no parapet on the cliffs, and—but you have no nose—the orange-flowers and the hot-house smell of the fig-leaves, and what can be wanted by the tourist?[1]

At Savona he read the Italian poet Chiabrera's epitaph and it seemed an omen.

> It has affected me very deeply indeed: I have often alluded (to you) to the struggle in myself between the poet and the priest, on account of the *absorbing* character of such a pursuit as poetry, and the *exclusive* character of such a calling as the priesthood. More than once I have desisted from composition, but in the end nature got the upper hand of holier resolutions. All this has been passing through my mind lately, and in the

acme of another struggle Chiabrera rises from the dead, and preaches from his tomb in San Giacomo at Savona. These are the words he ordered to be engraved:

AMICO, IO VIVENDO CERCAVA CONFORTO
NEL MONTE PARNASSO:
TU, MEGLIO CONSIGLIATO, CERCALO
NEL CALVARIO!

I do not think I ever got such a sermon in my life.[2]

It was a sermon he was to take to heart, but not immediately. The shadow of the cross had, however, already fallen on his life, little as he yet knew it. At La Spezia he confessed that he thought of that "low unprincipled scoundrel", Shelley, and it was not long before he was maintaining that the Riviera below Genoa was even more beautiful than the French Riviera which he had already described in such glowing terms. At Pisa he tried to shake off his delight in natural beauty. He had come, after all, as a pilgrim not as a tourist.

The great tower leaning like a telescope pointed *toward Rome*.

Italy was "a second Palestine, the Holy Land of the West."[3]

At Siena, "suffering severely from a bilious attack", he staggered about the streets in mingled pain and delight.

A red and stormy sunset was making its way into the [cathedral] through the narrow windows, and playing with the alternate stripes of black and white marble in a marvellous manner, while in the gloomy side-chapels the candles burnt like steady stars before the several altars . . . Altogether I am fascinated with Siena, and could write pages to you about it, were it not for the *tremblement de système* which my bilious attack is causing.[4]

And then came Rome.

From the lip of the crater of Baccano I saw the dome of St. Peter's: I have crossed the Ponte Molle, where Constantine vanquished Maxentius and established Christianity, and by moonlight I have prayed at the Tomb of the Apostles, almost alone in the metropolitan church of the whole world. To describe my feelings is impossible.[5]

He spent his time learning Italian. He read assiduously Italian books of theology and devotion. By means of his letters from Wiseman he visited many places quite unknown to the tourist. "There are", he wrote,

> two separate Romes; the Rome of the English, exclusive, frivolous, ignorant, surrounded with *valets de place* who think to please the Protestants by inventing scandals of the Pope or *amours* of the Cardinals or priests: eating ices, subscribing to reading-rooms, buying cameos, examining artists' studios, coursing over picture galleries, reading the last novel, going to Mass to hear music "not discerning the Lord's body". This is one Rome which lies mainly to the north-east, and of which I see only glimpses now. The other is made up of residents, native or foreign, quiet Cardinals, humble Jesuits, unobtrusive monks, pious scholars, kind-hearted, simple-mannered, erudite,—full of interest of all kinds—the existence of which second Rome ninety-nine out of a hundred of the English tourists no more suspect than that of a secret club at Ispahan.[6]

Among other places he visited the Chiesa Nuova where the body of St Philip Neri lies. The Oratorian father who showed him round apologized to Faber for kissing the glass of the case in which St Philip's little bed is kept as a relic. The priest explained how tenderly St Philip's children love their father and that that love was his excuse. Faber was greatly impressed by the atmosphere of the Chiesa Nuova and from this time he had a devotion to St Philip.

"It is natural that while thus adoring the Divine Footsteps in history", he wrote to Morris of Rome,

> and overwhelmed by the admonitions of such holy places, one's thirst for Catholic unity should increase to an extent which might lead one to undisciplined acts; living too with saintly men and hearing their affectionate eloquence on unity and Rome. Moreover, I am specially anxious to keep my mind open to conviction, and to expel all rude, unreasoning dislike out of my thoughts: for neither shame, nor station, nor interest would, I hope, prevent me from going where conscience

leads. But I do not find myself shaken at all, though in many ways humbled; and in proportion to the openness with which I lay myself out to receive impressions and views, I persevere in prayer not to be led astray, nor seek anything of my own will, and I find my attachment to the Church of England growing in Rome, the more I bewail our position. All arguments on the doctrine of indulgences etc. I have put aside, telling my friends that in reality the one thing necessary to prove was, that adherence to the Holy See was essential to the *being* of a Church; to the *well*-being of all Churches I admit it essential.

If this point were demonstrated by Catholic tradition, I apprehend the controversy is over with me. They did not seem quite to like this simplification of the matter; and have been quite unable hitherto to establish a case. One professor, whom I much esteem, urged upon me his own firm faith that I should not be saved: I said that of course it was most distressing to be told so, but afforded no ground to leave my Church, and that if we were humbly submitting ourselves to antiquity, and truly penitent for our own sins, and spoke no evil of our brethren, I could not but hope that God "would reveal this unto us also," if needful.

On returning home and reading the evening service, I was delighted on meeting in the Psalms the verse, "And no good thing shall be withheld from them that lead a godly life"; it seemed to come with great force and to justify the method in which I had put the controversy. In another discussion of a very grave nature, I said to the Rector of the English College†, "It is not right to press me in this way; before you urge me to leave my (so called) Church, you must *first* prove that she is no Church, or is unchurched, otherwise you urge me to what is, in your own moral theology a sin, viz., a disobedient act of self-will and self-judgment against an authority whose lawfulness you have not disproved. This is not right; you are urging my conscience to a sin." He took my hand, and said I was right; that so long as I felt in my conscience that I could not without sin leave my Church, he would never give me advice to leave it, or welcome my conversion.

† Charles Michael Baggs 1806–45; 1840 Rector of English College; 1844 Vicar Apostolic Western District in succession to Bishop Baines.

Thus at present I feel much benefited by my visit to Rome, and my allegiance to England quite unshaken. Of course I could not make any use of a *feeling* as an argument, yet I confess that sometimes when I am hard pressed I feel that there is a little fortress in the background quite unsuspected by the enemy, namely, recollections of Oxford and the good people there. I feel, however unable I may be to put it scholastically, that *there* is evident work of the Holy Spirit, whose sanctifying influences they would restrain, so far as any real advance in holiness is concerned, to the Roman Church . . . It is plain I am in somewhat of a dangerous position, yet from which I think it would not be right to fly, and in which I have not been shaken hitherto. I feel my chief security to be in continuing to regard the matter one much more to be decided by moral temper than by scholastic theology.[7]

He was now busily reading the lives of modern Italian saints. Dr Grant, another friend of Wiseman's, later to be a bishop in England, took him to

little obscure places where interesting memorials of them are to be seen, or at least where one can court *admonitus locorum* of an edifying sort.[8]

He wrote Frank a violent letter which turned almost into a sermon.

That there is plenty of Protestantism in the Church of England I am not wild enough to deny; but one cannot too *openly* or too consistently assert one's opinion that it is a spirit alien to that of the Church, condemned by the Church, and separable from it; just as a demon is separable from the sufferer whom he is allowed to possess . . . Depend upon it, we have a hard enough game to play with the Church of Rome, and nothing but a prominent bringing into view of the Catholic, i.e. anti-Protestant, character of our Church, can save our best, holiest and most learned members from leaving her. Protestantism has had three centuries of existence; in Prussia, where it rose, it has degenerated into a blasphemous rationalism, denying the four Gospels; in Switzerland, its second home, it has sunk into the worst form of Socinianism; in English Dissent it has degenerated into an impious caricature of the truth, and in the Church it is now fighting for its life against sacraments and good works. We must take our parts. . . . To take or allow the very *name* of Protestant, rejected by our own Church, is to disobey the Church, and so commit, if *knowingly* done, a *mortal* sin; and in proportion as our honest conviction of this is suppressed will be the number of our members who will leave us and go over to the Church of Rome. Now I pray you do not suppress this letter. If God prolongs our lives a quarter of a century, our doubts will be solved. Protestantism is perishing: what is good in it is by God's mercy being gathered into the garners of Rome; what is bad in it is running into blasphemy and unbelief. Whether our Church be a Church, be something *more* than that, something over and above a form of Protestantism, will be seen by the issue of the struggle: if she is not, God help us: we must go to Rome: if she is, which I BELIEVE, then are we Catholics, then do we enjoy the priesthood and sacraments of Christ's *one* (Ephes. 4) Church, without having to bend and break our consciences, to what modern Rome has reared upon the ancient superstructure. My whole life, God willing, shall be one crusade against the detestable and *diabolical* heresy of Protestantism, the very name even of which has been publicly and authoritatively abjured by my own Church. Arianism, Pelagianism, and the like are awful enough, and soul-destroying: but Protestantism is the devil's masterpiece. It has broken into the English pastures and must be hunted down. I will do my best in my little way, because I *doubt* the salvation of Protestants, and my office is to save souls.[9]

More than a hundred years have passed since Faber wrote this outburst to his brother. During these years many acute and able minds have grappled with the same problem. Yet it remains to many as intractable as ever. Faber's view may seem extravagant and his outburst ill-natured. But then the path from Canterbury to Rome had not been mapped as it is today. Rome and Canterbury, physically as well as intellectually, were further apart. Once the Tractarians had agreed that the Church of England was or should be Catholic, there was, as Faber clearly saw, one of two things to be done. Either the Church of England was to be considered too Protestant and be renounced as a man-made thing—or the Church of England must be made more Catholic. But this last inevitably meant imitating Rome. Rome of the past was one thing, but present-day, modern Rome—that was altogether another. Most Tractarians were content with a medievalized church. A Gothic east window, vestments and later on a little daring incense settled the matter. But Faber saw that it was not enough. The Church of England had to be contrasted not merely with the dead past but with the living present. Most clergymen were willing to be put off by stories of abuses and corruptions. This exonerated them from investigating for themselves. For what if the Church they were trying to build turned out to be nothing more than a man-made imitation of Rome?

Strangely enough a contemporary of Faber's, not a theologian and quite unlearned, in fact Queen Victoria herself, went straight to the heart of the problem and saw it with a clarity that would have astonished her bishops. The truth was frighteningly simple. She made the discovery that the Reformation in England had been left uncompleted. Doctrine, indeed, she found to be reformed. But that was as far as it went. Only half of the Reformation was accomplished. The hierarchy of bishops and priests, all the outward show of the old Church remained. Forms and ceremonies emptied of their content were retained. It is this dichotomy, this see-saw between the Catholic and the Protestant which is the very life (and dare one say it, the charm) of the Church of England. The Catholic party asserts episcopacy and then proceeds to the Real Presence. The Protestant party asserts Communion as a mere memorial and then proceeds to snipe at the bishops. Which is right? In truth the only plausible defence of the Establishment as a Church is comprehensiveness. It is both Protestant *and* Catholic.

But, of course, this modern solution was out of the question for Faber, though it does seem to have occurred to him. The Tractarians, and particularly the more extreme school of Ward, started with the assumption that the Church of England was or should be Catholic. What was Protestant had to be abolished, explained away or simply ignored. Failing this there was nothing but Rome.

Faber was by now in a condition of total bewilderment. Everything seemed to point to his submission to the Catholic Church. But he had learnt to fear his feelings. Was it not more than probable that he was under the spell of emotion? If only he could return to Oxford and see the good men there! On the other hand every theologian he consulted condemned Anglican orders. And if Anglican orders were invalid what point was there in Catholicizing the Church of England? One day he lost his way and it seemed to symbolize his position. He prayed at the shrine of St Aloysius on the saint's feast day and left the church speechless, almost unconscious where he was. When he came to himself he realized that either he must become a Catholic or go out of his mind. He gave himself three years to settle the issue. He prayed fervently to his guardian angel. Twice he was on the point of going out to the Collegio Inglese to make his submission. Twice a trifling incident intervened and he put off going. Were not these incidents obviously answers to his prayers? And yet already, dam up his feelings how he would, he was a Catholic in all but name—a Catholic outside the Church, without the sacraments, a minister of a Church in schism and perhaps in heresy.

The struggle was deep and intense. It left its mark for the rest of his life. Those few weeks in Rome seared him. He was never the same man again. The shadow of the crucifix had fallen upon him. Chiabrera's epitaph had proved prophetic. Parnassus in the shape of his beloved mountains and the Wordsworths was gone for good and all. The little hill of Calvary alone was now to be his.

But there was another agonizing struggle still to come. "We left Rome yesterday", he wrote to Morris,

> to spend a few quiet days at Albano, and this morning we were just setting off to bury ourselves in the woods, when my kind friend, Dr Grant, burst into our room. I said, "You here! What is the meaning of this?" He answered, "I have come all the twelve miles to fetch you back to Rome immediately." It appears that yesterday evening he called upon me, not knowing that I had left town immediately after the ceremonies

of Corpus Christi; upon my table he saw an official letter from
one of the prelates, which he thought it best to open; it was to
order me to be in full dress at the Vatican library at 5 p.m.
today, to have a private audience, which Cardinal Acton had
asked for without saying a word to me; and Dr Grant most
goodnaturedly came off early in the morning to catch me. In
five minutes more we should have been irrecoverably in the
woods, and what a mess there would have been! The Rector
of the English College accompanied me, and told me that as
Protestants did not like kissing the Pope's foot, I should not
be expected to do it. We waited in the lobby of the Vatican
library for half-an-hour, when the Pope arrived, and a prelate
opened the door, remaining outside. The Pope was perfectly
alone, without a courtier or prelate, standing in the middle of
the library, in a plain white cassock, and a white silk skull-cap
(white is the Papal colour). On entering, I knelt down, and
again, when a few yards from him, and lastly, before him; he
held out his hand, but I kissed his foot; there seemed to be a
mean puerility in refusing the customary homage. With Dr
Baggs for interpreter, we had a long conversation; he spoke of
Dr Pusey's suspension† for defending the Catholic doctrine of
the Eucharist with amazement and disgust; he said to me,
"You must not mislead yourself in wishing for unity, yet waiting for your *Church* to move. Think of the salvation of your
own soul." I said I feared self-will and *individual* judging. He
said, "You are all individuals in the English Church, you have
only external communion, and the accident of being all under
the Queen. You know this: you know all doctrines are taught
among you anyhow. You have good wishes, may God strength-
en them! You must think for yourself and for your soul." He
then laid his hands on my shoulders, and I immediately knelt
down; upon which he laid them on my head, and said, "*May
the grace of God correspond to our good wishes, and deliver you from
the nets (insidie) of Anglicanism, and bring you to the true Holy
Church.*" I left him almost in tears, affected as much by the
earnest affectionate demeanour of the old man, as by his blessing
and his prayer; I shall remember St Alban's Day in 1843 to my
life's end.[10]

† Suspended from preaching before the University on account of a sermon
on the Eucharist.

It may pertinently be asked why Faber at this point did not submit. It would have certainly pleased him to submit himself thus dramatically at the Pope's feet. But there were ties which prevented him. The love of the Anglican Church, its sober piety, its beautiful liturgy, the setting of a small plain Gothic church—to leave these things is to some people so difficult as to be almost an impossibility. But this was not Faber's case. He was possessed by an idea. He could not let himself believe that the Movement to catholicize the Church of England, set in motion with such high hopes by men whom he revered for their goodness and trusted for their wisdom, could prove in the end to be an illusion. The hand of God seemed to be in the Movement at every turn. He also distrusted himself. Who was he to set himself up before a Newman, a Pusey or a Keble? More and more it came to depend on Newman. And Newman was quiet, as he learnt from Morris's letters—even after Pusey's suspension.

"As to Pusey's business," Faber wrote home to his friend,

I feel an excessive indignation which has too much of temper mixed with it to be altogether right; but in what a state of corruption our Church must be, when one of her four universities can suffer a board of doctors, without instant excommunication, to pass such a sentence! Where can a protest be made? Where can the truth be authoritatively asserted? How can the Church show it is not her sentence? No way: there is no unity, no order, no authority, even where the honour of the Lord's Body is blasphemously slighted: we may explain it away, to be sure, on technical grounds, but *after all*, in the eyes of plain-thinking people has not the Church of England, in negligent silence, permitted the theological authorities of the University of Oxford to deny the Real Presence, and implicitly to assert the damnable heresy of Zuinglius? There is rottenness somewhere.

As to myself, nothing retains me but the fear of self-will; I grow more Roman every day, but I hope not wilfully. I used—and blessed it was—to invoke the Saints, but since the day last Lent, when you said you feared it was not justifiable on our system, I have desisted; for, please God, I will obey in all things while I can. But I do not know what the end will be indeed. I hardly dare read the Articles, their weight grows heavier on me daily. I hope our B. Lady's intercession may not cease for any of us because we do not seek it, since we desist for obedience sake. N[ewman]'s vision [that he should not leave the Church of England] is a consoling subject of thought. But I dare not keep my mind any longer on the subject. Whenever you see N. ask him to remember me in his prayers. May God bless us all and keep us in the right way and free either from self-interest or from self-will!

He added a postscript. Whytehead, his fellow clergyman and poet in the Lakes, had died of consumption in New Zealand on 19th March. "I am sure", Faber wrote, "Whytehead will intercede for us all at Oxford. He had it *much* at heart."[11] And that was where he had to leave the matter. Intellectually and emotionally he was already convinced. But he would not move till God shewed him clearly that he was not being self-willed. He bought rosaries for Morris and Dalgairns and explained how they should be used.

He set out for Naples his mind filled with the events that had taken place in Rome. Little scenes and incidents crowded into his mind. "The Pontiff, his eyes streaming with tears," slowly elevating the Host. "The ten or twelve trumpets, as from Heaven" in St Peter's at the Elevation pealing out "with a long, wailing timorous jubilee." Then he was rushing back from St Peter's to see the illuminations from the Pincian and back again to the Trinità steps. That had been his birthday and he remembered another birthday at Oxford which had also been the day of the Queen's coronation. At Mola di Gaeta he bathed in the Mediterranean "like a porpoise" and stayed in too long diving under water and doing other "aquatic tricks". In consequence he found the last stage of the journey almost unendurable.

The carriage became so hot it was like a furnace; not a twig or leaf stirred; clouds of white dust rose up from the horses' feet, and there being no wind lingered about the carriage, so we breathe dust, fire and dust mixed. We groaned, but all in vain; not a puff, not a breath, not a cloud, but the frightful sun shimmering away, and the cicalas screaming (I may say that) as if their trees were on fire.[12]

At Naples, as might have been expected, he fell violently ill. But as was his custom he as suddenly recovered. It was enough, however, to dispel any Neapolitan romance. "What a change," he wrote to Frank,

to come over the spirit of a man's dream. The solemn magnificence of old Rome, the silence, the holiness, the unworldly aspect of that Holy of Holies is left behind the Latin Hills, and here is the loud mirth, the extravagant splendour, the military glitter, the eternal revel, the *dolce far niente*, of this earthly Paradise. I feel quite oppressed; I feel as if I was smothered by the bad that is in the world, as if the devil had visibly got the upper hand, and had put down Providence. The effect is quite strange: at Rome the good comes uppermost; the nearest approach I can make to an imagination of heaven is that it is like Rome, not the Rome of the Piazza di Spagna, the tourists and their friends the *valets*, but the other true Rome wherein I dwelt. I know there is an immense deal of piety in Naples, but the beautiful, the voluptuous, the idle, the happy—that is the only Naples which meets the eye. Dear sombre Rome! the tawny Campagna, with its broken aqueducts is better than this Elysian seaside.[13]

From the Lakes came an inaccurate commentary on Faber's tour. Edward Quillinan, Wordsworth's son-in-law, wrote sardonically to Crabb Robinson:

The other day came a long yarn to Mr Carr in *Italian* from Naples, which Faber abuses as utterly uninteresting, detestable in climate and far over-rated even as to beauty and position, the bay being a very fair bay but nothing incomparable! He sighs for his *cara Roma* which he left by medical advice and so changed climate for the worse. From his *Cara Roma* the first letter he sent to Miss F[enwick] was dated Rome and that one word was all the mention made of Rome: not another allusion to the eternal city: it might as well have been penned from Geneva. But it was full of himself and his religious enthusiasm—for his parish in England. He, however, got afterwards much among the Cardinals and seems to have been all but converted to the true Faith. This between ourselves, and more of this hereafter; but he has rather retrograded; the Devil pulled him back a step or two from the Pope, and he stands again on the old new ground, if a man can be said to stand on a quicksand.[14]

Faber sailed from Naples to Leghorn to avoid the long land journey and stayed for a time in Florence. The sea voyage set him up and immediately on arrival he set about composing

a little course of parish lectures for the Eltonians [his new parishioners] on the sacred Infancy and Childhood.

With health all his vitality returned. He warned Morris and Dalgairns not to be disappointed with their rosaries which were not "anything grand or ladylike". He told them of his crucifix which was the "envy even of my R. Cath. friends". They were still to pray hard that he would not be tempted to marry. He had no thoughts in that direction and perhaps a new assault would rise up against him when he returned to the loneliness of Elton. "I hope", he added,

to conquer for I have been much altered since I came abroad this time but I am very, very, very Roman. I have learnt an immense deal both inwardly and outwardly and I hope it will lead to something more than feelings.

But a strange light is thrown on his theological position by his remarks on Pusey's famous sermon on the Real Presence.

Before I left Rome I made the acquaintance of a professor who has now seen the sermon. He says it is "abominable heresy" as contrary to the doctrine of Trent which forbids you to couple remission of sins in the proper sense of the word with the Blessed Eucharist. He said, If Pusey's sermon be admitted, then the *necessity* of confession falls to the ground, for he makes the Eucharist do the work of Confession, a most heretical confusion of the two sacraments. Now I think this is interesting, first because it shows the view of P.'s sermon taken by a far wiser Roman head than that of Mr Moore of Birmingham [a

Catholic priest]; and secondly by its very *indirectness* it shows how little P.'s theology is (in the bad sense) Roman, and how from its Patristic spirit it, as it were, unconsciously maims Romanism while travelling towards quite a different end. To all the English chaplains whom I have seen and who are frightened at the sermon, I have related this, and I think it has done good in some instances in quieting panic.[15]

He appears in this letter a convinced Anglo-Catholic. Was he less Catholic than he thought? Had he in reality been swayed by emotion while in Rome? Why, above all, did he want to quiet the English chaplains? It may be that Faber still cherished his liberty of judgment and the condemnation showed that Tractarianism was in reality a *via media* between Rome and Protestantism. Or was it that he regarded the sermon as a considerable Romeward step but fortunately not far enough to upset the waverers? His enemies would have explained it this way had they been able to read the letter. The nature of the Anglo-Catholic position makes the charge of hypocrisy plausible. But it is more likely that he was on the rebound from his Roman experiences. He was clutching at anything which seemed to prove him right in not making his submission. Oxford and Newman might, after all, be wiser than Rome.

He ended his letter

The motto of my life *now* is to be Chiabrera's epitaph:

> Amico, io vivendo, cercava conforto
> Nel Monte Parnasso:
> Tu, meglio consigliato, cercalo
> Nel Calvario.

At Bologna, however, he wrote a long letter (now lost) to Frank refuting Anglicanism. Frank took it to Newman at Littlemore for advice and Newman decided that it needed a reply. Frank knew that now there was no one else who could hold him back. "My dear Faber," Newman wrote,

I have seen your letter to your brother dated Bologna August 22 and while I am both surprised and put out at your very kind language about me (of which it is but a plain truth to say that I am quite unworthy) yet I will not deny that I could not help being much pleased, more perhaps than is consistent with the consciousness of what I am, at being spoken of in such terms by you.

I assure you, my dear Faber, as perhaps you can guess without my telling you, that I go very far with you in the matters of which your letter treats, much farther than I like; and that my heart leaps forward when I hear certain things said, so as to give me a good deal of anxiety.

One thing, however, I feel very strongly—that a very great experiment, if the word may be used, is going on in our Church —going on, not over. Let us see it out. Is it not our happiness to follow God's Hand? If He did not act, we should be forced to act for ourselves; but if He is working, if He is trying and testing the English Church, if He is proving whether it admits or not of being Catholicized, let us not anticipate His decision; let us not be impatient, but look on and follow.

Have you heard of that remarkable ordination at New York. I mean Mr Arthur Carey's? Surely we have no notion what is coming. Here is a man ordained by the Bishop of the most prominent American diocese, with the zealous co-opera-tion of nearly all her Presbyters, on his avowal that the Roman creed so little distresses him, that, if refused ordination in the Anglican Church, he will not say that he may not apply to the Roman.

Is it not the ordinary way of Providence both as a precept and a mercy, that men should not make great changes by them-selves, or on private judgment, but should change with the body in which they find themselves, or at least in company?

Ought not, moreover, a certain time of probation to be given to oneself, before so awful a change as that I am alluding to? E.g. I have sometimes thought that were I tempted to go to Rome, I should for three years pray, and get my friends to pray, that I might die rather than go if going were wrong. Do not suppose that I am recommending this to another; nay, I am not sure it would not be presumptuous in any case, but I put it down as an illustration.

Excuse this rude letter, which may disturb and annoy you rather than anything else—though I hope not. Be sure you have been in my prayers, such as they are, sometimes.

He added a postscript:

> I am bound to add, what we once touched on in conversation, how forlorn one's state would be, if any reaction of mind came on after a change. Surely one ought to be three years in the one purpose of changing before venturing on it.[16]

There was not, indeed, much comfort here. But Faber made the best of it. "Whatever be the end of my doubts," he wrote to Morris,

> (and Newman prays for me) I can already rejoice in one thing, namely, that I have *suffered*; one of the saints said, *patire e morire* but Sta Maria Maddalena de Pazzi went further *vivere e patire*; but it is not on this account that I rejoice; my suffering was for past sins, not the boon of being made like Christ; but I rejoice that the yoke of my past sins has been made a perceptible misery to me and I can recall particular and very fearful hours at Rome for which I now thank God most humbly. It has pleased and comforted me not a little that both N[ewman] and yourself have put the question, as I had already put to myself, as much more a moral than a theological one. But you put before me the heights of endurance, whose summits my poor imagination can hardly climb in conception, much less think of yet in practice, viz. R. Williams'† calm belief of the unreality of our Sacraments, and yet abiding with us. AT THE ALTAR, both at Rome and at Naples I received and gave with unhesitating faith the Lord's Body, God and Man: *there* I had no doubts: they were burnt up; and this was my consolation. But, my dear Jack, if I come to believe in only a gracious rite, not in the TRANSCENDING PRESENCE am I still to remain? This seems hard—at least to flesh and blood. If we are not now in the Church but in a Concubine (so long as it be a doubt) we may hope in the endurance of that last Mercy, Purgatory, to be knitted into the true Body; but if it grows beyond a doubt—what then? You will say, SUFFER, SUFFER, SUFFER. If it be so I must GO ON and God will reveal this also to me. If I try to pray, if I kneel without words in acknowledgement of God's presence, if I try to love Christ, if I meditate on the passion—all is in the mist and in the dark. I think—all

† Not traced with certainty.

this must begin with the One Church, are you in it? If not, of what good is all this? You have had it put before you—look at her catholicity, unity, sanctity, fruitful missions, clear miracles, wonderful saints, ancient things! In *one* age while we groaned under dryness and irreverence, were vouchsafed to her SS. Philip Neri, Charles Borromeo, Francis Borgia, Francis Xavier, Francis Sales, Ignatius, Felix of Cantalice, Aloysius, Camillus de Lellis!! You pray in vain, because you have not really humbled yourself before the Church so revealed to you, you confess in vain, you communicate in vain: all are shadows —So thoughts rush upon me. If in happy times I say, *Amore amoris Tui mundo moriar qui amore amoris mei dignatus es in Cruce mori*—then comes the chilling question, Why are not you in the communion where he was who said that and lived upon it?

But you will answer—You think too much about the salvation of your own soul, and too little about the Church. But, my dear Jack, I have not the consolation of thinking that I am running a risk (a most dreadful idea) for the Church, but of harming a number of misbelievers by not following the light given me to show me where the Church is.

But I daresay half of this perplexity is caused by my past sins and long worship of self will. It comes to this—to stay is misery at present, and I *dare not* go away—you must pray for me, you and Tom and Dalgairns; I do for all of you but I fear that will bring none of you any good yet.[17]

On the same day he answered Newman's letter. "I am much obliged to you", he wrote,

for your kind letter, and the important hints which it contains. I think my mind is quieter than it was altho' my conviction remains the same on all the details of the controversy; but I seem to have ascertained more clearly to myself the moral duty of being contented with *safety*, and not looking out for a more "excellent way," of which to say the least I am quite unworthy, or for a stricter rule, when I have not even approximated to our laxer one. Having been a spoiled child indulgently brought up, and lastly, since coming to years of discretion, a great worshipper of self will, it was a great temptation to me, as I became at all more serious, to go where I should find a system apparently far more calculated to mortify me than where I was; and this pressed very much upon me at Rome. . . .

I hope the end of it all with all of us will be the being led into all truth and that we may be patient during the dismal *Meanwhile* which is before some of us.[18]

It was in this frame of mind, thinking of the "dismal Meanwhile" that he arrived in his new parish at Elton, Huntingdonshire.

CHAPTER VI

ELTON

MY mother owned the inn there, "The Crown" [a description of Elton reads]. I had just returned after a considerable absence. On the Sunday morning I was looking out of the window when I saw a thin, rather austere looking clergyman passing towards the church. My mother said, "Tom, that's our new clergyman". She said that he fasted too much and that he was called a Puseyite, but she thought him a very good man. The first appearance of the Rector is still before my mind. The long cassock and M.A. hood were novelties to me. He seemed to have a broad white "choker" round his neck. The face was thin and pale, the nose long and above all a tall hat. Not a very favourable impression. He had the reputation of being a splendid preacher and in the afternoon I went to hear him. I have never seen the old church so well filled before. We were in the family pew just under the pulpit. Many of the Methodists who were strong in Elton were there, ready to catch the Rector in his Romanism. I was vastly struck by the preacher's appearance, with his beautiful white surplice and black and red hood, and stole, but above all by his bright piercing eyes, and what I can only call his heavenly expression. He was beginning a course of sermons for the young and his text was "Thou hast the dew of thy youth". I felt as if a personal attack was being made upon me. ... My mother was full of him but told me how he always kept his eyes cast down, and this was attributed to his peculiar religious views.

Tom Godwin, the writer of this description, was asked by Faber to go to the Rectory for an interview.

I got myself up very carefully for the occasion. I was shown into the study. He asked me if I would be willing to enter his service ... My choice was soon made, for there was a fascination and kindness in his manner which drew me to him ...

He noticed that I was looking at a picture over the mantlepiece. "You seem taken up with that engraving." "Yes, Sir, I suppose it is some eminent man?" "Yes, and he is still in the prime of life; it is the Reverend Mr Newman, who lives at Littlemore, near Oxford. He taught me all I know that is good, and is the greatest scholar since St Augustine!"[1]

There was also hanging in the house the romantic portrait of Lord John Manners.

Faber's household consisted of Old Molly who had been his father's cook and who always referred to Faber as Fred or t'lad, Tom Godwin's two sisters, Anne and Mary, William Webb who did the housework, William Rusher who helped in the garden, George Hawkes, and Tom Godwin who was valet and gardener. There were therefore seven servants, five men and two women. The Rectory, indeed, was a large Elizabethan building, picturesque and set in its own extensive grounds. The living also was considered to be a good one. But it was a strange beginning, these seven servants, to a life of austerity and holiness. There was talk of his sister-in-law coming, also of a curate. But these projects came to nothing.

Before long a change began to pass over the Rector's household. Little by little the men servants became a sort of Brotherhood, as Faber put into practice what he had learnt in Rome. There were spiritual exercises and readings from the lives of the saints. There was meditation, reading, visiting the sick. There were midnight prayer meetings when an hour was spent in reciting the psalter. On the eves of feasts the devotions were prolonged to three hours. As time went on the discipline was introduced on Fridays and in Lent. Other young men joined the exercises. They began to think of the Rectory as their "monastery" and themselves as monks.

The oratory which had been the study became the centre of the house. It had a painted glass window, a large crucifix and it smelt of cinnamon, as Faber recalled years later. The cinnamon apparently was an idea of Jack Morris's and was perhaps a substitute for incense. The clergyman-poet was soon discovered to have a genius for leadership and organisation. Everything was punctual to the minute, everything regulated to the minutest detail. Though autocratic Faber never found it difficult to delegate his authority. His household might inwardly rebel but they followed the Rector. What old Molly thought of it all is not recorded.

Meanwhile Faber discovered another talent. Now that he had two gardeners, or almost two, he set to work on the garden. He planted and cut down, drove pathways, erected fences.

> Through the trees, like pictures in frames could be seen the neighbouring towns of Oundle, Warmington, Fotheringhay and others. These were a constant delight to the Rector—each spoke to him of the days of old,

as Tom Godwin put it. In the end the Rectory garden had the air of a small park. The whole village was allowed to use it as such. On Sundays there were games of cricket and football. Faber would walk among his parishioners with a word for each of them. The choir would practise on fine days under a magnificent old acacia in the garden and Faber would preach long eloquent sermons. Tom Godwin remembered on one occasion a whole crowd under this tree singing the *Te Deum*, the Old Hundredth, and other psalms. On Sunday evenings the oldest parishioner would be asked to dine in the Rectory kitchen.

For recreation Faber strolled along the river accompanied by his three dogs, Leo, Dark and Spot. Although he had no horse he borrowed the gig of the Methodist Minister with whom he was on the friendliest terms. He and Tom would go for long drives in the country and he would drive guests to neighbouring places of interest. The gig had the minister's name and calling painted on it which Tom disliked—in case he might be taken for the Minister's servant.

But of course the church was Faber's chief concern. "The Lion and Unicorn", Godwin wrote later,

> were where the Holy Rood should be, and the beautiful west-end arches were blocked up. The centre arch was filled up with a choir gallery ... where the instruments ... a clarinet,

violin and 'cello were played in the worst possible style ...
Behind the Communion table were the Ten Commandments,
much dilapidated.[2]

Faber changed this in no time and the place began to look something like a Catholic church. He undoubtedly did some harm
with much that was good. He inserted a heavy stained-glass
window. He introduced an organ on which, he told Morris,
a curate "could play ad lib". The old orchestra which had been
such a part of parochial life was abolished and was not adequately
replaced by the formation of a choir. The Psalms were sung and
not recited, new hymns introduced, saints' days observed, and
Faber began to hear confessions.

In his sermons Faber spoke frequently of the saints and especially of St Philip Neri. In his spare time he translated St Philip's
life. It was his intention, fantastic as it may seem, to work his
parish, as he put it, "in the spirit of St Philip and St Alphonso".[3]
Faber was first and foremost interested in souls. That was what
mattered to him. As to the outward forms of ceremonial he was
indifferent. In the middle of the surplice controversy he told his
congregation he preferred to preach in a surplice but would preach
in his shirt sleeves if they liked. He called the Tractarian obsession
with ceremonial *playing at mass*, putting ornament before truth.[4]

This was the outward picture. It was not achieved, or indeed
lived, without cruel difficulties. "I am tumbled into a sad parish,"
he told Newman soon after his arrival,

> 800 people, and nearly 400 *rabid* Dissenters, who have found
> out that I am, as a hostile churchwarden expresses it, "tainted
> to say the least with Puseyism".[5]

"I am in a great strait: because of some of my parishioners,"
he wrote to Morris,

> partly on account of *Puseyism* and partly because the church
> property here by Dr Fisher's non-residence was miserably
> dilapidated and my agent is now raising the rents etc., and
> partly from the spiteful underhand proceedings of the Dissen-
> ters. It would be but a trifling matter to some dispositions,
> but it quite upsets my poor stomach ... I believe I am *getting*

on and the regular work of my parish is better for my own soul's health than my selfwilled occupations at Ambleside: but I fear getting bitter. I have *power* to crush some of my enemies and by withdrawing alms from the sick Dissenters and my custom from the village shopkeepers by going to Peterborough for things to punish all; and I fear being tempted to this. They think me a fool because I continue kind to people forward in spitefulness and they think they may do as they please with me. As soon as I hear anything unpleasant I always say a prayer for the person who has done and said it. Both my tenants have thrown up their farms; and I try to be quiet under it as my lawyer says all is just and equitable and *kind*. But what between oppressor, Puseyite, hypocrite, covetous man etc., etc., I am afraid I am growing rather peevish, and there is no Eucharist till Easter. So you must pray for me: it is a *little* trial, but little trials are great to little men. John Manners is coming to have Passion week quiet here: I am afraid it is too great a pleasure for that season. I have not done anything worthy of the name of fasting for 10 or 12 days.[6]

On 27th March 1844 he reported progress to Newman:

I have nearly 1000 people here, and *everything* wants doing. But I have no right to complain: the Dissenters are very violent: they *worship* the Sabbath and really seem to cheat and live impurely on weekdays, and none of their neighbours seem to doubt but that they are *the* elect. I get from 25 to 30 poor on Wednesdays and Fridays and Saints' Days, besides the children, and we average about 40 to monthly Communions. The weekday services seem a sort of *test*, for I find they just collect the quiet unobtrusive unboastful people—"the merely moral" as the Dissenters call them. One Sunday evening my choir at my request when at practice in the evening with locked doors, tried to sing the litany without organ, which we do in Church now: and it is believed that I shut myself up with them and celebrated Mass!!! altho' it chanced that I never went to the Church that particular evening. . . .

He ended his postscript with:

I could [do] all things in my parish if I were Roman, and had not my feet in the stocks of our system.[7]

It is doubtful if he was or seemed as weak as he made out to Morris. Unlike Newman he was not afraid of authority or of familiarity. "I remember," Godwin wrote,

> his teasing Ben Fowler about some ribs he had left on the grass in mowing it. Ben was a bit nettled and at last broke— he leaned on his scythe and said, "Sir, you are a poet, and if you will not be displeased I will quote some lines". "Quote away, Ben." "Well, Sir, 'the faults of other we easily *disarm* but our own faults are hard to larn'." I shall never forget the laugh and "Bravo, Ben," that followed.

Godwin also recalled how he found some boys throwing stones and asked which boy was responsible. But Faber overheard him and called out:

> Tom, don't put temptation in their way; they are sure to lie, give them a cut each, they are sure to deserve it.[8]

There was in Faber a streak of cruelty. He feared his own inclination to pleasure which made him severe with himself—and thus in turn severe to others. He thought much of the virtues of tenderness and kindness which he found exemplified in the lives of the saints. But he does not seem to have been able to put them into practice. Above all he lacked moderation. His love of exaggeration was too strong. He ruined his health by excessive fasting and habitually wore a thick horse-hair cord tied in knots round his waist. Part of the trouble was the lack of a director. Michael Watts Russell, rector of Benefield, a nearby parish, later his confessor, was unfortunately as ignorant and enthusiastic as himself.

In the middle of the Summer of '44 Faber wrote Morris a despairing letter after a visit to Oxford. He was lonely, ill and full of fancies. "Now I want advice," he began:

> Whatever am I to do without a spiritual director? It has pleased God sometime since to answer your prayers, and to deliver me wholly from even a half formed thought of impurity; so that I swim at ease in my own thoughts. How long this will last I do not know: I think I am very much more humble since my late miserable and hellish temptations; yet perhaps it is not humble in me to think so. Now, since I returned from Oxford,

I have fallen into the hands of another evil angel, *sadness*, a most unsettling sadness: and tho' the misery and aridity and loathing of prayer is very bad to bear, what frightens me is that Rodriguez says it is often an antechamber to unchastity. My visit to Oxford partly caused my sadness; I was amazed at the cheerfulness, the boisterous mirth of all of you, when I have scarcely smiled for months. You see I have no educated, no religious person near me: my solitude is, in *effect*, as utter as that of the Thebaid: the horrors without the honours of an anchoret.

Sometimes I see in this a penance, very gracious, for my peculiar defects: sometimes I do not: anyhow it enervates me at times, because I am psychologically eating myself. One while I think of betaking myself to read some mere intellectual book; but I have lost my taste for literature now, and it seems time lost to read anything but spiritual books. Another while I think of poetry, but with *me* that is too engrossing: except a few lines on you, and such mutations as Sir Lancelot wants in his passage through the press I have written no poetry since I came to Elton. Watering during the drought kept me cheerful: now that is past, and I cannot dig. And lately I have taken an undisciplined fancy into my head that I would write and ask Newman to remove his inhibition of invocating the B.V.M., as I think it would be so very joyous now that I have lost all sensible joy in our B. Lord: but N. must have seen something in me which made it wise of him to forbid me. What then am I to do? Struggle on, as I am, or take some step? Would it be well to look out for someone to live with me till Mackenzie [a proposed curate] could come?

It does not sound well for a priest to say that the poor are not company enough for him: still I *do* feel a want of those *entretiens de récréation* which even monks have; tho' do not think that I am presumptuous enough in a great Anglican parsonage to fancy myself a monk. However I should like to have some advice how to be cheerful with a great stone round one's neck. (I mean our cramping parochial system.) I daresay others would find my temptations very light, but I am really so vile, so little obedient to my conscience and such a mere tyro in holy living that the least shifting of Satan's wiles seems to bring me to the verge of shipwreck. . . . I am writing with a

Crucifix before my eyes, but it does not send those thrills through me which it used to do. I had a dose of blue pill 2 days ago, so I don't think my present temptation is stomachic.

Yesterday—perhaps it will sound very absurd—I was so depressed that I conceived a violent hatred of my servant's dog because it avoided me: I really had a difficulty not to kill it, and the feeling was so strong I could not get it away at prayers, and I was obliged with shame and confusion to pray about it. I am afraid you will think this looks more like madness than sin. O that my wretched nature had the yoke of S. Ignatius laid on it—there is nothing in our system to macadamize one. Strange to say I do not feel any temptation to omit duties, only there is no spirit in my doing them. But I have said enough.

He added a postscript.

Perhaps the devil is going to bring marriage temptingly before me: I pray him off for that. Let me do at least one solid act of penance; for celibacy never can be a higher thing than penance most inadequate for my past life.[9]

Young Tom Godwin had the audacity to suggest that the Rector needed a wife. The owners of the big house, Elton Hall, thought the same. A party for the Rector and some eligible girls was arranged. Faber accepted the invitation and then ordered Tom to cut his hair so that he looked like a convict. When he came home he told Tom that he had thoroughly scared them, but apart from his hair he was frighteningly pale and thin. The fasts and austerities were telling heavily on his none too robust health. "I have been lolling on a sofa in a very 19th Century way," he wrote to Morris on August 9th, "having had a huge boil on my seat of honour."[10] But instead of resting he spent the time revising his poem *Sir Lancelot* which was "longer by 3 or 400 lines than Par. Lost, by a 1000 than the Excursion," and was in fact nearly 11,000 lines in length. He was also engaged in writing lives of the saints for Newman's series. He asked Newman to take out anything that might cause offence:

I see no paper or review now, so I cannot tell what is strong and what not. I seem to grow more Roman daily and almost to

write out of the bosom of the Roman Church instead of from
where I am.[11]

"My poor", he complained to Morris,

> are out at harvest so I have not even their gossip. I scarcely
> speak out aloud all day except to say my breviary, and English
> service with the servants and a few orders daily.[12]

In the Autumn he went for a holiday in the Lakes with the
Harrisons but though he felt better his health was precarious.
He had been given "gray powders and opium" by the Elton doctor but the doctor at Ambleside suggested nitrate of silver. He
began to suspect that there was something more wrong with him
than "a knock up". He slept well and had "no remittent fever at
night" but he had "funny inward feelings of giving way at times".
He had described his symptoms to Newman as "liver won't act—
pains in the spine—cramps in the legs—and constant sick headache."[13]

Towards the end of the year he made a second request to
Newman to take off his prohibition against invoking the Blessed
Virgin Mary. But Newman was firm in his donnish way.

> I have great repugnance at mixing religions or worships to-
> gether. It is like sowing a field with mingled seed. . . . I do not
> like decanting Rome into England . . .

And having advised him against many Roman practices, including
"extraordinary degrees of asceticism," which he found dangerous
in a communion which did not create saints he characteristically
added:

> I am far too much perplexed myself in various ways to feel
> it pleasant to give advice at all—much more to suffer what I
> say to be taken as a decision. . . .[14]

All his life Faber wanted Newman to make decisions for him
which Newman was not prepared or able to do. Faber fussed
him by his direct enquiries which could not be answered (or could
only be answered badly) in the oblique way Newman liked. But
Faber accepted what he took as a reproof very humbly. "Like
most humbling things," he replied,

it has quieted me very much; and it quite seems to me now a temptation of Satan that I should have pined, as I have done, for Invocation. I have work enough of a far more common-place sort to do yet, for I appear to have done nothing but begin and begin over again. It is really very saddening to be obliged, as you say, to look on the inculcation of complete self abandonment and other saintly heights with jealousy and distrust; but I trust I shall get good out of your hints, for I believe a wish to imitate the Saints has been a great snare to me, and kept me in the very low state in which I am. Your words to me abroad, "surely a man should be 3 years in the *one* purpose of changing before he venture upon it" must, I believe, soon become practical to me; for I really fear I cannot carry this load much longer. I have said thus much, my dear Mr Newman, only that you may know the better how to turn your kind remembrance of me in your prayers.[15]

Newman wrote back that he was afraid he had been cold and unfriendly. But Faber assured him it was not so. "When others move," he wrote,

then I shall *begin* the serious consideration of what I am to do; I only wish to be where God wills me to be; but then sin deafens one; He may speak and I not hear: He may *have* spoken, at Rome, e.g., and I not heard. What they said about *finalis gratia* there sometimes runs like cold steel thro' me. Do what I will I cannot outgrow the fear of being "*damned*," as out of the Church; and so I too much overlook the risk of the same awful event thro' my own sinfulness and ineffective penance. I pine to feel *sure*, and that is self love again. Yet, if I can be confident of anything, it is that I am to *an extent* within reach of grace: whether corresponded to or not, I am sure it is offered; so I may well be patient. I cannot help fancying that the grace comes always or mostly thro' what in my life is borrowed from another system, not from what I have of my own, and so I feel as if I was living a dishonest life . . .[16]

But a new difficulty suddenly arose with the publication of St Wilfrid's life in Newman's series of British Saints. Newman had read the life in proof and having made a few changes had passed it. But both he and Faber were quite out of touch with the world. They had been progressing Romeward, as they both admitted, and as their intimates knew. But the world did not know and was shocked. And in fact Faber's Life of St Wilfrid is hardly compatible with his position as rector of a Church of England parish.

> He [St Wilfrid] saw that the one thing to do was to go to Rome, and learn under the shadow of St Peter's chair the more perfect way. To look Romeward is a Catholic instinct seemingly implanted in us for the safety of the faith.[17] He materially aided the blessed work of riveting more tightly the happy chains which held England to St Peter's chair—chains never snapped as sad experience tells us, without the loss of many precious Christian things.[18]

As anyone but Newman could have foreseen there was an outcry. Newman seems to have thought it sufficient to say that he was not now, strictly speaking, editor. Pusey and Marriott were scandalized, even Morris thought Faber had done wrong. Faber himself was, all things considered, not as upset as might have been supposed in spite of what he called his "morbid sensitivity". With the publication of Ward's *Ideal of a Christian Church* he could not see "the meaning of the honesty of reserve".

"It is quite clear to me that I must retire from the Lives," he did, however, write to Morris,

> and for a season from all writing. The whole business brings home to me very forcibly the culpable forwardness and presumption of my venturing at all to take an active part in a movement *the very avowed object of which is to unsettle men's minds, IS, HAS BEEN, and WILL BE.* When I know how miserably sinful and soft-living I have been, I ought never to have stepped out in the way that I have done ... I should keep to my obscure duties and great retirement here. E.g. Saturday night, just after Marriott's second letter, a very striking conversion and confession of a Methodist took place. On Sunday night, after your letter, a great grown up farmer who had never shewn any contrition confessed, and tho' above 6 feet high and very strong, he so nearly went into fits that I was obliged to fetch wine to restore him.[19]

Many thought the outcry would be the signal for his conversion. Bishop Wareing, the Vicar Apostolic of the Eastern District, wrote to him. Faber replied courteously but also evasively.

But there was another, darker and more significant cloud in the sky. Faber had written to Morris in December:

> Newman tells me Ward is to pass his Responsions today. Alack! Alack! I don't [know] whether to laugh or cry at the state of things—iniquity and puerility make such an unhealing poultice; from the far-off serene bosom of the H. Roman Church, how infinitely little must such squabbles in a duck-pond appear![20]

Ward's *Ideal of a Christian Church* had been published in the Long Vacation. Only with the reassembly of the University in October were any steps taken to combat his blatant praise of the Catholic Church and denigration of the Church of England. It was eventually resolved to put before Congregation three propositions: 1. A condemnation of the *Ideal*. 2. The deprivation of Ward from his Master's and Bachelor's degrees. 3. A condemnation of Tract 90. Faber's joke about Responsions of course refers to the second proposition. Morris wrote anxiously to Faber that he must at all costs be present in the Sheldonian theatre to record his vote.

Faber shrank from the ordeal of facing Oxford again but at length he agreed to come. "I am coming up to Oxford for a pure penance," he wrote:

> I am not well to begin with and I have a number of sick people whom I hardly like to leave, one woman in particular who is in a curious spiritual state. I had one of my attacks on Shrove Tuesday: Mr Westcott said it was the worst he had ever seen me in ... Add to which the snow is falling very thickly.[21]

When the time came he took Tom Godwin on the two-day drive and was a witness of the historic scene in the Sheldonian on 13th February. Ward made a long defence of his book but it was condemned by 777 votes to 386. The proposal to deprive him of his degrees was carried by 569 to 511. The third proposal on Tract 90, as is well known, was vetoed by the two Proctors amid a storm of yells and cheers. Ward stumbled in the snow as he made his way from the building and was cheered by the undergraduates. The Vice-Chancellor, who had brought the proceedings to an abrupt conclusion after the veto, was hissed and snowballed. But the snowballs, as Faber well knew, were not flung in honour of religion or for anything the Tractarians held dear. On the contrary the undergraduates were moved by the liberalism which Newman considered to be religion's worst enemy.

The cold weather, the heat of the Sheldonian, the excitement and the disappointment were too much for Faber. He became alarmingly ill. "Tom, I'm afraid I am dying," he said. "Tom, I have grave fears that if I were to die I should be lost." "If you are lost," Tom replied, "God help the rest of men." Still ill he set off back to Elton.

Elton was now his one consolation. His enthusiasm and leadership were beginning to tell. The parish was transformed. Elton now began to hold him back. To go seemed the abandonment of a duty. "There are," he told Morris in March,

> now 17 persons strikingly converted, all *confitentes*, some really being led in extraordinary ways, and *perfectionwards*: some confess weekly, 5 or 6 of them. 31 persons came to the *early* communion last Sunday; and the sermons on exam. of conscience seem to have moved the whole place: *numbers* come almost daily in grief and distress, and I doubt not many of these will become *confitentes*. I can hardly *open* a book now, let alone write; for seeing people here *privately* occupies 3 or 4 hours daily, or averages that. (I have just been interrupted by a confession.) People are beginning to come beforehand when they wish to communicate: the little children in the school by simple minute catechizing in the Passion open their little griefs and sins to me; the actual *face* of the village is changed obviously to worldly eyes, in sobriety and nocturnal quiet. I really cannot without anguish confront the idea of throwing this up, and leaving these souls to—I know not what—i.e. the ministry of Piers Claughton.[22]

Faber was both "cocky" and "dishonest", as he described himself, but the parish really was transformed, as Wordsworth and other visitors witnessed.

The success of his parish seemed to show that God intended him to stay where he was. He realized the significance of what he had seen in the Sheldonian but was unmoved. Pusey certainly influenced him as no doubt did Marriott who came to stay. Even his health which was getting worse seemed to make a move impossible. "Something is wrong with my heart," he told Morris in June,

> defective action they say; anyhow my feet will not bear the weight of my body and my heels have turned white and exude liquid. I can walk when the pressure is changeable but I cannot stand without great pain . . . I was 3 hours with Pusey in town, and I feel, which I wish you would tell him, much quieter even than when I last wrote to him. My dear parish gets on very well: it is quite humbling to have any hand in such a work, knowing one's vileness. I am working as hard as my poor feet will let me; and if my rickety carcase is going to tumble to pieces, I shall I hope be glad to be withdrawn from this distress, and I think I could lie quietly down and die with English sacraments.[23]

The parish went on so swimmingly that he had time to marry Frank and pay visits. "I am brimful of work," he was writing in August,

> people are beginning to come, gentlemen, from a distance to confess, i.e. 2 have done so, a 3rd went to Oxford by my advice, a 4th to Oakeley thro' me; and the parish work goes on. I have 40 penitents to guide; we grow a little *monastic* too in the house . . ."[24]

But by the Autumn he had become uneasy again and wrote for Newman's support.

> I need hardly say that my affections are with the Rom. Ch., my attractions towards Roman doctrine and simple temporal ruin on the back of apparently weakening health seems some little guarantee against self-will. Now on the other hand,
>   1. I have no definite argumentative convictions about our being in a state of schism or anything more than a blind feeling that heresy is permissively rife amongst us.

2. God appears to have been more with me, since I came here, than ever He was before. I do not mean to say that I am anything better than a most effeminate penitent, yet I feel to creep on—what I did not do before.

3. A wonderful work appears to have been done in my parish by confession, weekly communion and bodily mortifications. Is this any symptom of a vocation? Is the consideration what is to become of it all, if I go, an allowable *ethos*, as one loves certain penitents and contemplates injury to their souls?

4. I have vehement drawings towards Rome: I repress them, and for a season they die. Is this likely to be a stifling of convictions?

5. When the drawings come, they disquiet—have I a right to think this an *Ignatian* sign of their *not* being from God? Then on the other hand, again, the work that I have done in my parish has been, *sub Deo*, with Roman implements— S. Ignatius made easy and the like.

I cannot say that I have any feelings of dishonesty *now* to the Engl. Ch. because I work hard in her; but I sometimes think that there may be a duty to the *held down* party, whose doctrines I hold, while I revel in the comforts of the Establishment. Pusey seemed to think one's only duty was to the station we were placed in: might not a born heretic use this excessive view of hereditary religion? Then—once more on the other hand—I am frightened of my two old and yet untamed habits of self-will and acting on impulse. You see what a raw letter I have written and I feel as if I had no right in delicacy to bother you; yet when one has been accustomed to look up to a person and go by him one is quite at sea, if cut off from his guidance.[25]

This letter was written on 5th October. The reply from Newman written on the 8th was a bombshell. As Tom Godwin put it:

Everything was going on as well as possible in the parish and Father Faber was full of his schemes ... Mr J. B. Morris was staying at the Rectory, when one morning I was in the garden just after breakfast when Father Faber came out with a letter in his hand. He seemed much upset. "This is from the man to whom I owe all under God, Mr Newman, to whom we all look for guidance." He then read it to me.[26] "My dear Faber, I am this night expecting Father Dominic the Passionist whom I shall ask to admit me into the One True Fold. This letter will not go till it is over. Excuse this very brief announcement, as I have many letters to write—and believe the great affection I have for you and the confidence that you have your wish but to find and do His Will who seems to be calling us all one way. Ever yours sincerely, John H. Newman."[27] He seemed dreadfully cast down, and Mr Morris was crying and talking of St John and Dalgairns having gone over too. This news upset us all very much. From this time he seemed changed.[28]

It was the parting of the ways at a time when the decision was cruelly hard to make. It was Newman who had kept him from Rome for years. And now when he had just settled down as a successful Anglo-Catholic clergyman Newman himself seceded without warning. Faber replied on 11th October:

My very dear Mr Newman, your letter of course *requires* no answer, yet you will understand why I should wish to send you a few lines merely to express my great sympathy with you, and to hope you will remember me in your prayers. I am afraid of making any resolution under the influence of this shock, especially when I know that my secession will involve temporal misery which I have no right to suppose I have grace *readily* to confront: yet I *think* I see my way to fixing myself a period of 9 months for prayer etc.[29]

He ended the letter by asking whether on the probable conversion of Watts Russell, he should look round for another confessor.

Newman, however, did not reply and on the 24th he wrote again.

I suppose you did not think it was right of me in your position and my own to ask the questions I did. I have had a very suffering fortnight, and felt as if my health would give way, but I am better now, tho' a shocking correspondence with my eldest brother has gone deep into me. Russell's kind and attentive affection has been a great and undeserved blessing to me; and tho' I am not always quite in the same mind, I feel calmest when most resolved to go. Now and then future prospects disquiet me: I fear that an opening—or sometimes I *hope* it—may be given to me to go abroad, which it may be my duty to act upon because of my debts; I *fear* it because I think I should be taking a lower and more comfortable ground, religiously speaking, and because work might fall out at home where workmen are wanted. Sometimes I *hope* it, because I am weary and ailing; but I must do my best to keep both feelings out of my head, and keep to what is before me. What makes me write just now is that the fluxes and refluxes I have, frighten me lest for seemingly devotion's sake I should quiet myself forcibly, and I wished to beg you to pray for me, as being one who by your sole and simple authority over me kept me from joining the R. Ch. in 1843; and again it was your staying with us which retained me a year after when I had a 2nd conflict; and now that you are gone and I am left behind I feel as if I may have been doing wrong; and I shall be supported by the thought that you do pray for me during these months of decision, if indeed they are to be so many. Supposing that up to Xmas I should still remain growing in the *quiet* conviction that I ought to go, should you disapprove of my coming to Littlemore to have an hour's conversation with you about matters which could hardly be discussed by letter, and which indeed it would be an inconsiderate intrusion to trouble you about in the way of correspondence? I know you will tell me just what you think.[30]

Newman's reply to this letter has been lost but Tom Godwin to whom it was read recalled it

as to the effect that you know that it is the Catholic truths, drawn from the lives of saints which account for this (success in your parish) and you would be still more blessed in the Fold of Christ.[31]

A visit to Littlemore was agreed on.

Meantime there were other difficulties. Faber was hopelessly happy-go-luck over money. He had never possessed much. What he had he always spent recklessly and lavishly. In the Rectory cellars was £50 worth of wine and 50 lbs of pepper. When he had taken possession of Elton he had borrowed heavily from his family to improve the house and grounds. The improvements were real enough but were they necessary? He had loved planting the trees, altering the gardens, and tinkering with the old house and church. He had just begun on a grandiose scheme to turn the stables into almshouses. He had saved nothing from his income and had generously given away much of it to needy parishioners. Were he to become a Catholic, without his stipend, he could neither repay the interest nor the capital. Was it right that he should go in these circumstances? Or was it a snare to keep him back? He decided in the end that he should, in spite of the money, follow Newman, provided his conscience dictated that course. This unworldly contempt of money was rewarded almost immediately after his decision by a friend paying off the debt.[32] The friend had no leanings to Rome, which made the present the more generous.

Everything now seemed to demonstrate that he should go. He began to feel dishonest in staying. He was already in touch with Bishop Wareing and had visited various Anglican friends to explain his coming secession. He made, it appears, another visit to Pusey in London.[33] He still hesitated, however, almost but not quite decided. Watts Russell pressed him to go as a duty.

Poor Jack Morris, back at Oxford, tried every shift to get out of making a decision. He wriggled and turned like a hooked fish but Faber was remorseless. Whatever doubts he still may have had disappeared in his letters to Morris.

I really cannot exaggerate to you the intense cutting misery of last week about my most dear flock, but as Russell pointed out one's flock is not one's only duty to the Ch. of Engl. He said very truly that Pusey was quite unshaken for he claims to be in *suspense* about all Roman doctrines, instancing even Purgatory: but, my dear Jack, are you and I in suspense about them? Do we not honestly hold all Tridentine teaching for holy and true? Do you not practise even invocation? So, anyhow, Pusey's quietness is wholly inapplicable to us: he is on a different *doctrinal standpunct*. Now I *do* think that this consideration tells very materially (I do not say, decisively, but *very* materially) on the whole question of subscription. You hold your fellowship on a subscription of Articles XIV, XIX,

XXI, XXII, XXIV, XXXI, and the oath of supremacy; now just read those articles over quietly, not as Pusey may with his suspended judgment but as a man who would subscribe *ex animo* the Trent decrees tomorrow and see how they sound.[34]

Three days later he was writing:

My dear Jack, Many thanks for your letter which I confess takes me most completely by surprise. I think, if you will let me say so, that the suddenness of the quiet is very suspicious; especially when you say at the end of your letter that you think "*the utmost suspense*" needful. . . . At present N. thinks you not in the One True Fold which is most *awful*, as coming from him: so that you hold not with him: Pusey rests his quiet upon *suspended belief* in important doctrines about which you are religiously convinced; so that you hold not with him. . . . Indeed, indeed, my dearest Jack, your letter has made me feel very uncomfortable . . . I know it cannot be with *you* but it looks very like, not stifling convictions one way but *forcing* them another . . . Surely speaking in a simple way S. Ephrem [Morris was editing the saint's works] ought to be laid aside rather than you should lack time to reconsider a question which as you say needs the "utmost suspense and deliberation" and which may be one of life and death. . . . All that distresses me is that after years of N.'s influence and the most strong convictions, leading to extreme practices of Roman doctrine, after an "unaccountable dread" of which Pusey in another mood would have said (see Pope's letter) that it was from God—after N.'s frightfully calling the R. Ch. the One True Fold—after a letter the other way 2 or 3 days since—you should all at once go so very much the opposite way, and put off the question of Christ's One Fold as interfering with other occupations and rest so much as you do on sensible feelings of quietness.[35]

On 28th October he wrote to Newman again.

It is perfectly true that I have known for a long while of your intended change, still I find I did not realise it till it came, and it would be absurd for me to say that it has not worked strongly upon me. . . . I was using [at Elton] the spiritual riches of, what is amongst us, a despised hated minority and at the same time enjoying the temporal station and ease of the establishment . . .

Indeed I do not think you know what you have been to me ever since the day, I think Easter Day, when you preached the sermon in Vol. I on Resurrection of the Body in 1834–5. So far as I know of myself, I am in the state of one calmly convinced of the duty to move but wishing to put it to the test of time and prayer, from self distrust arising from a natural tendency to act on impulse.[36]

Newman was busy and worried and ill at ease in his new communion. He wanted to disengage himself from these long emotional enquiries. He may also have obscurely wanted to disengage himself from the younger man's open hero-worship. There is a frosty note in his crabbed enigmatic reply.

I had no wish at all to avoid any responsibility, nor do you think it, but of course one feels it is impossible, as a neophyte, to do otherwise, if one speaks, than to speak as others would speak; not from one's own judgment, if judgment I could have.[37]

The visit to Littlemore, however, was very successful so far as Faber was concerned. If Newman's manner was chilly Faber did not notice it.

"I was perverse enough", Faber wrote chattily after his return to Elton,

to catch cold at Littlemore and it has turned to rheumatism; however today my right arm is quite in scribbling condition; so I write to tell you that I have been so very very happy since my visit to you. Somehow you have quite set my mind at ease and I have not had the slightest change of feeling since I left you, and intend to put all doubts away now, by God's help, as sheer temptations which I am sure they are. Only I think it will be hard to wait till Xmas; tho' if I go sooner I fear my brothers will be sadly scandalized. I have written to them at some length. On my return home I found my young men more than ever confirmed in their intention of going, and it was quite touching to see their joy at the shortening of the period. Six young men and one of my maids seem to have clear and steady convictions on the subject; and tho' I am anxious about what will become of them yet they look so happy, I am as it were forced to be happy too. The two boys who will have to get away from their father will cause, I suppose, some strong criticisms; but they have no scruples themselves: and I do hope it may please God to smooth things so that we shall not have more to bear than our poor state of grace may be able to meet.

Knox [an undergraduate from Trinity, Cambridge] is at present with me; and we have agreed, D.V. to seek admission on the Epiphany, together, which is very pleasing to me, on account of his friendship with Whytehead. I suppose, if you so write to Russell, that he will be of the party on that day; so that eleven of us will form what even the Master of Balliol would consider a *"respectable"* congregation. Now do you think one place will be better than another? Northampton as the nearest is in some respects the most convenient; as I thought of sending my young men back by railway to the rectory to superintend the sale while I went on to Birmingham to see if I could find a house near St Chad's where we might live together for 2 months or so for them to be instructed, and to give us time to look about and see if there was any likelihood of our being able to realize the further plans I spoke to you about . . .[38]

But all was suddenly thrown into confusion by a letter he received from Italy on 11th November. It was from a rich English Catholic in Florence who promised financial assistance. This seemed to be the hand of God indeed and Faber dashed off a letter to Newman.

It leaves no manner of doubt that if I go to Italy, and see my kind benefactor, he will, if I feel called, let me return to England, as he himself says *ad majorem Dei gloria animaeque salutem.*[39]

On the night of 12th November he went to give communion to a dying woman. "As we were going home," Tom Godwin related,

my master said to me with much solemnity as to impress me greatly, "Tom, I have a strange feeling come over me, and that is that I am not a priest and that what I have been doing has not been a reality".[40]

The next day Faber and Knox drove over to Watts Russell at Benefield. They paced about the garden discussing plans for the future when they should be Catholics. Faber was filled with ideas about his "monastery". Watts Russell listened and encouraged but he could not hope to participate as he was a married man.

On 15th November all was settled.

I returned from Bishop Wareing today: all arrangements are made. Knox and myself with six young men and 1 woman of my parish, are to be received on Monday morning, to make our first communion on Tuesday, and receive confirmation immediately after Mass. My dear little flock will thus be *full catholics* before we, any of us, part. I will write again when all is over. Just now I feel as tho', if I dared, I would pray God to take me to Himself. I am all in darkness—cannot pray—can see no reasons for going, and such a horror of Roman people and things that it almost seems as if I should draw back at the last. I have begged my young men to put me forcibly into the carriage on Monday morning, if anything happens. Indeed, I have never, never known misery like this; I have hardly closed my eyes for some nights past, and I was so happy before.

For 2 days I had most violent assaults of impurity, and then to marry as a layman after my change: but my present state is worse than that. I have sometimes thought that if God loved me He would give me more suffering than He has done but here is a cup of bitterness which I quite draw back from in horror. Tomorrow I bid my people goodbye; not one of them suspects it, beyond those who go, and I fear a sad scene in Church. Perhaps there being no Communion will make them suspicious. ... O what I would give to have these three days over; for I am very very ill and wretched: I did not foresee such an encounter at the last. It is a comfort to think that you remember me;—but the bells are ringing the Saturday night's peal and I cannot write more ... By the way, they have said strange things to me about *claiming* me, and Bishop Wareing hinted at "ordaining me *per saltum*" which I parried as well as I could: but it adds to my nervousness.[41]

The next day, Sunday, there was no Communion Service and at Evensong he said goodbye to Elton. The portrait of Manners had been packed up and sent to Hope. It was a symbolic gesture. "His text was from Ruth," Godwin wrote:

"And Ruth said to Naomi, whither thou goest I will go, thy people shall be my people and thy God my God." He began by saying that all the world over goodbyes were going on. Some were parting with the hope of meeting again, but some were *farewells*. He was saying goodbye to them; this would be his last address in the dear old church. He asked them to pardon any neglect of duty, and said that if anything he had said or done had been of any use to them or inspired them to lead better Christian lives, he begged that they would follow the light and persevere in the narrow path. . . . He did not actually say that he was about to become a Catholic. There were not many dry eyes in the church when he stopped. After the sermon he took off his surplice with an evident sense of relief.[42]

The congregation does not seem to have wholly realized that he was going. But some of the parishioners came to the Rectory to implore him to reconsider his decision. They even said he could preach what doctrine he liked provided he stayed.

Early next morning a fly arrived at the Rectory. In this Faber went off accompanied by Francis Knox, Tom Godwin and his sister, while George Hawkes, another of "his young men", was on the box. Meantime the two Pitt boys, Webb and Strickson, walked to Oundle Station. Five followed and two came on later. "We were all very sad and depressed," Godwin wrote.

It was a cold, misty morning. In the village there was a family of orphan children to whom Father Faber had shown great kindness, and as we passed the house they cried out to him: "Goodbye, God bless you, Mr Faber." The effect upon my master was beyond words. I think it was the only time I ever saw him moved to tears.[43]

That evening the former Rector was received into the Church with his little band, eleven in all, by Bishop Wareing. On the following day they made their first communion and were confirmed. Faber did not forget Morris and sent him a note written by Hawkes as he felt too ill to write himself. But at the foot of the letter he put these words: "Peace—peace—peace!"[44]

CHAPTER VII

ROME AT LAST

FABER'S secession caused a good deal of comment and he was accused of treachery in staying so long in the Church of England. It was put about that he stayed in order to inveigle as many of his parishioners as possible into the Roman Church. It was also said that he celebrated Communion in Elton Church the day before his departure.

Why, in fact, did Faber become a Catholic so late? He was a Catholic at heart when he left Rome. He should have been received then. It was Newman, or rather the shadow of Newman, who kept him back. Newman had not moved—nor should he. Guarded as Newman might be, Faber insisted on taking every word or gesture as significant. Newman was wise, slow to move, careful, thoughtful—all that Faber was not. He needed Newman as a guide, to protect him from himself. At Oxford he had learnt with bitterness to distrust his volatile nature. Was he much more than a poetic gadfly? Newman could give him the serious ballast he needed. Newman, on his side, was not adverse to admiration but there had to be intimacy, warmth, sympathy. He could feel none of this for Faber. Faber was "too cocky", too sure of himself. Faber's directness affronted him. He was too good a man not to supply Faber with advice when he asked for it. But it was against the grain and the advice was very unsuited to one of Faber's temperament. For Faber the waiting, the uncertainty, the possible destruction of all the schemes by which he lived, was a purgatory which damaged his health and ruined his happiness.

If Newman had not become a Catholic, or had Faber venerated Pusey instead, it is probable he would have remained an uneasy Anglican for the rest of his life. He would have continued to think that "heresy was permissively rife", as he put it, in the Anglican Church. But he would have held that this could be remedied by the use of the sacraments and Roman methods.

There was in fact a very great difference between Faber's attitude to the Church of England as a Church, which may be called negative for a period of years, and his attitude to the sacraments of that Church. As late as 31st October 1845 he wrote to Beresford Hope that he intended having a Communion Service every Thursday morning as well as every Sunday morning. By that time he had all but determined to leave the Church of England though he anticipated his secession as coming after Christmas. He undoubtedly still believed in the Anglican sacraments. It was not till 12th November that he had serious doubts when he went to administer Communion at night to the dying woman. He did not know whether he should give this Communion and hesitated what to do. But he recalled the teaching of St Alphonso and acted on what he considered only a probable opinion. On leaving the woman, however, he had the feeling that what he had done was unreal. After that he never said the Communion Service in Elton Church again. He had ceased to believe.

What is much more open to question is why he suddenly ceased to hold an opinion which he had held for years. Tom Godwin thought he received the gift of faith at the moment of leaving the dying woman. But from the letters it is clear that he had his doubts before the Communion was administered. To the cynic it may be suspicious that he had heard from his Italian benefactor only the day before. That letter had opened out a prospect in Catholicism—the use of his Elton boys in a religious community—which before had been denied him. Did he cease to believe at that moment because it suited him not to believe? It is hard to say. More probably he regarded the letter as an act of Providence which removed his last anxieties and in the ensuing relief and excitement the belief vanished. Continuing belief in the validity of Anglican orders and sacraments would not, in any case, have prevented his reception into the Church. He had enquired of Bishop Wareing on this very point and the bishop had replied:

A member of the Anglican church, in complying with this form [of reconciliation] is not called upon *totidem verbis* to pass

any opinion upon the validity of his orders or his past minis-
terial acts.[1]

Nevertheless it was psychologically congruent to the man that
once a Catholic he would not believe in the Anglican sacraments.

Anglicans who did not make the distinction between he
Anglican communion as a Church and the validity of her sacraments were puzzled and angry with Faber. When his letters were
read with their sarcastic references to the Church of England
it looked as if he had been a spy in the fold. The angriest supposed
that he had really been received in Rome before he took the
living.

There was great unpleasantness with Pusey which Pusey was
not to forget in his *Eirenikon*: "It is not for me to think ill of
anyone but myself," Pusey wrote,

> but I ought not to leave any doubt as to my own line of duty.
> If any who have felt it their duty to leave our Church "take a
> position of active hostility" against her, all intercourse of all
> sorts, except prayer, must cease. If the step of leaving her
> implies "downright aversion" for her, or if people use such
> dreadful language as Mr Knox did in a note to me, "of the
> English church being a delusion of Satan" I should fear that
> another spirit had been busy, than the spirits of love and truth.
>
> I must not, either, mislead you, as if I were "reconsidering
> the grounds" upon which I stay. It is not for me to think how
> in Newman's mind what he once held so strongly should have
> given way: life is not given for continual review of first prin-
> ciples but for acting. While those grounds gave way in dear
> N. they strengthened in me. I cannot part with them; it does
> not depend upon me to part with them; they are wound round
> and are part of me. Believing the English to be a branch of
> Christ's Holy Catholic Church "how shall I defy whom God
> hath not defied"?
>
> God grant that none of you may by hard words or theories,
> blind yourselves to God's gracious work or set yourselves to
> undo it or to weaken their hands who are engaged in it.
> There is alas! more than enough to occupy yourselves in
> restoring by any gift which God may bestow upon you that
> Communion which you have thought it right to choose. Do

not mistake the tone of this note but I **must** not use com-
promising language about myself.

He added on 25th November:

It is to me quite frightful to think of one, one day, officiating
as a Priest at our Altars and then shortly afterwards speaking of
"downright aversion" and "an attitude of hostility" . . .[2]

There was a lot of talk in Oxford and Stanley, the charming
liberal churchman who had been Faber's friend at Balliol, wrote
to his sister on 7th December:

Claughton has taken Elton (Faber's living) which will vacate
the Head Tutorship at Easter, quite as soon as I shall be ready
for it, and he has been there once already to look after the
place, and one of the churchwardens has been here. The accounts they give are very curious. It seems that Faber had
devoted himself wholly to the parish, and with the great
energy of his character and fascination of his manners had
produced an effect on the people which I should think was
really very extraordinary, whilst the faults which his friends
knew did not strike them. He had lived on terms of great
familiarity with them, having the young men, etc., constantly
to dine with him, and read with him in his own drawing room,
and having pulled down all the divisions in the Rectory grounds
so as to turn it into a kind of park, and throw it open to the
whole parish to walk in, so that on Sunday evenings there
used to be promenades of one hundred or three hundred
people, the poorer classes, and he walking about from group
to group, and talking to them. And thus, while the old people
liked him for his kindness there had grown up a "young
Elton" which quite adored him, and most of whom (about
sixteen) have gone over with him, and when Claughton came
there he found these young farmer boys talking of "the church
of St Peter, out of which there is no salvation".
     The churchwarden described the last Sunday, and the
departure on the Monday evening, as the most piteous sight
he ever saw: all the people weeping and lamenting, and
following him along the road as he went, and wandering
about desolate all the next day. On the other hand he must

have gone to the verge of what was right, if not beyond it, in Romanising the people, while he was still himself doubting what he should do, nor has he behaved quite fairly since, it is said.[3]

As might have been expected an angry controversy involving lawyers' letters broke out between Piers Claughton and Faber. Claughton was a rich man and when he had taken the living, before Faber's acceptance, he simply claimed £800 dilapidations —either through negligence or because he thought he could expend his own money on the very necessary repairs. Claughton only stayed nine weeks and then returned to Oxford. Faber received no stipend for his first year which he claimed amounted to £495 and having taken over the £800 dilapidations found it totally inadequate. Instead of claiming more dilapidation money Faber borrowed from his family and spent at least (as far as he could calculate) £1,384. Claughton maintained that a lot of the £800 was used for remaking the gardens into a park and other work which was unnecessary. Faber argued that on the contrary he had increased the value of the living by £110 a year. He therefore claimed that he owed nothing to Claughton for dilapidations. The row took a turn for the worse when Claughton attended the sale, the proceeds of which was to be Faber's only means of livelihood. Claughton bought £50 worth of goods and paid for it. But he then bought £50 10s. 10d. worth of wine and £27 5s. 6d. worth of fixtures which he pointedly did *not* pay for. Faber seems to have been in some danger of arrest but the dispute eventually petered out. It is uncertain how it ended. The college and Claughton, in any case, were in a difficult position for Faber was now insolvent.

Meanwhile the little band of converts had separated. The young Eltonians returned to the village to superintend the sale, Faber went to Frank's rectory at Saunderton, and Knox returned to Cambridge.

Faber wrote on the 19th to Newman:

Thank God all is over, and I am happy and at peace in a way I never have been for long and long. My sufferings last Sunday were very great, and on Monday I had some vehement hysterical fits: but, mercifully, I got over the temptations to draw back which were very strong indeed. My people were in a terrific state; two went down on their knees at my feet, and would not get up, and several scenes of that kind occurred. . . . I have not yet heard from Elton about my boys, how they have been received etc., but as soon as I hear I will write to you at length and also about my own plans. At present I am almost engrossed by the sensible enjoyment of a *peace* to which I have so long been a stranger: all doubt seems gone, and on looking back I see nothing in the step, or in the approaches to it, which I regret. Excuse this raw letter and believe me, my dear Mr (I think this must be the last Mister I shall ever give you as I don't like converting you into an Oriel don, which you used to be in my eyes) Newman, affectionately yours Fredk. Wm. Faber.[4]

Faber and Newman grew nearer together. They corresponded frequently and met to draw up plans for the future.

Faber now went to stay at the house of Mr Moore, a well-known priest, at St Chad's, Birmingham. Newman had already written there a letter filled with warmth of feeling.

Do not measure my own great joy at your present position by the few cold words which I put on paper. I had almost resolved to come down to Birmingham today to see you but thought you might be Mr Moore's property. . . . Do not commit yourself if you possibly can help it. The future requires a good deal of thought . . .[5]

Newman was turning over in his mind the prospect of forming a religious community which the converts could join. Faber wrote back ecstatically:

I shall wait here for a few days till I hear from you to know where I can come to see you. I will come *anywhere*. I am so, so happy. God bless you for all your kind words.[6]

What happened at the meeting, or if it took place, is uncertain. On 4th December Faber reported:

My visit to the *neighbourhood* of Elton enabled me to land six more of my dear flock; my little sheaf consists now of

thirteen. *Deo gratias.* .... By St Thomas' day I shall have been
so venturesome as to have lodged eight in my little monastery—
but the wherewithal to keep them? I know of no resource for
money-making but that of Father Dominic [the famous
Italian Passionist who had received Newman]—a novena to
B.V.M. However if I can manage it for six weeks or two months
their trades will keep themselves, and then I shall be off to
Italy and leave them to try their vocation for a year or less. I
think only four will make *positive* monks. I am in a good deal
of trouble, abuse, rupture of friendships, calumny and the like;
but I am not, thank God, cast down; only very tired. I cannot
get Wm. and James Pitts; their father is violent and inexorable:
do pray for them. I look for great things from those boys.
Pusey has written to me rather a bitter letter because I said
that the step I had taken did of itself involve "the highest
disaffection if not positive aversion" to the English Church.
He says he wishes all communication to cease between us and
believes that "another spirit than that of love and peace has
been at work" in all this. ... Lord Carysfort's steward has
written to me to say that if I came to Elton just now, there
would be an *auto da fe*, in which I should play a painfully con-
spicuous part: what a chance for Pugin's designs![7]

Faber was hurrying about the country visiting new converts,
would-be converts and possible converts, brimful of plans and
enthusiasm. In spite of his lack of money he had by now leased
a house, 77 Caroline Street, Birmingham, near St Chad's, and here
he expected to start his monastery. There was, however, an
exciting adventure to be got over before the scheme got fully
into operation. On 10th December he wrote to Newman from
St Chad's:

I wish you very much to pray that God may soften the mind
of W. & J. Pitts' father and induce him to give them up to
me. Unable any longer to endure the persecution they have
run away, and their father has been here today, wild and
brokenhearted, poor fellow! He says they shall never be
Catholics, and he will confine them: he has employed the tele-
graph on the railway, and the police here. We cannot make
out whether he is in the town or gone to London: he says he

will search everywhere. Meanwhile the 2 little boys are no-one knows where, abroad upon the face of the country, helpless and homeless. I suppose they will surely make for me and then will be arrested, and I am in such a nervous state I can hardly keep still. Poor little fellows! they have their guardian angels with them; but I long to see them. . . .[8]

Two days later he was at the Passionist convent, Aston Hall.

I have found my boys who have had marvellous escapes and are quite knocked up—poor fellows! they were scrutinized by the police at Rugby, but escaped; and I ran off, not by railway, to Wolverhampton yesterday where we stayed till dusk with a Catholic family, and then got to Stafford by the penny-a-mile tram, and this morning got under the wing of Father Dominic, but unluckily the driver of the fly overheard Father Dominic and myself talking about the boys which may be a clue. It has struck me very much that when Mr Moore and all of us thought they had been arrested I went to the third Mass on Thursday at St Chad's and made a vow to St Joseph, and an hour after they came. They are so happy they don't know what to do and Father Dominic pets them and tells them funny stories.[9]

By now the escapade had got into the papers and there were angry letters about Faber and "the perversion" of his "parishioners". All this was most distasteful to Newman, coupled as it was with Faber's breach with Pusey. "Under the circumstances," he wrote sensibly,

I should recommend the boys going back to their father. His tyranny cannot last forever—if they are firm and he goes on keeping them from Mass the neighbourhood will be on their side—and he will be forced to relax. On the other hand public opinion will be sure to support him if the boys are secreted and Father Dominic will get into a difficulty. Expedience seems strongly to point out this course.[10]

But, as so often happens, events overtook good advice. Next day Faber was writing:

I am delighted to be able to tell you that all, so far, prospers wonderfully. I got back to Birmingham on Saturday half an

hour after Pitts (the father) left the house, threatening to arrest
me. He applied to the magistrates for a warrant to search the
[bishop's] palace and Oscott, but was refused on the ground
that they would not meddle in matters of religion. He then
took up his abode at the public house close by, and watched
for the boys and myself, and made a great stir in the neighbourhood, but people all went against him, even Protestants, and
the poor fellow was quite cast down about it. He heard that
I was here, and I sent to say I would see him whenever he
pleased; he said he would come on Monday morning, but I
answered he had better come that night (Sunday). He applied
for leave to go into the organ loft at Compline (which he *sang*)
and Benediction, and he came out of the Cathedral a *changed
man* . . .

Father Dominic has reluctantly unloosed his grip upon the
two boys—forced 5d. upon them tho' they had lots of money—
the whole convent began the rosary for them as they went out
of the house, and last night (Monday) the novena for their
father began there. At the present moment they are gone into
the crypt in surplices to sing the dirige at a funeral, as happy as
possible, but [with] two terrific *convent coughs*. Padre Domenico
has made James promise that if ever he enters into religion he
will take the name of *Dominic* after him; and he took such pleasure in seeing the hungry boys eat that he told brother Ansanus
that he would be sure to go to heaven if he brought them
plenty to eat because it was a *prime* work of mercy![11]

Birmingham soon became a centre for converts. Its central
position and nearness to Oxford, but above all the presence of
Wiseman as coadjutor bishop at Oscott, made it an obvious
meeting place. St Chad's house near the Cathedral was filled with
those whose allegiance to the Church of England had become
"rickety". Among the visitors was William Antony Hutchison,
an undergraduate from Trinity, Cambridge. Hutchison's father
had been head cashier of the Bank of England, and dying young,
had left his son a rich man. At Cambridge young Hutchison had
early been attracted to Catholicism through the Ecclesiological
Society. Faber's name was well known in Cambridge owing to
his connection with Beresford Hope and Manners but he had

criticized the Ecclesiological Society and was unpopular. Hutchison, in fact, particularly wished to avoid him when he came to Birmingham. But this was not to be.

"I went up to Mr Moore's room," he wrote later:

> There I saw a person on his knees before the fire trying to make it burn up better. His hair was grey, he was dressed in a long black coat and tweed trousers, and he looked to me hungry and worn. I thought, this is some poor fellow they keep here out of charity and as there were a good many books round the room I took it into my head that it was the library and this person was employed as the librarian. What other views I should next have taken I don't know for Mr Moore proceeded to introduce me to him and to my astonishment he proved to be Mr Faber. I little thought then that that was really the most fortunate moment, as it has been also the turning point of my life. . . . It secured my conversion. I had many long walks with Mr Moore. . . . I was not sufficiently in earnest, however, to make up my mind to be received at once, and perhaps I should have drifted away from the Church after all, had it not been for Faber.
>
> I did not get on well with him the first day from shyness, but afterwards we became more intimate; and then, when he began to talk to me about Our Lord when dying on the Cross, thinking of me individually, and shedding His Blood for me as if there had been no one else in the world, he made me realize all this in a way I had never done before. From that time I made no more excuses for delay.[12]

It was the beginning of a life-long friendship between opposites, for Hutchison was as prosaic as Faber was poetic.

Michael Watts-Russell, Faber's former confessor, had now also become a Catholic together with his wife. Faber persuaded him to come to Birmingham and he took the two Godwin girls in the Eltonian band as maids in his household. They had been something of an embarrassment to Faber as he could not take them into his "monastery" and he did not want to turn them away. The girls were pleased with the arrangement as they wanted to be near their brother Tom and (unknown to Faber) Ann was in love with George Hawkes.

On 19th December Faber moved into 77, Caroline Street. "I write to you in amusing confusion," he told Newman:

I have this night taken possession of my little monastery; we are only three tonight, tomorrow we shall be nine. We have made some tea in a jug, bought a quartern loaf and some treacle, and have got three straw mattresses on the floor to lie upon, close to one another, and we have heaps of filth all round. We had some difficulty in kindling a fire, as we had forgotten to buy any chips; but now that we are well heated the two monks are indecorously merry; however I am going to try my hand upon pease soup tomorrow, and it is more than probable that I shall turn out some genus of food which may diminish their mirth. William and James Pitts are still with Mr Moore, envying the monastery. ... P.S. Our day has just closed; the room which is to be the chapel is full of filth yet, but we reared our dear Elton crucifix on a chair amid the dirt and recited the Litany of Loreto and the prayers for England, by way of an inauguration; and now we are going to bed, having got a bad cold apiece.[13]

The remaining members of the community arrived from Elton the next day. "Father Faber", Tom Godwin remembered,

wrote ... that as many of us as were prepared to take up our cross daily might live (at the monastery) rent free, but that we could not depend on him for more as he would have to do something (himself) for a living.

Faber's idea was for the boys to get jobs and so earn their keep. He hoped that they would be used as assistants to the clergy, in visiting the sick, giving instruction and in similar duties. They were to be trained as lay brothers and would live together under Faber as their superior. There was no idea at first of a definite rule. "Nine of us", Godwin continued,

went off to Birmingham. The rector and J. Pitts received us when we arrived. They had been preparing our frugal meal ... When he came to open the door it was evident that he was acting as cook—the meal consisted only of vegetable soup. "My dear boys," he said, "I have nothing very luxurious for your dinner but it is a fast day." I may add that I . . . have a conviction that cooking was not his strong point.[14]

"Tell St John", the cook wrote to Newman a few days later,

> that . . . the pudding he *sneered* at today was highly esteemed by my boys and I should think from its *weight* must have been *fearfully* nutricious.[15]

Hutchison, now a Catholic, visited the community a few days later:

> Preparations for dinner were going on. The Superior (Faber) was acting as cook and though terribly scorched by the fire, was perseveringly stirring without ceasing a kettlefull of pea-soup. He and the brothers wore long black cassocks of the Anglican pattern which they had brought from Elton. I remember well the impression that John Strickson (afterwards Brother Chad) made on me. He wore a cassock made of some very woolly shaggy material, and looked so gaunt and hungry that I thought him the very beau-ideal of a wolf in sheep's clothing. I have since found him, however, to be a most innocent and excellent wolf. The furniture of the house was very scanty; they had certainly a chair apiece, and a long deal table for their meals: each had also a knife and fork and mug; a benefactor had given them some pewter spoons with the temperance pledge stamped on them, and as they were too poor and too ascetic to drink anything stronger than tea, the pledge was not likely to be broken. A small round three-legged deal table, split across the centre, and a windsor arm chair completed the furniture of this room the front parlour, which served as a refectory, recreation room and parlour for guests. The armchair and round table were for Faber. On it stood the ivory crucifix which used before to stand in his oratory at Elton, and at this table, he was busy when not cooking or writing . . . Behind this room was a miserable back kitchen and upstairs four small rooms. One of these was used as a chapel. It had no furniture whatever, not even an altar, but only a crucifix on one wall. Here they assembled at fixed hours and recited various litanies and other prayers. The other rooms were dormitories; the beds were all on the floor as they could not afford to buy bedsteads and there was an old second hand

chest of drawers in which Father Faber kept his clothes; his bed was on the floor like the rest. It will be understood from all this that the life they led was an extremely hard one; in fact I believe that they depended in a great measure at this time on alms for their daily food. Still, everyone seemed very happy and cheerful, Faber especially so, though his health was suffering a good deal. . . .[16]

Meanwhile the work of conversion was going on. Jack Morris was not forgotten. There was a good deal of comment at his intention to preach before the University in his "rickety" state. On 5th December Faber had written:

While every day adds to my happiness and the sense of Catholic communion dilates within me like a new life, I feel more and more the *want* of your conversion. How long is it to be delayed? How long is the unhelpful bondage of that communion with nothing and with nobody to keep you from the open possession of all those sweet truths which you have lived up to better far than I have, and which form your secret life at this day? . . . I cannot tell you how every day, every Mass, seem more and more to show me the greatness of the peril from which I have been so mercifully rescued; and natural it is that I should yearn the more intensely, while on the hilltop I watch for the angel leading those I love out of the burning Sodom.[17]

The end came early in the New Year and Jack became a Catholic. There was much rejoicing in Caroline Street.

You would, I am sure, have been much pleased with the joy of G. Hawkes, Tom and Wm. Webb and at the fervour with which all the Wilfridians† said the Te Deum for you in the chapel . . . What Pusey may call the suddenness of your move only satisfies me the more that you are following a divine call. I have seen much of these vocations lately and there are some striking features about them; one is that all are under such circumstances that the real motive is hidden from those you leave, and they will misjudge you.[18]

† Faber's name for the members of his community.

It was the logical conclusion to Morris's diatribes against the
Church of England up in his room at Exeter College tower. But
with his conversion the shadow of the "awfully grand crucifix"
fell on him. His life as a Catholic was a long journey from one
chaplain's post to another. He was a misfit in his new communion.
In 1850 Faber wrote:

> You know we all, *cum Patre nostro*, groan often and say, "Poor
> Jack! He's the only convert who hasn't found his place in the
> Church yet. He's wasting life."[19]

But in January 1846 Morris could not see ahead. Nor could Faber
or Newman. To each was given a different path of suffering, for,
as Faber was to write, God rewards our love of Him with suffering.

Faber now set to at the "small, round, three legged table,
split across the centre," with the Elton crucifix on it to write
the apology for his conversion. Written in the form of a letter
to a High Church friend it was entitled *Grounds for Remaining
in the Anglican Communion*.

It is a violent amorphous piece of writing ill calculated to
help Anglicans still in doubt. New converts are seldom attractive
and Faber was particularly disagreeable for many years after his
conversion. Once he had changed his opinions he was incapable
of seeing any good or attraction in what he had discarded. It is
true that Pusey and his friends attacked him as a renegade who
had made the change on a sudden sentimental impulse—which
was absurd. But on grounds of expediency alone it was not sensible to counter attack with such vigour. In Faber's defence he
was sorely tried and unwell.

> I am regularly beaten down by another afflux of persecution,

he wrote to Hutchison,

> which comes on me when weak with overwork at my pamph-
> let.

He had also received at the same time a worrying letter from his
Florentine benefactor which seemed to put his future plans in
jeopardy.[20]

"Why should it seem to you", he wrote in his pamphlet to his High Church friend,

> so unnatural that those who have left you should feel anything rather than loyalty and affection to a system, or anything but kindly reminiscences of a dreadful position, which they were forced from by the simple fear of everlasting ruin? Where do I owe my Christian allegiance? Is it not to the Church of my baptism? And surely *you* at least cannot be so foolish as to suppose that anyone is baptised into any particular insular, national or provincial part or branch of the Church or into anything short of the Catholic Church of Christ. It is there my allegiance is due, and it is there your allegiance is due also. A false system took me from my Mother, as soon as I had either sense to do overt acts of schism or wilfulness to commit a mortal sin: that system nurtured me in hatred of the Holy See; it nurtured me in false doctrine; it has had the strength of my youth and formed the character of my mind and educated me in strange neglect as well of doctrinal instruction as of moral safeguards: and now do I owe allegiance to the Mother from whose breasts I was torn, and whose face was so long strange to me? or to her who tore me from her, and usurped a name that was not hers, and whose fraud I have discovered?[21]

Answering the well-known Tractarian conception of their difficulties as providential trials he wrote:

> We are to be cross-bearers; but where are we ever led to be prepared for anything so terrible as that our Church is to be our Cross?[22]

He accuses his imaginary correspondent of what he himself had been accused of:

> You are living on Roman books, on Roman devotional practices, on Roman ascetical usages ... you are uniting the temporalities of established Protestantism with the spiritualities of depressed Catholics.[23]

He made hay of the branch theory with:

> Are all the Churches *branch* Churches? Is there no *trunk* Church? If there is which is it?[24]

As to those Tractarians who did not move because Pusey or others had not moved—were, that is, behaving as he had done:

> Can it really be that this is a ground whereon a reasonable accountable Catholic Christian holds communion with his Church? If this is not that calling man "master" which is condemned by Our Lord, which is such an especial note of an uncatholic spirit, I do not know at what the words can be aimed.[25]

He dismissed the Caroline Church as an Anglicanism untried, and "Young England" as an impossible hope without the Catholic faith. He poured ridicule on the plea sometimes put forward by harassed Tractarians that they were not good enough to become Catholics.

> Now comes a charge, which, whether it be against old Catholics or converts, pretty plainly intimates your more real opinion to be that the Church is not worthy of *you*.[26]

Even if the sacraments of the Church of England should be valid,

> yet *valid sacraments do not give safety:* there is the *injury of schism*.[27]

A particularly insulting charge (made also by Mark Pattison later against Pusey) was that the secret of the confessional was not inviolate among Anglicans.

The causes of the imaginary friend remaining an Anglican are listed as

> a secret subtle and intolerant pride . . . a most profane, sickly Puritanical mysticism . . . a keeping at arm's length the simple penitential humbling anxiety about your own soul . . . and a fretful disobedience to your present position cloaking itself under the garb of a mournfully humble endurance of it.[28]

The pamphlet ends:

> You are not a Catholic, and so much belief alone is yours as St Ambrose speaks of, (how long shall it be true of you and yours?) *Credis quod tibi prodesse praesumis; non credis quod Deo dignum est*.[29]

There were some palpable hits but the pamphlet was written in a harsh tone of polemical triumph. The Anglican position might be all that Faber made it out to be but why, people asked, had he held these same theories so long if they were worthy of so little attention? Faber might be a charming and persuasive person to meet but it is doubtful if his pamphlet made a single convert. Had the pamphlet been written as a confession of past mistakes to which he had found a solution its reception might have been different. As it was it infuriated the Anglicans and upset his friends.

"Nothing ought to disturb me," Newman wrote to St John,

else I should say that Faber's pamphlet would do so. If anything could stop the Movement it would be such writings. It is the recipe, the specific, to close simply and certainly the hearts of such as Pusey—to have the most powerfully deleterious effect on such as the Kebles—and to be a marvellously useful drag in the hands of quacks, as Sewell & Co. But I must not go on, or I shall get fidgetted. Of course the Church has the credit of it with all Anglicans—for Faber must necessarily be under a staid director who knows perfectly well what he is at. I would tell F. my mind but, poor fellow, he has so many people upon him that it would be cruel ... I don't mind Jack [Morris] knowing it.[30]

Morris duly informed Faber, as apparently he was meant to do. "I am very, very unhappy", Faber wrote,

at having done anything to displease Newman, and actually miserable thro' the fear of my being the cause of anyone's drawing back from the Catholic Church because of my exhibition of evil temper. Doubtless it was a want of proper humility which made me come forward in the matter at all; and the thought that I should already have done mischief entirely discourages me as to my future plans at Birmingham. I shrink from undertaking any sort of responsibility; it were better for me to be back at Elton than making mistakes where mistakes are so fatal. Indeed I do not know what to think, things have been very different since I became a Catholic, different on the wrong side, and when one strives as much (as far as one can see) it perplexes one how such can be the case, certain given premises being true ...[31]

By the same post he wrote to Newman:

> I only write these few lines to express my very, very deep
> sorrow that I should have done anything which has displeased
> you, or from want of proper humility have come forward at
> all. . . . If you think it well I beg you will tell Toovey, to stop
> the sale of it [the pamphlet], and I will find means to make up
> anything he may lose by so doing.[32]

He was sincere when he wrote this but was he convinced? It is
doubtful. A few months later he was again writing to Morris:

> Perhaps Newman does not regard the English Church with the
> same *horror* as I do, nor so utterly and undoubtingly respue her
> pseudo sacraments and orders as I was taught at Rome to do . . .
> I did not and do not see his objection to my pamphlet but to
> be safe I immediately wrote an apology.[33]

Faber had intended from the time of his conversion to visit
his benefactor in Florence. The little community could hardly
hope to survive, even with all the young Eltonians at work,
without some endowment. Faber was getting more and more
troubled by the fear that the community would soon break apart
of itself. "Three are head over heels in love," he wrote to Newman,

> *direction* they have none in the proper sense of the word;
> and there are daily fresh symptoms of the work thawing away
> under my hands. I have had a very long interview with the
> bishop today [probably Wiseman] and another is to follow.
> He seems out of heart and non-plussed about it. However my
> patronus St P. Neri used to say, "Are there no difficulties?"
> No. "Then it can't be good for anything." If however on my
> return the scheme does not seem feasible and only 1 or 2 remain
> with vocations I shall offer them to you as lay-brothers and take
> refuge at Santa Maria in Vallicella (S.P. Neri's Church)—*non
> in Roma ma in Oscotia*, that is to say if you will take me.[34]

Newman replied rather guardedly. He was not sure of his own
future except that he was to live at Maryvale with other converts.

Of course we should be too glad of the gain which a change of your plans would bring to us at Maryvale as you will believe, I hope, without my enlarging on it—though I shall not be surprised, even though you joined us, if you find yourself ultimately called elsewhere. I cannot help thinking you should be a distinct centre of operation and collect people about you.

He went on to say that Faber might take the opportunity when abroad to spend some months in a continental seminary. This would dispel any feeling among the old Catholics that Maryvale was to be a new school of Catholicism. "I have long felt", he continued,

> special reverence and admiration for the character of St Ph Neri, as far as I knew it, and was struck by your saying that his Church at Rome was in Vallicella. I wish we could all become good Oratorians but that, I suppose, is impossible.[35]

Newman was writing from Littlemore but he was preparing to move to Maryvale. The similarity of the names Santa Maria in Vallicella and Maryvale was not likely to be missed by Newman. The hand of God could be read in such things. And, indeed, in other ways the letter was prophetic.

Faber determined to visit Florence as soon as possible. He left Caroline Street in charge of Mr Moore and set off with the young convert Hutchison on 2nd February. They intended to learn more of Catholicism besides seeking material aid. There was also a typical project of Faber's—a short visit to the Holy Land. But the little Eltonian community was never far from his thoughts. "After the miserable foothold which the world and the flesh have gained in our little household at Birmingham", he wrote to John Strickson,

> I believe my absence is very necessary, as a trial to you all, to prove who is to do God's work in the world *without self*, and who is not. Those who are honestly seeking from God a saintly vocation will have temptations of a very dangerous sort to go through ... Now you must put steadily before yourself *this one thing*—that your present position is an awkward and in

some respects an uncomfortable one, which is to be your trial *till I come back*, and no longer: if then it be four months, or six or nine, be patient, and think that if God does give you the grace and the happiness to become a monk at last, this waiting will really have been but a small price to pay. You will not, cannot get what you look forward to, till I come back; bear this in mind.[36]

The two Englishmen visited Sens Cathedral and venerated the relics of St Thomas of Canterbury. During the previous days Faber had had doubts about the Catholic faith. He felt he had been mistaken in leaving Elton and even began to doubt Christianity itself. But in the Cathedral, owing as he supposed to his invocation of St Thomas, all his doubts left him and he was flooded with "divine love". His mind seemed suddenly to clear and he jotted down the whole rule for his order as he left the town. At Lyons the travellers read a pastoral letter from the Archbishop directing thanksgivings to be made for the recent conversions of Newman, Oakeley and Faber. They then travelled to Leghorn from Marseilles.

> I was very much affected when I saw the mountains of Italy; when I was last at Leghorn I was Rector of Elton, returning to reside there, and with my head full of plans for the spiritual welfare of my parish: now how different all is! I feel fifty years older, tired and broken down, and no longer in love with life, for life has nothing to offer, but I feel still an unbated desire to do God's will, and a daily increasing hunger for hard work, and hard work in England. I confess that just for one moment, when I saw the beautiful mountains, and the glorious blue sky, and the church towers of Italy, I felt as if I never, never would go back to the difficulties and disturbances and enmities and evil speakings of England; but it was a mere temptation which passed away.[37]

Mr F. J. Sloane, "the kind benefactor" whose letter finally tipped the scale at Elton, and from whom so much was hoped, acted as Faber's host in Florence. Hutchison went to lodgings. Sloane had come by his money in a romantic way. According to Adolphus Trollope he had been tutor in the household of Prince

Boutourlin. The rights in the copper mines of the Volterra region had been granted to an incompetent company and the tutor, who had a knowledge of geology, was asked his opinion. The upshot was the cancellation of the previous concession and the granting of it on favourable terms by the Grand Duke to the tutor and an English banker. He was now one of the best known figures of the English colony. A fervent convert he had helped build the new Campanile of Santa Croce and had contributed largely to the recently completed façade. He was on intimate terms with the Grand Duke and fully at home in ecclesiastical circles. According to Trollope he gave magnificent dinners on Fridays in order to show what feasts could be given without infringing by a hair's breadth the ordinances of the Church. Sloane seems to have wanted to adopt Faber. Was he prepared to adopt his community as well? Faber had taken this for granted but he soon found he had been too optimistic. There had been a warning letter in January.

> My kind benefactor here has received me more like a father than anything else; nothing can exceed his affectionate goodness to me.
>
> But even in the sunshine God provides trials for us. I have opened my plan to my good friend but at present he by no means approves of it, for many reasons which I will not trouble you with, and partly it is a disappointment to him as he had looked for something *higher* for me. For one moment a deep feeling of dismay came across me; but our Rule came to my help: the Will of God![38]

Faber's appearance at this time is described by Frances Trollope in a letter after dining with Sloane. It is strangely at variance with that of Hutchison.

> In the way of *brilliance*, by far the most brilliant person with whom I have made acquaintance is Faber. He is, I think, the most eloquent person I ever heard talk. I dined with him at Mr Sloane's last week and on Thursday he dined here. On both occasions I sat next to him, and have rarely listened with such *wonder*, and I must confess, with such admiration to any one. I did not know, until he told me, that his education began at

Mr Gibson's near Penrith. Then he was at Harrow while Anthony was there, and then, as you know, at Oxford. He told me that Mr Cunningham gave him his earliest religious thoughts—but that he always had a sort of misgiving that he occasionally talked nonsense.

The first sermon he heard at Oxford was from Newman. He says the effect of it upon him was equally sudden and profound. All this, and a great deal more, in the same strain was exceedingly interesting,—yet nothing could be less like what I should have expected from him. He is thirty-one years old, but looks considerably younger. He is fair with light hair, and has a *lively good humour* that is very pleasing. But the charm and *power* of his countenance is in his mouth, which is not only peculiarly handsome, but has a variety of expression that is quite extraordinary. That he is perfectly in earnest, it is impossible to doubt:—the great sacrifices he has made prove it sufficiently, and every word he speaks on the subject of his conversion confirms the impression. Yet there is something of playfulness in his phrases now and then, that is rather startling. He talks, for instance, when speaking of the party he has left behind, of "their rush towards rubrics". But he is, in all moods *brilliant* and agreeable. He talked to me freely about our dear Grand Duke's want of Popish strictness; and said that the Pope had told him that he had more trouble with His Highness of Tuscany, who was Catholic, than with His Majesty of Belgium, who was Protestant! He spoke with very sanguine hope of the speedy conversion—or *re*conversion—of Great Britain to the old faith; and said that he was returning to England, after Holy Week, to establish a monastic house at Birmingham—where there are already three for women. He invited me earnestly to visit them.[39]

However brilliant and fascinating Faber may have appeared to Mrs Trollope, Mr Sloane's attitude did not change. But Faber was unmoved. He was convinced all would come right. An emotional friendship at the same time sprang up with the young Marchese Leopoldo Bartolommei. Faber hoped that he might join the new community. They had long earnest conversations on prayer and holiness. "I love you as if you were my own brother," Faber told him, and wish I could always be with you, and so you might by your sweet example lead me forward in spiritual life.[40]

But Faber added that God had continually given him

> things to love and set my heart upon, and then He takes them away from me ... I love and then He bruises my love, so I must take the Infant Jesus in my arms.

In the meantime Hutchison and Faber visited all the churches and ceremonies they could. At first they were not much edified, particularly as regards the abstinence in Lent which was dispensed except for Fridays. This seemed a sad lack of strictness. Faber went so far as to say that he preferred English to Continental Catholicism. But he was very impressed by the Quarant' ore which he described to John Strickson in detail. As Tractarians, their taste was, as Bowden put it,

> what is called Gothic, and they were consequently disposed to criticize unfavourably some of the ecclesiastical arrangements which came under their notice. Such dispositions, however, gradually disappeared under the influence of the edification which they received, and before they returned home their fastidiousness had given place to a hearty admiration of the material as well as the spiritual developments of Italian piety.[41]

This conversion, or perversion as Pugin would have called it, from the Gothic to the Classical was to be of some consequence later. And from this time dates Faber's exuberant fondness for Italian devotions which was to prove such a difficulty with his fellow English Catholics. However that may be, Faber's love of Italy certainly let in rays of sunshine into his spiritual life.

He wrote home:

> We shall have no midnight services, and fewer bodily severities in our new monastery, yet it will not be very unlike the rectory. The chapel, however, will be much more beautiful, for I am promised all manner of grand ornaments for it; and we shall be as happy as monks, who are in reality by far the happiest people in the world.[42]

He now called his rule "merry and sunny".

At length when no more was to be gained by staying Faber and Hutchison set out for Rome. Mr Sloane remained kind as ever but unmoved. This community of raw village boys in the middle of Birmingham was beyond his comprehension. A slight detour was made in order to visit Loreto and its Holy House. Here Faber asked

> a great thing of our dearest Lady in the Santa Casa, and she got it for me in ten minutes.[43]

What he asked is unknown. It may have been a more fervent love for Our Lady in the same way as Coventry Patmore asked for it at Lourdes (see page 149). Hutchison always regarded the incident, whatever it was, as mysterious and miraculous. Hutchison who was a rich young man had offered himself several times to Faber in the course of the journey as a member of the new community. But Faber had refused to receive him in case he should not persevere. It is possible that he finally made up his mind at Loreto.

They arrived in Rome before Holy Week and drove straight to the English College where Dr Grant was now rector. They spent their time, as they had done in Florence, visiting churches and attending ecclesiastical ceremonies. But Faber's main concern was naturally his community. There were many consultations with Dr Grant and Cardinal Acton. They were very sympathetic, "but," Faber wrote,

> it is uphill work and truth to say, I am worn out, worn out, worn out. My last year's complaint in my feet has broken out again, and I feel more than ever the burden of beginning life over again at my age, standing alone and surrounded with uncertainty. Then again I find here that there are a host of *canonical* objections to the Rule and Congregation, and I hardly know how to turn myself. I am like a tired-out spider, whose web has been demolished so often that he is inclined to give up spinning it over again. St Wilfrid seems to get for me a kind of dogged cheerfulness and so I go on and on and on; and perhaps I may not live much longer, and then it will be well to have worked up to the last moment.[44]

He wrote in the same despondent tone to Bartolommei:

My spirit is a little oppressed now by the work which lies
before me. I am 32 years old; I have spent a life of very active
work, and you see it has all, all been vain, all wasted in a
wrong direction; now I am weary and have a feeble body, and
yet I have to begin life over again as if I were a boy. Where
are the spirits and the gaiety and the young strength to come
from? Alas! it is a fearful prospect: a child of 32 to make a new
life, to fight the fight over again which he has already fought
till he was soiled and bleeding and fainting. But where is the
consolation? Why in this reflection! That I am but a lump of
flesh with a soul in it, and He who made it has a right to squeeze
it and to throw it about and to trample upon it as He pleases.
I am not my own: I do not belong to myself; that is the
luxury of religion. O to be trodden underfoot by the sweet
Will of God,—that is my *delizie*! So back to England I must go
and work and work for my dear dark country till my strength
is spent.[45]

He even had thoughts of becoming a Jesuit and throwing up
the Birmingham community. But on Easter day it was agreed on
Dr Grant's advice that Hutchison should join the community
when they returned to England. This decision finally put an end
to Faber's financial worries. After Easter the two Englishmen
were presented to the Pope. "His Holiness," Hutchison wrote,

received us most kindly and was reminded by Dr Grant that
some years before, Faber had been presented to him when he
was an Anglican, and that His Holiness' blessing had not been
without effect. When the Pope learnt what was the annual
value of the living which Faber had given up, he seemed a good
deal impressed and slapping him on the shoulder, said "Ah!
That was a fine patrimony!!" The interview ended by his
giving us his blessing, and telling us to go back to England and
convert as many of our friends as we could; words in which
we pleased ourselves in seeing a certain mission and authoriza-
tion of our plans.[46]

Faber at this time was convinced that much larger bodies of
Anglicans would become Catholics. It was indeed the general

belief. To Watts Russell, who had some damping things to tell, he wrote:

> I do not wonder at there being a pause and a lull just now, but there will be another throng, a second harvest, depend upon it.[47]

His plan was to be a labourer at the harvest. He was encouraged to hear that Watts Russell considered his pamphlet was doing good in spite of Newman's criticism. It had, however, met with a characteristic reception in Rome. The religious censors stopped its distribution on account of its title: *Grounds for Remaining in the Anglican Communion*.

On 25th April Faber and Hutchison set out for home. As they left the city they stopped at the Chiesa Nuova to make a parting visit to the body of St Philip Neri. Hutchison wrote of their feelings as they reached England.

> I suppose no one can approach London by the river from the sea, the only fit way of approaching it, without being deeply impressed by the immensity of the great city, with its perpetual canopy of smoke, which seems to conceal and yet perhaps magnifies its vast extent. But to us, who could but look upon it as the great sinful capital of heretical England, the sight of it was painfully interesting and almost depressing; for what could *we* hope to do toward furthering the conversion of this great empire and yet it was with the view of devoting ourselves to this work that we had now come back to England.[48]

They arrived late in the day of 16th May at Caroline Street laden with a large store of rosaries, medals, crucifixes, holy pictures and books of Italian devotions.

CHAPTER VIII

BROTHERS OF THE WILL OF GOD

ON Faber's return a move was made from Caroline Street to Colmore Terrace. Watts Russell had decided to leave Birmingham and Faber took over his house together with the lease of the house next to it. It was not, however, till June that the two houses would be knocked into one.

A chronicle was started in the true medieval style.

Annales Fratrum Voluntatis Dei, Congregationis St Wilfridi, Ultimorum et Minimorum Servorum Ecclesiae Sanctae Romanae. IN NOMINE PATRIS ET FILII ET SPIRITUS STI. AMEN.

Benedicta sit Stã Humanitas Jesu et Immaculata Conceptio Mariae.

1846. On Tuesday, 26th May, the Month of Mary ✠ Brother Wilfrid of the Humanity of Jesus [Faber] having received the blessing of our Holy Father, Pope Gregory XVI at Rome, and the relics of several Saints, on the 24th April, the Feast of the Translation of St Wilfrid's relics from Ripon to Canterbury ✠ we entered our monastery in Colmore Terrace Birmingham with the knowledge and consent of the bishop. We were as many in number as the Holy Wounds of Jesus—Brothers Austin of the Ascension [Henry Mills, a Cambridge convert] (Choir), Chad of the Sacred Heart [Strickson], Frederick of the Will of God [Tom Godwin], Bernard of the Immaculate Conception (all three lay), and Wilfrid of the Humanity of Jesus (choir) [Faber]. Blessed be God for His grace, and Mary for her help, and Joseph our Superior for his efficacious patronage. Feast of SS. Austin and P. Neri.

Friday, May 29th. In answer to our prayers we heard today, not officially, that the Bishop had examined our Rule, and was favourable to it. Deo Gratias.

Saturday, May 30th. The Eve of Pentecost. We began to recite the Divine Office in choir at the first Vespers of Pentecost;

we also commenced a novena for 2 persons. At night Brother
Antony of the Blessed Sacrament [Hutchison] who had joined
the Order at Rome on Maundy Thursday, came to us. Michael
Watts Russell presented us with a monastery seal.

Sunday, May 31st. The Feast of Pentecost. We made a communion of thanksgiving for the Bishop's approval of our Rule.
The last day of the month of Mary: we part from it with
sorrow: the consolations of these 1st days of confusion and
beginning will not soon be forgotten by those whose souls
have been filled with such peace and sweetness. Viva Gesù,
Giuseppe e Maria!

Monday, June 1st. We began the Month of the Precious Blood,†
giving all the indulgencies to the Holy Souls in Purgatory.
We went out for the first time in our habits, to the Confirmation, and were very little insulted, the Holy Ghost giving us
boldness. At night we heard that one of the 2 persons for
whom we were making a Novena was received into the
Church. Blessed be St Joseph, our beloved Warden. Brother
Ignatius of the Mother of God joined us today. . . .[1]

It was religious fiction that there were only five members
of the community for there were plainly more. Faber found on
his return that "the spirit of the world" had been at work among
the Eltonians and three soon left, but even so there seem to have
been about twelve brothers. The somewhat rapid rate of turn-over
makes it difficult to say how many there were at any one time
but there were probably never fewer than eight.

The Wilfridians set out to provide a body of priests to undertake the charge of any good work the bishop might find for
them. They were also to have their confessionals open at all times,
in this imitating the Oratorians. (The lay brothers no longer
went out as they had done in Caroline Street but worked in the
house.) The three simple vows were taken and property was in
common. Brother Wilfrid (Faber) was not called the Superior,
that title being given to St Joseph. The brothers wore black
cassocks, buttoned in front, with wide sleeves and on the breast
a cross between the letters V.D. (Voluntas Dei, Will of God)
in red cloth. A cloak was worn over the habit with the same

† Then apparently June.

device on it. Round the waist they wore a leather belt from which
a rosary was suspended. The choir brothers wore the Roman
collar, the lay brothers a stock without collar. They had clumsy
and uncomfortable birettas made locally. At first by mistake the
lay brothers wore these as well as the choir brothers and there
was some little difficulty over giving them up.

Mr Moore, who had been in charge of Caroline Street in
Faber's absence, was for the brothers' launching out into various
useful activities immediately. He had pitifully few workers at
St Chad's and he wished to use the brothers without delay. But
Faber considered that the community would certainly fall to
pieces unless it was allowed time to grow together. The rule had
to be understood and the particular objects of the order appreci-
ated. There was a conflict of wills. Mr Moore used his position
as confessor to press his point of view. The *Annales* discreetly
screens the conflict in these words:

> Brother Wilfrid of the Humanity of Jesus had a long conference
> with the Bishop at Oscott; the result of which was to place the
> Congregation on a much surer basis, better to secure the ob-
> servance of the Contemplative part of the rule, and to check
> what Claudius Aquaviva calls *the nimia effusio ad externa*. Blessed
> be Jesus for the kindness and love of the Bishop.[2]

In other words with the help of Wiseman Mr Moore was ousted.
When asked what V.D. stood for on the habit of the Wilfridians
he replied briefly: "Very Devils." He was furious when later on
Italian vestments arrived from Bartolommei.

"We had three abstinence days in the week," Hutchison
wrote,

> and breakfast, to an Englishman usually the most comfortable
> meal, was very much the reverse by being taken standing, in
> silence, and consisting of dry bread and tea without sugar.
> Butter and permission to sit were given on festivals, to whose
> coming, I, for one, used therefore to look forward with satis-
> faction. We rose at half-past five. At six we assembled in the
> room fitted up as a chapel for half-an-hour's meditation in
> common. Then the Choir brothers said the Hours, after which
> we went to St Chad's to Mass, in parties of two or three.

After Mass and Communion, we returned to Colmore Terrace to breakfast; then came a short visit to the Chapel, after which the lay brothers were busy in household work. At half past twelve the Choir brothers said Vespers and Compline, and the others came to join in some devotions. Then came dinner, during which there was spiritual reading. This was followed by recreation, up to which the rule of silence was observed from the beginning of the day except on Sundays and Festivals. The afternoon was left tolerably free till about five, then came Matins and Lauds. After tea and recreation we generally assembled in the Chapel to receive instructions in mental prayer, examination of conscience and such subjects from Brother Wilfrid. After this followed the giving of the meditation for the morrow, the Rosary of the Seven Dolours and other night prayers of the Community. The brothers were encouraged to practise other devotions during the day and to use the discipline in their own rooms. A triduo or a novena was almost always going on, and a relic of a saint exposed on the altar. We went out but little except to Mass at St Chad's on week-days, and to the High Mass and Vespers on Sundays, when the Choir brothers occupied seats in the stalls. At first we went through the streets in our habit, but at Mr Moore's request this was discontinued. Inside our house, I think we succeeded to a great extent in doing what Brother Wilfrid proposed, ignoring the existence of Protestantism, and living as if we were in Italy.

Perhaps it was because we were still in the first fervour of our conversion, but certainly in those early days we seemed to live almost in the companionship of the Saints and of the Madonna. We led a most unworldly life, and I do not think it was unreal, notwithstanding perhaps a little occasional eccentricity. . . . We adopted many Italian customs and practices in devotion, especially to the Madonna. The devotion of Maria Desolata was observed every week from Friday evening to Sunday morning. On the Vigil of the Assumption the Chapel was adorned with an abundance of candles and fir trees . . .[3]

It was a happy time and a successful one. Faber indeed was offered a house and chapel in Nottingham for a second "monastery". The project was abandoned for lack of money. It was too soon, as well. Faber even offered to hand over his community to Newman so that the converts could be united. Newman politely but firmly refused.

The summer of 1846 was extremely hot, Colmore Terrace was low lying and the brothers suffered a great deal from over-crowding. But towards the end of June the second house became vacant and an internal doorway was constructed. A large room was set aside for the library and Watts Russell's bedroom became the chapel. It was decorated in the Gothic style with red walls and a blue ceiling. An altar by Pugin was imported. The brothers now had a large forlorn garden planted with soot-laden fruit trees and evergreens where they could exercise themselves without going into the town. To the despair of the gardener it was also used for processions and ceremonies. In the evenings poor Catholic boys came to play in it, their games always ending with the Litany of Loreto sung in procession. It was in some ways an idyllic life, however uncomfortable. There was much cheerful-ness, in contrast, Hutchison noticed, to the atmosphere at Mary-vale. There were a few incidents in the round of prayer and duty. A leg of mutton caught alight and the monastery was nearly burnt down. A bad piece of meat was bought by mistake and the community was poisoned. They recovered by what Faber called "*almost* a miracle". Newman commented that Faber had more adventures than anyone else.

> To be sure the blue sky, and the green fields, and the river side, and the grey gables, and the idolatory of Elton,

Faber wrote,

> are far other than the smoke, and the dense streets, and the denser mass of unbelief and utterly abandoned souls, and the stifling sick-rooms, and the hooting and pelting of Birmingham, yet the last is more to my mind *now*; and I hope God may bless us and quicken our love for these poor English artisans more and more. . . . I hope you will find Brother Wilfrid walking the smoky lanes of Birmingham, with the boys cutting jokes on his habit, a being not a whit less gay than the Frederick Faber of the Lakes. . . .

"Life is now little short of heaven," he wrote later,

and the bliss increases daily, because the calmness of it deepens daily. . . . My mouth waters when you "babble o' green fields" and "St Catharine's by the silver lake"; and the thought of the *awful* gulf that is now betwixt me and flesh, blood and places I idolized before sends a cold chill over me, but the red cross on my rough habit must keep that little beater down, and bid it beat, not less ardently but for Jesus only—Jesus, my daily Guest, my Lord, my Life, my Love, my All. . . .[4]

Yes, as always, there was another side. It was not easy for the converts to be assimilated into the Catholic body. The old Catholic priests, solidly English, conservative, unenthusiastic, were suspicious of the new-comers. The converts, on their side, were painfully aware that the priests were not gentlemen. There were only about half a million Catholics out of a population of seventeen million. But Catholicism was much more of a minority religion than even these figures imply. Catholics had played no part in public affairs and were out of the stream of national life. Moreover at least half of the total figure was composed of poor Irish labourers crammed into the new towns. The proportion of Irish to English, owing to the potato famine, was steadily increasing, creating in men's minds the image of a Church of the poor, the ignorant and the uninfluential. By contrast the Catholic aristocrats who had played so large a part in penal times were all powerful. They tended to regard priests as their chaplains. In such an abruptly contrasted society in process of rapid change it was not to be supposed that the Tractarian converts would immediately find their feet. Some indeed failed to do so. Others found aristocratic patrons or put themselves under Wiseman's kindly wing.

Catholic priests who came to visit the monastery raised their eyebrows when Faber referred to Our Lady as "Mamma". If this was Catholicism, they said to themselves, how was it neither they nor their fathers had known it? Faber's exuberant nature delighted in the Italianate devotions he had discovered. "To me," he wrote to Morris,

one of the most striking things is that the more Roman I get, the more I seem to recover, only in a safe way and with make-weights, of old boyish evangelical feelings instead of the cold gentilitising ethics of Williams and others which never came natural to me.[5]

It was these boyish evangelical feelings which the old Catholic priests found distasteful.

"Here", Faber continued to his friend,

> we have lots of strange priests almost daily, and they ask one's view downright, and speak of the Rule, and one can hardly help speaking dogmatically without in a short visit getting that character of jealous reserve which old Catholics fancy they see in most converts, and by which they are specially disgusted. They come at all hours, stay meals, take one by surprise, throw one into a hurry and I must not deny that they have not infrequently put me out of temper. . . . As to the word Mariolatry, all I meant to say was, that we spent all our time in teaching people what we were *not* to do to Mary, instead of pushing forward the ardent worship of her, as we ought to do. . . . In good truth it is odd that I should go to Loreto to beg devotion to our dear Lady, and that afterwards in two solemn communions I should have vowed my life, health, strength, intellect and senses to be her slave and to spread her devotion, in great measure because I feared converts relapsing from want of that *gran segno di predestinazione*; and then that, on that account, it should be thought I should be like one who *never* "warmed", as a bishop expressed it to me, to Mary; and whose fall is considered to be owing to that.[6]

He wrote more personally and more emotionally to Bartolommei.

> I am but a mere convert, one who has spent 31 years in rebellion against Holy Church, and has employed all his talents and influence against her; and now instead of being hidden in some monastery to do long and safe penance under obscure obedience I am placed partly by circumstances, partly by the bishop's orders, and partly by my inordinate pride in the position of superior. Some of the old Catholics say I shall fall away and become an Apostate, because I push devotion to our Blessed Lady too far. . . . Surely Mary will never suffer that my love for her should be the cause of my destruction. In

truth I do love her with a most fiery enthusiasm, the fire that was kindled, my dearest brother, when I prayed for you and myself in the Santa Casa of Loreto.[7]

The brothers were thinking of building a larger chapel in which they could hold popular services, after the manner of the Oratory. There was even talk of a move. And then everything was transformed by a new and totally unexpected event.

"I must tell you", Faber wrote to Watts Russell,

that we do not seem to get on here for reasons too long to enter into; and I have vowed my life to my dear Lady, body, soul, and spirit, to spread her devotion; and we are keeping a Novena to her mother S. Anna with great fervour, and are learning God's will about buying a site, etc., etc.

Faber put his letter down at this point and then later continued excitedly.

O—would you believe it, on Tuesday, Lord Shrewsbury has an enthusiastic I don't know what for me and for my Order and sends to offer me as a free gift a piece of land adjoining the Church at Cheadle, which he has given £1750 for!! and Cotton Hall for the *Maison de campagne* of the Order, and Newman rushed in to tell me the news.[8] I hesitated, because God's Will is my Rule. But Newman is for it, and so is holy Mr Heneage [the Wilfridians' confessor]; Mr Moore, of course, against it; Dr Walsh for it, Dr Wiseman not at home. We are praying and communicating and Mr Heneage saying Mass. Brother Antony [Hutchison] (a secret) offers me £5000 to put into Pugin's hands to fulfil Lord S.'s condition which is—to build at Cheadle!! Newman and Mr Heneage think our spiritual good and likelihood subsequently to affect the country are in favour of our going: but strange to say! Saturday is the last day of the Novena to the glorious S. Anna and Lord S. has oddly fixed to come over to me from Alton Towers on *that very day* to have my final answer, and Mr Heneage has ordered me to decide nothing but that when Lord S. speaks God will put into my mouth what to say.

You may judge of Lord S.'s kindly feelings by the tone of his last. "Dear and Revd. Sir, I am much obliged by your

Father Faber cooking in Caroline Street

From a pen and ink sketch

A Brother of the Will of God

From a pen and ink sketch

This is that Priest so remarkably stout
Who makes all the Novices so devout

Father Faber with the novices at St Wilfrid's

From a pen and ink sketch

A Father defending himself with his
stick from a wild crab on ye sea-shore
Fr. R— S——. Lancing 1850.

Scene on the shore at Lancing

From a pen and ink sketch

kind favour, and I shall do myself the pleasure of calling at
the *monastery* between 5 and 6 on Saturday afternoon if that
will not be too inconvenient an hour—that is if I hear nothing
to the contrary. Lady S. is also very anxious to make your
acquaintance, and as I presume your Rule excludes ladies from
your precincts we must hope you will be able to find a moment's
leisure on Sunday to come and see us at the Railroad Hotel
as you were good enough to offer to do. I trust to hear that
you have not altogether turned a deaf ear to my message
through Mr Newman. I have just spoken to our good bishop
on the subject, and *he* at least approves the project, and I shall
hope before long to show you the localities as we cannot yet
(*I had refused his invitation*) renounce our expectation of seeing
you here (Alton Towers) on occasion of the dedication of St
Giles! Believe me, Rev. and Dear Sir, very truly and faithfully
your Shrewsbury." It is but a few months since two Protestant
parsons gossipped over a crude dream in the garden at Benefield
—and but 7 months since the founder was a beggared expect-
ant of a prison from his Protestant successor: surely God must
have a purpose upon us. Today Newman and I are to have a
thick conference. . . .[9]

The Shrewsbury who made the offer was the "good Lord
Shrewsbury," the church builder. He had succeeded his uncle in
1827 as 16th Earl and lived at Alton Towers, a huge fantastic
palace by Pugin. Disraeli described it in *Coningsby* as "a pile
of modern buildings built of a white and glittering stone. Its
striking situation, its brilliant colour, its great extent, a gathering
as it seemed of galleries and halls and chapels, mullioned windows,
portals of clustered columns and groups of airy pinnacles and fret-
work spires . . . with its . . . chapel in which art had exhausted all its
invention and wealth offered all its resources." Here old Catholics
and converts met to discuss the longed for conversion of England.
   Lord Shrewsbury's offer was very tempting to Faber. It would
give him the opportunity of leaving the publicity of Birmingham
and of consolidating his Order in quietness—but was it God's
will? He put all the factors in the situation before Watts Russell
in order to clarify his mind. But in the meantime the new Order
was undergoing its natural time of uneasy growth:

The Blessed Sacrament came to us last Sunday which was St Anna's Day, and you may imagine the burst of fervour and spirit of penance which it has produced among these good lay brothers. Our novena to St Anna was most fruitful; it gave us the means of getting rid, with more gentleness than I supposed had been possible, of 2 brothers who had no real vocation for us, Brother Bernard of the Immaculate Conception, an Irishman, and Brother Gabriel of the Heart of Mary, the fat fellow from Maryvale, whose vocation consisted of love of me. He has for the present returned to Newman. The same Novena brought us an Aloysius in Brother Vincent of the Holy Cross, a choir brother of 17, and not a convert, and who seems all love to everyone but his own poor body, which he disciplines *frightfully*. It also brought us Lord Shrewsbury's princely offer; and then ended by the coming of our Love to dwell with us, in what was your room, where He is almost perpetually, in the daytime at least, worshipped in His tabernacle which is just where the bedhead was. I tell you the localities because they will naturally interest you.

Lord Shrewsbury came on Saturday week, and then Lord and Lady S. came on Sunday as I preferred her coming to us to my going to an hotel. But I am so startled by the possibility of not doing what is God's sweet peaceful Will, that I have begged for time, and Lord S. has kindly granted it. The Birmingham people are affectionately up in arms against our going, and Lord S. found the feelings so strong that he said he would be contented with a filiation, and says I may divide his offer, if I please, and take Cheadle without Cotton, or Cotton without Cheadle, if I can't manage both. Thus the offer has been the means of showing us that we are more esteemed here than we had any notion of; but I don't see how a filiation can well be managed so early. They do not like the idea of being separated from me, any of them, and think they are not sufficiently trained in the spirit of the Rule and Order. Then again comes the question whether the change of locality will not necessitate some amount of change in the Rule and so in the peculiarity of the Institute! Indeed the pros and cons are balanced with a perplexing nicety. . . .

When the burden of government is heaviest, one can gaze on the glittering door of the tabernacle that holds our willing

Prisoner of Love, till one can almost fancy one hears the huge Will of the Supremely Blessed making melody as it moves along and wheels round us, and sparkles in its rapidity, giving light for a moment to its own beautiful movements, and then leaving us on our knees in the darkness once again, with the music of the same perpetual Will all round about. But, after all, the hot choking *allezo* [*sic*] of Birmingham with the weary sacrifice of limb and spirits to our neighbour are sweeter with that music of THE WILL in them, than the solemn woods and sighing yews of Cotton, however, it might seem that we should be more with Jesus there.[10]

It is not known what finally caused Faber to make up his mind. Perhaps it was Wiseman's decision. It may have been weight of numbers. Jack Morris was against the move but as Faber wrote to him:

You and Mr Hardman and Mr Moore are on one side, Newman, Mr Heneage, Mr Fowler and Bishop Walsh and Michael Russell and Mr Tempest on the other.[11]

On 1st September Faber with Hutchison and another brother were present when Pugin's church of St Giles at Cheadle was dedicated. They were given some part in the ceremonies and were of course in their habits. Newman and Oakeley were also present. It was probably while at Alton Towers on this occasion that Faber accepted Lord Shrewsbury's offer. He gratefully accepted the house and grounds of Cotton Hall for the purposes of the new order but declined to build near the new church.

The house which dated back to the seventeenth century is in a delightful rural countryside which retains its charm to this day. It is intimate country with rolling hills, small woods and rich pasture land. Cotton Hall, or St Wilfrid's as it was now to be called, stood high up on the side of a valley the lower part of which was filled with thick woodland. From the front windows there was a fine view over the woodland and up to the opposite bank crowned by a clump of Scots firs. Faber called it in a letter to Bartolommei "a wild and beautiful solitude among the hills of Staffordshire". There was a large garden with many trees in front of the house, a sloping lawn, and the little Anglican parish church in Regency Gothic stood in the grounds. It was an idyllic place for the poor Eltonians who had been exiled in Birmingham from country things. The move, which took place early in September, acted as a tonic on Faber and he was soon scheming changes in the place. New walks, gardens and plantations of trees were laid down. A terrace was made in front of the house. Tom Godwin was kept busy and the rest of the lay brothers were set to work. There were of course alterations and additions to the house, and a new church by Pugin was started.

"You can scarcely form an idea", Faber wrote to Watts Russell on 5th October,

> of the confusion, hurry, work, I may actually say, *ubiquity*, which have been required of me during the past weeks. From Alton Towers to Cotton, at Cotton from the house to the garden, from the new church to the new school, from the quarry to the wood, from bricklayers and carpenters to painters and glaziers, from Dr Winter the Dominican to *Mr* Winter the steward, from Lord Shrewsbury to Brother Chad, trees, walls, windows seemed to echo Brother Wilfrid, Brother Wilfrid and the unfortunate Brother Wilfrid was everywhere but in the one place where he ought to have been, viz. before the Blessed Sacrament.[12]

This whirl of activity did not go without its punishment, for Faber continued:

> Well, fratello mio, for I conceal nothing from you, not even what must be secret as death—in the midst of all this confusion, hard work, inability as yet to keep their Rule, the poor lay brothers were distracted and when I was overwearied, God reserved a fresh token of His goodness in trying me; a conspiracy was formed in the monastery against my extreme severity and want of fatherly consideration, and failing (though only just) to draw in Brother Frederick (T. Godwin) Brother Aloysius (an Irishman) and Brother Stanislas (Camp. Smith's man) *all* the rest [of the lay brothers], headed by Brother Chad, broke out into open rebellion and abusive insult, and prepared to return home. I was stunned for one moment—spoke to Brother Ignatius; he insulted me! I then gave one look at the

awful width of public scandal at their return to Elton and
Birmingham respectively—rang the chapel bell myself and in
the presence of the Blessed Sacrament gave them leave to go
home and stripped the rebels of their habits, which I claimed
as my property, freed them from their obedience, and offering
them money for their journey, I said with the utmost calmness
that come what would, I was not to be daunted by numbers,
and that I would not suffer my red cross and V.D. to appear an
hour longer on the breasts of those who could worship self
so basely as this; and in another half hour the choir brothers
and Mr Wells were seen digging at the foundations of the
church, loading carts with soil, and every office in the house
filled. The burst of enthusiastic union among the 5 choir
brothers was to me an unspeakable consolation; the rebels
dispersed I knew not where; I took no notice of them at all
and would not speak to them; I understood they were going
in 2 or 3 days.

When all was quiet I began to give way, but I went and
threw myself prostrate before the altar, and in my bitterness
I blessed Jesus that He at least could not leave me, as He was
a prisoner of love in the tabernacle, and I rose comforted.
About noon or after, the choir brothers who seemed more
drawn to me than ever, met in the chapel and we recited the
7 penitential psalms and the Litany of the Saints for the rebels,
and during this I seemed to have an interior assurance that it
was all an actual possession of the devil, which made me
redouble my prayers for the poor fellows. The next day there
were evident signs of distress and misery, and a hope that I
should speak to them, and offer some compromise; but though
I *yearned* to do it, I would not; I spoke to none of them; they
got their meals in plain clothes; they were allowed to do no
work, and I ordered the choir brothers to avoid them: meanwhile I begged of God to beat down their pride, and one by
one, some almost at midnight, unable to sleep, threw themselves
at my feet in tortures, declared they were *possessed by a devil,*
did not know what they were doing, nor what cause they had
had—I summed up all my kindnesses and sacrifices for them,
I taunted them with the most cutting language, and renewed
my permission for them to go home, till they were goaded
almost into fits; neither did I finally relent till they threw them-

selves on the floor in the refectory before the rest, acknowledged the satanical influence under which they had been, and
implored mercy in the most abject terms. I then laid my hands
on each one (after an address of about a quarter of an hour)
saying Benedicat te Maria, and restored them their habits. It
is now more than a fortnight since peace was restored; we are
again observing our rule; obedience is more perfect than ever;
but I am overwhelmed with spiritual direction, for each soul has
suffered the withdrawal of some of its graces through the anger
of God, and they must fight their way through mist and tears to
the recalling of it; and I, like a spider, must repair my web.

This is *one* page of our history. I can say no more now than
1. that I am to receive minor orders with Brothers Antony
and Austin [Mills] at the Towers on Monday. 2. that the
Bishop fixed St Edward's day but it ultimately turning out
inconvenient to Lord Shrewsbury it will now be, D.V. on St
Wilfrid's day, 3. that on the same day the bishop with mitre
and crozier will walk round the foundations of my new Church
of St Wilfrid and bless it, and sing the Litanies over the rising
walls: Pugin says it will be the "only perfect chancel in
England" and with "an East Window he could die for". . . .
Pray also for the Catholic clergy that they may have more of
the ecclesiastical spirit and be less like *ministers,* that God may
raise up Newman or someone to get us a *seminaire* as distinguished from our present Oxford-mimicking colleges. . . .[13]

The story of the revolt could not be kept secret and in his
next letter to Watts Russell he wrote:

I am said to have *strangled* one of my monks: the story is all
over the land and is believed: it has led to a rupture between
the Bullers and the Shrewsburys. Mrs Buller came to see
me at St Wilfrid's "to see the man"; and glaring at me in
silence like a tigress she told Lord Shrewsbury and Lady
Arundel that I was *quite* capable of all she heard, and that her
faith in it was established! Brother Antony's brother has sent
a Scotch physician here to inspect and report; the said Brother
has also written a letter in which I am "an ambitious villain
and a hellish ruler," and that wherever he goes in London "the
finger of scorn is pointed" at me. . . . I *beg* you never to say a
word in my defence to anyone. I keep a most tranquil silence;

I feel most for the poor fratelli who mourn in silly sympathy for me.[14]

All these troubles were followed by a retreat given by Father Cobb, a Jesuit. "The unbroken silence, the long hours of solitary meditation of the Retreat," Faber wrote,

> have been more than I could bear; I suffered considerable mental anguish in my general confession, and an intensity of doubt, terror and uncertainty about my present vocation, and as to whether I was not called to be a Jesuit. I am afraid therefore that I shall shock you a little when I say that after battling with a burning brain all yesterday I took to bed, no one in the house but the Jesuit father, about 6 in the evening; after a struggle my whole body was paralysed except my head; by this time another priest had come; after the ringing of the Ave dei Morti I received absolution and extreme unction and lay in the arms of God in excessive happiness: from this it was His Will I should recover; for half an hour or so I got life back and then was again convulsively paralysed, all but my head, my mind was clear and calm; I made my profession of faith, bade the poor wretched Brothers goodbye, lay in the arms of one of them, and received the last benediction and papal indulgence, while Brother Antony thrust Pope Gregory's crucifix into my lifeless hands. I seemed to pass through death: God was all around; I was inexpressibly happy till I heard like an inward voice (nothing at all supernatural, mind) say I was to return to life, and I mourned. I believe the Holy Oil has done it: tonight I am very very weak but out of all danger and the like ... Jellies, soups, jams, etc. come pouring in from poor distressed Lord Shrewsbury. Father Cobb is a capital nurse and the medico is a Catholic. The poor brothers had a sad night besieging the tabernacle with Miserere's and Litanies of the Saints but are now getting right. I keep even the good Jesuits laughing round my bed and am in high spirits.[15]

But although his recovery was quick it was by no means complete. From this time Faber's health deteriorated. He gradually changed from a thin poetical-looking man into what he described as a "mountain of flesh". His letters scarcely mention the alteration in his appearance and he does not seem to have regretted the

loss of his good looks. Faber of the Lakes and the Catholic Faber
from about 1847 onwards were not recognizably the same man.
His constitution was peculiar. His father and mother died young.
Both his brother Frank and his grandfather were what he called
"never very well". George Stanley Faber was delicate. Faber's
enormous energy, the frequent physical collapses, the late sexual
maturity, his delight in exuberant exaggerations of all kinds may
have been caused by a glandular or hormone disorder or it may
have been that Bright's disease from which he eventually died
had already gained a hold on his system. The distortions of the
disease could not, however, destroy the music of his voice or the
characteristic expression on his face.

Convalescence took time and was filled with troubles. "I
was given up to such awful temptations of the devil", he wrote,

> as banished sleep, and were fit to carry me away by their terrific
> impetuosity: add to this that in myself, and nearly all the
> brothers, the intensity of the retreat was succeeded by a most
> distressing disgust of spiritual things: mass seemed abominable,
> communion nauseous; and one day in genuflecting before the
> tabernacle I felt all at once an impulse to dance before it, and
> then strike it out of mockery of the *imaginary* Presence within.
> You may well conceive the terror all this caused, while I was
> weak and ill; but I dragged myself up to communion, in
> misery and disrelish, trusting in its hidden strength; then came
> the wild tempest of the flesh, till I was sick, beaten down,
> despairing. The prayers of my kind friends must have kept me
> to God; I almost ceased to make an effort.
> Then on Saturday one of the choir brothers resolved to leave,
> and treated me most strangely. I set another brother to speak
> to him; but we could not get at his heart; his outward manners,
> even face were changed; on Sunday he was for tearing his
> habit off. I told the others he was possessed and wished the
> bishop was here to licence me to exorcise him. O what I
> suffered! At night, broken-hearted, I spoke to him in my cell
> about his leaving, which was decided on, and I told him he
> was possessed. You should have seen his look. I then said to
> him in a loud tone, "kneel down, and beg my pardon, and curse
> the spirit of pride in your heart". He fell at my feet; I said,

"Have you cursed him?" He answered in a faint whisper, "Yes"; then embraced my feet and kissed them, and then writhed on the ground in a fit. I dragged him to a bed, where he soon became senseless and stiff. I laid him at full length and ran to call for help. (I ought to say that during the day he had been guilty of great irreverence to the Blessed Sacrament.) As I was going through the next room I heard a loud noise in his cell, [and] running back I found him lifeless, rolled up like a ball near a priedieu. To this day he knows nothing of how it was. The medical man arrived from Alton in an hour; but he was himself by that time. I went to bed on Sunday night wretchedly ill, and on Monday I was in bed nearly the whole day in acute suffering. The poor brother came to my bed, flung himself on his knees, and cried and kissed my hands; he said his heart had been *hard* for some days, but that it grew soft as I spoke the night before, and the fit came when he cursed the devil in his heart: now he is all gentle, docile, humble, loving.

Well—on Monday night, after this day of burning in my brain, I was myself either possessed or something very like it: I heard noises (and in the morning Brother Austin said he was sure the devil had been to him in the night) and I felt the Enemy in my room. I was torn by temptation too horrible to relate, so that at one, ill as I was, I jumped up, lit a candle and got the life of S. Juliana of Retinne but it was past three before the Evil one gave me any respite. On Tuesday night when I was asleep at 12.30 the whole house was roused; it was a livery servant all the way from my brother in Bucks; of course I thought he was dying but it appeared that in some extraordinary way a paragraph had appeared in the Oxford Herald, stating that I was lying at death's door from paralysis. I had never written to my brother, so in an agony he sent off his servant express. This was another shock to my poor nerves: it was strange to say! the very night [last] year I was called up at midnight at Elton to give the communion to a sick woman, in which service I seemed to see that it was no sacrament, and the next day, St Martin's day, came over with Knox to you at Benefield. . . .

Now a word on the congregation, the dear congregation. I am too tired to tell you all the processes of mind I went through in the Retreat—how near I was to becoming a Jesuit—how Father Cobb discouraged the new scheme—with what mental agony I was agitated—how I rushed into Father Cobb's room one night, etc., etc., how humility seemed to suggest joining another order—how the calumny I pray for might come best in the ridicule and scorn which would be raised about me—but enough, enough. What I feel now is that I am all at sea about the congregation. The great town development seems impracticable; all clearness and speciality seem gone from me. In a word I am at sea.[16]

As if what had happened was not enough rumours circulated that Father Cobb had been discourteous to the new congregation. Faber was distressed as he was under great obligations to the Jesuit's tact, kindness and good advice. Father Cobb may indeed have used his influence to mitigate some of the austerities. He was not, however, consulted about the stand-up breakfast which was Lord Shrewsbury's *bête noire*. Lord Shrewsbury put down many of the troubles which had befallen the congregation to this austere breakfast. He took the matter up with Faber and with the bishop. To Faber's disgust the bishop eventually decided against the breakfast and it was discontinued. Faber made a bad impression by writing a sarcastic letter about "couches and ottomans".

In January a new choir brother arrived. Frederick Wells, from now on Brother Alban, was just twenty-one. He was the grandson of Lord Carysfort whose place, Elton Hall, had been in Faber's former parish. (Tom Godwin, it may be remembered, chopped off Faber's hair before a party at the Hall.) Wells had met Faber at Elton and while still an undergraduate at Trinity, Cambridge, had become a Catholic. Being under age he was put in charge of a clergyman but on reaching his majority he joined the new congregation. He had already been a frequent visitor both before and after the move from Birmingham.

There was still a considerable turnover in the new congregation. In November Faber was writing:

Brother Philip has been obliged to leave the order for health and Father Cobb has cracked Brother Bonaventure's vocation and he has gone.[17]

The Brothers, however, had the advantage of having a resident priest, at first Mr Kennedy who had assisted at the Eltonian's reception at Northampton, and later Dr Faá di Bruno.

Faber had received the tonsure and the four minor orders after the lay brothers revolt on the day the bishop came to bless the foundations of the new church, 12th October. He received the order of subdeacon on 19th December. He now prepared for the priesthood in the early months of 1847 with characteristic energy and determination. He read till all hours and undertook heavy penances. In the result he further undermined his health. Hutchison thought this mental overwork ruined his chance of a true recovery. He was, of course, now able to preach again and already a number of local people, mostly Protestants, came to hear him. On the fourth Sunday in Lent he spoke as follows:

> For eight years of my life I have been a Protestant clergyman, with important parishes entrusted to my care, until it pleased Almighty God of His infinite mercy to show me the dreadful errors and unscriptural doctrines of Protestantism, and to lead me into His true Church, and give me the unspeakable happiness, a happiness which increases every day, of being a Catholic. During those eight years I gave up my life to the poor, lived among their children, was continually in their cottages, or at their death-beds, and, as an Englishman bred and born, no object was so dear to me as the English poor, so miserably neglected, ill used, or coldly treated as they are now; and now that I am on the point of being ordained a Catholic priest, I feel even more strongly than ever the desire to devote all my health and strength to win my poor countrymen to the true light of the Gospel, to console them in all their tribulations, whether of body or of soul, to sacrifice my own ease and comfort for them, and knowing so well as I do the trials and difficulties of the poor, to endeavour to make religion as easy and as kindly to them as possible—to make the yoke of Jesus what He Himself called it, a light yoke and merciful.[18]

The idea behind leaving Birmingham and coming to Cotton was, as he explained to Bartolommei,

> to get a secret retirement to prepare ourselves to work in the large towns.[19]

"I believe", he had written while still in Birmingham, probably to Roundell Palmer,

> the large manufacturing towns will be converted and that their weight will decide the rest of England.[20]

Cotton was to be a *casa di campagna e noviciato* only. There was no question of converting the rural neighbourhood. But already Faber had begun to let down roots. Stations of the Cross were put up in the garden and large wooden crosses on the hills on each side of the valley. Later on he erected a statue of Our Lady with the Holy Child in front of the house and called it the *Virgo praedicanda*. It overlooks the valley and was meant as a challenge to Protestant England. The crosses were in Faber's mind a challenge to the neighbourhood. The countryside he had learned to love was to have the Catholic faith preached in it again. A boys' school with 46 pupils had already been commenced and they were making a start with a school for girls. A night school for adults was soon to be opened. But the real campaign that Faber was already scheming could not get under way till he had been ordained at Easter. Good though all this might be it was a change of direction which Faber later acknowledged.

In the meantime there was another adventure. "In a word," he wrote to Lord Shrewsbury,

> we have been a prey to fire but by God's great mercy are saved —persons, effects and house also. At about 9 this morning I was washing some corporals in the study, as subdeacon, when Mr Kennedy came in great alarm to announce that his room was on fire. I saw he was in a great panic, so I said, "Never mind—Our Blessed Lady will take care of it". I could not of course leave the corporals but I finished them as quickly as I could, and then setting Brothers to work with pick axes discovered that the timbers of the roof were on fire, and the wood work in Mr Kennedy's room wall was white hot. As soon as I discovered that the *house* was actually on fire I detached 2 brothers from the work, and the abbate, and myself, and removed the Blessed Sacrament with torches, surplices, veil, and all formalities, of which I would not have one omitted. Having deposited the Blessed Sacrament in the school-

room with a Brother to decorate the place as quick as he could, I returned to the scene of the fire. The heat was tremendous but the Brothers worked gloriously and we made awful havoc in a very short time, and at last laid all the fire bare; so that in two hours we were safe. . . . You must excuse any more for stairs are running down with water—inflammable articles such as bundles of newspapers, etc., are lying in the snow under the windows—mists of lime and steam—chalices, vestments, etc., lying on benches anyhow in the schoolroom: so that the superior has plenty to look to.[21]

That evening

all in surplices, with torches, we took the most High out of the schoolroom, went in procession through the yard, out of the large gates into the grounds, and so to the front of the house singing the litany of Our Lady. It was a dark still night, and the bell and lights and singing and the flashing *ombrellino* had a most touching effect among the trees. We deposited our Lord in His own tabernacle after receiving His Benediction, and when the tabernacle was closed, we stood up and sang the Te Deum.[22]

Conversions in the neighbourhood through the agency of the schools were beginning. Faber jocularly put down the fire to the devil being angry at the success of the Brothers. "I am tired", he wrote on Septuagesima Sunday,

with having given a most vehement lecture for 1 hour and 10 minutes to a crowded chapel of Protestants on our dear Lady and Confession. They were immensely attentive to it all. I am really, my dear Lord, worked to death by young men from Oakamore and all parts: from 25 to 30, several grown up, one of 40 to 50 years, come to the night school to hear the *fervorini* I give every night, and then they come crying up to my cell with tales of hideous guilt. They hardly know there is a God and even in this retired spot we are all overworked. I catechize publicly twice a day except Saturdays; then there is Sundays' *conversazione*, and hours of private talk to these young men. Last Sunday Richard Goldworthy, 20 or 21, was received into the Church; on St Francis of Sales, the very day you wrote

your letter, I presented Mr Kennedy with 7 more, and last
night I at last overcame Moult, the shoemaker, at Oakamore
(though Miss Rag has been to him and is going to persecute
him and get his custom away) and he made his confession and
was received: then the mother of two of my converts has been
brought by them, and was received yesterday. Thus we
received 10 into our flock last week, God be praised! and Mr
Kennedy speaks in the highest terms of their dispositions.

But I am pretty well come to the end of the tether of my
strength; and what is to be done? It is a kind of work one can't
control; a young grimy smith comes at 8 or 9 p.m. after his
work, from Oakamore or elsewhere, and says, "I want Brother
Wilfrid". Well—what's to be done? Wanting Brother Wilfrid
means that the poor wretch is terrified out of his wits and on
the verge of confession. He can't be sent off; and he won't see
another. So an hour or so goes teaching him the Trinity, etc.
and how to confess; and then perhaps it takes a week to get him
fit for absolution.[23]

A week later he reported four more confessions and "the
huge consolation" of the converts' first communion. The labourers
in the neighbourhood were desperately poor and seem to have
been left very much to themselves both by the Church of England
and Nonconformity. It was only when Faber's successes began to
make a stir that interest was taken in them. In a letter to Lord
Shrewsbury Faber wrote:

There are many in need of shoes and stockings and other
apparel. We had a brace of brothers with only one pair of shoes
between them, and they came in the one pair alternately;
neither had stockings.[24]

As the ordination grew nearer Faber became more and more
nervous. Lord Shrewsbury with the privilege of the Catholic
aristocracy which had kept the faith alive during the dark penal
years told him bluntly that his health was too low either for
fasting or abstinence that Lent. "I am immersed in tribulations
and difficulties," Faber wrote to him,

harassed by uncertainties and doubts and exposed to attacks
which it will be hard to stand against: at present we are in

perfect darkness about the future. . . . We are in a mess too about our Congregation: we could not hold them yesterday and the floor of the Chapel gave an *awful* crack during Compline *just under me.*

There were unpleasant interviews with neighbouring clergymen. "I was very sheepish," he wrote after one such interview,

> though plainspoken, and would not let them be angry, and I made them both shake hands with me before they left the house. I hear there were two more parsons waiting at the outer gate; I suppose lest I should hang or disembowel Mr Hendrickson. I think they were very unreasonable with me. I am *much* out of spirits, hardly able to bear up against all I have on me; but I will do my best, as I know it is a duty: but I am not a little wretched.

It was war to the knife. Mr Hendrickson proposed that no conversions should be made by either side. Not unreasonably Faber refused. A Protestant school was set up and got thirty pupils— several of Faber's boys leaving to go there. An ugly note is struck in the postscript to the same letter.

> For the sake of the mission, my dear Lord, do not without well thinking of it let Prince have a *lease* of his farm. Brother Antony has been made Procurator and has refused to take Prince's butter. . . .[25]

If the Catholic cobbler was to lose his trade so was the Protestant farmer.

As if further to harass Faber news arrived immediately before his ordination that Newman had become an Oratorian in Rome. The Oratory of St Philip Neri is not an order in the usual sense of the word. Each Oratory is a separate community of priests living under the rule inspired by St Philip, having a common table and times for prayer in common. They are not vowed to poverty nor is any Oratorian bound to his congregation by "any vow, oath or promise" as the constitution lays it down. The Oratory grew out of the religious exercises of St Philip Neri carried out in Renaissance Rome. It is characterized by a light-hearted spirituality, affection for Our Lady and devotions in the vernacular. It will be seen immediately how attractive the Oratory must have appeared to Faber.

"Whether what Newman has done will necessitate any change in our Rule or not I cannot tell," he wrote anxiously:

> If he wishes the large towns to be given up to him, of course, as juniors and in every way inferiors we will do so; but nothing can be decided on till N. comes home. It is clear we must not clash.[26]

By the same post he wrote to Newman:

> The news of your becoming an Oratorian of course raised a little fresh assault on us, as we ought to follow your example and merge in an old order, etc., etc., and it was rather curious that I had proposed to Dr Wiseman to make an Oratory but he discountenanced it, and we gave it up a little bit grumpily ...
>
> You perhaps may know that our Rule as revised and presented to Dr Wiseman at Xmas was a *mélange* of Padre Filippo's and St John of God and had almost exclusive reference to towns. Now we have taken no vows under this Rule, nor in any way pledged ourselves to it, except as a temporary measure of our community life. Consequently when you return we could have a Conference, and if it still seemed advisable, as the bishop said, that we should not be merged in another institute, then let us (as juniors and inferiors naturally ought, and we most cheerfully will) cede everything which might interfere with you or the spread of your houses (I suppose *filiations* they cannot be called according to S. Philip's rule) and occupy whatever ground discretion and holy obedience may point out. We shall have a greatly increased difficulty to make our ground good as a *new* institute, since we lost your shelter; but as I have just refused the new Orphan asylum in the London district, we have no engagements on hand; and could be shaped afresh, when you return, if we are found to stand in your way. Anyhow if any of the odd or ill-natured things people say just now reach you, do not be uneasy on our account. We have now quite given up our notion of returning to Birmingham, and nothing shall be settled permanently till I see you.[27]

Faber was ordained by Wiseman on Holy Saturday and returned that afternoon to St Wilfrid's. "We arrived from Oscott", he wrote to Newman on Easter Monday,

King William Street Chapel about 1850

Oratorian. "Is your Mistress within, my dear!"
Maid-of-All-Work. "Oh, help! help! here's a Bogie, Missus! help! help!"

Scene on ye shore at Lancing 1850

From a pen and ink sketch

about 9 at night; about ¾ of a mile from St Wilfrid's two guns were fired to our no little astonishment, and then the carriage was stopped by a huge crowd of peasants and labourers; strange to say! I was sitting next my old lay helper at Elton whom I had accidently invited from Birmingham, and whom I sat next to, I think, in the fly on my memorable retreat from Elton. This crowd, composed almost all of *Protestants*, took the horses from the carriage and dragged us home amid volleys of guns and fireworks and a brass band; a series of really most tasteful triumphal arches were reared along the road, with illuminations and crosses on them; under each of these we stopped, for cheering and music. I was very weak and ill and the unexpectedness of it all completely overcame me. However when we got into the yard, I mounted some steps, spoke a few words to them, and gave them my blessing; and they seemed much affected . . . The poor Protestant minister had to pass to his chapel under the triumphal arches: he had only seven to preach to, and coming away with his seven he met under the first arch the whole community, cross, torches, and a dead body—while we were singing the *officium defunctorum*: really it was rather hard for him.[28]

But the triumph of his ordination had really been spoilt by the news from Rome. Agonizing doubts about his vocation returned. Would he not have done better to have been under the guidance of Newman all along instead of superior of an order which was going who knew where? But the sheer momentum of the work of St Wilfrid's (together with the spiritual hunger of the people) carried things forward.

Districts were marked out and assigned to the brothers, who each spent a good part of the day making systematic visits. The people were invited to the services and given preliminary instruction. Faber reported to the Bishop that many of his converts had been half prepared before he came—presumably by Mr Kennedy who had been chaplain from 1845 to the previous tenant (John Campbell-Smith) of Cotton Hall. There was a First Confession Brother, a First Communion Brother and a Further Instruction Brother. There was a Confraternity of the Precious Blood and a brass band. During the summer of '47 Faber preached under a beech tree in the garden or in a yard near the church as the chapel by this time was too small and Pugin's church had not been completed. It is said that after a few months of these operations there was only one Protestant family to attend the Anglican church. Hutchison wrote exultantly:

> We have converted the pew-opener, leaving the parson only his clerk and two drunken men as his regular communicants.[29]

This statement is surely as exaggerated as it is distasteful. But perhaps it is excused by the heat of the battle. A minister of the Primitive Methodists pushed his way into a house and insisted on hearing what a dying man said to Faber in confession. It was only with the greatest difficulty that he was ejected and then only after Faber agreed to discuss points of doctrine at another time. When Faber left the house another squabble ensued outside. A formal meeting was proposed, the Minister insisting that the Bible alone in the Authorized version should be the subject of discussion. Faber, understandably but in the circumstances rather meanly proposed to use only the original Greek. The formal meeting therefore never took place but the Minister pursued him with abuse and calumny.

Faber was at length goaded into print and he wrote an open letter to his religious enemies:

> What has been the policy of our adversaries, and the fashion of their warfare? One clergyman of the Establishment rides into our garden on his pony, and refusing to bow or return my salutation, tells me that because I persist in trying to convert his people and visiting them in their own homes, my "conduct is neither that of a Christian, a gentleman, or an honest man"; that he is "on the look-out to catch me breaking the penal laws, and to make an example of me".
>
> You and yours are far more effective Catholic missionaries than we are; and I assure you, hardly a week passes without some one or more stragglers being driven into the bosom of the Holy Roman Church, declaring themselves fairly wearied out by the incessant curses fulminated against us from the pulpits of the State Church, and humbly echoed back with fury even wilder still, from the Dissenters' chapel and camp meeting, and desirous to seek refuge where they hear only of

Almighty God, of the love of Jesus, and of duty, charity, peace, and kindly affection towards all, whether Catholic or Protestant. . . .[30]

Like all Faber's controversial writings it was calculated to annoy rather than to soothe. The Protestant attack, he said,

> was like an angry child beating the huge buttress of a strong stone church, because it has hurt its foot against it, breaking and bruising its own poor little knuckles and then crying, half with pain and half with spite, because the hard old church will not tumble down for its puny knocks.[31]

Summer turned to Autumn and things seemed at last to have an air of permanence. Perhaps it seemed too permanent with the house and garden in order. The church was nearly finished. Father Dominic the Passionist gave a retreat. When asked by Faber what he thought of the Brothers of the Will of God he replied jokingly that they were Brothers of the Will of Faber. Faber was not offended and always openly called him a saint. It was decided that Faber and Hutchison should visit Wiseman, who was now administrator of the London District, in Advent and pronounce their vows. The rest of the Community were to make their vows later. Meantime news arrived that Newman would soon be home as superior of the Oratory. At this eleventh hour Faber's doubts returned with redoubled strength.

"Last Tuesday week night," he wrote to Watts Russell,

> which was the feast of St Andrew, St Wilfrid's patron saint, I chose for my next morning's meditation St Joseph's delay about putting our Blessed Lady away, and his sorrow, and reflecting on my most responsible position I asked as the fruit of my meditation the gift of counsel and the grace of prudence: you must know that our Wednesday's meditation is always on St Joseph. The next morning I rose at 5, and made my meditation: it was full of distractions but I took pains with it, although I had no particular sweetness in it, nor was there anything signal about it in any way. Towards the conclusion when making my colloquies, and repeating my petition for counsel and prudence, when nothing was farther from my thoughts, all on a sudden I felt an interior call to join the Oratory of St

Philip; and in one instant all the perplexity of the faculties of my soul which I had experienced for some weeks was calmed. I ought to have told you by the way that we were just preparing to take our vows.

I immediately set myself to work on my knees to argue against this call, and to combat it in every way. I appealed to St Joseph our own special patron and superior but he seemed to answer that God's Will was his great end, and that we were to go, with other like things. I then took the relic of St Philip and I appealed to him as now enjoying the beatific Vision and having no self love about his own institute, but he seemed to answer that all had been his doing hitherto, and now as the consummation, that I had begun to translate his life at Elton, that he had been my model there, that my rule was only an expression of his spirit adapted to England, and that now the Vicar of God had himself modified the Oratorian Rule for England, that he had gradually displaced St Wilfrid as *foremost* in our devotions, etc., etc. I then tried to throw myself back upon the strong repugnance I had always felt to Newman's men, but I found it was gone, thawed away in some mysterious manner. I then went and said Mass for the Anime Sante, though I could scarcely tell what I was doing, yet it was wonderfully calm. My *ringraziamento* was of course entirely occupied with this matter; Elton was to come over again; the Will of God was to hunt me out of my new home, to snap all ties, so I passed, little indeed to my thinking [expectation?], once again to the calm broken-heartedness of the past, and I let God strip me as He pleased ... How everything seemed changed when I went out! everything had ceased to be mine; the rising spire of our magnificent church, the young trees, all seemed buried in the one thing, God.

I had now to face my choir brothers whose aversion to N.'s people was very vehement, and as we were to take our vows shortly no time was left me to prepare things. That same day, Wednesday, I took Father Hutchison out, and told him the whole: he immediately said, "It is from God. I will go with you". His repugnance was utterly gone. The same happened with Brothers Alban and Austin: this seemed wonderful. I then proposed that I should go down to the Jesuits to make a retreat, and to make out if all this really came from God. The next morning a letter came from Dr Wiseman fixing that Father Hutchison and I should come up to town on the Immaculate Conception B.V.M. to take our vows. This letter made us consider how far it would be well to go down to Stoneyhurst without Dr Wiseman's knowledge and permission as he had been our director all along. So Father Hutchison and I started for London at once. Strange to say! the first Oratorian in England, Father Stanton, in the habit, arrived just before us and was with the Bishop in Golden Square.

I was up with the bishop till midnight on Friday: he solemnly approved of the whole as coming from God, and being His Holy and adorable Will. The next day, S. Francis Xavier, we both said mass for it, and afterwards the bishop pronounced definitely that so it was to be. You will not be surprised now at my falling ill. I could not get my breath in London, vomited violently, etc. so I asked the bishop to let me go down by railroad to Tring to sleep where I could breathe. Father Hutchison, also white as a corpse and very ill, set off with me on Friday at 2 p.m. but when we got to the Euston Station we were obliged to go to bed. In the evening we got up, and went all the way to Derby, arrived here on Sunday evening, in time for the Confessional. And now all the lay brothers and catechists, Elton and non Elton, follow me, and N. Darnell of New College also, 17 in number. It is at present a profound secret, as we do not know whether N. will accept us; you know he refused me at Maryvale. The bishop says St Wilfrid's can, by the Pope's modifications, be kept and become an Oratorian house and he has pledged himself to me that our most prospering mission will be carried on. What the people will do without "poor Father Fable", as they say, I know not; they were all in misery at a foolish report that I was going to be made a bishop. However *Fiat Voluntas*! And now, fratello mio, you must pray hard: I shrink from the prospect before me, very, very much, to fall from founder and superior to novice, and a novice who must naturally be an object of extreme jealousy.[32]

"My dear Faber," Newman wrote on the last day of the year from London,

Dr Wiseman has told me of your most welcome offer and I wished to have written to you by the first post, but in London this was impossible. I now write before daylight this morning to secure doing so at all. Today I go down to Maryvale—so write to me there. (Maryvale *Perrybar*). You may fancy the joy with which St John and I heard the news that you proposed we should be one—I should say "gratitude" except that the confidence of course is not shown to us simply but to St Philip.

He went on to point out the contrast of spirit between the Oratory and St Wilfrid's but concluded:

I am so desirous of our coming together that I wince while I put down these objections but no good will come of it if we don't consider the matter first in all its bearings.[33]

Faber replied:

You should consider us as giving ourselves over to you in the spirit of surrender, that you should take us as so much raw material for Oratorianism and make what you can of us in the way you think best and fuse us down as you think will be most convenient into your existing body. There is nothing in what you say about Oratorianism which takes any of us by surprise; neither have we anything ascetic or poetical about us now. In Caroline Street and Colmore Terrace there were relics of the *savagery* of Elton, but either prudence or lukewarmness or both have long since worn those away.[34]

The letters went backwards and forwards and at last all was fixed—not quite without a struggle, for Faber speaks of "mutineers". What might have been the first English religious order for men brought into being since the Reformation, and the second in the history of the Church, came to an end.

"Four of our lay brothers", Faber wrote,

have gone to Maryvale; and tomorrow night I expect Father Superior [Newman] with F. F. Ambrose and Richard [St John and Stanton]; they stay Sunday here, and on Monday, St Valentine, the day on which 2 years ago I visited the relics of S. Thomas Cantuar at Sens and drew up the first draft of the Wilfridian rule, we shall all be solemnly admitted Oratorians. My courage fails me a little; I am to remain here a few weeks and then go as "a strict novice" [this was Newman's phrase] to Maryvale, and I understand I am *never* to return to St Wilfrid's. So away goes home, church, flock, Eltonian children and all. The people are up in arms about it, memorializing Father Superior, the Shrewsburys are vexed, the neighbouring priests are writing letters, the lay brothers are downcast: as to Father Wilfrid himself he hopes he is happy. Certainly rickety and ailing as my health now is, I have occasional fits of low spirits; I cannot move my library to Maryvale, so I shall be separated from that as well; neither will Maryvale be my settled home. In my first spoliation I kept my books and my Elton children; now I lose these too; Deo gratias a beato Philippo! ...

I have had a house full of temptations and repugnances to govern for some weeks past, and one actual rebellion but by the grace of God and dear Mamma's help I hope to steer my little crew into the port of San Filippo without a loss. ... You know what a desperate fellow I am for local affections, and St Wilfrid's represents 18 months of arduous and interesting struggle, besides its own excessive natural beauty. The trees I have planted, the walks I have planned, the streams I have turned—every one has got a shockingly tight hold upon me, and all the 200 converts! ...

Thursday, 17 Feb. F. Superior has now left us, all in our Filippini habits with turn down collars, like so many good boys brought in after dinner. In the solemn admission on Monday morning he gave a most wonderful address full of those marvellous pauses which you know of. He showed how wonderfully we had been all brought together from different parts, and how in his case and ours St Philip seemed to have laid hands upon us and taken us for his own whether we would or not. Since my admission I seem to have lost all attachment to everything but obedience; I could dance and sing all day because I am so joyous; I hardly know what to do with myself for very happiness. F. Superior too is as merry and simple as a schoolboy, and affectionate to us beyond description. . . .[35]

CHAPTER IX

ORATORIAN

I

THE transformation of the Wilfridians into Oratorians was not without its difficulties. There was from the first a certain lack of understanding, though not of sympathy, between Faber and Newman. A leader of men must have a touch of ruthlessness but from the start Newman feared to ask too much of the Wilfridians. Faber for his part was as much determined to see a leader in Newman as he had been at Elton. "We have no *Terms* to come to," he wrote,

> but the great thing is whether we shall suit you, or have the grace to carry out the spirit of surrender in detail, as it may be wanted. So please bear this in mind:—we do not come to you as a community asking filiation, asking to be constituted into an Oratorian House at Cotton, in other words, asking to get under the shelter of an approved institute with the least amount of self-will sacrificed; this would make us much less useful, and possibly endanger or thwart you:—but we offer ourselves to you as eighteen postulants for the Oratory (together with our house and the Church) to be removed and distributed just as meets your views, and desirous to undress ourselves of any habits or traditions we may have as quickly as we can do so with safety. This is what I particularly begged Dr Wiseman to make clear to you.[1]

It was typical of Newman to suggest that Faber should make the change in the lay-brothers' clothes, bit by bit, tactfully. Faber, however, replied with unconscious briskness.

> I think we had better start at once with the short cassocks, and I don't think I shall have any difficulty about it, and the change seems safest in being simultaneous.

Faber was never frightened of action once he had made up his mind. The lay brothers all obeyed him even when they were drafted about from place to place according to Newman's convenience—except "the Rosminian cook" who gave notice, "which", Faber commented, "is very awkward".[2] But it was the beginning of the end for the original Eltonian lay brothers. There was no satisfactory place for them in the Oratory and they gradually drifted away except Brother Chad (John Strickson). They all, however, remained good Catholics and on friendly terms with Faber.

But the great problem was what to do with St Wilfrid's. It could not become an Oratorian house because an Oratory has to be in a town. It could not be used simply as a summer residence because the Wilfridians had bound themselves to Lord Shrewsbury to keep up the mission. Newman hoped that another religious order would take it over, or that Lord Shrewsbury would buy it.

St Wilfrid's was an embarrassment to the Oratory but Newman shrank from taking a drastic decision—even if he had been able to do so. "Father Antony", Faber wrote,

> tells me he *fancies* you do not feel quite at ease in legislating for us and seem (very kindly) to fear to exact too much sacrifice from us. Now you must please to remember the language of my former letters which was not offhand. Of course it would be foolish and insincere to say that we shall not feel giving up St Wilfrid's very keenly; it became our home when we had given up our homes; it was our first work as Catholics; we are greatly beloved by our people, and we as tenderly love them; it is a very beautiful place, and it has the associations of eighteen months of hard and interesting struggle within and without. . . . I told you before that we bring no plans, no projects with us; to ask you to Oratorianize our community and then set us free again would be a poor and ungenerous thing. I question whether you as a founder *could* at the outset do so to another community, and it would weaken the Oratory instead of strengthening it. Yet from something you said to Father Antony it seems to have come to your mind that that was our wish: *it never has been our view from the first, and we put it away knowingly and after talking of it.*[3]

But the more Faber insisted on surrender the more responsibility there was for Newman. It was an extremely intricate situation. Lord Shrewsbury who had at first welcomed the Wilfridians joining the Oratory changed his mind. He was significantly cold. He may have heard that Newman was thinking of temporarily leaving St Wilfrid's to two priests.

Meanwhile on 21st February Faber was called to the noviciate at Maryvale to learn to be an Oratorian under Newman's guidance. He is said to have made ungainly attempts to play ball with the other novices. He had already grown extremely fat and awkward. To his surprise he was suddenly returned to St Wilfrid's after a few days. The situation was already getting out of hand.

"As for me," Newman wrote despondently,

> besides the many anxieties and sorrows which I must have, this matter of St Wilfrid's is to me, as to you, a great trouble. It can't be helped—it was not possible that so great a good as your joining us should be effected without pain on both sides— and the union is worth the pain. Consider my side then as well as yours—see how for years and years, nine years (to say no more) during which *instabiles sumus* with no certain prospect before me; wishing for rest and quiet and not getting it—first moving to Littlemore, then to Maryvale, then sent to Rome— with two movings of my library, and considerable damage the last time. Then at length I come here for a little peace— having got all my papers in their places and my closets completed. And now I am called to move again and that with *no prospect of being settled then.* . . .

But he could not bring himself to a decision.

> To decide, then, *at once* on removing to St Wilfrid's is, I feel, quite out of the question. On the other hand to give up St Wilfrid's would be equally *rash*, to say nothing of any claims which either you or Lord Shrewsbury have upon us. I don't see then that it is *possible* to do anything else than to put off the decision. . . . Keep up your spirits, my dear F.W. and help us to keep up ours—be sure it will all come right if we are patient —and remember us at the altar as we do you.[4]

He asked everybody's advice but still could not decide what would be for the best.

Lord Shrewsbury broke off negotiations with Newman and began writing to Faber whom he accused of backing out of his undertakings. The three-cornered correspondence grew more and more complicated. Faber was placed in an awkward position between his benefactor and his superior. Inevitably he was thought ungrateful by the one and disobedient by the other. Newman had asked for more money from Lord Shrewsbury which Faber considered wrong. Newman, for his part, never seems to have grasped the complete situation. He had come in at the last. Much had happened which had been agreed verbally. Lord Shrewsbury maintained, for instance, that his lawyer had omitted to state that St Wilfrid's should be in the hands of a religious community, but that this had been taken for granted. He also understood Newman to feel that Faber and St Wilfrid's were a burden to the Oratory. Faber not unnaturally was upset when this was repeated. Newman was indignant. "You are made the scapegoat," he wrote:

How could you fancy I should have said anything to Lord Shrewsbury such as you quote from him. I used no such words. I will send you copies of my letters to him. You must realize more than you do, how much I admire and love you—and how we all do the same. How can you suppose we think you a burden? . . . Believe me if the trouble of St Wilfrid's were ten times what it is it would be far more than repaid in your giving us *yourselves*.[5]

With his ability to see every side of a situation he, however, wrote another letter on the same day in which he criticized the St Wilfridians with a good deal of asperity.

"I feel, my dear Father Superior," Faber replied contritely to the first letter,

that I have wronged you very much in allowing myself to fret as I have done over Lord Shrewsbury's severe and cutting letters to me; but one feels so acutely what people *ought* to think of one that one is inclined to believe that they do think it, and strange fears come over me sometimes that I am hardly able to control. Lord Shrewsbury himself seems to think he has treated me rather harshly; at least he has written again yesterday in a different tone apropos of nothing. . . . I certainly have for him a very tender and lively affection; he has completely won my heart, and of all things I most shrink from doing anything to hurt him. It has been a great pain to me to differ from him in all this McHale† business, and he has felt it so also. You do not know, my dear Father Superior, all we went through while you were away, and it would be difficult to explain it now, but there was misery, petty harassment and persecution enough to break one's spirit, and it was he who supported us through all, especially while Dr Wiseman was away, and our enemies had Dr Walsh's ear. On one occasion I was summoned at the instigation of some clergy and received a severe rebuke from the dear old Bishop [Walsh] for what he himself had *proprio motu* praised and thanked me. In a word we should have been mastered, and forced either into Rosminians or Jesuits had it not been for Lord Shrewsbury. All that we had of peace, of comfort, of respectability, nay, my very ordination was through the station he gave us; add to this the numberless daily little kindnesses, especially when in the November of '46 I was hanging between death and life.

I feel the warmest personal love for him, and I also admire him and his character excessively, and to me of course it is not hidden or defaced by the perversity of his pen; though I can see his faults as plainly as others. No part of my past life has left such furrows in me as the last eighteen months, and he is bound up with it all. So you must please put this as part of my excuse: and I will try to think less of things. . . . Perhaps it is self-deceit and touchiness which makes me sconner so, as we say in the north, at the idea of seeming heartless and ungrateful to Lord Shrewsbury, because I feel that I *ought* to have seen he was misunderstanding you and exaggerating your view of us.[6]

On the receipt of Newman's second letter, however, all was in confusion again. "I am afraid", Faber wrote,

† Lord Shrewsbury wrote an injudicious letter to the Archbishop of Tuam about the attitude of the Irish clergy during the potato famine towards English landlords.

you will think us very stupid but neither Father Antony nor I can understand your letter: we do not see the drift of it, what we are to do, or where we stand. Is it this? We surrendered ourselves unconditionally to you last January—now we want to back out and qualify that surrender—you give way—we are no longer to speak as novices but to make fresh proposals—and you will see if you can accept the bargain. This amazes both of us not a little: we must have made some very great blunder to cause such a misunderstanding. I will try to explain, but I despair almost of doing so to your satisfaction. . . .[7]

It was an enormously long letter which ended:

I have taken the utmost pains to go through everything; that is all I can do with what I cannot understand.

Newman apparently wrote a soothing letter in reply for Faber answered:

[I] am very thankful to you for your note this morning; I have been so wretched the whole week that I have hardly slept, and scarcely opened a book, but have wandered about quite *distrait*; and I had already come to the resolution, if you asked me any more questions to beg of you to take the matter into your own hands and consult me no more. There could be nothing wrong in that; in controversy with superiors there is difficulty in avoiding sin. . . .[8]

Newman had his difficulties, too. He had thought of St Wilfrid's as an asset. It was turning out a liability. He had not understood the strings attached to it and felt Faber had acted dishonestly in not telling him. In a moment of bitterness he seems to have been betrayed into saying that he would never trust Faber again. The remark was repeated to Faber by Father Joseph Gordon, and Faber, who could never keep his mouth shut, may have responded in kind. The response was also repeated by the same person to Newman. The trouble was a misunderstanding. It was characteristic of the exuberant Wilfridian not to mention the difficulties—he was probably only half aware of them. He certainly did not act with deliberate dishonesty. It was also characteristic of the unworldly don not to have gone into the question with Lord Shrewsbury until it was too late. Faber was obviously not a man to be trusted in a business transaction. For many a year St Wilfrid's was to be a bone of contention and the wounds of the misunderstanding, though concealed, did not heal.

Pugin's new church was due to be opened immediately after Easter. Faber had hoped that Newman would spend Easter at St Wilfrid's but Newman seems to have been nervous of a quarrel with Lord Shrewsbury. He did, however, preach at the opening on Easter Tuesday while Bishop Wiseman sang the Mass. It was a colourful spectacle but the happiness was sadly marred by uncertainty about the future. There were, moreover, other troubles. Faber had preached in London, he had worked very hard at the arrangements for the opening, and had been extremely distressed by the quarrel with Lord Shrewsbury. He now fell ill with a violence which was characteristic of his constitution. "A most impetuous diarrhoea came on in the afternoon," he told Newman,

> and drained my strength away. Doses of laudanum were given every hour as well as some astringents besides, but in vain and at last three large suppositories were forced in one after another before the fury of the purging would give way. This forcible stoppage caused my body to swell, horrid perspirations to come on, and at 1.30 this morning Father Antony was called up to see if the Doctor should not be sent for, lest inflammation of the bowels should take place. However after some hot arrowroot and being rubbed again with cod liver oil I was enabled to lie tolerably quiet, but nearly sleepless.[9]

Father Hutchison's account was more matter of fact and mentions the cod liver oil treatment which gave Faber "a very ancient fishlike smell". A few days later he reported:

> I am glad to say the medico thinks Father Wilfrid is getting rather better, though he still suffers much pain from his rheumatism. Brother John, however, still goes on applying the atrociously smelling oil with frightful perseverance. They want completely to cake Father Wilfrid over with it, and then they think the rheumatics will depart. Meantime he is not allowed to leave his room and he mayn't if he wished do any work; of course this idle life will soon make him look and feel as well as smell like a fish out of water.[10]

The lay brothers had begun a novena to St Philip and before long Hutchison could report:

> Father Wilfrid's health, thanks, I suppose, to St Philip is rapidly improving, the Doctor even talks of letting him come downstairs tomorrow and more than this he even holds out hopes that he may shortly be allowed to wash off the terrible oil, to the inexpressible relief of all the community.[11]

But the slow recovery did not come without great suffering. Faber describes himself as feeling half drunk and wanting to blaspheme. As to the doctoring "it is all experimentalizing—I see that". The one consolation was the frequent visits and kindnesses of Lord Shrewsbury.

Meanwhile Brother Stanislas Besant who had joined the Wilfridians in Birmingham was dying of tuberculosis. While Faber was ill Mr Besant arrived to take his son home. Father and son were reconciled but Brother Stanislas refused to move. The move was impossible on medical grounds but Faber discovered the father's real motives. "I have just heard from Mr Tomlinson, the *protestant* doctor," he wrote excitedly to Newman,

> that Brother Stanislas' father's *real* wish is to get him back into the hands of the ministers of his own religion—a traitor!! and Brother Stanislas appeals to me against his own father. All is however quietly and amicably settled, and old Mr Besant returns *solus* tomorrow.[12]

The illness was not yet conquered. The rheumatic condition, which was now called sciatica, returned with insomnia. At the same time he suddenly began to put on more weight. He grossly overtaxed his strength at the dying brother's bedside. Death when it came was agonizing, and trying to the onlookers.

> He kept throwing one of his arms round my neck and drawing my face close to his, saying, "Father Wilfrid, how long will it be now? Will it be long?" and if I just whispered: Patience, my dear child, or Wait God's time, or Think of Jesus on the Cross, or Call on Mamma in your heart, he immediately made an effort to calm himself and squeezed my hand as if in token of it . . . He lost the power of speech about half an hour before

death, and had a great struggle: that ceased and he went off like a little child, so gently that we scarcely knew when. He breathed twice after I had closed his eyes, and so I held a looking glass to his mouth, and my hand to his heart, for some minutes before saying the *Subvenite* and the rest of the prayers. I then got up from my knees and lifted his head on the pillow and kissed him, and there came on his face the loveliest smile that can be imagined. The lay brothers cried out for joy and there it is upon his face still to this moment. He lies with his habit on, his hands clasped in prayer, the white collar, and his little skull cap, and it is really *most* beautiful. The lay brothers can hardly leave the body, they seem all in joy and light-heartedness and say they cannot grieve. . . . For myself I quite envy the brothers their happiness; but I feel sadly depressed: it is the *first* death, and it seems as if an enemy had broken in and committed a sacrilege; there is a feeling of broken clausura somehow; and he was with us in our troubles at Colmore Terrace, and it seems hard that in our day of holyday and triumph, just when the new church was opened, he should be struck down at our feet to sober us . . . I wish [the lay brothers at Birmingham] could see him smiling now as I have just seen him, with all the little [school] boys kneeling round him saying falteringly Hail Marys for him, their old Master.[13]

A new squabble now arose round the infant Oratory. The old Catholics had always disliked Italian devotions used by Faber. But Pugin and Ambrose Phillipps saw in these practices cause for more than mere dislike. If Italian devotions why not Italian architecture? And if pagan styles of architecture were to be allowed where would it end? Gothic architecture was in their eyes a living embodiment of Catholicism, almost Catholicism itself. While Faber was still ill Ambrose Phillipps called at St Wilfrid's. "Ambrose Phillipps tells me today", Faber wrote,

that Formby has written to him. It seems you have not captivated him, and he won't Oratorianize, so Ambrose is going to ask him to be his parish priest at Grace Dieu. Has Father Ambrose [St John] terrified him by his Italianism? Ambrose [Phillipps] was most pleasant today: screens were not the subject of our converse.[14]

About the same time he wrote:

> Mr Gubbins tells me that for a long while A. Phillipps has, at his own table, spoken against the Oratory. He has invited himself to spend a morning here shortly so I must be very pacific.[15]

Ambrose Phillipps was a convert but of a much earlier date and held what were considered to be liberal opinions. He was an old friend of Lord Shrewsbury and, like him, a rich and ardent Catholic.

Faber described his visit in the company of Pugin to St Wilfrid's in a long letter.

> Ambrose has got his view, and outed with it: *poverello* me! What have I done to the Oratory? Caused it to be cursed! But you, who as Ambrose says *or say*, have in *Loss and Gain* "sunk below Dickens" must not complain. Exeunt from the Church Ambrose, Pugin and Father Wilfrid:
>
> *Amb.* Why is there no screen?
>
> *F. Wilf.* Why we are great people for Exposition, and besides Father Superior wished us not to have a screen: he prefers it without.
>
> *Pugin.* My dear Sir, my dear Sir, I hope he will be served out.
>
> *F. Wilf.* Why, Pugin, you might as well treat the Blessed Sacrament as Henry VIII's people did, as do what you do at a Benediction at Cheadle.
>
> *Pugin.* Now, hear him; my dear Sir, I never saw such a man as you are: it's beastly, it's positively beastly.
>
> *Pugin receives a crack on his back from Father Wilfrid.*
>
> *Amb.* We ought to have reverence: there is none in your Church; we have no right to see the Blessed Sacrament; we ought to bow down; the Church desires it.
>
> *F. Wilf.* But, my dear Mr Phillipps, what do monstrance and Exposition mean?
>
> *Amb.* It is the same as in the Pyx; people must have faith.
>
> *Pugin.* A function, my dear Sir, never should be quite seen.
>
> *Amb.* You are copying a wretched people (Italians) who are now throwing off the faith, and persecuting the Church.
>
> *F. Wilf.* O surely, Mr Phillipps, we handful of puppyistical English Catholics always tearing one another's eyes out must not sit in judgment on others.

Amb. But I *do* sit in judgment on them; we have the faith: with us all things are reviving; with them all things are decaying.

Pugin. My dear Sir, what would you do with all the screens of the sixteenth century?

F. Wilf. Burn 'em all.

Amb. (very angry) You are setting yourselves up in opposition to your bishops who are putting up screens.

Pugin. My dear Sir, your own Dr Wiseman ordered one worth £12. etc. for St George's.

Amb. You have no business to thwart the wishes of the Church, and disobey your bishops, and throw slurs on the received opinions now in vogue.

F. Wilf. Live and let live: I will let you alone behind your screen: you let us alone without one.

Amb. The laity must be separated from the Sanctuary.

F. Wilf. And yet tailors in copes and black whiskers occupy the stalls at St Chad's.

Amb. That is the fault of the building of the Church. *A glance from Pugin.* I tell you, you are setting yourselves up against bishops and old Catholics and introducing new usages.

F. Wilf. Mr Phillipps, you have no right to speak to me in this way; this is not amicable criticism on art.

Amb. Sir, I am in communion with the Pope, and I have a right to utter my sentiments, although you are a priest: (*voice louder*) you are a Catholic of but a few months and I of twenty-two years.

Pugin. Come, come, my dear Sir, be moderate: upon my life I'm the only moderate man in the country.

F. Wilf. Mr Phillipps, you have no right to speak to me in this way.

Amb. (Opposite *Mamma's image*) Father Faber, God for your pride destroyed and brought to naught your first effort. (*Stamp, fist to heaven*). He will curse and destroy your order, and it will perish if you go on thus.

F. Wilf. He knows best, Mr Phillipps.

Amb. You have insulted me.

F. Wilf. No, Mr Phillipps, I have not; but I appeal to Mr Pugin, if you have not insulted me.

Pugin. My dear Sir, why must I stake out the ground—Now

come, my dear Sir, come, hold your tongue; my gracious, what a thing—upon my life—really—well, I always thought I was the only moderate man in the world.

Amb. I'll never set foot in this place again (*Stamp, fist heavenwards—silence—Pugin fretting*).

In five minutes Ambrose puts his hand into mine. I retract—consider the words not spoken—he speaks for three-quarters of an hour of the 1260 days; the unburied witnesses, God's forbearance with the Church to let her vomit "the pagan Renaissance", the removal of the Holy See to Jerusalem—he eats much veal with us, and somewhat of suet pudding, and talks kindly and departs—leaving me ill, shady, and vexed with myself that I should care a boddle for what he said, or perhaps by tartness called up his bile. When he comes to Maryvale don't let Father Bernard [Dalgairns] see him on any account. Ambrose tells me that you were made by Kenelm Digby, and that the theological move arose out of the ecclesiol: etc. whew-ew-ew-ew. The Northern Nations threw off the faith because Italians took to pagan art!

When Ambrose retires to the Towers four Oratorians are seen near Mamma's image, making an act of faith composed by one Padre Ambrogio della Vallicella in Inghilterra—one Lord, one faith, one baptism, *one chasuble*! O I feel quite gaseous and inflated with the immense amount of *views* which have been poured into me—mixed with a galling remembrance of our Lord in our Lady's arms in our beautiful Genezzano Madonna being got up with his hair dressed like a boy for after dinner at home, while his Mother was undevotional looking! The order cursed—the Italianism blighted—the bishops revolted against—the Church thwarted—the bodies of the two witnesses now lying in the streets unburied, and we somehow connected with their non-interment—and the Superior "down to Dickens". You must be a manful man to work your way through all this: one remembers Johnson on being abused puffing like a grampus, shaking his waistcoat, ventilating himself with his coat flaps, and saying to Bozzy, "Sir, are we alive after all this?"

Like old Mr Talbot, the meteor will pass on from St Wilfrid's and appear at Maryvale; muzzle Father Bernard, in case the witnesses should still remain unburied and the *man* of sin, ("scantily clothed *Madonnas*") should still be out upon the earth.

The jolly thing about it all was to see how a good man retracts the instant heat is passed, and victimizes himself to eat veal with us rather than a good dinner at the Towers. This *did* really edify me.[16]

Phillipps went to Maryvale and talked of Faber. On his return he wrote:

> I was sorry not to be able to finish our conversation about Father Faber the other day: I hope he may become less violent and excessive in his ways and ideas. If he does he will render to the Church those solid services which his abilities and his zeal qualify him to render, but if he does not, I tremble for the result; forgive me for my presumption in thus freely speaking my mind about so good and so able a person, whom I regard and respect with all sincerity.[17]

"I am sure, my dear Mr Phillipps," Newman replied,

> you will let me speak freely to you—and the more so, because you have most kindly spoken to me with freedom about Father Wilfrid. It seems then you cursed the Oratory. Now if this was the case, did it become a person who had used strong language of this kind to treasure up and divulge the strong language of another? ... I could say much about the grief I feel at the neglect I see, of that so good and true maxim, *In necessariis Unitas, in dubiis libertas.* How is it, my dear Mr Phillipps, that you understand this so clearly in doctrinal questions, yet are so slow to admit it in ritual? I do not say you, but are there not persons, who would be more distressed at a man's disliking a chancel skreen than at his being a Gallican?[18]

Phillipps replied:

> [Faber's] statement that I "cursed the Oratory" is a most unjust representation of my words and of my thoughts. I am not going to defend what I did say, it would have been better unsaid, but it was no curse, and Mr Faber must know that ... On the occasion before alluded to at St Wilfrid's I did not quarrel with Father Faber because he had no skreen, but he shocked me by his awful expression in denouncing the skreen at Cheadle. The intolerance was not on my side.[19]

Newman admitted that the words "cursed the Oratory" were too strong but he insisted that Phillipps was intolerant.

> Please, let me ask, is it not somewhat exclusive to call Grecian or Italian [architecture] Pagan, as you do? For the word Pagan surely is used, not historically, but as a term of reproach. If it be Pagan, it is Popish too, for I suppose the Pope has given quite as much sanction to it as he has to Gregorian music, which by the by seems to be Pagan in the same sense that Italian architecture is.[20]

He finally wrote a long letter to Phillipps about the whole question of Gothic architecture. Phillipps gratefully thanked him and called it "affectionate and parental". He avowed his friendship for the Oratory. By the end of the year the breach between Faber and Phillipps was also healed. Kind letters passed between them. Neither side, however, altered its architectural opinions.

Faber's health did not improve quickly and Newman sent him with a lay brother to recuperate at Scarborough. After the first week-end he wrote

> I am already *ennuyé* and don't know how to get the day over, and there are such a quantity of ladies on the beach that Brother John and I dare not venture there except in unfrequented spots . . .

This was presumably when the two went bathing.

> Old Mr Waterton has fastened upon me; and it appears that nearly all the old Yorkshire Catholic families are here just now, the Stourtons, etc. I find that Sibthorpe† preached here or in the neighbourhood as a Catholic priest, and gave great disedification by having nothing *distinctive* in his sermon, and so people *watched* me; however I was lucky enough to give Mamma a good word or two, which Mr Walker tells me gave unlimited satisfaction; so my fellow-countrymen pronounce me safe, which is satisfactory . . . Brother John is weary to death and very lame; he cannot shed his amazement at York

† R. W. Sibthorp (1792–1879), a convert clergyman who, to the end of his long life, could never satisfy himself as between Rome and Canterbury that he was "in the right way". Charles Waterton (1782–1865), naturalist and eccentric.

Minster; he had no notion Dearly beloved brethren had such homes or attempted to fill them.[21]

He got on very well with the old Catholics and gave "a kind of Oratory" to the female members of the Stourton family. "I am told", he added,

> to expect some hits in the next week's York paper: the offence being that I dare, as an apostate, appear in my native county and preach in schism shops![22]

He was able, too, to spend a few days with his brother at Stockton-on-Tees. He could not, however, visit his uncle George Stanley. All Catholic Fabers were "placed under the same ban". The old man had decreed that they could not visit or be visited.

II

Faber had written ecstatically of the old Catholics in his conversion pamphlet. His enthusiasm was short lived. He soon found the English Catholics cold, rational, anti-Italian. The clergy held minimal views on Mariology and the papacy, while the laity had little respect for a clergy it had so long been in the habit of controlling. Both clergy and laity bickered incessantly among themselves. Even bishops were treated with contempt. The Catholic body may have been solidly English, and it was not Irish or Italianate, but it was provincial and lifeless. Centuries of disappointment and isolation had made it more like a sect than a living organ of the Universal Church. It lived in the past, infected with a Gallicanism fast disappearing from the Continent after the Revolutionary upheaval. So it appeared to Faber and his fellow converts. There was, of course, another side. It was the period, in the words of David Mathew, "of those happy years for the English Catholic clergy which lay between the granting of Emancipation and the submission to Rome of Archdeacon Manning".

The clergy were perhaps too happy. The task of converting England had not been abandoned so much as shelved. The task was too gigantic to be seriously entertained at that time. The fields might be white but what hope was there for the harvest? There were too few priests to cope with even the moderate trickle of conversions which was going on all the time. "On coming out of the cathedral [St Chad's]," Faber wrote,

> I was accosted by a melancholy looking young man, whom I recognised as a convert I had sent from Colmore Terrace to one of the priests; seven months had elapsed; he had been conditionally baptized seven months ago, and since then had never been able to get the priest to give instructions, had never been to communion, hung on to the Church in half despair; I went to the priest; he could not tell whether he had absolved the poor fellow, *who had made a general confession*; that probably he had *not* done so!!!! In fact it is absolutely impossible for the priests to *compass* their work there.[23]

Gentili, the Rosminian missioner, who had criticized the English priests came at the end of his life to admire them. He admitted that he had not fully understood their difficulties. Nevertheless the clash between the new Catholicism and the old was not simply a mistake on the part of the former. It went much deeper than that. It was caused by a difference in approach.

Faber had been impressed and all but converted by what may be called the ordinary arguments for Catholicism. But it was the new Catholicism which he had seen at work in Rome which really effected his conversion. The spirit of this Catholicism was almost the antithesis of the spirit of the old Catholics. It was a Catholicism brought to birth in, and in opposition to, the world of 18th-century rationalism—warm, enthusiastic, romantic. It hated the least hint of Erastianism. It emphasized devotion to the humanity of Christ and to His mother. It sought the closest connection with the revived papacy. It was essentially evangelical, a revival of personal religion. The clash between Faber and the old Catholics was roughly reflected in the Anglican mirror as the opposition between the Evangelicals on the one hand and the High and Dry School on the other. It was indeed a clash between Italianate and English ways but only accidentally and to the extent that tenderness in religion is associated with Italy and the Pope lives in an

Italian city. Ultramontanism as a word is too narrow to be descriptive. It was the new versus the old, the nineteenth versus the eighteenth century, Romanticism versus Classicism. If the Church in England was to live, the clash had to come. The blood of the new Catholicism had to be transfused into the old.

It is always sad when the past, having served its purpose, has to go. And of course there were unfortunate losses. The Church of Pio Nono had the defects of the Church in Italy—defects so deadly as to make modern Catholics overlook the virtues. It was illiberal, out of touch with the world, liturgically blind. But was the Church of the old Catholics so much better in these respects? It is doubtful, except perhaps in liturgical matters, but even there the superiority of the old Catholics was not so marked as is generally believed. And if the new Catholics could see little good in the old, the old could see little good in the new. A remark of Provost Husenbeth about Faber is amusing but inexcusable. "Faber was there," he said after a visit to Cotton, "with a few young men of some indescribable order which he was setting up at the time: I think they called themselves Wilfridians." The converts were always being told not to make the old Catholic clergy "jealous". But, as Newman said, what business had they to be jealous?

Faber was not merely a natural enthusiast and Romantic who loved showy and emotional ceremonial. He was well aware of what may be called the facts of the problem confronting the Church in England and characteristically he set out to solve it. *The Lives of the English Saints* edited by Newman, in which series Faber had written the controversial life of St Wilfrid, had been a Tractarian attempt to bring the Church of England into touch with England's Catholic past. Faber hit on the idea of a similar series of post-Reformation saints to bring English Catholics into touch with the Continent. *The Lives of the Modern Saints* were to be translations of original works, the translators were not to be paid, and the volumes were to be sold as cheaply as possible. The object of the series, as stated in the prospectus, was to act as a check to the deadening spirit of materialism, and to present to Englishmen samples of the fruit produced by the Tridentine

Church. The miraculous and heroic features were to be translated literally and not toned down in any way.

Watts Russell was a key figure in the scheme. He was not only
to be used as a translator, but he was also to procure books in
Italy from which translations could be made. Faber mentions the
scheme on 13th November 1846. "My gigantic notion", he
wrote,

> of the lives of the saints in English we hope to begin next
> year, and bring out at least five goodly volumes a year. I
> believe it will do immense things towards the conversion of
> Protestants and the perfection of Catholics ... It is rather
> irksome work, but then one keeps offering up all the pushes
> it may give to poor heretics, all the good thoughts it may give
> to Catholics etc., etc., in union with the merits of our Blessed
> Lord, as a penance for past sins. I suppose also that one gets the
> special patronage of the Saints whose honour we laboriously
> strive to spread. The more I think of the work the more I feel
> its importance: only think if we should live to see 100 volumes
> of the lives of the Saints in small 8vo. volumes, cheap because
> the translators are unpaid, from the Italian, Spanish, and French.
> Am I not a dreamer?[24]

By July 1847 great progress had been made. Bishop Walsh
had indeed been "so frightened" by the life of St Gertrude that
its publication had been deferred. But Faber plunged boldly on
with his scheme. He soon found however that the bishop's
timidity was the prelude to a storm. "Our lives of the saints", he
wrote to Bartolommei,

> are meeting with dreadful opposition, especially from Catho-
> lics, and I almost expect they will be forcibly stopped soon.
> From living so long amid controversy and en face with Pro-
> testants the faith has become deteriorated in the minds of many
> and miracles and visions and ecstacies meet with ridicule and
> unbelief even from the sons of Holy Church.[25]

"I have been reproved by Dr Walsh", he told Watts Russell,

> for the life of St Philip Neri, because some old Catholic priests
> found it too popish. Lord Shrewsbury is also scandalized with

the supernatural character of it, and I believe some fellows have got to Richardson the publisher, and teased him, and he is inclined to hang fire. I have written a very firm letter to him, and I hope by dint of firmness and gentleness combined that I shall be able to carry the matter through. All this is only a proof that the series is already doing the work we intended it to do, and that opposition should arise in so unexpected a quarter and upon so clearly right an action is extremely consoling and goes far towards proving the Divine approval.[26]

"Lord S[hrewsbury]", he wrote in December,

has turned against us, and has delated me to both the bishops: he is quite in the hands of some cold jealous unitalianizers and is now quite violent about me. Dr Walsh has written an odd but kind letter to me; I immediately wrote, and made my submission and offered to discontinue the work. I think the B[lessed] saints will not let matters come to that and I hope Dr Wiseman will be firm. I have now 40 writers, of whom 19 are ecclesiastics of more or less distinction; the sale is advancing rapidly, and in America the series is doing great things. If I could get St Ignazio out early it would perhaps get the Jesuits to our side. ... I am constantly in hot water about all this, and what with coldness, jealousy and persecution am worn out: instead of being able to think only of God I have to fight with my crucifix for charity, charity, all day long. Yet I am sure that all these people think me a wild dangerous ultra lad, grievously needing curb and snaffle, and that they are doing God service by snubbing me: and perhaps they are. I ought to get holiness out of it all, and yet I do not.[27]

Faber's reply to Bishop Walsh was far from meek. He listed the good the series had done and put the opposition down to Ambrose Phillipps. Phillipps, he said, had stopped many conversions. As it happened Faber's bitterest opponents were all converts but they spoke for the old Catholics.

The dissolution of the Wilfridians and their entry into the Oratory complicated the situation. The continuation of the series was now no longer Faber's sole responsibility. "The success of lives", he wrote in February 1848, is greater than ever; but Dr Walsh has crushed them again, and again they have risen. They say Father Superior [Newman] will be against them lest they should bring the Oratory into trouble; I do not know, because he tells me nothing. . . .[28]

But Newman approved of the lives. It would have been strange had he not done so. His *Lives of the English Saints* which he had edited as a Tractarian were filled with extraordinary miracles and strange austerities. This *penchant* for the marvellous was characteristic of the early Tractarians and was the ostensible cause of Anthony Froude's break with the Movement.

With the publication of the volume containing the life of St Rose of Lima the trouble came to a head. Faber had foreseen that it would be so. "The judiciousness of publishing in England," he wrote in the preface,

> what are actually classical works of piety in Catholic countries is a further question which the result alone will decide, and that possibly at no very distant date ... A Catholic, do what he will, cannot weed his religion of the Supernatural; and to discriminate between the supernatural and the superstitious is a long work and a hard one, a work of study and of reverent meditation.

He warned those who might be startled at the life of St Rose to be sure that they were not victims of their environment and victims of Rationalism. The reader should not say, What will men say of it? but, "Is it true? ... Ought not my views to be deeper than they are."

Pierce Connelly, a convert clergyman from the United States, whose wife had become a nun and was foundress of the Society of the Holy Child Jesus, was installed as chaplain at Alton Towers. He was a plausible unstable personality who soon exerted a sinister influence over his not very clever patron. His views at this time were more than liberal. Having read the life of St Rose he scored under the passages he objected to and thrust the book into the hands of a visitor to the house and asked him to review it severely. The visitor was Edward Price, a priest, a convert from Presbyterianism and editor of *Dolman's Magazine*. Instigated by

Connelly he wrote a long and intemperate article which displayed
a good deal of theological ignorance. It came out in the September issue.

"Those in the house," he quoted from the Life of St Rose,

> who heard the sound of the blows she inflicted on herself had
> a horror of this cruel treatment. Father John Laurenzana, her
> confessor, being informed of the manner in which she treated
> her body, commanded her to use moderation, she obeyed;
> but she begged so earnestly that he could not refuse her the
> permission she asked to take five thousand more stripes in the
> course of three or four days (p. 33). Five thousand stripes with
> two iron chains! The imagination sickens under such a revolt-
> ing detail—under such an extraordinary permission so sought
> and so obtained . . . Reader, as an English Catholic, we may ask,
> and we trust without offence, are these austerities approved of,
> or even sanctioned by the Church? *We trust not.*

He described the saint's austerities as "more than charnel horrors",
not consonant with the Gospel or with "a merciful Redeemer".
Moreover he maintained that one passage sanctioned prayers
addressed to statues. This was true but it was never satisfactorily
decided whether it was due to looseness of language, the translator's mistake, or a misprint. He accused Faber of idolatry and
protested against the series as a whole in these words:

> In the name of all those who know their religion, in the name
> of those who revere it in its innate and immaculate purity and
> truth, we protest most solemnly against this and suchlike
> publications. However painful to our feelings, we must not
> shrink from a public and sacred duty in thus exposing the
> dangerous tendencies of this species of modern hagiography.[29]

The review pleased no one except perhaps Connelly. It was
obviously "temerarious" as Faber's friends quickly pointed out,
for had not the Pope spoken of "Rosam totius Evangelicae per-
fectionis exemplar"? On the other hand the old Catholics objected for different reasons. They would have liked the authentic-
ity of the narrative to have been called in question and they
feared the reaction of hostile Protestants. In fact *Punch* was later

to quote from the book in a very disedifying (and amusing) way. And, of course, it was, and is, highly questionable whether the popularization of extraordinary austerities is desirable.

Meantime Lord Shrewsbury, who had campaigned against the *Lives*, began to have second thoughts. "Lady S.", Faber wrote to Newman from St Wilfrid's,

> has just been here with Miss Tempest in a great state of excite-
> ment, and on a mission from the Earl. This morning [Oct. 6th]
> for the first time they have heard of the article in *Dolman*:
> as far as I can make out some noble guests have brought it
> under their notice, together with the report that it emanates
> from The Towers ... The Earl has not come over; he says he
> is pained beyond measure lest I should have thought he was
> privy or in any way concurring in the attack. It appears that
> he and his chaplain have already had words ...[30]

The violence of Price's attack rallied many waverers to Faber's side. Shrewsbury, when he saw Faber a few days later, was "*very affectionate*, nervous and confused", even Connelly was "most polite". Ullathorne, who had succeeded Walsh as Vicar Apostolic in the Central District, told Faber he found the article "offensive and disgusting". He also disclosed that Price had written a peni-tent letter.

Newman at first was nervous and suggested that the bishop should have a veto on the series or should even appoint a censor. He was especially worried about the misprint or mis-translation or whatever it was concerning prayer to images, and proposed editing the series himself. At last he had an interview with Ulla-thorne and wrote of it indignantly to St John:

> Well, then, the Bishop has stopped the *Lives of the Saints*.
> *Without my asking him*—for what I put before him was, that
> *we* could not go on, *without* the Bishop's support. ... It is
> *shameful* to recommend us to stop the Lives *before* they have
> made Price eat his words publicly. But it is our destiny and
> blessedness, thus to be treated ever. I thought of trying to
> set him against Price, but I somehow think that Our Lady and
> St Philip will take our part if we do not take our own—and
> even humanly speaking we shall be sure to have defenders if

we do not defend ourselves. But this is almost clear, that we must send someone to Rome—at least I don't see how we can escape it. I know I have at present the Pope's ear; and I think he might be made to see that a socalled Englishman may speciously conceal under screens and roods a great deal of doctrinal error. We ought to (and might) get full leave in our rescript to keep up the Italian traditions of the Oratory.[31]

Faber was not informed of the interview but he came to hear of it by mistake. Father Henry Formby was staying at St Wilfrid's and was in correspondence with Newman. One of Newman's letters contained the indiscreet sentence ". . . and we have decided (I tell you in confidence for what particular reasons at the moment Father Wilfrid himself does not yet know) that they [the Lives] are to stop . . ." Father Formby thoughtlessly gave Faber the letter to read, forgetting this sentence. Faber immediately wrote to Newman explaining how he had come to hear.

It would be hypocrisy in me to say I do not feel it most acutely, more acutely than I like to find myself feeling about an earthly thing at all. But so it is; it has been the scheme of years, an Elton scheme; it has mixed itself up with my devotions, and it has become more endeared to me because of the difficulties it has surmounted and the blessing I thought it was being to many: and I feel that the suddenness of the blow after your letter of the 14th the other way, and the humiliation of the triumph of others, and the slur on my character as a priest from the circumstances under which it was done, find me not so mortified as a *good* son of St Philip should be.[32]

"You may be sure, Carissime," Newman replied by return of post,

I will stand by you and no reproach shall fall on you which does not fall on me, too. Everything will be easy, do not doubt it.[33]

A circular was now sent to subscribers. In it Newman declared to Faber:

No-one can assail your name without striking at mine.[34]

Not unnaturally Ullathorne, who had not been informed in advance, was deeply offended. The situation was not helped by an article in the *Rambler* by a convert on the educational short-comings of the old Catholics. Ullathorne (wrongly) took this to have been inspired by Newman and Faber and wrote a severe criticism of it. "All the clergy about here and at Oscott", he told Wiseman,

> are much offended at [the circular] ... Mr Newman after all the kind and familiar confidence shown him both by other Bishops and myself, stands stiffly to his own opinions.[35]

The circular indeed was taken to mean that the series had been stopped by ecclesiastical authority and Ullathorne wrote to *The Tablet*. He said that although he had considered certain changes advisable in future volumes he had never refused his approbation. At the same time he expressed his dislike of Price's article.

Newman, however, was not appeased.

> The article in *Dolman* contains the words of one of my brethren: "If this is not gross palpable idolatry, we are still ignorant of the meaning of the word. Has Mr Faber forgotten the words of his catechism?" ...
> On the article in which these words are contained Your Lordship remarks; "I do not approve of the *general tenor* of the remarks in *Dolman's Magazine* in reference to the Lives. ..."
> Is it presumptuous in us to entreat Your Lordship to consider how such a negative statement published to the world, must wound us as coming from Your Lordship?[36]

Meanwhile Faber wrote to Bishop Wareing:

> You will get this on the morning of St Hugh, the day you kindly received me into the Church. ... It is a sad confession on the part of the Catholic authorities that the English Catholics are unable to digest the literature of Catholic countries, and start away from what is not found too strong for their *Protestant* countrymen.[37]

Ullathorne was not a tactful man but his goodness of purpose would not be concealed in his next letter to Newman. "Old Catholics," he wrote apologetically, familiar with all our habits, will consider that I have strongly censured the article in Dolman's and marked the author for life.... The sensitiveness of the circular, regarding as it does the lives of the meek and humble servants of God, has widely left a painful impression. Shall I say how this is? It is the manifestation of sensitiveness in holy religious men, personal sensitiveness, "the blow struck at *me*", for example, in a matter concerning the edification of the world by the lives of those who perfected themselves in patience by long suffering, in many trials, and whose obedience, so sweet, so tranquil, so humble, knew no touch of bitterness. My dear Mr Newman, I can with difficulty refrain from tears whilst I write. I love you so much and yet I feel so anxious for the spirit recently, I think, indicated, a little, to say the least.... Believe me, that a little of human nature is to be found fermenting in this sensitiveness...[38]

Ullathorne was Newman's bishop. Nevertheless it was a courageous, unworldly letter to write to so famous a man. In spite of his Australian experiences Ullathorne was unknown to the great world and was five years younger than Newman. This letter is said to have been the foundation of their future friendship but if it had any good effects later it had none at the time.

Next day Ullathorne wrote a very different letter to Faber. He had perhaps heard from Bishop Wareing. "I trust", he wrote,

we have nearly reached the end of this unpleasant affair, which has led to exhibitions of bitter zeal, not, I fear, altogether in the spirit of the saints.[39]

Newman sent Ullathorne's letter to Wiseman although it was clearly intended to be confidential. He was presumably offended. Wiseman remarked after reading it that Ullathorne had no right to lecture Newman. The remark was retailed to Newman who wrote again to Wiseman:

Not only he as a bishop, but *any* one may lecture me and I should be obliged for it. What I had to remark in Dr Ullathorne was that he spoke about me *without knowing me*. It stands to reason that no one can know a person of my age in a moment—and the Bishop has had no experience whatever of persons in my circumstances—and he spoke of me on a *theory.* I sent you the letter to see, that you might know how we stood.[40]

Luckily Newman's ruffled feathers were smoothed by a happy turn of events. An article by Price was inserted at Wiseman's instigation in the December number of *Dolman's Magazine* in which he apologized to Faber. Newman and Faber did not think the apology sufficient but Price excused himself on the ground that he had had to write his article at great speed. Privately he apologized more profusely. He now realized he had been led astray by Connelly. Connelly was already talking of filing an action in the Court of Arches for the return of his wife. For a priest this was tantamount to apostasy. The unfortunate Price was no apostate. "I may have written heresy," he told Ullathorne, "but I will not be a heretic."[41]

The series was restarted under the auspices of the Oratorian congregation as a whole on the Feast of the Epiphany, 1849. Newman later repented of his advocacy of the Lives. "If", he wrote to Pusey,

> at that time I was betrayed into any acts which were of a more extreme character than I should approve now, the responsibility of course is mine; but the impulse came, not from old Catholics or Superiors, but from men whom I loved and trusted, who were younger than myself. But to whatever extent I might be carried away, and I cannot recollect any tangible instances, my mind in no long time fell back to what seems to me a safer and more practical course.[42]

In fact he had come round to Ullathorne's view. But a great deal was to happen before his opinions underwent their gradual change.

CHAPTER X

TROUBLES IN THE ORATORY

AT the beginning of July 1848 Faber was present at the opening of St George's Cathedral, Southwark, with Bernard Dalgairns. On the 22nd he was dispensed from the noviciate and soon after made novice master. He wrote at this time a long letter to Newman about the Oratory. Newman, he maintained, had, whether he liked it or not, a unique role to play among English Oratorians. He was the founder of the English Oratory. But since he could not be in several places at once his effective power was limited. The local superior would tend to override Newman's unique authority. Faber therefore proposed that wherever he (Faber) might be Newman should be his superior. "I for one," he wrote,

> want you now to take me as simply and absolutely yours, and to consider that I give up all power and choice wishing to remain with you, or go *locally* from you, just as you may judge best for the interests of the Congregation.

He recalled Newman's words to him at Littlemore before his conversion, "You are meant for a separate theatre of influence".

> It seems to me that the question, so far as regards those *haunting* words of yours, is not so much whether I am *intended* for a separate centre, as whether I can get grace and humility enough to forgo being a separate centre; and I think I *can get* it— because of what I have felt and experienced of additional peace, joy, confidence and strength against evil, since I have been no longer a superior but under obedience.[1]

By August of 1848 the Oratory had ten priests and four more about to be ordained. Maryvale with its long corridors and stair-cases in unexpected places was too inconvenient and too small to house the whole community. On the other hand it would have been ruinous to keep both Maryvale and St Wilfrid's. Since no suitable property was forthcoming in Birmingham, Newman ordered a move to St Wilfrid's in the Autumn. Meanwhile the integration of the Wilfridians had been steadily going on. Contrary to what has been written on the subject by Wilfrid Ward (and those copying him) it was a work well done. Faber could not but be a centre of influence in the Oratory, but he and the Wilfridians did not form a party at variance with Newman. Dalgairns who had been at Littlemore with Newman was every bit as much an admirer of "Continental forms of popular devotion", to use Wilfrid Ward's words, as was Faber. And so was Ambrose St John. When Newman said later that under the influence of younger men he, too, had rashly taken up with these devotions he was not referring to the followers of Faber. He meant simply what he said—"younger men"—and these younger men were his own followers as well as the former Wilfridians. Father Richard Stanton, another of the men who had been at Littlemore and who was with Newman in Rome, is singled out by Faber as too insistent on Italian ways in ceremonial matters.[2] There were, it is true, great troubles in the Oratory at this time but it was not between Newman's friends and the former Wilfridians. The difficulties arose over the impetuosity of the young Oratorians, both ex-Wilfridians and ex-Littlemore men. They were tired of waiting and wanted to get down to work. Their leader, if they can be said to have had a leader, was Francis Knox, who at this time was at least as much linked to Newman as he was to Faber.

Newman had lost control of the situation and was far from happy. He found himself immersed in a flood of practical matters with which he had little or no experience. He had to give decisions on matters he had never thought about and he found it hard to make up his mind. Above all Faber was a trial to him. He was for ever demanding excruciating decisions. For Faber to give a decision one way or another was all in the day's work. He did not realize how hard Newman found his new life. Newman's dislike of practical responsibility explains why Faber's protestations of complete obedience met with only tepid responses. Moreover Newman was intensely shy and sensitive. He responded like a chameleon to atmosphere. With a few intimate friends whom he could trust he was at ease, but now he had a collection of men about him many of whom he hardly knew.

"My head", he wrote to his intimate companion, Ambrose St John,

is so stupid today, that I take up my pen, as the only thing I can do, even if that. I have a little cold, but independent of that, my head has been worse since you left ... It makes me languid and drowsy, and then I can't do my duties, and people think me reserved, etc., when I don't mean to be.

At times the sense of weight [of responsibility] and of desolateness has come on me so strongly, that I could fancy it might grow equal to any pain; and I thought what the Pope must suffer. It is useless to tell you on paper all the little trials which constitute all this and it is ungrateful in me not to be more cheered with the improvement of things in some quarters. My great trouble is some of the *giovani*—not that anything new has occurred, but they have so repelled anything between us but what is external, shown so little kindness when I have done things for them, treated me with so little confidence, as to throw me back upon myself—and now I quite dread the fortnightly chapter day, when I have to make them a little address, as being something so very external, when I have no means to know what is going on in their minds. In consequence I feel as if I was not doing my duty to them, yet without any fault. I don't know what influence I am exerting over them. It is as if my time of work were gone by. Except that one has been led step by step to where one is, beginning in 1841 with going to Littlemore, one is tempted to say: "How much happier for me to have no liabilities (so to speak) but to be a single unfettered convert"—but if this had been so, I should not have known you, Carissime—so good and evil go together.

The above I wrote before dinner, and suddenly during dinner my deafness, etc., went away completely on my taking some cayene pepper, which I had speculated upon using for some hours before, and for the time I am better than I have been for a fortnight past—how odd it is—whether nervous, or what?[3]

"It is true", Newman wrote in a letter to Faber

there are persons who can by their manner and bearing *claim* to be loved and obeyed; and so would solve the problem at once. I feel deeply I have not that gift, and, so far, am unfitted (as also in many other ways) to be a Superior.[4]

A further difficulty was Newman's friendship for Ambrose St John on whom he fell back for comfort and advice. "I have also seen Brother Philip (Gordon)," Faber wrote,

whose vocation I had heard was unsettled. He loves you most *tenderly* but thinks you do not care for him, and keep him at arms' length; and this I think is very much the case with Father Antony. He fancies that you will not let him get over with you his affair at Maryvale [Faber described him as having "kicked up his heels"] ... Somehow I *do* wish the *giovani* and Fathers were more mixed up. You will remember months ago I asked you to talk with them, not in a formal body, but now with one, now with another. The difficulty on their part is to make advances to a Superior. They are afraid of forwardness if *they* make advances. Is not this natural? Then here is another grief: Advise me about it. Several of them have what amounts to a positive dislike of Father Ambrose; it seems that occurrences at Maryvale, before I came there, have soured their mind with regard to him. ... They acknowledge his great goodness; but say they cannot get on with him; for his manner is either a series of snubs or a "condescension", I am using their own words, which is quite "insulting". You would think I exaggerated if I told you how strong this feeling really was and still is. Then they consider him as identified with you— they say he colours your view of them, and if they can't get on with both, they think it useless to try with one—that you are different with him from what you are with others—that he stands between them and you. When I spoke to the Gordons about a particular friendship growing up between them the answer was that you set the example with Father Ambrose....[5]

Newman replied in a long letter that what Faber said was true but he said pathetically: "I can do nothing to undo it, unless I actually did cease to love him as well as I do." Faber's answer was not that he should cease to love Father Ambrose (he himself loved Hutchison) but Father Ambrose should not be allowed to influence Newman's decisions as Superior. Newman then questioned that Father Ambrose did in fact influence his decisions. It was a painful correspondence which both parties felt ought never to have been necessary. It was a time of torture for Newman which he could never forget.

Wilfrid Ward in his great but misleading biography relates what perhaps was an attempt to remedy the situation.

[Father Philip Gordon] told me that after some weeks, during which he and Newman met daily without a word, when he was wondering as to the cause of what appeared to be a real breach between them, the Father Superior one morning put into his hands the following note: "My dearest Brother—It is strange to write to you and write about nothing; but such is my fate just now and for some time, that, since I have nothing to say to you, I must either be silent or unseasonable.

"Many is the time I have stood over the fire at breakfast and looked at you at Recreation, hunting for something to talk about. The song says that 'love cannot live on flowers': not so, yet it requires material, if not for sustenance, at least for display—and I have fancied too that younger and lighter minds perhaps could not, if they would, care much for one who has had so much to wear him down. All blessings come on you, my dear Brother—in proportion to my waning."[6]

He also wrote to Hutchison excusing his shyness—"what that is, only shy persons know". He promised to move faster "in my outward ways" than it was his nature to do.

The whole community arrived at St Wilfrid's in October 1848 but in January 1849 Newman took a house in Alcester Street, Birmingham. Four fathers moved back to Birmingham with him. Faber was left at St Wilfrid's, still novice master and in charge of the mission. Hutchison also stayed at St Wilfrid's with the rest of the community.

Plan after plan for a London Oratory had been discussed and rejected but the idea was still very much in the air. With Newman's departure a feeling of uncertainty sprang up. "Nobody

knows whether we shan't split and who will be where", . . . Faber
had written,

> Neither to be *in* work nor to *see* any work going on, that is
> our present state, and it can't last round to this time next year
> without loss of some valuable subjects.[7]

"It grows on me", Newman wrote wearily.

> for many reasons that separation is the only cure of our
> difficulties.[8]

His idea was to let the *giovani* have their head in London or some
other big city. Faber could not help seeing that such a separation
was inevitable as matters stood but he bitterly deplored the
necessity.

"What you say of separation is all very well *theoretically*," he
wrote,

> but I don't see how it's practical. These excellent *giovani* can't
> go without me, and they think they shall have me. Now I *do*
> protest *con furia* against being victimized and separated off from
> you and others, especially at such unseasonable time. I have no
> confidence in them, however much I love them. At present
> I am not ruler over them, except in matters of counsel and
> support and all that is soothing in the spiritual life. Suppose I
> were *superior* of a London house do you imagine that the eyes
> which can discern the specks on your brightness would not
> soon discover a very continent of blackness on mine? I should
> be arbitrary, self-willed, crotchety, impatient of difference,
> inconsistent, Jesuitical and the like. What they have done to
> you they would *a fortiori* do to me; and however great my
> sins may have been I feel that such a penance is above my at-
> tainments. If we are to separate, we are not ripe for it now, and
> I don't think you ought to cut me away from yourself at all.
> The more I think of it the less I like it; and it is hard to be as
> you tell me "calm" about it. One of the *giovani* so far forgot
> himself as to insult me very grossly this morning because I
> reproved him for discussing these matters with another *giovane*;
> he told me [that I was] grossly and culpably unjust, etc. I made
> no answer *per la grazia di Dio*, and I must wait till he cools
> down. Pray write and tell me that you will not dispose of me in

the event of a separation, or count me as of the house to which you do not belong. Indeed as to separation at all, the more I think of it the more I doubt the feasibility of it at present, from the untempered state of the mortar with which we should be built. Do go on with your ragged ragamuffins there [at Birmingham], and let the pot seethe here, and boil over, if it will. I don't say this is *nice*, but the other seems impossible . . . I am tired of the whole business and sick of these rows. I am bent on reading a spiritual book or two now; I have earned it and am reckless about all else for the present. . . .[9]

The pass to which things had come may be seen from one of Newman's letters.

Last November Brother Francis [Knox] who was in the February before admitted a member of the *Birmingham* Oratory, went out of his way to make a voluntary proffer of his obedience to me, which, being out of the way, implied something more than what he was bound to by being a member of the Birmingham House, and moreover included of course an obedience of heart, spirit and the *razionale* as well as of external conduct.

Three months after this, I put this surrender which he made of himself to its *first* trial—and find, that, though of course he does not mean to withhold the external obedience, yet it would be so dissevered from any submission of heart and mind that you, his Director, judge that the external act had better not be required of him.

However, the act of obedience which I asked of him was nothing of those extraordinary deeds which his voluntary surrender would seem to promise but simply what was *essentially* included in the original act by which he made himself an Oratorian, *that he would come to his own Oratory.*

I asked him to come to Birmingham, no more; the reasons you give me against his being urged on this point are such as the following—(1) that he has a repugnance to coming to Birmingham, (2) that he cannot pray for the Birmingham Oratory, (3) that he has an aversion, so strong that you fear if you attempt to state it, you shall seem to exaggerate it, to one of the Fathers, who, so far from having any such feeling towards him, is unconscious of its existence and has been wishing him here, (4) that he thinks the said Father colours my view of him (Br. F.) and is too much in my rooms, (5) that he cannot feel himself an Oratorian till the Oratory is in a normal state (which it can never be at St Wilfrid's, and can only be, and tends to be, in Birmingham).

Moreover, besides these strong feelings against taking up his place in his own Oratory himself, he grudges others going there, and says, "Why cannot they (i.e. *his Fathers*) do without *more*?"

Moreover he implies as a reason for our doing without the rest, that the rest can very well do without us.

He finishes by expressing unbounded love and attachment to me, founded on the memory of many years.

You "indorse" all this, by assuring me he is very affectionate and eminently devotional, and ask whether "I see my way" to writing him a line.

Save me from such affection and devotion and give me a little more tenderness for others, and a little less self will.

Your letter has just come but I shall go on with these notes before reading it—to get my view off my mind . . .

I had written to you a second letter which on second thoughts I don't send; at least not now.

Meanwhile contemplate carefully on this in all its consequences. *I don't leave Birmingham.* I don't leave Birmingham for London.

And while you take in this with its bearings upon us, think of this too, that we must decide, not by natural affection, but by reason and judgment, *which ever way they* direct—for I am not determining which way.

I am not advocating *separation*—I wish it *discussed* and the notion has risen *not from me but from Brother Francis* and those others who have said, "Why cannot they do without us?" I had *no idea* of proposing separation till then. Nay, he has not only taken this for granted, but gone on to deduce *therefore* he must look sharp lest he go to Birmingham and so get separated from those he likes best. All this is very offensive: (1) because it implies that we should have no regard to his feelings, but treat him like a bale of goods, (2) because this suspicion and impatience is so utterly inconsistent with his voluntary surrender of himself to me in November. I am very much grieved about him for his own sake, and in small measure for your sake, since he has caused you such anxiety.

As to your anxieties as Superior, my notion was that, if we were called to separate (but I say it in *the strictest confidence* for I throw it out to hear what you say) Father Rector should be Superior [Robert Coffin] and you director, etc.

Don't suppose that it would not be a most dreary miserable thing for me to be separated from you—but consider the state of the *Giovani* and meditate on the fact that I don't go to London.[10]

But Faber was still against separation if it could be avoided.

I do not suppose matters have come to such a pitch as to present us with separation or loss of subjects as the horns of our dilemma. But if it were, let the subjects go. I say this not in heat but deliberately, and loving extremely those who might leave us. We are not fit to separate. Putting myself entirely out of the question—nobody could govern these men as their superior half as quietly as they are governed now. I who know them best, and love them sincerely have no confidence in them, and the way in which all the recent business has been trans-acted has destroyed the confidence I had. Nothing but force would now drive me into an Oratory with them, apart from you ... I must say a word for myself. You said to Father Bernard—Put Father Wilfrid at the head of the London House. Now can you really see your way to this? Observe—and it is very remarkable—the tendency to split not into Oratorians and Wilfridians. Take even the instinct of liking. Father Antony is amazed people don't like Father Ambrose. People predicted I should never dovetail in with you and yours: has it been so?

And look at the responsibility you take. Think of the past. When I was at Oxford I loved you most intensely when your manner to me shewed openly that you did not think well of me—and rightly. Still it did not alter my feeling. When I was converted in heart at Rome, your sole word stayed me. When I was on the brink of the Church, I begged you to take me; I had nowhere else to look: you would not! When I might perhaps have kept Knox I sent him where I wished to be myself—to you.

I found no rest for the sole of my foot among English

Catholics, and was forced on a seemingly wrong and presumptuous independence, and carried my points with triumphant obstinacy; when the opportunity offered, and the *moment* it offered, I came to you. Is it only to go off again? My dearest Padre, you don't know how sick I turn at all this. When I joined you I was an active missioner—preaching, etc., in all directions: you threw me into a different groove. Quiet, hidden, indoors, pensive work has been mine ever since I have had work at all in the Congregation; and it was hard to curb, and hard to snub the many risings of my old restless *effusio ad externa*. It was the first time I had worked under obedience; it was counter to my whole nature and I believe it was and is the will of God, and would not have it changed. But what supported me was the thought Baronius had when he said: *Ad te, pientissime rector, vitae nostrae deferimus gubernacula.*

To know you and to be with you was not all I wanted, as I told you at Maryvale; but to work with, under and for you. I do not know a heavier cross God could give me than separation from you. Think of all this before you decide to cut me off from those I love and those who love [me] to go and govern men who will neither confide in me or bear with me, when I go a different road from theirs. I have been their slave these ten days past, and have written and said all they would have me write or say, and I have let them do the same, in order that they might have their *sfogo*[?]; and I have taken their part with you and kept back all that would prejudice you against them, and I can make a pretty tolerable composition of place of what the new Oratory would be like. I have now put a forcible stop to it all—forbidden it as a subject of conversation, and enforced exclusive attention to spirituals.[11]

The cause of the trouble is contained in one of Newman's letters at this time—namely his waiting for God's will to be made plain.

All that Father Rector says tends to hasten on this separation which I would fain have delayed to a distant day. My own day was ten years hence, as I proposed to name to the Holy See— but you all seem to feel that, if we are to divide, it must be done at once.

I am not disputing the justness of this conclusion, and I

am not combating an impression which is a *fact* but it fills me, my dear Father Wilfrid, with sorrow—the more so, *because* I *cannot* combat it, for I cannot make minds patient and hearts contented and imaginations quiet and wills subdued, which are not so. *I* could live ten years with you all, knowing that then there must be a separation from some—you all cannot—*I* would consent to leave it to the course of events, that is, to Providence, gently to work our separation during that time as fruit ripens on the tree and falls; you all force me to take a knife and cut it off. I repeat I cannot fight with facts—but I will not allow anyone to say that I am the direct and immediate author of this proposed separation, for I lament it.[12]

Newman's waiting on Providence was precisely what the *giovani* disliked. Would Providence *gently* work the separation in ten years' time? Was it not more likely that with no decisions arrived at the Oratory would have disintegrated? Besides, what was going to happen in the ten years? Was the waiting on Providence really a disguise for indecision? Was not anything better than uncertainty? These were the questions the *giovani* asked themselves. Faber's position lay between the two. Temperamentally adverse to indecision he nevertheless could not bear the thought of separation from Newman. In justice to the *giovani* it must be conceded that Newman acted with a hesitant weakness which must have been galling to young and impatient men.

Such was Newman's extraordinary ascendency over his fellows that no one saw that he was ill fitted for his position. Faber never understood that for a man of Newman's genius, a writer, a thinker, a man of intuition—his position as Superior of these unruly *giovani* was little short of hellish. He also never grasped the irrational femininity of Newman's character. "My very dear Padre," he wrote,

if the idea of early separation causes you sorrow I beg of you, if you love us, to say no more of it ... The very strong wish of FF. Richard, Rector, Antony and myself is that you should take matters into your own hands and act as you think best.[13]

But it was because Newman felt unequal to the situation that he wavered and asked everyone's advice. Faber's equation of his decisions with the word of God only made him the more nervous.

The correspondence dragged on and on fraying everyone's nerves. Faber kept falling ill. Newman's dialectical ability made him read depths into the simplest propositions or again and again simply to misunderstand what was proposed. Faber kept up a rearguard action against being sent to London. A Roman Father, that is one who had been in Rome with Newman, was wanted as Superior. He (Faber) was only fit to work under some-one else.

> The great thing is to avoid anything like a split, or appearance of split, between you and Wilfridians.

But, as Newman pointed out, there was no principle of unity in the Oratory except Newman himself and Faber. Therefore Faber must go to London. A tentative list of the two houses was drawn up. Some of the community objected. Finally Newman wrote five alternative lists which covered every possible arrangement. These were voted on and it was almost unanimously decided that the fifth should stand. This was as follows:

Birmingham: Newman, Penny, St John, Bowles, Mills, Darnell, Joseph Gordon, Whitty, Flanagan, McQuoin.

London: Coffin, Dalgairns, Stanton, Knox, Faber, Hutchison, Wells, Philip Gordon, John Bowden. The last two were novices.

One ex-Wilfridian and Darnell who had been associated with Faber at St Wilfrid's went to Birmingham. Two ex-Wilfridians (excluding Faber) went to London. The London fathers were really nearer to Newman than to Faber. Stanton had been at Littlemore and then in Rome with Newman. Philip Gordon had joined the Oratory in Birmingham and on account of Newman. John Bowden was the son of Newman's Trinity friend. Coffin never went to London though technically he remained a London father till he left the Congregation in 1850.

Dalgairns was especially close to Newman. He was, indeed, rather out of favour with Newman at this time but the friendship with Newman was very deep. "I think with dismay on London," he wrote. When he left, Newman was downcast.

Father Bernard is just gone. Curiously enough I have set down seven years, for a long while, as the term of *Contubernium* with my friends. Froude was with me from 1827 to 1834. Rogers from 1833 to 1840 and when at the end of that time I saw him get on the Oxford coach for the Continent, I thought of the seven years and wondered whether I should ever be with him again. Now F. Bernard came up to Littlemore on the Eve of St George 1842 and he leaves the Oratory here on St George 1849. Don't mention this, as I have *before now* been afraid of Fr Ambrose getting hold of it—he is so fanciful.[14]

"With regard to myself I should like, speaking according to *feeling*," Faber wrote,

to be in the house no. 4 [with Newman at Birmingham] but I doubt the London house standing. . . . Of course I'm floored; however my chief consolation will be to think that after all I shall be doing *your* work in *your* way instead of in *my own* way.[15]

But a few days later he was feeling depressed and ill:

Yesterday and today the agitation of my mind is so great that I am worse; and then the toothache kept me awake, so that may account for a great deal. I shall be very glad to come to you, and will try to take an interest in the Oratory; but my spirits are so beaten down lately that I doubt my taking an interest in anything. Ever since the plans have been proposed I have done nothing but sit and brood over difficulties and various separations, till I have been quite oppressed; and Office and Mass have been distracted by it. I think I shall be better when I have got fairly away from the poor people in whom I have taken such very deep root this time, and who *seem* to depend upon me more than ever. My Chief wish now is to get to London; Caroline St, Colmore Terrace, St Wilfrid's, Maryvale, St Wilfrid's, is flitting enough for three short years, and I am sick of it, heartily sick. Besides which my health gets worse, i.e. more rickety and I can stand uprooting worse.

Having arrived at a conclusion Newman now began to tinker with the lists. Faber pointed out the excited state of the Fathers and novices at St Wilfrid's and added anxiously:

If, however, my dearest Padre, you fluctuate in your mind, don't write word of it to anyone here; your notes this morning, especially the one to F. Rector quite created a fermentation ... It is a great responsibility; a large community of men, young, almost without training and discipline, long Protestant habits of selfwill and private judgment, very little *respect* for each other, no experience, little sobriety, less patience, imperfect knowledge of the institute they are in, having joined it most of them for the sake of one person not from *attrait* to the institute, with their minds on edge—to divide these into two organic houses is a huge difficulty—and yet as matters stand now, delay seems to me to be worse than difficulty. But enough. You must take this letter *cum grano salis* as it is written with a sick body and a sicker mind. ...[16]

On 10th April, Easter Tuesday, 1849, Faber and Hutchison left St Wilfrid's for Birmingham. They passed a few days in Newman's new Oratory there and then went on to London. It was the end of St Wilfrid's as far as Faber was concerned. He did visit it but it was never again his home. Unhappily the squabble as to its future continued. Ullathorne complicated the issue still further by claiming it as the property of the diocese—apparently with some legality. Lord Shrewsbury was furious when the Oratorians suggested that the parish should be served by two secular priests. "It would be perfect sacrilege", he wrote to the bishop,

> to divert it from monastic purposes. I gave it to them [i.e. the Wilfridians] *because* they were a community, because I always felt that a religious community alone could convert that neighbourhood. This Father Faber knew from the beginning. ... I approved of their joining the Oratory, because I considered it would strengthen their community, not dissolve it ... I did not then know the rules of the Oratory, nor Father Faber either, I believe, and least of all did I think it would induce them to act as they have done since and wholly frustrate all my views in giving them the property ... The very possibility of St Wilfrid's being abandoned appears to me so shocking that I can only attribute Father Faber's letter to a certain aberration of mind; indeed we have often suspected him of being hardly sound.[17]

Newman had thought of turning St Wilfrid's into a school and many other projects were proposed. Father Robert Coffin looked after the mission in the meantime. In 1851 St Wilfrid's was taken by the Passionists who, however, did not prosper there. In 1855 they left and the parish was almost abandoned for more than ten years. In 1868 part of Sedgley Park School took over the Hall, having already bought additional land in the district. In 1873 the final transfer of the whole school to Cotton took place. The school, founded in penal times, has been there ever since and has flourished exceedingly.

CHAPTER XI

LONDON

O N arrival in London Faber and Hutchison found that
three friends, David Lewis, George Fullerton and Lord
Arundel, had not been idle. Lewis was a well-known
Oxford convert, Fullerton a convert guardsman and Arundel
the future Duke of Norfolk. Lewis in particular had gone round
with John Bowden looking at various premises. The most
suitable seemed to be 24 and 25 King William Street, Strand.
Faber immediately visited it.

> The chapel is smaller than I expected, about 60 ft. by 25. It is
> a gin shop; there are twelve *good* bedrooms, besides four or
> five good community rooms. Some things would want
> humoring, but altogether the concern is marvellously suited.
> The rent is £400 per annum, a lease of twenty-one years. It
> seems, however, that there is little doubt that the British
> Architectural will take the premises on Friday. ... The
> Irvingite Chapel in *Newman Street* is very eligible; Stewart
> the bookseller will see one of their body on Thursday; it
> seems they are going to move in to a grand church. Mr
> Fullerton is moving heaven and earth to get us a *nido*, and
> talks of a tennis court behind Trafalgar Square; he thinks a
> tennis court and a church very cognate buildings. O my feet
> are so sore! This by way of parenthesis.[1]

He was soon wondering how they would manage to live if they
found a suitable house. He reckoned the London Oratory would
have a guaranteed income of something under a £1000. Mrs
Bowden had promised £250, which included the board of her
youngest son Charles aged thirteen whom she proposed should
live with John and the Fathers.

> Mrs Bowden says she will *do more* next year and that John
> will be of age, and come into £400 per annum of his own,
> independent of what she may allow him; and he says he will

do great things. Then Father Antony's aunt is not eternal. Old Mrs Butler may give something, Mr Zulueta and others.

But besides the income there was very little for buying furniture, crockery and so on.

Brother Edward (John Bowden) thinks he would get a trifle of his pocket money. Lord Arundel is selling a farm. I am going to be unconscionable enough to ask him for a donation towards the outfit; but most of his money has gone lately in a different direction. I shall ask Dr Wiseman; it will be vain. I dare not speak to Lord Shrewsbury till I see how he takes our move at St Wilfrid's. O Padre mio! What a work this begging is— it goes against my proud grain terribly; and these calls and small talk, little courtesies, and dinners and luncheons![2]

"We have been high and low, advertised, enquired," he wrote a few days later,

and nothing but these King William Street premises would do. The Association of the British Architectural empowered their committee; the committee took the premises; all was over: lo! the Association has met to ratify the Committee's work; and unexpectedly a majority has floored the Committee. I have therefore made a regular treaty to-day which binds till Tuesday morning.[3]

On 24th April he wrote:

I have got one of my beautiful headaches. I am going out no more to $\frac{1}{2}$ 7 dinners; I can't stand it; and I get no sleep at nights, nor digest what I eat, and I hate everybody that calls, and I hate still worse everybody I have to call on. My present life is one huge proximate occasion of sin. Yesterday we were thrown on our beam ends by Rushworth the agent taking against us as Catholics, and letting Scoles [the architect] know pretty plainly that if he was the owner he would not let us have the premises; and in these remarkably uncouth dispositions he went up to Mr Nurse the owner, in Regent's Park, who is lying motionless, but speechful, in paralysis. It appears that the organ will be a great nuisance, which is good, seeing the house has been almost, if not quite, a brothel, and the large whiskey room used to have orchestra and dancing almost every night. Item—a Catholic chapel crowds a street with the lower classes, and deteriorates the surrounding property. These last items remind one of the devil witnessing to our Lord's divinity. Well—we *poveri maledetti* must take these kicks.

This morning we received answer. They have thrown overboard every principle of equity and honor. They do not positively refuse us the premises, but, considering the "Catholic chapel" they break their covenant and treaty with me, which was (in force) up to this morning, and consider themselves at liberty to treat with a museum company which has meanwhile come into the field. I have sent in a definite proposal. . . . I have offered Faber, Hutchison, Coffin, Stanton and Bowden for tenants, with Lord Arundel and Mr Fullerton for referees; for our two officers in the Blues are still staunch, blessed centurions that they are; Jack Morris shall never preach in the Oratory that sermon on the brutalizing effects of the military life. . . .[4]

"Rushworth", he wrote next day,

has made his profession of faith—"I wish to avoid Mr Faber. Your priests may be very good moral men, but they have no money. Mr Faber is a man of religion. I am a man of pounds, shillings and pence"!!!

He has been here. O such a man. He deplores Mr Nurse's letting us have the premises, and "to be consistent," as he calls it, he and the solicitor have protested. I was so quiet with him that he positively became cowed; I got all my conditions and have signed the rough draft of the lease and we shall have the keys in an hour. Now I must get to work and work till late at night. Did you ever read *Dombey*? If you remember Carker you know Rushworth. Direct—The Oratory, 24, King William Street, Strand—in time we can drop the number.[5]

"Another headache", he wrote on the 26th,

I suppose from the hours spent in consultation with Scoles on the premises yesterday. He can greatly improve us in the way of light and air but we must wait even for those two things, till we have money. F. Antony and I had a bit of a dispute about painting the chapel; I was sour and cross, and he grumpy, but I carried the day. Decoration will come in gifts when we are once started . . . I am buying beds, mattresses, chairs, tables, pans, pots, fenders, etc., today—linen and blankets are *en route* from St Wilfrid's, just enough to start with—a round of beef and a ham are to come from a cookshop in St Martin's on Saturday. How to get water and gas turned on, and to get *en rapport* with a baker, butcher, milkman and greengrocer, these are my present straits . . . I think if I could get *into* the house without chairs, or tables and squat on the boards, like a Hottentot in his own Kraal, I should be happy; this life of dinners and of calls is purgatory . . .[6]

"I wrote you a hymn last night," he told Newman next day,

to help you in your month of Mary. There is an *embarras de richesses* of tunes. It will go to "Sound the loud timbrel" of Moore, or the "Meeting of the waters", or Byron's "The Assyrian came down like a wolf on the fold", or a song in the Beggar's Opera . . .

Our bargain is off again in the most scandalous way and that when the Brothers are coming up tomorrow. . . .

My sense of the ridiculous is exceedingly tickled with the figure I shall cut tomorrow with Philip, Ignatius and John Lewis, no end of blankets and not a house! They had actually promised possession on Saturday, and Scoles took steps accordingly; but they are not bound by law, and equity is nothing to gents who don't go to confession . . .

¼ past 11. The last question which Rushworth has just sent us is, "What hostages have you for your country; you have neither wife nor children!" He is now off to examine the deeds of St Wilfrid's at Bagshawe's, which deeds, another joke! were burnt in the Lincoln's Inn fire some weeks ago. The worse matters look the more confident I get . . .

Afternoon. A conclave has been held at Mr Nurse's, the owner of the property, in Regent's Park, who has had a paralytic stroke. Mr Nurse entered into none of Mr Rushworth's objections, and accepted all our conditions. The estimable agent however started a fresh hitch; all Catholic communities give alms, and we should annoy the other inhabitants of the street by so doing. Lewis said we were not like Trappists, and were not by rule an almsgiving community and gave no alms beyond what all Christians are bound to give. Rushworth: That may be your view of Christianity. (The place remember was *worse* than a brothel before.) This however was over-ruled. He then objected to our having the power of subletting. But this also Mr Nurse conceded. . . .[7]

But at last the lease was signed.

"Your *figliuoli* are at last safely housed", he wrote on 29th April,

amid dirt and disorder, but very happy and comfortable. . . . We did not get into the house till about five, and then we had to borrow a few chairs from a policeman; we got some beef from a cookshop. I sent John Lewis out to buy a tin kettle, and by nine we got some tea, and about midnight reared F. Richard's great picture of S. Philip on the wall, and the B. Sebastian at the side altar, tabernacle and crucifix; and this morning Lord Arundel and Lewis joined us at eight; I said Mass, and F. Antony followed me. Lord A. and Lewis stayed breakfast, and drank milk out of a washing jug; and a very, very happy morning we have had of it.

I am extremely tired; but when I go into the little chapel (the future sacristy) which has no light but a glass louvre, and kneel down before the Blessed Sacrament, with the beautiful S. Philip behind, and my old Elton ivory crucifix above, and hear the distant roar of London (for it is at the back of the house) I can hardly believe it is not all a dream. God grant it may be the beginning of a great work! . . . St Martin's clock is so like Durham Cathedral. It minds me of old times . . .[8]

The property the Fathers now found themselves possessed of consisted of two houses on the street with a large building, divided into an upper and lower floor, at the back. This building which had been an assembly room and then a shop for the sale of whisky was approached by a broad passage from the street between the houses. The rooms were large, 60 ft. by 30 ft. The upper room, the one destined for the chapel, and approached by a flight of steps, had no windows, but was lighted by three sky lights. It was 15 feet in height with an apse at the West end and a recess on the North side. The lower room, similar in shape, was intended as a second chapel but it was extremely dark and airless.

It was eventually used as the Refectory and little Oratory. The frontage on King William Street was fitted up as two shops and these had to be removed.

Faber fixed 31st May as the day for the public opening, allowing scarcely a month for the transformation. The community consisted of six priests: Faber, Dalgairns (who arrived late), Stanton, Hutchison, Knox and Wells, the two novices, Philip Gordon and John Bowden, and three lay brothers, Chad, Ignatius and John Lewis. Charles Bowden, aged thirteen, also arrived to join his brother and carry on his education. Everyone had to work as they had never worked before and it was not long before Faber was ill again.

"I could not bear", he wrote on 16th May,

> to be more than a minute off my bed: want of food, vomiting, and a burning head, an incessant flux of cabs and drays over a granite pavement below, teddy talers at my door breaking doors through into the rooms, the gas pipes broken and the house ineffably fetid with the same, and interruptions nearly every ten minutes for orders ... I had chosen for myself a delicious little back room, about the size of yours at Maryvale, looking over the chapel roof, and commanding the free area of the Charing Cross hospital; FF. Richard and Antony have turned me out—declare it will be a great inconvenience to the Congregation—unfit for visitors and the like. Yet it was quite as big as yours at M'vale; peaceful as Paradise, and London sounded only like the roaring of a hyena with a very bad relaxed sore throat; whereas my front room, 16 ft. square, is bleak from want of furniture and the roar is intolerable: I never felt so badly with a headache before. I think if a little experience does not immune me to the row which the cockneys Antony and Philip never hear, I *must* go to the back.
>
> I have put Charley into the attics to his Mamma's delight, and Br. Edward into the south attic next Charley. Mrs B. flits about the house, visits me in my bedroom, inundates us with floods of devout Irish charwomen, groans over the dirt, and is a positive mother, the S. Elizabeth of our Chiesa Nuova.[9]

Meanwhile back in Birmingham Newman was receiving a flood of news, not only the almost daily bulletins from Faber but letters from the other Fathers as well. He grew fidgety. "I am rather anxious", he wrote to Hutchison on 2nd May,

> how you get on with your habits in London lest you should be soon voting them a bore. I don't see why you should and the Oratory has so little of a penitential nature it is a sort of mortification but I have been feeling for poor Philip walking up to the Regent's Park. Yet would he not be more wonderful in the mongrel archideaconal dress of a secular priest?[10]

Writing later, Philip Gordon said:

> I remember very well the first time I went up Regent Street in it [the habit], wondering what would happen. I kept saying to myself: "the first boy that gives a yell, and I'm like a dog on a race-course." But as a matter of fact, the boys did not insult us or do more than chaff us, the insults came from the gentlemen who would do so from their carriages.[11]

At this time it was the gentry and middle classes who were most anti-Catholic. The talk of converting England applied practically only to the working classes. "Mr Fullerton says," Hutchison reported,

> that people began to talk at dinner now about "the Jesuits" whom they have seen walking in the Streets. The Jesuits are no other than ourselves. We have as yet not found the habit at all a bore, but quite the reverse. The London boys don't make such personal remarks on us as the Birmingham ones do.[12]

The Fathers in Birmingham who also habitually wore their habits in the streets had much the same trouble, or worse. It is even recorded that Newman had a sack of flour emptied over his head. In London "the habit seemed to excite wonder rather than amusement", Philip Gordon wrote.

> I remember once walking with Father Faber when we met a small butcher boy, who could do nothing but gape, and finally expressed himself thus: "Well you must be a—fool"[13]

As for Faber he expressed himself thus:

> I walk down the street in my habit and I feel I dispel invincible ignorance wherever I go.

All the exuberant letters frightened Newman.

> You have been too go ahead with the Bishop and I say it the rather because if you do not look sharp you will be carried off your legs. I hear that dear Brother Edward spreads out his cloke like a peacock's tail in the sight of Sir R. Inglis [the Commissioner for Woods and Forests and a prominent Evangelical], while the *Tablet*, before you are well in your saddles in King William Street advertises you to the universe as its destined saviour. All this will create fear, odium, jealousy —and you may have the Newspapers or the Woods and Forests step in and do you a mischief. The Woods and Forests might at least pull off your habits for you. [Newman feared that there might be a clause in the lease which would allow the Woods and Forests to interfere.]
>
> Then again avoid slang. F. Bernard slangs the Confessional. F. Alban slangs Our Lady, F. Francis slangs the Puseyites, and F. Antony slangs the Bishops, and poor dear innocent F. Wilfrid is carried away, and slangs right and left in consequence.
>
> I was not pleased at your talking of Dr U[llathorne] as a little man—it may be a fact but it is [a] sort of dogmatic fact which the Church may rule contrariwise. I suppose the Church may rule he is a tall man—in the eyes of the Church he *is* a tall man.[14]

This letter was followed by another marked "Private". He complained again of the article in *The Tablet* about which he felt he should have been consulted. "And now again," he continued,

> you take it for granted the opening is to be advertised, and perhaps my name is to appear, yet I have not been asked about the advertisement ... The word "Philippine" is an innovation of the same kind though perhaps without your knowing about it. Depend upon it, Charissime, you all need my control over you in little things at this minute, more than you have yet or will again.[15]

The article in *The Tablet*, it appeared, was by David Lewis. Faber was under the impression that the adjective "Oratorian" might be thought "Jansenist."

"What you say about our needing your control is most true," Faber replied:

one chief discomfort of our present position is that we none of us know either what or where we are, or what we can, or cannot do, and so many things have to be done daily. I wish you would say something definitely about this; I feel it most disheartening to have so much to do; nobody near me seems to acknowledge the slightest responsibility except myself, and I have no powers . . . You have never given me any instructions; you have given me a very hard work to do viz. to start the house, and you have not laid down any *modus*; you have left it all undefined, which harasses me extremely; I have felt over and over again that I should be making some *sbaglio*, and then that you would come down upon me; and yet I feared to ask you for definite instructions lest I should be teasing you, or showing want of confidence.[16]

Newman answered kindly and to the point. He was worried that

Sir R. Inglis stared at Brother Edward! The Jesuits may have an excess of caution but they are wiser in these matters. My very wish that you should wear your habit in London makes me fear wanton display which may look like a bravado and strip you of it.

I feel what you say about want of control. Be then at once and hereby Rector of the London community and I will write to F. Minister by this day's post and say what I have done and that he is now naturally F. Minister and Missioner as he has lost all his subjects. And be absolute in all internal matters. Only, as I have said, I should like to have an opinion on the services (*when they are out of the way*) and on public announcements.[17]

Faber's gratitude for Newman's confidence is not on record. His next letter on 18th May merely thanks "for your very kind letter" and awaits his arrival.

"We have got a hitch about the opening now," he wrote on 18th May:

The man of whom the benches were ordered a fortnight ago has made none; and finds he shan't have time to do them! Mr Gibson, the solicitor, tells me the Woods and Forests can do nothing; but we can't advertise this week.

Poor Brother Edward does not, I think, mean to make any pomp of his habit; but he walks with his mantella not wrapped round him on account of heat. I have not been in the street, but once for five minutes, since last Saturday fortnight, and they say I am looking very white. Augarde the hatter has called to say that Mr Reardon of Spanish Place has ordered a hat "like the Oratorians" and he (Augarde) has begged to inspect our hats. How odd Mr R. will look with nothing below to correspond! Perhaps it may be the beginning of ecclesiastical dress.[18]

There was less than a fortnight till the public opening at which Wiseman was to preach in the morning and Newman in the evening. Nothing was ready. It seemed impossible that it could be. And there were other anxieties. Faber had written an injudicious letter to Ullathorne about St Wilfrid's and was forced to apologize. Newman was seriously annoyed.

You seem to wish to show the world that after all there is something unmanageable in you, that you can't be relied on, that you are fickle, take up schemes, give them up, insult benefactors, are heartless and wilful. Now though such an accusation is of course absurd yet I do think you have given countenance to it—I don't wonder if people so think:— "A clever man but you can't depend on him." I am sure this is said.[19]

But Faber's apology when it was written was so complete that Newman was astonished. "How naughty of you", Faber wrote,

to make merry with my wondrous *humility* to Dr U. *Here* also my debut in the character of *lamb* was not received with becoming gravity.[20]

Happily the bishop accepted the apology but it caused Faber a lot of worry.

On the feast of the Invention of the Cross Faber had written: "We have found our cross today." Out of the blue the architect of the Woods and Forests informed Faber's architect, Scoles, that a Catholic chapel could not be opened without the permission of the Bishop of London. Luckily it was discovered that this was not so. Then there was illness in the house owing to the heat. Brother Chad fell ill, then Brother Ignatius with "some horrid cholera" and finally Faber was "doubled up with rheumatism".

Faber however was not downcast. Perhaps on the strength of being Rector he moved into a back room again.

> I have got into a back room and am happy. The sun never shines there, and fresh air is at a discount; but a bright yellow and red paper creates an artificial sunshine, and F. Antony has bought me a *glowing* rug, and a *gleaming* chintz curtain, and Burns has given me a brilliantly painted St Joseph—and there is a water-closet in my room; in fact my room was the lobby to the refreshment room water-closet. It will make a nice confessional. The white paint gives me perpetual headaches and pains in my back. The faster ones are to have mackerel and asparagus in honor of Santo Padre [May 26th, his feast day] ... I find Brother Edward was going to trot Charlie about the streets in his habit; and I have forbidden it, till you rule about it. Won't it make us all ridiculous if he goes to feed the swans in St James' Park in cassock and mantella?[21]

In the midst of "the filth and dirt" he was writing hymns by way of a "pastime". He told Newman he had one hundred and fifty pages of them.

On the day before the opening, benches were arriving all the afternoon. (Faber had had his way with the bench maker.) The organ was being tuned. But a number of its pipes were strewn about the floor. Some of the Fathers were erecting the altar. They were, Faber said,

> white, tired, sleepy, dyspeptic and irritable except Brother Ignatius who looks ten per cent. better for his cholera. Chad looks interior and grumpy, so I suspect his bowels are out of order.[22]

A bishop's throne had been borrowed. A gallery, Fullerton's gift to the Congregation, had been set up at the East end and the scaffolding was only just being taken out. In fact workmen were in the chapel almost up to the commencement of the Mass. "The Bishop [Wiseman]", Newman wrote to St John, preached a most beautiful sermon, in composition and logic a perfect sermon, and with great feeling; he preached from the altar [there was no pulpit yet]. The music was composed by Capes expressly for the occasion. It is now close on five, and the carriages are setting down their burdens. Birmingham is a place of rest. O! that I had wings like a dove, for I do dislike this preaching so much.[23]

His sermon preached at Vespers was called "Prospects of the Catholic Missioner".

The Fathers now found themselves inundated with work. "As I am not quite dead," Faber wrote on 4th June,

and the rest of the house is more nearly so than myself I must write to report progress. Somehow or other every Father and every brother has more to do than he could do. We were so devout that we forgot to make a collection at four of the Masses; the other collections brought us £14 17s. and some odd pence. This we mustn't expect every time, of course. F. Bernard and I took two sermons apiece; the crowds reached out into the street, and of course the heat was fearful. We had poor at the early Masses, nobs at H. Mass and afternoon lecture, and shop-keepers at late Benediction.[24]

"Confessions are increasing", he reported two days later,

and the numbers at the weekday Mass, and we have worshippers before the Tabernacle *all day*, and quite thick towards evening. I have done little work myself; the heat makes me faint, sick and sleepless: yesterday it was like the atmosphere of a lion's cage in Wombwell.[25]

"My time is now completely engrossed by *convertendi* or *ae*," he wrote on June 8th,

for they are chiefly Puseyite ladies ... My whole afternoon is spent in controversy; and I have no time to prepare my sermons, and am so weary at night I can hardly keep awake in the Confessional. ...[26]

Letter after letter speaks of work beyond their endurance. Faber maintained that even with double their numbers they could not get through it.

But the effects of the heat and overwork began to tell.

> Chad has behaved *very badly*; he has talked at recreation of a
> rebellion at St Wilfrid's; when we first set up, when I stripped
> them of their habits and says it will come over again here soon.
> ... Certainly I never knew such a change; I can't manage them
> a bit; they are rude to me, with the greatest coolness; and the
> least rebuke makes them sulky, and they complain of their
> food, which is better far than they used to have, or would have
> as labourers at home. Of course workmen, confusion, etc.
> are very much against them ... When I ordered some mince
> for dinner (cold meat to be used up, or wasted) I was told it
> could not be; the *brothers* have had mince twice lately and they
> won't eat anything but joints ... If it had been in old Wil-
> fridian times John and Chad would have been in the railway
> for Elton by this time.[27]

There were other difficulties, too. Stanton was dictatorial,
so Faber thought, about the arrangements in the chapel. There
were quarrels as they settled down together.

> Father Alban is very bumptious, F. Francis very captious,
> while even Charlie gets notions and Edward has to snub him.

There were "particular friendships". Then there was unpleasant
gossip that Dalgairns had "a regular passion" for hearing people's
confessions—which Faber described as the very worst that could
be said of a convert priest.

> I am very anxious about F. Bernard. I have told him that I
> think he fishes for penitents and looks greedily about him when
> sitting outside his confessional,

he reported.[28] It seemed almost as if their critics were right when
they said the Fathers were too new in their Catholicism to hear
confessions. When Faber returned from a short visit to his
brother Frank he found Knox with the beginnings of

> a bad nervous fever brought on actually by lying awake at
> night and imagining difficult cases in the confessional which
> he could not solve.[29]

Later it turned out that he had malaria.

John Lewis, the lay brother, "can't get a notion of cooking; I help him in certain things, but he is a dirty greasy fellow", which probably, together with the heat, explains a "second cholera" which he reported on the 27th. The heat made the whole house languid.

> The heat of the house and chapel is of the nature of Calcutta Black Hole. I lie on bed all day. Scarcely any of us can eat. I am going to give them all wine regularly. The heat at night interferes with their sleeping. F. Bernard grows tame. F. Richard's siesta is prolonged. F. Antony is querulous, Br. Philip looks wan. Bass' Pale Ale supports Edward and Charles. The *fratelli* are weary with work and unrule; we are only just through the Woods and Forests. I can't write more; any chorus of Euripides will put you in possession of my despair. Our choir has deserted us; alas! penitents do not desert us.[30]

"We have had a regular blow up among the brothers", Faber wrote on 5th July,

> now that we have got back to Rule. William Pitts even went so far as to scrape the floor with his foot, etc., etc., in the refectory, by agreement while the brothers laughed. Brother Gregory, that perpetually troublesome spirit, seems to have led the way. They struck work and none but John Lewis would wait at dinner. At last I found it spreading so fast, B. Ignatius got so excited, and B. Wilfrid flushed and flustered, that I offered any who chose money to go to you at once, or to go home as they talked of doing. The fact was that I was frightened of any of the stout rebels staying in the house till there was time for reference to you, and preferred running the risk of their going to the whole thing being blown up. The consequence is Brother Gregory is gone without seeing me (so I find) and *home* to Elton.[31]

By the next day he was probing at the cause of the trouble. As an experiment it had been decided to go without beer in the house except on Sundays and feasts. Brothers Philip, Edward and Chad, however, were given stout for reasons of health. They drank only half of what was bought and this Brother Gregory seized when it went down and bottled for himself.

This amazed me, it shaved so close upon stealing; none of the Brothers had dared tell me and Brother Ignatius in extenuation of Br. Gregory's conduct said that Br. Gregory sometimes gave some to the other brothers!! After this Brother Gregory said that Br. Philip had refused beer; he said this in the kitchen, so for a fortnight Philip had *none*; the brothers gave him none. He spoke to them, and Br. Gregory said, you refused it and some other rude speech, and still they gave him none. F. Antony called my attention to this, and I found Philip's beer had been got from the shop, yet not given to him. The brothers prevaricated—I never could get at the bottom of the affair . . . At last Br. Gregory told the brothers he would not do his work unless he had beer neither would he keep silence at work times. Then the whole thing broke out; for two days no brothers went to Communion. No sooner did Wilfrid come [from St Wilfrid's] than he was laid hold of and in two or three hours was as black as thunder and sulky as a bear.

It was agreed that Wm. Pitts, as not a brother, should assert his rights, and that in the refectory, by scraping the floor with his feet, jogging the tables, etc., while the Brothers were to laugh, which accordingly took place . . . Then came out a host of grievances: Wm. Pitts was not adequately clothed by F. Antony; F. Alban did not understand music, and ought not to be prefect of music; F. Richard was tyrannical and hard to please in the sacristy and chapel; as to myself I had been quite changed by the Oratory, harsh, stingy, careless of brothers' healths, etc., etc.; and that they could never have me for a Superior . . . When Brother Gregory found nobody was allowed to go but himself, I fancy he was considerably sold— the brothers had deserted him and let him in for it.[32]

The Oratory was a phenomenon to Catholics as well as Protestants. Up to 1849 no religious body or community had been allowed to open a church in London. Even the Jesuits had no public work assigned to them. Farm Street Church had not yet been opened. The devotions of the Oratory also caused a good deal of surprise. Popular services on weekdays were then unknown. When the Exercises of the Oratory began with new hymns, new prayers and a new style of preaching they were considered Methodistical and were denounced to the bishop.

The chapel was kept open all day for private visits to the Blessed Sacrament and for confessions. This was considered in the middle of hostile London to be the height of imprudence. As had happened before, Faber's devotion to Our Lady was looked on with suspicion. There were, of course, many pictures of Our Lady in Catholic chapels but only one statue in a public place, that at St Mary's, Chelsea. To decorate a Lady altar with flowers or to burn lamps or votive candles before her picture was absolutely unheard of. This sort of thing might go on in backward countries and for the benefit of emotional Italian peasants—but in the middle of London it was a positive incentive to disbelief. Faber was what we should now call appallingly "illiturgical". But those who opposed him were by no means models of liturgical excellence. The clash was only incidentally liturgical. Ultramontanism went hand in hand with an unthinking mimicry of Italian ways of worship at a time when Italians were practically blind to the liturgy.

Pugin criticized for other reasons. "Has your Lordship heard", he wrote to Lord Shrewsbury,

> that the Oratorians have opened the Lowther Rooms as a chapel!!—a place for the vilest debauchery, masquerades, etc. one night a masqued ball, next Benedictus. This appears to me perfectly monstrous and I give the whole order up for ever. What a degradation for religion! Why, it is worse than the Socialists. What a place to celebrate the mysteries of religion in! I cannot conceive how it is allowed. It cannot even be licensed or protected by law, since they only have it for a time. It is the greatest blow we have had for a long time; no men have been so disappointing as these. Conceive the poet Faber come down to the Lowther Rooms! The man who wrote "Thoughts and sights in foreign churches"!!! hiring the Lowther ROOMS! Well may they cry out against screens or anything else. I always said they wanted rooms, not churches, and now they have got them. Sad times! I cannot imagine what the world will come to if it goes on much longer.[33]

The opposition of the London clergy was more important. The intensity of the hatred was extraordinary. Besides what may

Father Richard Stanton

Father Antony Hutchinson

Father Bernard Dalgairns

Father John Bowden

Father Francis Knox

J. Newman in 1852. returning to Birm^{ham}
in J. Faber's French coat
N.B. The coat is brown, with black
braid, and a hood of bright light blue.

Newman in Father Faber's coat

From an album at the London Oratory

Newman at the time of the
Achilli trial, 1852

be called the opposition on theological grounds there was also fear that the Oratorians would cause a diminution of collections, dislike of convert clergymen teaching them what to do, and anxiety lest Faber should provoke a Protestant reaction. "We are hearing on all sides about ourselves," Faber wrote in October,

and the hatred against us. There is not a day passes but it comes to us, both in the confessional and out of it. When I say in the confessional I mean, not in confession, but persons coming to say they can come here no more, because Revd Mr So and So says he won't visit them when dying if they do, and such like things. I have been quite surprised with some recent indications of bitterness. One person has been talking against me for preaching "*heresy*", because he says "I said that a man in a state of lukewarmness was (omitting 'in a certain respect') more hateful to God than one in mortal sin". At last he mentioned it to Monsignor [Wiseman], who put him down, and said, "It is you who have misunderstood it," and then reminded him of the text in the Apocalypse . . . I could mention some things on the part of *good* people almost incredibly ungenerous: one priest, e.g. said the suspicions against us were cruel and unjust, but recommended another priest to avoid us lest he should narrow his sphere of personal influence by being supposed to be our friend . . . It shows two things—(1) that we must be wary and trust nobody, and (2) that we must not think of any place which will loosen our connection with you, but hold all together. I don't see how they can harm us, if we are all one. Certainly our confessionals have been affected by it lately, but we shall live that down; and we are striking out roots every day.[34]

A month later he wrote that Wiseman had confided in him.

It is hopeless to try any more to get ourselves recognised by the secular clergy. He said, "Father Faber, you don't know the narrowness, spite and jealousy there is, etc.": he says the younger clergy are making a movement against the old coves, and he will spur them on; but he has no power in the matter.[35]

Not long afterwards, however, he wrote to Morris:

We are in the full swing of work! lawyers, medical students, etc., pouring pell-mell into the Church. I have received twelve

quite lately; but we keep them snug. I am worked off my legs
... The success of the Oratory has certainly been most marvellous.[36]

The Oratory could not have succeeded without Wiseman.
When the attacks were at their height Wiseman announced that
he was coming to the Oratory and would preach after Vespers.
The Fathers were fearful that he would take the opportunity of
reprimanding them for being too bold. The presence of a considerable number of clergy made the possible humiliation worse.
Newman had been talking of the London house taking in their
sails and going down to the cabin. But, Faber reported,

> the bishop was extremely eloquent, and gave us his imprimatur
> in the most unqualified terms. He thanked God that "here you
> are taught night after night sweet and tender devotion to
> Mary"—"from hence you go forth as apostles of love each of
> you into the dismal city"—"before this perhaps you thought
> her a saint, here you have been taught to love her as a mother,"
> "here I know you have been taught again and again not to be
> suppliants only but fond children of Mary". . . . The chapel
> was densely crammed two hours before the service; we thought
> the bishop would never have reached the altar . . . Really, what
> blessings heaped on blessings we have had since last Purifica-
> tion year: yes—this afternoon last year when I ran out of the
> gate at St Wilfrid's to meet you as you came along the lane.[37]

But with the success came fresh difficulties. "The poor",
Faber had written,

> seem turning out all those *honestioris et nobilioris conditionis*; I
> suppose the propinquity of stink and dirt does it, even though
> reserved seats may be had. I regret this, because I am sure a
> great part of our mission ought to be the higher classes; and
> yet the poor turn them out even from the afternoon lectures
> which are specially directed to the educated.[38]

These were the days of the potato famine in Ireland. Starving
Irishmen were pouring into the country and where they did not
lapse into indifference or Protestantism they overwhelmed the
few English priests available. Apart from the specific instruction

of the Pope mentioned by Faber that the work of the Oratory should be directed to the upper classes there was a great loss of income with the chapel "equally crammed". And yet the Fathers could not possibly in any way discourage Christ's poor.

But the poor, particularly the Irish poor, caused great discomfort. Faber writes of getting up in the night because of the fleas, and later:

> The house is dreadful: the paint has driven the fleas out of the chapel, and so they have come into the house. Br. Chad catches them by *handfulls*. F. Alban has just been to tell me that B. Chad has had a haul of *thirty* at a go.[39]

"The heat and crowd of our chapel", he was writing in August,

> cause fits nearly every night: Miss Gladstone [Gladstone's sister] has left us saying she can't stand it . . . The offertory has sunk to between £5 and £5 10s od. The Irish are swamping us; they are rude and unruly and after many complaints the Catholic tradesmen are leaving us . . . I have invented a ticket system: F. Richard is strong for the Italian freedom. I maintain that people of a certain class in England are made physically ill by contact with stench and filth: old Ward even is made ill in our chapel. F. Bernard says that the English love of cleanliness is only part of our pride and national exclusiveness, and he talks at a great pace. At the same time he is bored by not having decent auditors for his discourses . . . At present there are, what F. Bernard happily names, immovable *belts* of stink in the chapel, and no wonder people faint and go off in epileptic fits.[40]

"We are so plentiful in bugs", he wrote next day,

> that they walk about our surplices and take possession of gentlemen's hats.[41]

By the Assumption it had become clear that the lack of ventilation was a danger on account of cholera and the chapel was soon afterwards closed for alterations. At the same time a system of tickets was introduced which was to operate from the time of reopening. The tickets were, of course, issued free.

The Fathers had now been in London four months and the

chapel had been open only three months. Yet such had been the avalanche of work and the bad conditions that by this time there was much illness. All the Fathers were strained and overtired. Father Bowden showed signs of consumption and had to leave temporarily. Although it was not yet suspected Wells was also consumptive. Faber himself, fat, white in the face, harassed and irritable, still a tornado of energy, suffered from terrible headaches. The doctors could do nothing with him. No remedy did him any good, perhaps because he was already suffering from Bright's disease, incurable then as now. He went with Hutchison and Wells for a fortnight to Belgium to recuperate.

When he got back the work was behindhand and the chapel could not be reopened immediately. There was still trouble from dirt although the chapel had been closed.

> The frontals of the altars it appears are filled with bugs, and the room in which they were put is swarming with them; and alas! so is the sacristy linen. We are going to consult a chemist today; and four women are already in the house brownsoaping the fleas. It is really quite Italian in the number of black-hopping fleas.[42]

The heat and the influx of destitute Irish had caused numerous outbreaks of cholera. The Fathers received an urgent summons to go to stricken Irish hop-pickers in the parish of Henry Wilberforce (the philanthropist's son) at East Farleigh, Kent. Two of the Fathers went immediately and others followed later. Faber wrote that they had anointed forty-six. Thirty-four in the end died. Newman and St John were also at work at the same time at Bilston where cholera had broken out.

With the reopening of the chapel, better ventilated now and decorated "quite exquisitely", the Fathers began to publish small books containing prayers and hymns appropriate to the various seasons. These little books played a large part in propagating the Oratory devotions. Faber was a great believer in these popular evening services. He is even said to have maintained that Vespers and the High Mass could go but that the night services should be maintained. He was busy writing hymns at odd free moments.

An edition of forty-three hymns was published with the title *Jesus and Mary* during 1849. Many of the hymns were intended to be read rather than sung as he was often at pains to make clear. He projected a life of St Philip in verse which was never published. He had no very high views of his hymns and admitted that many were slipshod. But he enjoyed writing them and especially enjoyed the excitement of hearing them sung for the first time. Wells, as Prefect of music, and William Pitts, as organist, concocted tunes to suit Faber's words. They were not always successful. A story is told of a novice who gave out the hymn at one of the night services. After two verses he was seen to bolt from the chapel. "I thought they had all gone mad," he explained,

> then it occurred to me that they couldn't all go mad together, so it must be me.[43]

"I wish you could have seen Ward" [whose great delight was opera], Faber wrote to Newman,

> over the Gazziniga hymn; he fell back in his chair, covered his face with his hands—"Awful, you'll excuse me, Faber,— positively shocking." It has nearly made an atheist of him again.[44]

The next years were passed in many trials and difficulties. Illness dogged the little community in their unhealthy house. John Bowden was continually away. There were recurrent money difficulties owing to the very high rent. But little by little the Oratory became part of the established landscape of London. Somehow there was always just enough money to scrape through and when there was not some friend, such as W. G. Ward, came to the rescue. It was a time of great activity. Faber at this time is described as

> working like a steam engine more than a man. Whether he is well or not I don't know, I hope he is, but his work is something prodigious. He has got up twenty-six sermons for Lent, is now giving a Retreat, is getting up sermons against Transcendentalism, has written devotions for Jesus risen, is to give the Tre Ore, and has poured out verses on Santo Padre by the mile.[45]

In the Lent of 1850 he gave a retreat for what he was to call his "Belgravians", Catholics living in the world who wished to lead more spiritual lives. Three hundred people attended and there was a string of carriages down the street. The keynote was that the spiritual life could not be regarded as primarily for religious— it was for all men, even the moderately good. The day after the retreat the Quarant' Ore took place. The chapel was magnificently decked out and Faber claimed that there were four hundred candles. Lord Arundel was so alarmed that he brought down a portable fire engine which was kept charged in the Sanctuary.

In May and June Newman delivered his lectures on Anglican difficulties in the chapel from which the Blessed Sacrament had been removed. A distinguished audience attended which included many Anglican clergy, Thackeray and Charlotte Brontë. Newman arrived from Birmingham every week, delivered the lectures on two consecutive days and then returned. Wiseman was present at the opening lecture, and is described as swaying to and fro in his chair beaming hugely. He was dressed in a cope. Unlike the previous lectures in London which had been such a painful failure these were a great success and had far-reaching effects. Faber at this time preached three sermons on St Philip which were later published as the *Spirit and genius of St Philip*. Dalgairns also gave a series of discourses on the Sacred Heart which afterwards became the well-known book. In July 1850 the Confraternity of the Precious Blood was formally erected and played an important part in the Exercises of the Oratory.

By the end of 1849 Faber had been thinking of a country cottage for the Fathers where they could recuperate from their gruelling London existence. After a drive to Clapham he wrote to Newman:

> I am determined now never to be happy till somebody gives us a cottage on Clapham Common, or Lavendar Hill, or at Wandsworth, where a bus would let us down. An old man and woman to live in the house—and a rum little garden at the back, with arbours of shells, like yours, and an old figurehead of a ship—and a distant view of the water and gasworks at Vauxhall and the flat over which the Portsmouth railroad passes.

I have now got a real earthly wish, and life will be imperfect till it is realised. I saw several such cottages, with magnolias trained round the windows—white dimity blinds and such a sweet-tast[ing] wind.[46]

The wish came true in the Summer of 1850 when W. G. Ward made over a small house at Lancing for the use of the Fathers. Lancing was then a small place and the inhabitants were amazed by the Fathers' "long clothes". The position in London was also eased by the acquisition of another house in King William Street.

The Oratory was, of course, in the thick of it at the time of "the Papal Aggression". Wiseman had been called to Rome as he thought to become a Cardinal in curia. Actually when he arrived he discovered that he was to return as Cardinal Archbishop of Westminster at the head of a restored hierarchy. His flamboyant nature responded to the situation by issuing his famous bombastic "pastoral from out the Flaminian Gate". It caused a storm of anger in England. Protestants thought confusedly that the country had overnight become a papal fief. The old, long dormant anti-Catholicism was fanned to a blaze. There were serious fears of a recurrence of the Gordon riots especially as the indignation grew to a crescendo by Guy Fawkes day. *Punch* fastened on the Oratorians as particularly odious intruders into Protestant England. There was a cartoon of John Bowden being mistaken by a maid of all work for a bogey. Fun was made of Faber through his life of St Rose of Lima and Thackeray wrote an article called "A dream of Whitefriars". Dicky Doyle who was a Catholic and who had designed the famous cover of *Punch* resigned in protest. A man actually broke into the Oratory looking for the Cardinal.

The Vicar General, who was in charge till Wiseman returned, called on Faber on 4th November. He told him that an attack was likely on St George's Cathedral and the Oratory on the 5th. Faber refused to shut the chapel unless expressly ordered to do so by the Vicar General or by the police. He promised, however, to see that the Blessed Sacrament was removed after the last Mass. He had already written to Scotland Yard. "St George's", he told Newman, is barricaded which is like tempting the mob *m[e] j[udice]*. The streets are filled with placards—"Englishmen! will you be governed by Cardinal Wiseman or by Queen Victoria? Rise, Englishmen, your liberties, etc., etc."

Faber was really enjoying himself. "Several of the old priests", he wrote contemptuously,

> are getting cowed which is a bore. Tonight (Monday) we have been pestered by a parcel of low blackguards warning people not to enter the chapel; and all day it has been absurd to see how people have stopped and looked up at the house: that may be partly owing to the Oratorian picture in *Punch*, and that fearful article of Thackeray's . . . Our police are here but as yet nothing but Guys and hootings and crowds—no glass smashed. No-one has left the house of course . . . P.S. I now find myself with a detachment of police under me, some in plain clothes and some in uniform, with orders from the superintendent to carry out Mr Faber's intentions!![47]

On 6th November he wrote:

> We are all safe and sound, having only been carried (in effigie) as Guys and duly burned—crackers thrown on the roof of the chapel and the like. We gave our policemen supper, Brother Ignatius acting host . . . Merivale called yesterday, and Drury the Harrow Master, after *years* of estrangement: they were excited and in *fear*.[48]

On the 10th, he reported:

> The excitement increases here, and is laying hold of the lower orders . . . Things seem pointing more at us:—"Beware of the Oratorians" "Down with the Oratorians, Banishment to the Oratorians, Don't go to the Oratory"—are now all over the town. In Leicester Square is a gigantic placard, "No Popery, Down with the Oratorians, No religion at all,"[49]

which he described to Watts Russell as being of "singular truthfulness". "We are cursed in the streets," he told Russell,

> even *gentlemen* shout from their carriage windows at us . . . There is talk of our prelates changing their mode of life, assum-

ing more dignity, etc., etc. Alas! if God does not stop this, and I only hear of it among laymen, *conclamatum est*. Of late in praying for the Cardinal I have felt strongly drawn to pray that he may have a great share of the spirit of mortification. That is what we need . . . [50]

With Wiseman's fine "Appeal to the English people" which was published in extenso by *The Times*, to the paper's great credit, the disturbances died away.

The Papal aggression, as it came to be called, probably did more good than harm to the Church. Many educated people were ashamed of what had happened and they examined the Church with new interest. The Gorham affair† also caused the secession of many Anglicans, including two of the Wilberforce brothers and Archdeacon Manning. Manning, whose name has been systematically blackened, was to carry on Wiseman's work of raising the status and spirituality of the secular clergy. Two months after his reception into the Church he was ordained by Wiseman. "He is here several hours daily," Faber told Newman in May 1851,

> I am teaching him how to say Mass. He and Lord Dunraven dined here yesterday. We are all quite in love with Manning and he has made himself quite *di casa* with us.[51]

Meantime the Fathers and Hutchison in particular had turned their attention to the poor. They had felt deep qualms at having to resort to a system of tickets in the church. A day school for about two hundred poor boys, in imitation of the Protestant Ragged Schools, was therefore opened. The success was so great that soon over a thousand children were at the school in Dunn's passage, Holborn. One scheme led to another and Hutchison threw himself so unsparingly into the work that his health gave way. But before this had happened he established St Patrick's

---

† The Rev. C. G. Gorham was presented in 1847 to the living of Brampton Speke but the Bishop of Exeter refused to institute him on the grounds of heterodoxy. Gorham appealed to the Privy Council, who declared his views were not contrary to the doctrine of the Church of England and he was eventually instituted by the Archbishop of Canterbury.

Confraternity for the poor living in Wild's Court. The services consisted of spiritual readings of the simplest kind and the recitation of the Rosary.

The Oratory was now established in London without fear of failure. The next years were to consolidate its position.

CHAPTER XII

SUPERIOR

FABER'S ascendancy among the Fathers in London was great but not unquestioned. At the end of 1849 Hutchison told Faber things were going wrong:

that my headaches were not as bad as I made them out to be—that as my brother [Frank] was hypochondriacal so probably was I—that I ought to bear up better, not to go to bed—but do my work in spite of it—that I had things sent up to my room when I was ill and did not eat them when they were cooked—that the Fathers had not been sufficiently consulted about printing our little books . . . and a great deal more to the same effect, all displaying an utter want of confidence in me as superior . . . It has left me quite miserable. I confess my own impression is that it is most unfair and unkind—that I am always forecasting to make them all comfortable—that as to any cordial or real subordination to me they have never shown any—that I suffer more than they are aware of, work many days with headaches, hate lying in bed, often feel hurt at the total neglect and want of sympathy I meet with, that it is perfectly true I often ask for some dinner and when it comes it turns me sick and I can't eat it, yet it is not thereby wasted, that as to money I often hardly know what to do for want of it: I wore my nightshirts till they were rags, at last I told Br. Chad to get me four calico ones, he did and brought me the bill; I told him I could not pay it and he must take it F. Francis or F. Antony; so with my shoes, I gave the bill to F. Antony, and said I had no money to pay it. He once promised me some money, and gave me £10 at Easter, of which he took £5 back at Birmingham, and the rest was spent on my journey . . . Mrs Bowden gave me £5, part of which I spent in going to Frank in the Summer, in cabs, and steamers down the river, lucifers, spirits of camphor, and some razors and shaving soap. F. Antony gave me another £10 some months ago; and I have paid a bill of Keats the tailor at Cheadle, and my journey to Bath, and have some left. He has forgotten what he said about a regular allowance and talks now of making one to Philip; but he makes so many grand presents to the chapel, frontals, etc. that I don't suppose he has much ready money. This is my financial case, and as I have given my books to the house, which was all I could raise money upon, they must either give them back or clothe me. As to the little books they were consulted . . .

I have thought of nothing else, all day and *all night nearly*. I hope I want to see as much truth in what he said as I can, and to forget what I wanted (but now cannot) say to him, that he is so overbearing and fond of having things his own way that he throws a gloom over me by his temper when I thwart him . . . I distrust everyone; they distrust me; they, as I know, talk of me and criticize me behind my back. What can I do? Could nobody else take my place? . . . I shall be perfectly wretched the next headache I have, I shall hardly dare to send to F. A(ntony) to ask for my meals upstairs; and now that he has mentioned this suspicion about money [that Faber spent money for the community on himself] which cuts me to the quick I don't know what I shall do . . . My pride has several times been sorely put to it to go and ask F. Antony for things: I was obliged to ask for a bottle of ether the other day and he reminded me he had paid 5d for a bottle of something when we first came to town . . . If it be *possible*, my dearest Padre, I wish you would release me from my office here. I confess myself to be quite disheartened; it is now four years and I have had no rest, and I am ill and cowed. I am sure if it were not for my intense love of you I don't know what I should do.[1]

But Dalgairns, who had read the letter, wrote to Newman two days later:

I think the Rector [Faber] exaggerates very much the want of confidence in him. Father Antony and F. Francis both think him autocratical and expensive in money matters; but they have full confidence in him in other respects. In fact they know perfectly well that take him all in all they cannot possibly do without him. They know quite well that without his energy and strength of character the London Oratory would go to ruin. When they heard today of his letter to you, their only fear was lest you should accept his resignation.[2]

The trouble, as Dalgairns saw, was partly Faber's natural love of exaggeration. He was also thoroughly unwell and could not see things in perspective. Money worries harassed him all the time. The other Fathers were overworked, too. But there was a deeper *malaise*. The machinery of government within the Oratory could not function properly. Though Faber was Rector he referred everything to Newman in far-away Birmingham. Newman had made it plain that he need only do so in external matters but there were many internal affairs which Faber thought it right he should know. The internal affairs of the London house were discussed at what Faber called "informal palavers in my room" for, as it happened, the deputies (the four priests deputed to help the superior) appointed in February 1848, were divided between London and Birmingham. The result was that the London house in practice fell absolutely under Faber's control.

The formal division of the two houses which was bound to happen (and everybody agreed was bound to happen) was hastened by a complicated series of incidents. The knotty problems connected with the disposal of St Wilfrid's caused the first rift. Newman's proposal for an Oratory school at St Wilfrid's was not welcomed in London. Newman asked for views and the London Fathers answered with unthinking frankness. Dalgairns wrote:

I loathe literature ... In a word my intellect has disappeared. Now F. Superior's view of the Oratory seems to be much more intellectual than mine.[3]

The London Fathers considered intellectual work and especially education would make the Oratory diverge from the rule of St Philip and make it resemble the very different French Oratory (Oratoire de Jésus et Marie) founded by Cardinal Bérulle. Newman's conception of the Oratory had arisen before and caused bad feeling at the time of the division. Faber had vainly tried to persuade him to come to London. But Newman had made it plain then that it was his wish to remain in obscurity so that he could have leisure to study and write. None of the London

Fathers understood how strongly he felt about the school. He reacted with considerable heat to the letters and in his bitterness brought up the question of his jurisdiction which the London Fathers were very far from questioning.

"It is not quite pleasant", he wrote to Faber,

> to find a *name* given, "French," to a certain view or supposed view. I fear a course like this:—viz. first an agitation among you to be a separate O., originating in the same *impatience* which first refused to be quiet at Maryvale and St W.'s and next wishes simply to ignore St W.'s, then a feeling that the F. Superior of the London house must be wholly London's, and under no external influence; else he is no real "Superior:" he is but half a "Father;" a family is one and complete, it shuts doors and windows, it enjoys the *notos vultus et id genus omne*. And then, bolder grown Our Brummagen cousins take a *French* view of the O.—let us have no order or regularity, it is French; no pre-paration for sermons, it is French; no care for what friends or enemies think of us, it is French—no guard lest our words or deeds give scandal, it is French—slowness is French, go it if you would not be French; disgust the lay brothers as you fear to be French, for we all know what came of the French O. *not that* we anticipate the like of the Birmingham.[4]

Newman meant that the French Oratory had been tainted with Jansenism.

Faber was stunned by the unexpectedness of the onslaught and the bringing up of so many matters about which Newman had written critically but which had long been settled. He wrote a pained reply pleading that he had been misunderstood. Newman answered, as was his way:

> You know well enough I don't dream of *your* wishing inde-pendence, but I am not so certain of others. [He was thinking in particular of Knox.] There will be a strong *prima facie* case for it from the extreme inconvenience of the present half arrangement . . . For your comfort I can't help wishing you a real Superior that you might exercise a full authority.[5]

But Faber did not now take the matter very seriously:

> We could no more stand without you than we could fly.[6]

He did not see the depth of the hurt in Newman's heart. The very obscurity Newman had sought in Birmingham had become a difficulty. The Oratory, as Faber rather tactlessly pointed out, was in men's minds the *London* Oratory. Newman was held responsible for what he (Faber) did. Therefore, he argued, Newman should remain in a position of authority. But this was not how it looked from Birmingham. The Birmingham Fathers felt that they had been left on the shelf. The London Fathers on the other hand felt that their own methods were successful and that Birmingham's were not, all of which created an uneasy situation. Stanton's legalistic mind was another factor. He wanted things *en règle*. Regulation was needed, everybody admitted, but when and how without a quarrel?

Newman's plan for a rotation of Fathers from the two houses to look after St Wilfrid's caused disagreement. The London house felt itself too weak and poor to support the scheme. Newman with some justification considered it was backing out of an obligation. But Newman's painful feelings exceeded the provocation and he made of what was only a difference of opinion a breach of friendship. "It is a thing done and cannot be undone ..." He was especially annoyed at the plea of poverty. They should have asked money from Ward for travelling expenses instead of taking the Lancing cottage "merely for the convenience (something certainly) of being able to run up and down for a day". When he had come to London he had been shocked to find that Faber was proposing to go to Lancing for three weeks. The implication, of course, was that if he could go to Lancing for three weeks he could well go to St Wilfrid's.

> I *can't* make you all wish to keep up intimacy with us all if you won't so I must give this up. In saying this I know quite well that you love *me*. I know quite well that some of you love some of us; but I know too that the continuance of that love depends on intercourse which you are now breaking off.[7]

Then there was a correspondence between Faber and Newman over the relative costs of the two houses. When Newman showed that he fed his house far more cheaply than the London house,

Faber replied that he could not think how he did it. Newman took this as an implication that he starved his subjects and Faber had some difficulty in assuring him that he had meant nothing of the kind.

But though there was a tendency, at once emotional and logical, not to say inevitable, to separation the idea was resisted as long as possible. Faber was strongly opposed to it and was probably the most opposed to it in the London house. He was a dominating character but Newman's presence in the background (as Newman himself pointed out) was a help to him. He was not a man to hanker after the show if he had the reality of power. It is doubtful if he wanted power at all. Moreover his veneration for Newman was far too strong for him to think of any real separation without pain. It is the theme of all his letters. "I don't think", he wrote in June 1849,

> that any practical inconvenience can arise to people here from my subordinate superiorship.[8]

In September he wrote:

> For us to be separated is *impossible* at present; I could not go on if it was so.[9]

Even Stanton never proposed a complete separation. He envisaged a Superior in London who would automatically be superseded when Newman came to the house. Newman might petition Rome to be made Superior of all houses for life as founder of the Oratory in England. While Newman was in Birmingham, London would operate as a normal Oratory with deputies under the Superior. It was, however, one thing to be under Newman, quite another to be under the Birmingham deputies. When Newman talked of setting up the Birmingham house on a legal footing both Stanton and Faber saw the danger. "If absence and distance", Faber wrote,

> cause passing fits of jealousy and captiousness about you whom we all so really love and can have no difficulty in bowing to, whatever would it be with old Joe legislating for us with his dietic finger? Or F. William objecting as *praefectus aedifiorum*

Father Faber about 1860

Newman about 1865

Both from an album at the London Oratory

Father Faber about 1860

From a pastel portrait

to our new ventilation or the flushing of our sewers ... and with what kind of open arms should we welcome F. Bowles arriving with plenipotentiary powers to visit us?

He summed up his view in these words:

You must hit off some way of making this house independent of your deputati, yet not independent of you.[10]

The letters went backwards and forwards between London and Birmingham. Dr Grant, Bishop of Southwark and Faber's old friend in Rome of Anglican days, had a finger in the pie. He offended Newman by saying that Newman interfered with the London house. Newman later took this to have been at Faber's behest but there is no evidence that Faber wanted the separation. The evidence is that he did not want it. Half measures were taken but were not enough. Newman became convinced that separation was an inevitable necessity while Faber fought every inch of the way to prevent it. But in the end the separation took place, hastened by the fear of Wiseman's departure to Rome. On 9th October 1850 Newman and the Fathers at Birmingham, "with much regret and sorrowing hearts" released the Fathers in London from their obedience and deputed them to elect a separate Congregation. In order to retain as far as possible their hold on Newman the London Fathers drew up a bye-law. The bye-law, as drafted, gave Newman sweeping powers, almost as great as he had enjoyed before. But Newman amended it to three clauses— that he should have the right to advise; the right to propose through the Superior matters to be voted on by the General Congregation of all the Fathers; and that a minority of two in the Deputy Congregation should have the right to refer to him. The bye-law was to remain in force for three years only and was to be cancelled in the event of his ceasing to be Superior at Birmingham.

On paper it was satisfactory enough. But Newman seems to have felt a certain bitterness caused by the interminable difficulties over St Wilfrid's. Dalgairns wrote to him:

I do feel that you are angry with us, and I think all of us feel it ... You cannot tell what a damper it would be to me individually in all my exertions if I thought that we were set up as a house with your displeasure upon us ... You seem to wish to mark your last acts, as our superior, with coldness and displeasure as if disgust with us was your reason for separating us from you ...[11]

"I cannot deny", Newman answered reproachfully,

there has been in the London House's treatment of St Wilfrid's what has pained me ... To all this is added a still deeper sorrow arising from the frustration of all my wishes for some sort of moral union between the houses. But I trust Santo Padre will guide it all to good; may he ever bless you with his most tender affection.[12]

On St Wilfrid's day, 11th October 1850, Faber was elected Superior. "When you come back", he wrote to Lord Arundel and Surrey,

you shan't know me again. I will be so grave and recollected and mortified and queer and holy.[13]

Newman jocularly addressed him in a congratulatory letter as "your very reverence". But the letters still went to and fro with very little difference in tone. In December Newman was warning Faber against being satirical and in May was once again giving cautious warnings to Faber, Stanton and Dalgairns.

All your papers mark the difference between your house and ours ... You bring out programmes of lectures and services, systems of preaching and celebrating you post up over your recreation fireplace. You print copies of works by the 1000, you revolutionize chapels, sacristies and refectories as by a magician's wand, and a choir, nay a double choir starts up, like Cadmus's men, only more harmoniously from as scanty and unlikely a sowing.

Hence, when you would have an Orat. Parvum [the little Oratory in which spiritual exercises for laymen take place] you ignore it except in its integrity—you will not let it be born and grow as human beings are—but it comes forth, or ought to do so, like the goddess of Wisdom from the brow of Jove *totis numeris*.[14]

Was there just a hint of envy mixed with the criticism?

Gradually the Oratory in London was accepted even by the old Catholics. Little by little opposition died away. Wiseman preached on St Philip's day 1851, and according to Faber "when in full tog he looked like some Japanese God". He said the Oratory represented the modern church and that St Philip was the type of modern times and modern charity.

> No carved pinnacles should intercept our view of Philip's love, Jesus in the Eucharist—no longer could we pray in dark corners of Churches intercepted with pillars. We in England have been in chaos, now that we are emerging we must look at Rome and Italy and see what the Bridegroom has been whispering to the Bride these 300 years.[15]

From this time onwards Catholics began to understand that the Oratory stood for the new life of the Church and was not an eccentricity. Its prayers and devotions were gradually copied. Within a couple of decades the new ways had all but swept the old Catholicism out of the Church.

Faber continued to feel ill throughout the year and on 14th October he wrote to Newman:

> Our unhappy house is in no slight confusion. Mr Tegart [the doctor] is apprehensive about the state of my brain from long excitement and overwork and insists on my leaving the Congregation for not less than six months, or he won't answer for it ... That I am and for three months have been more than usually out of sorts, I acknowledge; but I cannot think my nervous system so deranged as Mr Tegart says, and I always recover quickly.[16]

He was, however, forced to obey and set out for the Holy Land with Father George Ballard on 17th October. Stanton fell ill at the same time and had to go abroad too. "St Philip knows what he is at," Newman commented,

> but it is very mysterious that both your house and we should have so many invalids.[17]

At Marseilles Faber reported that he was no better, feeling slightly drunk and wanting to be back. At Malta he fell ill again

and gave up the journey to Palestine. But he told Newman,
"I was never so thoroughly a fish out of water", and gave him
an outline plan of travels to Catania, Syracuse, Messina, Palermo
and Rome to look at various Oratories. His letters home were
full of entertainment. He said Mass at the Oratory on the island.

> After this we went into choir to sing Terce. What a trial it was!
> The Preposito walked up and down the choir, behind the
> curtains and altar, occasionally treating us to a verse, and oc-
> casionally blowing a boy up in Maltese ... A certain Canon
> Psaila has written an answer to my Uncle's *Difficulties of Roman-
> ism* in 780 pages; a copy is coming to me to read! I am said to
> have written *The Difficulties* in old times, and priests cry over
> me, and say *Che grazia*! At first I denied it, but found I was not
> believed; and on Monday the two antagonists Canon Psaila,
> and *Dr* Faber are to meet. *Il Canonico è molto consolato* especially as
> he says the *mala fede del Faber* about the early Fathers was dread-
> ful! I shall have it all to explain, and then he will be so *scon-
> solato*.[18]

With his usual extraordinary resilience he was soon travelling
about perfectly well, eating "ferociously", feeling as if he had
never been ill, and pining for home. At Palermo he called on the
Shrewsburys and had a warm welcome. All bitterness was now
forgotten. It was their last meeting for "the good earl" died the
next year in Naples. In Rome he had an audience with Pius IX
with whom, as might be expected, he got on well. The Pope
asked what privileges he would like. "Nothing for myself, but
whatever your Holiness pleases to give my Congregation." He
then produced a petition for a daily plenary indulgence for the
Church of the Oratory.

Pius IX: "This must go to the Congregation of Rites."

Faber: "Ah, Holy Father, you can do it yourself if you
will."[19]

The Pope laughed and signed the paper. At the Chiesa Nuova
the shrine of St Philip was opened and lighted up for him. On
26th December he was in Turin and back in London on the 31st.
Instead of the six months ordered by the doctor he had been away
less than two and a half.

The Oratory in London had been left in charge of Dalgairns
and neither he nor Hutchison approved of Faber's quick return.
Dalgairns had confided in Newman that Faber ruled the London
house so completely, "at all events as far as opinion goes", that
no one dared tell him his faults. He was alarmed at the thought
of Faber returning in a worse condition and making life in the
house more difficult than before. Newman thought of sending
Faber to America. "If he comes back as ill as he went", Dalgairns
replied,

> he certainly is better away. He only remained in his room
> creating rows in the house and living apart from the community.
> At the same time no-one but you can do it. I cannot conceive
> what he will do when he comes home, in the first joy of getting
> back and finds out the present feeling of the house. He will go
> wild unless you come and help us. He will accuse us of con-
> spiring rebellion and treachery.[20]

Newman was under the mistaken impression that Hutchison
and Dalgairns wanted to depose Faber. He wrote in alarm that
this could never be and that Dalgairns exaggerated the situation.
Hutchison and Dalgairns as a matter of fact were not in agreement. Hutchison thought Faber acted without consulting others.
Dalgairns on the contrary thought he consulted others too much.
"The practical effect of it is that he consults us," he wrote,

> he is opposed, and then he chafes and is irritated. If you ask me
> what his faults are, I believe they lie far more in the *modus*
> than in the things done. He brooks no opposition. If there be
> any he goes from room to room painting the opponent's
> conduct in the most extravagant colours. He throws the most
> bitter contempt upon the slightest word expressing a difference
> of opinion. He governs the house by sarcasms and not by *dol-*
> *cezza*. If any evil exists, he thunders in the most eloquent man-
> ner against it and sets everybody in the house against the
> unhappy individual, who is the object of his censures. You
> may think this is a ludicrous grievance; but I can assure you that
> it has either irritated into secret opposition or broken in spirit
> everyone in the house ... A sermon more than usual will
> almost arouse a rebellion. I agree far more with F. Wilfrid if he

would but do things quietly; but as it is I dread his return, simply because I know it will cause a series of rows which will be quelled but will leave sores behind. Such has been our life hitherto; we have been kept together (1) by success (2) by F. Wilfrid's strong character (3) by a certain feeling of sticking to S. Philip.

As for myself I am broken in spirits ... I cannot be certain that anyone will not turn round upon me at any moment and be rude. I utterly disapprove of our blurting out to each other what we think. Merciless criticism and unsparing ridicule is what we meet with from each other's hands under pretence of English bluntness. But, above all, there is no peace in the house. Perpetual rows rise up. I say to myself "Peace, peace" and there is no peace. When I read the Lives of the Oratorian fathers, I see that peace, joy and mutual charity are their characteristics.[21]

In another letter he wrote:

There is certainly a deep feeling in the house that F. W.'s rule has become quite unendurable from his restlessness. This feeling was kept under by sheer funk of him but now rises to the surface. The house has been kept together for some time by its success externally, and by fear of F. W. St Philip's *carità* is not the link that binds us ... F. Wilfrid has always made me suffer intensely by his restlessness. There is no security against his stalking into one's room at any moment, and painting something that was going on either in or out of the house in such vivid and exciting colours that you were carried off your legs you know not where. Latterly he was so restless and excited in his way of talking that he quite frightened both F.A. and me.[22]

But Hutchison knew Faber far better, was deeply fond of him, and was moreover himself far less temperamental than Dalgairns. "I cannot conceive," he wrote,

how he will be able to settle down quietly in his smoky, dingy room after so lately tumbling in his yellow berline over the mountains in Sicily. If he comes back no better than he went he cannot be allowed to stop here and I should have thought that if he would undertake it, a tour in America would be just the thing for him . . . I am sure his present attack must have been a good deal brought on by the illregulated way in which he has been working and he wants to have his work and his time for work laid out for him by obedience if the thing can be done. For instance after a day spent in bed with one of his tremendous headaches he would perhaps find himself free from it at about five in the afternoon and then with his brain quite hot and excited he would set to and devour some book, generally some one of Chapman's infidel series [Faber maintained these books were much more interesting than Protestant works] and work away at this till two or three in the morning. Whenever he works he always seems to do it too hard and with too much eagerness. I see no cure for it but the being put on a system through obedience.

I have always thought and once ventured to say to him, though I had no business, that his health has also suffered from the way in which he takes his meals—such quantities sometimes and eaten in such haste and in such a huggermugger way in his own room—such frequent draughts of hot tea also must be prejudicial . . . This is what I have for some time felt and yet from affection to F. Wilfrid, which grows stronger as the time of his return grows nearer, I feel sorry to put forward such a proposal [resignation on grounds of ill health or put under some discipline] because though I only do it out of anxiety about his health yet I fear it would look to him like a mark of unkindness and want of confidence. He has been the *Preposito* of the London Congregation at the different Oratories he has lately seen and was presented as such to the Pope. He has been gathering together facts relating to his office and the government of the Congregation and is now I daresay returning with a number of different schemes and plans. I fear then that to ask him to resign his office would be a great shock to him and he would attribute the request to some very different motive than the right one. He would say, I fear, that everyone had deserted him, that he could trust no one, etc., etc . . .

As regards the views of the other Fathers—F. Rector [Dalgairns] is disinclined to give any opinion—his position is rather awkward as he would probably in case of any change be elected—he suggests waiting and taking no measures till the Father [Faber] actually breaks down again, but this seems rather unwise and unfair to F. Wilfrid—besides the House would go on rather uncomfortably meantime while we were in suspense as to whether he was going to break down or not. The others, I think, are somewhat inclined to the same view as myself. . . . In what I have said about F. Wilfrid's being recommended by you to resign I trust you will understand that I do not *wish* it—but the reverse.[23]

Newman was hearing the state of affairs from all sides and knew that Dalgairns was depressed and exaggerating. He pointed out to him that difference of opinion should not destroy brotherly love. But he went on:

Your complaint about the want of tenderness, gentleness, courtesy and sympathy in your congregation is, alas, most true, and I think most unphilippine. Had you not said it, I should not have ventured to have a clear opinion that it was, but directly you say it you collect together all the scattered surmises of my mind as in a focus, and throw from my own impressions a clear light upon your own testimony. Yet here again A[ntony] is very different from what he was, this is a matter of common remark. Again, I am sure Ph[ilip's] turn of mind is not such, but, whatever be his faults of character, he is gentle like yourself . . . It would seem then as if some overbearing influence, or bad habit, or youngness, or want of experience of trouble, has been here or there the cause of this . . . I will remind you that all *acclimation* is painful . . . No one but a Jesuit or Trappist knows what a J. or T. go through in becoming a J. or T. but the vow binds them and they must go thro' it. What do women go through in accommodating their lives to the will of a husband! When they have done it, it is their happiness . . .[24]

"You did not suppose", Dalgairns replied,

that I had any formal design of leaving St Philip. What I did conceive was that if this state of outward restlessness and interior suffering continued, it seemed in my present mood as though it would turn out to be unbearable . . . Would it not be well for you to say to F.A. what you have said to me about a "basis of carità", about rudeness to each other, etc.[25]

All unawares Faber returned. He found a letter from Newman awaiting him.

> I am going to write you a very ungracious letter, that is, to express my *sorrow* at your return. The truth is, I have been fuming ever since you went at the way you have been going on. I wrote to Malta to protest against your preaching—the letter missed you . . . then suddenly you were making for Rome which was *forbidden* you, and before a letter could hit you, you are against all medical orders, in England.[26]

Faber was contrite and "put out", he would leave the next day. But he pleaded:

> I am not well when I *halt* abroad for I fidget and mope, and I can't control it, try as I will . . . I can hardly ever say Mass; people are near, or they see my face, and I get flurried and break the rubrics, and I have left out Glorias even and Credos. New altars distract me and I am never very well when I haven't said Mass.[27]

Faber may have been more annoyed than he admitted at Newman's letter. He may even have thought of it as an illegitimate interference. Contrary to all expectation he really was better, even much better. Far from being a disturbing influence now he was back things seemed to go on more easily. Dalgairns himself wrote to say so.

It was, however, decided that he could not remain in King William Street. "Of all places London is a place to bring on again the excitement of his brain" . . . Newman wrote to Hutchison:

> You live on nothing but oxygen (moral not chemical) in King Wm. Street. There is no repose there, no quiet. Did things go on like the Solar system, silently and surely, it might be another matter . . . but the cares of such a house as yours will drive him out of his senses in no time. He is not a person to take things easy . . . If he is not well his subjects will annoy him and then it stands to reason he will annoy his subjects . . .[28]

A few days later Newman came to London to see how matters stood and Faber must have got wind of what had been going on in his absence. Eventually it was decided to lease a small country house.

"I have fixed", he wrote on 10th January 1852, "on Spring Rice's house at Hither Green near Lewisham."[29]

He was installed by the middle of the month. "Spring Rice's fat old housekeeper", Hutchison told Newman,

> is in the house and manages everything and does the cooking and does it *well*—she has a girl to help her I believe and Isaac Ratcliffe, [Brother] Wilfrid's brother, is there to wait on the Father, wait at dinner, etc. There is a nice garden and the country is very pleasant. The Father is all day out of doors, takes long walks, is in excellent spirits and seems in better health than I ever remember, but I suppose he always would be well if he lived in the country in a *civilised* house and with good food . . . He is certainly desirous of letting things go on much more quietly than heretofore, though to do so is so contrary to his nature and that of many of us that it will I am afraid be rather difficult . . . We shall be still exposed to the Father's old danger, that of deciding on things with too much precipitation. This has been the fault of *all* of us here and unless we are gradually getting wiser by experience I don't see the safeguard we have against it.
>
> I wrote to you before the Father returned, speaking of the possibility of it being necessary for him unless his health was better, to resign his office:—Happily he has returned much better than we expected and there seems to be no occasion for it. But besides this I confess that now he has returned and one sees him along side of the other Fathers it seems it would have been quite impracticable (unless he had indeed been deplorably out of health) he so completely in every sense outweighs the rest of us, he is like a first-rate line-of-battle ship sailing among a lot of frigates.
>
> F. Bernard has been rather unwell but is better now. The responsibility when he was Rector seems to have floored him a good deal, though it must have been the *dread* of what *might* happen in the way of rows either externally or internally rather than anything that actually *did* occur that must have alarmed him.[30]

Faber himself was extremely happy. Mrs Bowden had given the community a piece of land at Sydenham where it was pro-

posed to build a country retreat. Faber spent his time at Hither
Green scheming about the new house. In the meantime he relaxed
and enjoyed himself. "I am nearly blown away by the cold winds",
he told John Bowden (who was still in Malta on account of health
and behaving, Faber said, like a salamander),

> which send health and joy thro' every limb and fibre. I struggle
> across ploughed fields, and wade thro' the liquid mud of the
> lanes in my patent clumped shoes, to my heart's content. I
> eat like a wolf, I sleep like a top, I am in immense spirits, and
> how my digestion goes on I am unable to tell you, for I am
> never in any [way] reminded of the existence of a stomach,
> except when I stoop to tie my shoes, an operation which is
> daily becoming more difficult. O my dear John! this is the only
> pure air in the world, a dear, clear, cold whistling wind that
> blows one's hair about, flies one's hat over hedges, goes up the
> arms of one's coat, wars in the chimney and pipes thro' the
> keyhole! None of your nasty hot suns, withering siroccos,
> cloudless skies, for me. Yesterday I walked out without my hat
> in the rain; and it was delicious beyond expression. I can't
> conceive whatever induced me to enter into a town-living
> congregation. The feelings of the past week here recall the
> health and strength of young days, never felt since I have been
> a Catholic...[31]

But there was all the time serious work at Sydenham which
was after Faber's heart. Serious it was. Stanton was only just
recovering from his illness, John Bowden was still in Malta,
Wells was on his way to Madeira in a vain attempt to stave off
consumption, Dalgairns had had to have a holiday and Hutchison
was very far from well. The rows and troubles were largely due
to overwork, but the premises in King William Street were so
bad no one could stay there long without falling ill. A country
retreat was an urgent necessity. The foundations of St Mary's,
as the new house was to be called, were laid on 2nd February 1852.
There were the usual troubles with lawyers, builders and vendors
of the land. But Faber was constantly on the site, encouraging,
bullying and threatening. By the end of March it was completed
up to the first floor and by April the roof was nearing completion.

Sydenham was then in the country and the garden had to be made out of rough common. For the third time Faber set to with his usual drive laying out gravel walks, planting trees and making orchards. A cemetery was laid out. "You will long for your nine feet of it", he wrote, "when you see its pensive cypresses and its holy calm."[32]

He had a pond dug and the clay was burnt and used for paths. Ragged boys from the district collected stones from the fields and made the foundations of the walks. The house was formally opened on 10th August after an ordination in King William Street. Wiseman, Dr Grant, Ward and Lord Arundel and Surrey were present. After this Faber, who had left Hither Green for London in May, spent part of each week in Sydenham. The community now went backwards and forwards as a regular routine. It is noticeable that after the opening of St Mary's there was much less illness—especially among the younger Fathers.

The Oratory had now been in King William Street more than three years. Many proposals had been made for another site on which a basilica in the Italian style could be built. In March 1852 negotiations were in progress for the purchase of Argyll house, the property of Lord Aberdeen, near Oxford Circus. It was nearly bought and then the purchase fell through. At length in September 1852 a site at Brompton unexpectedly came up. The Fathers made an offer on their own initiative as Faber was in Ireland. Two days later it was accepted. Kensington was then a district of fields and gardens. Nightingales could still sometimes be heard in Brompton churchyard. Fruit trees overhung the road. There were milkmaids in their picturesque dresses, fruit vendors crying their wares, and flower carts filled with every sort of bloom. It remained almost a country place till the Exhibition of 1862. "The site . . .", Faber wrote to Newman,

> adjoins Iron's Church, is in the main street, and a few hundred yards from the street branching off to the Fulham road, Thurloe Square, just finished, is within a stone's throw, Belgravia is nearer than Warwick Street Chapel was to K. Wm. Street, and the trees of Kensington Gardens are seen from the back of

the house, I am told, and it is nearer to London than Bayswater with a better neighbourhood and growing. The land adjoining this is the land the crown has purchased for the National Gallery which will make it a great resort.[33]

After much discussion it was proposed to build the house first and to be content with a temporary chapel. Faber of course had lavish schemes which had to be toned down. By February 1853 the site had been cleared. A strip of land in front of the property (where the road now runs) had to be sold to the Royal Commissioners in order to prevent encroachments. Then there was a fear that a row of houses would be put up on it in front of the house. Troubles of one kind or another, indeed, went on for the next ten years. The authorities of Brompton Parish church did everything they could to prevent the Oratory being built. The government was petitioned on the ground that a Roman Catholic establishment would ruin the district. Then an old act of parliament was said to forbid a dissenting chapel being built within three hundred yards of a Church of the Establishment. "*Punch* deprecates any attempt to prevent fair competition", was Mr Punch's liberal comment. As late as 1860 there was talk of forcing the Fathers to sell out by Act of Parliament to make way for the 1862 Exhibition buildings.

"The queen and the prince are bent on ousting us,"[34] Faber wrote in despair. But in the end, one way and another, the opposition faded and the Oratory at Brompton came into being. Building began in March 1853 on the house, library and temporary church. In a year they were ready for the Fathers.

In the meantime arrangements were made for the closing at King William Street, the "Great Shutting" as it was called. The lease of the main premises was taken off the Fathers' hands from Michaelmas and the first ceremonies took place on Sunday 11th September. High Mass was sung by Dr Wareing. "Crying and sobbing was awful ..." Faber told Lord Arundel and Surrey: "The old Padre came up to our close and cried away famously."[35] In the evening the usual meeting of the Confraternity of the

Precious Blood was held and Faber preached. "Four years ago",
he said,

> we came here as strangers and converts, with a new and untried
> institute bringing apparent novelties and foreign ways ... A
> chapter is closed; a day will come when we shall be in heaven,
> tranquil and safe for ever. The work begun in the Oratory
> will have ended in that—we shall be near St Philip and can
> tell him so. We shall have a vision of the earth, of the great city
> passed away like a blot effaced, and amid the beautiful fires of
> the Beatific Vision, and the songs of the angels and the soft
> flashings of the light of glory, and the magnificence of Jesus and
> the queenly splendours of Mary we shall see the old chapel, with
> the echo of its long silenced hymns, and the poor ornaments
> of its well-remembered festivals—St Philip by the altarside
> busy with his Mother, and our Lord dwelling there, like the
> Ark of God, for four years—nay even the worn benches and
> the dingy stains upon the walls which are tokens and witnesses
> of the presence and freedom of the poor. It will not mar the
> vision; it will be full of God, of Jesus, of Mary ...

"We remember reading", *The Tablet* commented,

> of one of the Norman princes, who, in a storm at sea, said he
> was not afraid, for he knew the monks in some monastery
> he had founded were at that hour saying the divine office.
> Something of this feeling connected itself with the Oratory
> in the midst of the tumultous sea of London streets.[36]

> Once the chapel was closed there was a mass of practical details
to be seen to.
"The neighbours", Hutchison told Lord Arundel,

> are amazed at the quantity of property we have sent off, the
> quality was not so striking. One whole van was filled to over-
> flowing with "fine old brown windsor chairs". It was a perfect
> Alp of chairs. The Two Thieves also attracted a good deal of
> notice.[37]

A friend and parishioner told Faber that all the hassocks should
be burnt as they were full of fleas. Faber was nettled. He replied
that the chapel was perfectly clean and that there was not a single

flea in the place. When the move was completed, however, he
wrote:

> Though I must apologize for contradicting you the other day
> I still maintain my opinion. We were both right however;
> there was not a single flea in the chapel; they were all married,
> with large families.[38]

Fathers Gordon and Balston were able to camp in the Brompton house on 27th February 1854 for the first time. Faber followed
the next day and Mass was said in his sitting room on 1st March.
There were still 240 workmen on the site, according to Faber,
straining to get the work finished for the opening of the church.
The house outwardly was much as it is today but the temporary
church was inconceivably different. It was a long low building of
yellow brick, 181 feet long by 40 wide and only 27 high. Faber
described it as "a tunnel". *The Tablet* wrote that it was like

> one aisle of a huge railway station, and the extreme lowness of
> the building makes it very ugly indeed. This, however, was
> not a matter of choice but depended upon the provisions of
> the Metropolitan Building Act ... The open wooden roof is
> left in the church and is coloured chocolate and blue. The sanc-
> tuary is thirty feet deep and forty wide, and there is one side
> altar just below the sanctuary steps for receiving the Blessed
> Sacrament during great functions when it is not right that it
> should be at the high altar. Then come two recesses the height
> of the whole building, one containing a regular Oratorian pul-
> pit with two staircases like the ambo of an old basilica, and
> the other an image of the Madonna. There are nine recesses
> on either side of the church for confessionals, so that eighteen
> fathers might be hearing confessions at once.[39]

When finished it was found to be very dark and badly ventilated.
The opening took place on 22nd March, the transferred feast
of St Joseph. It was not the grand affair that the opening at King
William Street had been. Canon Maguire, the Vicar General,
sang the High Mass. Newman and five of the Birmingham Fathers
were present in the Choir. Faber was exhausted by his exertions
and by fear that all would not be finished in time. "The Father

was very ill all day on Tuesday," one of the Fathers wrote to Lady Arundel and Surrey,

> and about 11.30 Fr Antony sent me to go and fetch Mr Tegart (the doctor) as the Father had been found lying on the floor and groaning most piteously. He had gone to bed about 8.0 and as we were all busy in the church nobody had been to see him till Fr Antony and Fr Philip went to him at 11.30. Mr Tegart came and said his illness was from extreme exhaustion and debility, and that it would be impossible for him to preach at the opening. When he saw him again yesterday morning he said that if he had to preach he would certainly fall down in the pulpit and that it would be on the conscience of the Fathers if they allowed him to try. Still we did not despair, but began the Mass and when it was near the time for the sermon the Padre who was with us went to Fr Wilfrid and advised him to come and preach which he did and after the sermon was very much better. He preached again in the afternoon ... The anxiety about the Father had the effect of stopping all inclination to laugh at the Vicar General's singing for we were all occupied in making vows of Masses and rosaries to St Joseph to have noticed anything else. It was really quite a "grazia". Fr Camillus vowed to put up a picture or statue of the saint in the church if he would help us ... We were to have begun the daily Masses today but at the last it was found that room had not been left behind the altar for the priest to carry up the Blessed Sacrament and the wall had to be knocked down and a recess built ... The dear Padre who is still with us ages very much and seems to have very little strength.[40]

The work of founding the Oratory in London was now over. The rest was consolidation. It was Faber who settled each problem as it arose and his work may be seen in the London Oratory to this day. Indeed the Oratory in London is his work. Without Faber's drive and perseverance it could not have flourished in the way it has. When Hutchison and Faber returned from Italy to set up the Wilfridians and arrived in London by sea they were appalled by the thought of how little they could do. And yet within ten years the foundation had been laid of an institution which quickly grew to be as much a part of London as St Paul's.

CHAPTER XIII

AN UNHAPPY QUARREL

FROM the 1850s onwards there was much less intimacy between Faber and Newman. They now wrote infrequently. While Faber was still at Hither Green in 1852, when the purchase of Argyll house was under consideration, he had written to Hutchison:

> I have quite made up my mind not to come to town to see A[rgyll] H[ouse]. I don't want to have another correspondence with the Padre like the last. I never write to him now, nor he to me. It was a sort of finale, and luckily there is no row.[1]

It is probable that he was referring to the correspondence over his illness and holiday. This in itself can hardly have affected his attitude to Newman so radically unless he was wrongly under the impression that Newman wished to depose him. But these few critical words were the prelude to a storm. Before this Newman had been above reproach. Faber's illness and the consequent necessity for Newman to write to other London Fathers on Oratorian business may have caused something of a breach in their friendship. The most likely explanation is that Faber had outgrown his dependence on Newman and had begun to be annoyed at the elder man's cautious criticism. Gossip seems to have been incautiously repeated. But whatever irritation Faber may have felt, at bottom he still loved and revered Newman. It is, however, clear that there was a rift as early as 1852.

The trouble began over a novice called Plater who had been in touch with both Newman and Faber. Birmingham was in rather a forlorn condition owing to the death of Joseph Gordon, ill-health, and two Fathers leaving the Congregation. "I find", Newman wrote with suppressed anger on 28th September 1853,

> that you have given Plater a consent, conditional on my assent, to take him at the London Oratory. Whoever has negotiated

the matter between him and you, has, I think, been very in-considerate. Whether you finally resolve to take him or not he is spoilt for us—he is lost to us. We could not keep him though you retracted.

Then consider our state. See how we are over-worked—how destitute we are of preachers—how sickly our novices. I do not mean to praise Plater so highly as to call him the Prophet's ewe-lamb, which would be somewhat extravagant, but we took him up when he was literally in a low estate, and, when we have set his way straight before him, he is suddenly taken away.

So strongly at the time of dear Fr Joseph's death did I feel our destitution that I got F. Ambrose to sound you about giving us up Father Bernard. I felt that I had given you up too many on whom I had a claim in the division of the Houses. When nothing came of this an obvious delicacy prevented my pro-ceeding and I did nothing.

Fr. Bernard found out this application of which I had not said a word to him: and asked me what it meant. I do not say he expressed any wish concurrent with mine though he had ever wished *before* the final division to be with me—but I shall express what I mean if I say that (*had* he) there was nothing in my reply to encourage it. And this is all which has passed between us. Now, however, under all the circumstances, I think I may ask of your charity to give us Fr. Bernard.[2]

The loss of Dalgairns was a blow not to be lightly considered. Faber wrote by return.

I can hardly say how very much your letter . . . has hurt and wounded me because of its injustice.

He pointed out that Plater was never given even a conditional consent to join the London Oratory because the Fathers did not wish that he should do so. Stanton while at Birmingham had noticed that Plater had talked with affection of the London house—that was all. "With regard to F. Bernard," he continued,

1. I am not aware Ambrose ever "sounded" me about him.
2. I was not aware that F. B. knew of your wish, or had had any communication with you on the subject. It was a secret to

me till your letter this morning and I repeat that it has been so. 3. I will lay your proposal before him, and will put no manner of obstacle direct or indirect in his way. More I cannot do. He is free.

As to your letter I must say that the cruelty and injustice of it are to me as hard to bear as they are unexpected. The very language imputes the worst motives to me—"he is spoilt"—obviously by someone external, i.e. myself—"retract"—"negotiation"—"the ewe-lamb". What have I done to deserve this? You judge me before you have heard the defence: you assume the facts. Now after the last 7 years, I might have put in a plea for at least suspension of judgment. You know how hard it is to keep two Congrs. of the Oratory right, witness Rome and Naples [in St Philip's day]; and I really have had no object so much at heart as to remain yours, and to keep ours in heart and soul with you. You know this to be true; and that I have taken no slight pains on our side. Yet you can suspect me of kidnapping your ewe-lamb, of negotiating with your own people, of sharp practice with you on the very subject matter in which you had been, as we have always felt and openly said, so generous with us. You ought to have known that I would sooner have been left without a Father than done such a thing. However the matter is done and is simply irremediable.

Under these circumstances you will excuse my not coming to Birmingham. I cannot come. I go to town on Saturday to give F. Bernard time for his decision before the elections.[3]

Faber was referring to the election of a Superior for the London house.

Dalgairns also wrote to Newman.

I fully made up my mind that I would not stir from the London house without its full and distinct consent. I determined to take it to be the indication of St Philip's will. That will is now most clear to me. I was even startled by its clearness when Father Wilfrid said to me yesterday morning that all agreed that the House must give me up to you . . . I need not tell you what a wrench and uprooting it is that I am transplanted. I did not know myself till now how I loved all here . . . I do hope that I am a perfect peace offering to you from Father Wilfrid.

I cannot tell you how bitterly I have felt all the misunderstandings which have taken place between you. Do believe me when I say that nothing can exceed the generosity with which he gives me up and that solely out of devotion to you. It is his doing; I never should have stirred without him; nor would the house have so unanimously and cheerfully spoken its mind if his had been different. The only drawback to the comfort which I feel in being a present from him to you is this miserable business over Plater. Indeed, my dear Padre, do let me say who know[s] the whole circumstances that Fr. Wilfrid is as innocent as the babe unborn of any negotiations with Plater . . . Another thing I deeply regret and that is, that Fr. Ambrose did not openly propose to him in February that he should give me up to you. So little did he do so "distinctly" that I am perfectly convinced that Fr. Wilfrid did not understand him. I have all along been astonished and annoyed at Fr. Wilfrid's not having mentioned your application . . . Whatever he may be in the way of impetuosity and precipitate talking, indeed he is not treacherous. He is at bottom most loyal to you, as his giving me up to you proves convincingly. And he does so at a time when we are more than ever one . . . at a time too when all his natural man is sore and hurt at what you have said about Plater.[4]

Various letters passed between the Oratories. Then Faber wrote to Newman again.

As to our Father you will feel with us in our sorrow for the loss of our best man, and the undoing of so much of the last four years, though you will hardly realise how keenly we feel it, because you are hardly aware of the internal condition of our House, or of its real necessities. You must therefore be kindly forbearing with any word or look of sadness by which, in spite of ourselves, we may betray our grief . . . Asking your blessing for the House, and the new elections and myself yours affectionately F. W. Faber.[5]

"My dearest Father Wilfrid," Newman replied,

I had sat with all your letters before me, not daring to open them, when James came and told me of your conclusion, and then I found you had enclosed me the decision of your congre-

gation. Since your last letter to me, last Friday or Saturday,
when I have taken up the Blessed Sacrament at Mass I have
thought that perhaps at that very time Father Wilfrid was
taking it up too, and I have prayed Him who has given us one
possession of Himself to make us more and more one in heart
and love. And now your letter so surprises and overpowers me
that I do not know what to say. For I did not think you would
have come to a conclusion so soon, and then I had not realized,
even though I had contemplated, the thing which I had asked
for.

If martyrdom washes away all stains will not such an act as
you have taken of self-sacrifice obliterate, I will not say any
fault of any of you, but of all that in the way of misunderstanding has hung about the matter? Nay will it not plead for all
those manifold imperfections of mine which the searcher of
hearts sees in me in the course of it? This alone I will say that
the thought of the pain I was giving to all of you has afflicted
me, and will afflict me, in a way which you cannot believe. At
present I will only ask your pardon, my dear F. Wilfrid, for
every unkindness or want of consideration I may have shown
you in the business and beg you to suggest to me anything I
can do to show you the perfect love and gratitude which I feel
to you and all of you.[6]

"God bless you for your letter," Faber answered happily:

What token of love could you give more than this? Not an
hour has passed since the decree in which we have all of us
felt St Philip did it his own way, and the joy that we have not
failed you when you tried us far surpasses the pain of the
sacrifice. I do not think we have ever felt to love you so much,
when once our struggle was over; and you must remember it
for us whenever we may happen to be cross or restive, as we
have so often been.[7]

But Newman still felt very unhappy.

I know how much you love me—and I am not worthy of it.
Whatever I have done or thought wrongly in this matter, for
every unkindness I may have committed, for whatever rash
judgment I have formed, and for whatever else in me God has
seen inconsistent with the truest and purest charity I pray you

to forgive me. Do believe how pained I have been throughout. One of my penances will be that people cannot believe how I have been pained.

And the next day he wrote again.

You say that I must bear with all of you if you are sad. How little you know or can estimate what I have felt in this matter! Part of my pain, indeed, which has been great and continued, has been about myself—because nothing I could do, as I ought and wished to do but mixed the most miserable rudeness and inconsiderateness in everything I did ... and now I am overwhelmed by a double feeling, by shame at my own request and by the most keen yet tender emotion of surprise, admiration, and love at your granting it. When shall I be able to look into your faces again? ... Never, for an instant, I solemnly declare, did I mean to accuse you of treachery. Never did I accuse you of any deliberate act of unkindness. Never did I doubt your love of me, nor impute anything to you inconsistent with the substance and reality of that love. My head is in such a whirl that I cannot write as I would for there is much I could say.[8]

He wrote by the same post to Hutchison:

What can I say more than that your Father is one who comes out nobly and heroically on great occasions.[9]

Hutchison summed up the matter with his usual common sense. "Let me end", he wrote to St John,

by looking at the whole affair in a sheep stealing point of view—and remarking that while we are defending ourselves from the charge of having tampered with your ewe-lamb, you fellows have basely bolted with our old bell-wether.[10]

The London Fathers had scarcely moved into their new home when Wiseman wrote a long emotional letter asking them to hear the confession of nuns. He pointed out the good the Fathers would do and Faber felt he could not in all honesty refuse the Cardinal's appeal. The difficulty was whether hearing the confessions might not run contrary to the Rule of the Oratory. The Fathers differed as to whether it was lawful or not and a letter

was sent to Propaganda in Rome. They asked first for an interpretation of the Rule on this matter or for permission, if necessary,
to relax it. Newman had been faced with precisely the same question in Birmingham and he had tried to evade the issue by
allowing his Fathers to give retreats and direction to non-
moniales—as for instance to Sisters of Charity and Dominican
nuns of the 3rd Order. He was on shaky ground legally and his
own congregation decided that what he had permitted was in
fact contrary to the Rule. Soon afterwards the Birmingham house
heard that London was making enquiries and shelved the matter
till the London house had had a reply. Stanton maintained that
Newman knew that the London house had applied to Propaganda. Stanton in fact had mentioned it to Newman on 7th
September 1855. Stanton was not the sort of man to make a
mistake on a matter of this kind. Newman, however, maintained
that he understood the application was not to Propaganda but
merely to the Chiesa Nuova or other Oratories. The difference,
of course, was very great. A reply from the first was binding and
decisive—and a reply from the second merely an opinion and in
no way binding. Propaganda was at this time the controlling
agent in Rome for the Church in England.

Apart from this initial misunderstanding there were two
complicating factors. The two houses had grown apart and, generally speaking, differed as to the advisability of seeking a relaxation
of the Rule. London was in favour of hearing nuns' confessions,
not from preference but in deference to Wiseman: Birmingham
was not. Newman was now busy in Dublin and intercourse
between the two Oratories had grown more tenuous than ever.
The second complicating factor was Dalgairns. He was now a
member of the Birmingham house but his heart was in London.
It was natural that he should be used as the intermediary between
the two houses. Unluckily he was strongly *partis pris*—in favour
of the permission being granted. He knew that London had
applied to Propaganda but did not tell the Birmingham Fathers—
presumably for fear they might scotch the application. His conduct was the more reprehensible in that he told everything to the
nuns at Stone.

The quarrel would never have taken place had Faber consulted Newman at the beginning. Considering how closely he had consulted Newman in the past it is odd that he did not do so, though of course, with the separation of the Oratories he was not bound to do it. According to Hutchison the Fathers did just think of telling Newman—and then decided it was unnecessary. In any case Newman was very busy in Dublin. Newman later maintained that Faber had told him on his death bed that he (Faber) had vainly tried to get the London Fathers to consult Newman, that the London Fathers had been so headstrong they would not have taken any notice of Newman's advice in any case, and that Faber had therefore had to acquiesce. It is difficult to know how much importance to attach to this story. It directly contradicts the story of the London Fathers and Hutchison in particular. It is also difficult to reconcile with Oratorian procedure (see p. 338, Chapter XV). Whatever the truth may be, in the light of what happened it was an error of judgment not to have consulted Newman and a lack of courtesy for the London house not to have informed its founder.

Faber wrote on 14th October 1855 of a project he had for training novices and was fidgeted by getting no reply. In fact he became quite unwell. He realized that Newman was angry but did not know why. When he later discovered the true cause— that Newman had heard of the application to Propaganda—he was at first relieved as he thought the matter of little importance. The novice scheme was straightforward enough but Newman saw in it little less than a plot. "Father Faber's letter", he wrote on the 30th to Father Flanagan, one of the Birmingham Fathers,

> seems to show me, that, were I gone, he would attempt to get over you, N. and Austin as his novices, despise (?) F., talk over Ambrose, laugh at H., rule Robert through Bernard, and then care nothing for Edward or William . . . I fear I must say what I have felt ever since [the time when] dear Father Joseph not long before his death opened my eyes to it that I utterly cannot trust Father Faber. I have never said it to anyone but Ambrose.*

Faber asked Father Flanagan to sing the Requiem for Frederick Lucas in London but Newman peremptorily refused to let him go.

Propaganda consulted Wiseman and several English bishops including Ullathorne, on the advisability of granting permission. All the answers with one exception were in favour of permission. The Pope, however, was against it and a compromise was arrived at by which the London Fathers were granted the permission for three years only. Rumours began to circulate and Newman became more uneasy. He sent Dalgairns to enquire. The London Fathers were so little apprehensive of trouble that they handed over all the documents. The Birmingham Fathers looked at them but did not get in touch with London. Newman, however, was roused. He had heard accidentally from a nun at Stone of the application *as if it was a secret*. From this time he became convinced that there was a conspiracy against him.

He made enquiries of Wiseman and Ullathorne. Wiseman did not reply which was later thought suspicious but the Cardinal was notoriously unbusinesslike. Ullathorne had lost the question from Propaganda but replied that he had answered in favour of the permission being granted. And here the matter might have rested. The London house would have received their permission without further trouble. But there was an unfortunate interference.

The Rescript, as the permission was called, was granted in Rome on 21st October and Ullathorne who had heard about it took it into his head to call on Newman. He told Newman that the Rescript would apply not only to London but to Birmingham as well. This was what he wished, for he was keen to have the help of the Oratory in the direction of convents—but it was untrue. He had received only one communication from Rome and that was the question he had lost. Dalgairns who may have inspired Ullathorne's visit now openly maintained that all was settled and that the Birmingham Fathers were bound to accept the Rescript. Ullathorne was not, of course, acting in bad faith. Having been consulted in the first place he was probably under the impression that the Rescript would naturally apply to the Oratory in his diocese. He may even have been told that it did so. Dalgairns probably also thought along the same lines—the wish being father to the thought. Even at this point, after Ullathorne's unlucky and clumsy intervention, things might have been put right had there been any personal intercourse. But Newman was away most of the time in Dublin. Flanagan meantime was doing all he could to fan the flames. Newman believed that the London house and Faber in particular had deliberately hoodwinked him. It may seem that the trouble itself was trivial enough. The original request and the permission, indeed, were not in themselves very important but a question of principle was now involved. Was it right that the London house should, as it were, legislate for Birmingham? As Oratorians took no vows, was not the Rule their all?

It was this question of principle and the fear that Faber had somehow outmanoeuvred him which now took possession of Newman's mind. The drafting of a letter to Faber on the subject assumed a quite unreal importance. Drafts were written and rewritten, submitted to the Birmingham Fathers and altered. Faber became more and more of a villain. Flanagan feared that he would

> write a splendid reply, consent to anything and everything, ask your pardon and then all would be over.

To Flanagan's way of thinking this would not "attain the end for which we are working". Newman began to believe that the separation of the Oratories in 1850 had been forced upon him. He implied that Dr Grant, as Faber's friend, had been at the bottom of it—under the pretext of stopping Newman's interference with the London house. "Ha! ha!" he added in a letter to Flanagan of 31st October,

> as if *I* were the quarter whence domination were to come! . . . I am getting in truth more and more to see Fr. F's ambition.

St John thought one of the drafts Newman proposed to send was too mild and

> might elicit a strong letter of 3 pages from F. W. disclaiming any intention of interfering with us at all, etc., etc. Meanwhile the Rescript would come and we should be nailed.*

Flanagan actually thought that Faber was about to send two of the London Fathers to Rome, although at this time Faber was utterly unconscious of the gathering storm.

At last Newman's letter was ready.

"My dear Father Faber," he wrote from Dublin on 8th November, a form of address he had never used even at the beginning of their friendship,

> I write this letter to your Congregation. I transmit it through you and hope you will read it to them. We have learnt at Edgbaston within this last several weeks that an application of your Congregation to Propaganda for a relaxation or suspension of one portion of the Rule of the Oratory, has been, unintentionally on your part, misunderstood by the Sacred Congregation to come from us as well as from you. In consequence, to our surprise, we learn from accidental information, confirmed by our Bishop, that he has received, or is to receive, in our behalf a relaxation or suspension which we neither desire in itself, nor desire should come to us without our asking for it.
>
> It is desirable for your sake as well as for ours, that such misconceptions should not recur; for, as your House has unintentionally involved us so we unintentionally might involve you. Suppose we were to petition Propaganda (to take a parallel case) that the Birmingham Oratory might claim the private property of each of its subjects, and your Bishop received a letter empowering the Oratory at Brompton to exercise a similar power over its own subjects, and you were suddenly informed of this by an accidental channel, after the transaction had been going on for months over and around you, I think you would consider our act at Edgbaston a great inconvenience to you. Therefore for your sake as well as ours, writing as Father Superior of the Edgbaston Oratory, I think it fitting to ask your Congregation to draw up a formal petition to Propaganda to beg the Sacred Congregation to recognise, in some way as is suitable to its forms, that fundamental principle of the Oratory of St Philip, whereby its houses are entirely independent of each other, and what one does is not the act of the other.
>
> And as being the person who brought the English Rule of the Oratory to England and has given it to your Congregation and set the Congregation up in the Archdiocese [London]

I think it right to ask that your application to Propaganda should be put into my hands to transmit to Rome. Moreover, I think your Congregation will see that it is fitting to draw up the supplication at once. And I shall feel the kindness of your writing me word, almost by return of post, that your Congregation intends doing it. Yours affectionately in Christ, John H. Newman of the Oratory.

The letter was sent by registered post.

The next day Newman was back in Birmingham and in the course of a statement to the Birmingham Fathers said:

Here was the London House and neglecting me, neglecting the Congregation at Edgbaston and acting with the Cardinal Archbishop, the Bishop of Southwark [Dr Grant] and our own Bishop, *about us* and without us, nay, against us and against me ... If one part of our Rule can be suspended while we sleep, so may another. We may wake in the morning and find that the Fathers at Brompton have demanded a virtually new rule, and imposed it, through Propaganda, upon us ... Moreover it is obvious that any *ambitious spirit* should such arise in any one Oratory (which St Philip avert) might, proceeding in this way, and gaining the ear of certain Bishops, throw other Congregations in England into utter disorganization, and rise upon their ruins ... And, as a finishing stroke to the whole, while Fr Faber was keeping silence in his correspondence with me on the subject which so intimately affected us, he was on those very days when they broke upon us for the first time sending me a letter to consult ...

Faber was unfortunately ill when Newman's letter arrived and felt disinclined to answer personally. It was answered on 10th November by Stanton as secretary to the Congregation of Deputies in London.

My dear father, The Father has received your letter and has communicated it immediately to the Cong. Dep. who have deputed me to answer it which I do without loss of time. I need hardly say that we should all regret your being involved by us, however, unintentionally, in any misconception of Propaganda ... It appears to us, according to the best of our judgment that we cannot consistently with respect to Propaganda, write to it on the subject until we have received its answer and know what it has done, and how it has understood us. . . . With respect and affection. . . .

The refusal seemed to confirm Newman's suspicions. He replied on 13th November:

I am very sorry your Congregation of Deputies declines to make the application to Propaganda to which I invited them. I cannot, will not, believe that they will persist in this refusal. It is a fact which none of them can deny, that, *in consequence* of a certain application which they have made to Propaganda (the matter of which I do not dispute with them about) Propaganda and our Bishop have been in correspondence about a certain suspension of a portion of the Rule of the Oratory at Edgbaston; and that our Bishop has recommended the measure without our knowing anything about what was going on.

Moreover, within the last few days our Bishop has said to one of our Fathers, in explanation of his own conduct, that "after all we must recollect that one of *our own Superiors* asked for the suspension", showing that even now he is impressed with the idea that the two Houses are connected, and that Father Faber has actually something to do with us. You have (unwittingly) done us an injury. We feel it. We ask you to repair it. You can. Do as you would be done by. What has once happened may happen twice unless it be prevented. If you will not prevent it, you *will be acquiescing in it, you will be anticipating it.* I repeat then my request, distinctly, formally more earnestly. Rather, since justice comes in, I make it a demand.

Two days later, on 15th November, Newman wrote to Wiseman who had still not replied to his previous letter.

My dear Lord, I wrote to you on a matter affecting almost the existence of the Oratory in England. Will you break down what you have built up? Has anyone slandered me to your Eminence? You are too just to punish me except for some offence.

Wiseman had seen Faber already and now sent on Newman's letter with the following note:

I send the enclosed which I have answered in the kindest possible manner without *alluding to my having seen you.* If possible therefore say nothing on this, and let us exert ourselves to the utmost to heal and soothe this noble wounded spirit.

The London Fathers replied to Newman through Stanton on the 17th. They respectfully declined to approach Propaganda again and gave their reasons. 1. That no Rescript had yet come from Rome. 2. That Propaganda knew that all Oratories were completely independent. 3. That if the Rescript should be found to include Birmingham Propaganda might have good reasons for so acting and it was for Birmingham to take the matter up. "And lastly," the Fathers added,

> that we cannot enter these resolutions in our Registers without recording at the same time the pain and reluctance we feel in thus being compelled to refuse any request made to us by him who is our Founder and to whom we are under so many obligations.

Faber meanwhile replied to Wiseman on 18th November. "I am so very ill", he wrote,

> that I am sure your Eminence will excuse my dictating this letter to Fr Bowden instead of writing it with my own hand, which indeed I am quite unable to do, as my nerves are completely shattered by the events of the last few days.

He then explained how the request to Rome had arisen out of his (Wiseman's) letter.

> We wrote to ask it. We did not even mention it to your Eminence, as to have done so would have destroyed the gracefulness of our compliance. There is not one Father of our Congregation who has any attraction to this work of Convents. We took it as *your* work. ... Have we done anything which indicates in the slightest degree a desire to change St Philip's Institute? What can be the meaning of such words as that "the very existence of the Oratory in England" is implicated in our act? If we may not trust Rome what may we trust? Can you tell us what our Padre means? Can you intellectually understand his position? My dear Lord Cardinal, we are cut to the

heart. *You* know how we have loved the Padre and how loyally we have served him. There is nothing we could not sacrifice to him except the rights of our own Congregation which we only hold in trust for others. We make no complaints. How should *we* who owe so much to him however much we may have to suffer? I have asked St Philip that we may have the grace so to bear it that nothing shall wring from us one complaining word against the Padre, even though he be bent, as it seems, to cast us from him altogether. But why should he hold so cheaply the loyalty and reverence of a large community whose members, with whatever amount of wayward temper and self-will have never been otherwise than completely *his in heart*?

On 19th November Newman wrote from Dublin to the Fathers in London.

My dear Father Secretary, Assure the Fathers of your Congregation that I really do not think I have, after the receipt of your letter, any but the warmest, tenderest, most affectionate, and most grateful feelings for them. I pray for every blessing upon them—long years of service, many graces, abundant good works, and much merit to carry with them out of the world. May they increase as I decrease. Tell them I never loved them so much as now when they have so exceedingly wounded me. But if you please you will oblige me by not answering this.

On the same day he wrote to St John:

I don't think I feel anything but tenderness for those poor fellows at Brompton but my feelings about Father Faber depended on nothing at this minute. He has acted but according to his nature.*

On 23rd November Wiseman wrote to say he had seen Newman and that all had been settled amicably. But the London Fathers were deeply shocked that Newman had come to London without telling them. A draft of a letter to Wiseman shows how deep the quarrel had now become:

Father Newman, under the title of Founder, has corresponded with your Eminence, unknown to us, in matters which concern simply our own Congregation—he has desired your Eminence to write to Rome on the subject—he has got you to forward his letter to Propaganda praying that we of this Congregation may not have what we have asked, he has persuaded your Eminence to write in the same sense, and finally he has arranged with your Eminence that if any Rescript comes to you for us we are not to receive it until he has had time to get an answer to his letter. In other words he has used his influence with our Ecclesiastical Superior to hinder our free intercourse with Rome, and to interfere with the private business of our Congregation which by St Philip's Rule is entirely independent of him.

The Fathers of the London Cong. of the Oratory beg, most respectfully to your Eminence, to protest against this conduct of Fr Newman, as being practically an attempt to exercise an act of *generalate* over us and thus as being destructive to the fundamental principle of St Philip's Institute, viz. that each Congregation of the Oratory should be completely independent. We consider that St Philip's rule and our own rights have been greatly violated by what he has done, and that it is of importance to the future of our Congregation that we should attempt to obtain from Rome the acknowledgment of our right to communicate with the Holy See directly and independently of him . . .

This letter briefly expressed the standpoint of the Fathers of the London Oratory. They felt that if they were obliged to consult Newman or anyone else before approaching the Holy See they would no longer enjoy the fundamental freedom of an Oratory. The dispute may be conveniently summarized: Birmingham maintained that one Oratory should not involve or legislate for another: London maintained that one Oratory, if really independent, must be able to approach Rome without consultation with or interference by another Oratory. The principles involved were real enough but were not both Oratories right? Legally no doubt there was much to be said for either side. Unhappily the dispute cannot be judged by legal criteria alone. More, much more, was involved.

As it happened the Rescript went direct to the London Oratory. It was now clear that Birmingham was not included in it. Newman was informed of the terms of the Rescript in a letter from Rome

signed by Cardinal Franzoni and Monsignor Barnabò, dated
10th November. But Newman was not interested in the origin
of the quarrel and was convinced that a real danger had arisen.
He proposed to Wiseman that the petition of one Oratory should
not affect another and that no interpretation of the Rule should
be made by one Oratory without consultation with other
Oratories. Faber's attitude on the contrary was that the matter
had long since been settled by St Philip and that Newman was
now simply filled with hostility to the London house. "He has
never written to us," Faber complained to the Cardinal on
15th December,

> notwithstanding his admission to you that he had been mis-
> taken about his facts. Our own belief, perhaps mistaken, from
> past experience is that he is egged on to all this by Fr St John.
> Anyhow the manner in which, as far as we can fathom the
> business, he *seems* to have treated us, has produced a more
> complete alienation from him in our minds than I should like
> to describe to you. He appears resolved that no reconciliation
> shall take place. Deeply as he has wronged us it seems as if he
> were becoming actually hostile to us. However, the one thing
> *I* want to avoid now is an open appeal to Rome against him as
> attempting to alter the Institute and to bring in a generalate.

The two Oratories were completely at loggerheads, each accusing
the other of the same thing.

Against the advice of Monsignor Barnabò Newman determined to visit Rome. He passed through London on 27th December with St John, without, of course, visiting the Oratory. The
London Fathers began to get alarmed. When they heard he was
going to visit various Oratories on the journey they drew up a
circular letter. It contained an account of what had happened
from their point of view and was designed to give information,
advice and a warning against Newman. Newman had been so
moved and upset by the quarrel that on his arrival in Rome he
walked barefoot from the *diligence* to St Peter's before going to his
hotel. He then pressed Propaganda for a ruling that all Oratories
were independent. Barnabò, however, pointed out that any ruling

from Propaganda would be ill advised, unnecessary, and would in any case weaken Newman's authority. In the event Barnabò wisely refused to make any ruling and persuaded Newman to relinquish the project. Newman felt that he had been unfairly treated by Propaganda and had not been received with sufficient courtesy. He was, however, pleased at the time with an interview with Pius IX. But it was an unfortunate episode. It prejudiced the authorities in Rome against Newman and led to a whole chain of misunderstandings and troubles. Looked at from the Roman point of view Newman was behaving tiresomely—as, in fact, it was considered, English Catholics had behaved since the Reformation.

In March 1856 Newman sent a subscription to Hutchison for the Ragged School. Hutchison took the opportunity in acknowledging it to try and end the quarrel. He wrote at great length and went over the whole controversy. "I cannot help supposing," he ended,

> that some, perhaps a great part of your displeasure with us is really connected personally with our Father. What the grounds of this may be I cannot tell, but if you think that among us all there is one who really has more affection for you than he has I am sure you do him wrong. I would appeal to any Father here or to any of our friends as to the affection with which he has always spoken of you, and I have now in my memory instances where he has refused his consent to what others have proposed because, though the thing might be good and unobjectionable yet it would not be kind, or fair, or respectful, or so forth to you ...

The rumour that Newman was to be made a bishop had come up some time before and the London house sent him two mitres as a present. They were returned but no message of thanks was received. This incident was never forgotten in London. Newman, however, told Flanagan that he had written a letter "to the sacristan", who of course was one of the London Fathers. The message may have been very curt. In any case his reply to Hutchison's letter was unhelpful. "I thank you", he wrote on 4th March, for your letter just received, but I shall not and cannot read it. Anything on the subject of that act of your Congregation must come to me from your Secretary.

Ludicrously he was forced to add:
By mistake a duplicate of this has got into the post.

On 8th May Faber made another attempt at a reconciliation.

I am just beginning to recover from a long and painful illness, and you will not wonder that I should write to you. My last letter to you last St Wilfrid's day you did not answer and in your first note to me about the application to Propaganda you cut me off entirely from you, called me by my surname, and told me that you did not write to me but to the Congregation through me. I was ill and broken at the time, and so was fain to acquiesce in the separation your letter implied. I will not deny that many a time since I have felt much bitterness, that even now I cannot but think you have treated us with considerable harshness, that I cannot feel without strange feelings of your writing to the Cardinal, without one word to us, that we were destroying St Philip's work in England, and that many little actions, such as returning the mitres, and the way in which you returned them, have been such as to startle me in *you*; I should not be truthful if I did not acknowledge this.

Still, I cannot forget that to you I owe all that I most value in this life, and to you simply I shall owe my salvation, if I am saved; nor can I forget that I have once loved you as I never loved a friend before. You have cast me from you, perhaps justly. I do not doubt you have had much to bear from me, more than I remember, or than in my rudeness I was ever aware of. But I have never been untrue to you, tho' this is what you seem to think. It was bitter for me when you told Fr Joseph Gordon that the Wilfridians "had been a dear bargain to you, and that you never trust me again as long as I lived"; [see Chapter IX, p. 179] and I see now that all that has happened during the past few months has had its root long since, I know not how. I feel as if there were in your mind a long series of jealousies, doubts and misconstructions which it would be hopeless for me to remove, and it is the kind of despair which this thought has engendered which has kept me silent so long.

But as the load of my late physical suffering is taken off I feel also that I should make some attempt to get the two houses upon better and more affectionate terms, and if it might be so, soften your heart somewhat towards myself. At the beginning of the year I took St John the Evangelist for my year Saint, because of his being your patron, and in the hope of his bringing us together again, and so, what I am going to ask of you, I ask in his name. I know you well enough to know how you must yourself have suffered all this time. Now, is it quite impossible for you to forgive us, to be a father to us again, to destroy the scandal of unvisiting houses? What exactly is it in our conduct that has angered you so greatly, what can we do to repair it, is it such as to justify a breach among St Philip's sons? Surely we are your sons, fathers must suffer for their children, must bear much from them. Has our conduct exceeded the measure of what your charity and long-suffering can or ought to bear? I do not want to make any excuses. You have never let us make any explanations. We hardly know what to explain. You have taken the initiative in everything as if you had got your view and made up your mind. I do not want therefore to make any defence; but I ask you to remember the past, to be considerate for your own work, and not let our house grow up with a habit of alienation from yourself. Let us be treated as if we were altogether in the wrong, if you will, it is what we all are with God, and yet from Him we get not forgiveness only, but far more than forgiveness.

I do not know what more to say. The sense that you deem me false to you fetters me. And if nothing more comes of my letter, it will be a melancholy satisfaction to me that I occupied the beginning of my recovery in thus writing to you, to whom I owe all things, and in asking your forgiveness, which I do with all my heart, for all the pain I have ever caused you, for my disobedience, temper, conceit and waywardness. True to you I have unfalteringly been, and the Congregation you entrusted to me is my witness that I have striven to keep it loyal to you. You cannot or will not refuse me that forgiveness I hope you will give me, or if that is beyond what you can do, at least our house, far more, St Philip, my dear Father, will mete to you good measure for your tenderness to us. I am here alone, and no one knows I have written to you. Oh! that St

Philip's day might see his English children one again. Believe me ever affectionately and gratefully yrs F.W.F.

Newman replied on 9th May from Dublin:

My dear Father Wilfrid, It is a very great satisfaction to me to see your handwriting; and tho' this is May and I wrote you in November your writing now is more than a compensation for your utter silence then. I put it down to your continued indisposition, which has grieved me very much, and which I have been for a long time in the practice of remembering at Mass and before the Blessed Sacrament. I must not allow you to exaggerate matters or to fancy that there is any alienation between the members of your and my Congregation. I am not at all aware of it, I believe it is not so; I shall be very sorry if any act implying it can be ascribed to us. I trust nothing of the kind will ever happen. As you will wish me not to call you "Father Faber" I readily consent. Nor can I let you for one moment fancy that I own the words which you attribute to Fr Joseph Gordon. Nor does any letter I wrote to you or to your Congregation's Secretary in November last, nor any act of mine, justify the imputation.

As to what then passed between myself and your Congregation it lies where they put it, with their Secretary. The initiative is with them through him, and with no one else. No one can take his place; if you have anything to say they can say it, and through him. Great confusion arises from going to and fro, beginning formally, continuing informally, and thus dissipating responsibility; as I am sure you will see. I am startled to find you talk of scandal having occurred; if I, or any of my Congregation is at fault I am sorry for it. Talking freely is the common source of scandal. I do not think we have done so.

"You will not wonder", Faber replied sorrowfully on Whitsun Eve,

at the pain the perusal of your letter has caused. Why! my dear Father, almost every word of it seems full of alienation. But I must not be discouraged ... Have you any objection to telling me, either as one of the congregation or as superior what it is you think our congregation, through its secretary ought to do—what you wish? We do not know what to do ...

Surely you will not refuse to tell me *what* it is which is our fault, and what we can say or do to get forgiveness. . . . If you leave it as your letter to me today leaves it, it will be refusing us peace.

But Newman replied on 13th May:

If you recollect the last letter I had occasion to address to your Secretary last November you will have an assurance, I think, that I shall receive with the greatest kindness and affectionate sympathy anything which he may have to convey to me from your Congregation on the matter which is the subject of your letter received this morning. There is no part of that letter of this morning which might not have come through him if it was necessary to write it at all. I recognise no-one but him as the person with whom I am to correspond upon the matter to which it relates if the correspondence is to go on. Pray understand my meaning here. I do not wish to say again what I said to you last week and to Fathers Richard Stanton and Antony Hutchison last February.

Faber replied on the 14th:

I am obliged for your note. I trust St Philip will bring a blessing out of it. I hope in a few days to be able to go to Brompton and I will then bring the matter before the Congregation, and, meanwhile, as you desire, I will not touch upon it myself.

"My dear Father Wilfrid," Newman wrote on the 15th,

Your note pleases me and I thank you for it.

That was all.

The General Congregation of the London Fathers met and unanimously agreed on a letter sent on 22nd May. They expressed their sorrow at having offended him, said that they had not wished to do so, and asked him

for the love of St Philip to forgive this and everything else by which [we] may have at any time grieved you.

Newman's reply on the 27th represented no change in his attitude. "I said", he told the Fathers, that even after the receipt of their letters, I had not any but the tenderest and most grateful feelings towards them. I added that their very act, which had so much affected me did but make me love them more. That act remains in force . . .

He reiterated his views on the danger of one Oratory legislating for another.

Meanwhile several letters passed between Newman and Faber as to the facts at the beginning of the quarrel. The London Fathers answered Newman on 5th June. It was not a very explicit letter and they did not offer to write to Propaganda as Newman intended they should do. But how could they have done so? Newman had himself been persuaded by Barnabò to desist from the very same project and he must have known that no good or change could come of it. It is probable that he wished the Fathers to make the gesture of compliance which he saw as an act of reparation for their conduct. After it had been made he would perhaps have told them they need go no further as he had forgiven them. Caswall had brought up the same question in a letter to Newman. What exactly, he asked, did Newman want the London house to do? Newman replied that it should pass a decree saying (1) that it would not seek any relaxation, etc. of the rule without making it clear that it was for the one house only; (2) that in such cases it would inform other British Oratories. If Newman had made this clear to the London house the quarrel would surely have come to an end. But he did not do so. He did ask Faber to preach in Dublin but the invitation was not a peace offering. It was Newman's way of allaying the scandal the quarrel was causing. In any case Faber declined to go.

Newman saw the answer of the London house as an evasion and wrote to Wiseman on 10th June. "I am led to ask", he said in the course of it,

whether they [the London Fathers] themselves could have prophesied in 1850, when I set them up, that they would have carried themselves toward me as they are doing in 1855, 1856.

He sent a copy of this letter to the London Oratory. Faber retaliated by sending Wiseman the letters sent by the London house to Newman asking his forgiveness. The quarrel was further embittered by the Birmingham house formally breaking off relations with London and enclosing a long document written by Newman retelling for the benefit of the Birmingham Fathers the course of the rather tedious dispute. It ended:

> Pray for the welfare of their Congregation; but keep clear of them.

(See Appendix I.)

The London Fathers replied to the Birmingham Fathers on 4th July. "Some misunderstandings", they wrote,

> time alone can clear up. ... If you have seen the whole of our correspondence with Fr Newman you [will] know how humbly we have apologized to him for any pain that we may have unintentionally caused him by the steps which we thought it our duty to take ... We did our best for peace, according to our light and we have failed. The ties of confidence and affection are broken. Alienation and coldness are henceforth to take the place of devotion and love. The memories of the past, dear still as memories, are not to live over again in the present. Such was not our choice or our wish. It is your act.

And that was nearly the end of the unhappy business. The Birmingham Fathers answered stiffly that they had indeed been shown the whole of the correspondence. This was merely formally acknowledged by London.

The alienation between the two houses was now complete. The London house became convinced that Newman was about to set up another Oratory in London. Newman probably had the legal right to do so and Mrs Bowden thought it had been agreed. There was talk of Oratories in Liverpool and Dublin. Newman certainly played with the idea of another London house as is shown in a letter to Caswall of 20th January 1856,* but Birmingham had not as a matter of fact sufficient subjects. The threat, however, together with a general feeling of uncertainty prompted the London house to seek an Apostolic Brief in Rome which was granted on 24th September 1856. It was not apparently

noticed that the London Fathers were almost doing what Newman had wanted at the start. (Appendix 2.)

Newman came to see the dispute as the culmination of many
incidents, as he explained to St John on 7th July 1856.

> As to Faber himself, he now finds himself as he was before
> he sought the Oratory, independent, with all the additional
> advantages, which St Philip, [?] reputation and years give
> him. When he first heard in 1847 that I was joining the Oratory
> his first feeling was as if I were encroaching on his province.
> Such was the tone of his letter to me at Rome (see p. 166).
> On my return he came to me, joined the Oratory, seized some
> of our most valuable subjects, went off, and now simply sets
> up for himself. I don't mean to say that all this has been of set
> purpose.*

There was one final matter to be settled. Dalgairns found himself in a difficult position at Birmingham. "The Father Superior
(Newman)", he wrote to Père Ravignan in Paris,

> has long shewn me a coldness such as none but he can shew.
> Without pity he inexorably breaks down that which I do for
> the glory of God, and that which does much for souls. Lately
> he has humbled me to the ground. This is what he did just
> before I left for Paris. He assembled the deputies and put out
> a decree that (1) I have not the spirit of the Congregation
> (2) that I am obstinate, that I am always in the right (3) that I
> try to introduce this spirit into the Congregation, and especially
> by leaguing myself with persons who do not belong to it. It
> concludes by saying that I must wait until he has taken steps
> to eradicate this bad spirit. Probably on my return he will
> deprive me of my offices of confessor and novice master . . .
> I went to Fr N. to open my heart to him, threw myself at his
> feet and acknowledged my faults. At the same time I said to
> him that I could not but wonder if this was a warning from
> God and asked leave to make a retreat. He embraced me very
> tenderly and though he thought it unnecessary gave me leave . . .
> [Fr N.] has not that zeal for souls which a place like B[irming-
> ham] calls for. In all I say do not think that I do not love
> him or admire him. He has heroic qualities, he is all for God,
> he has patience, confidence, firmness. But I have never seen

in him the zeal of souls which we see in S. P[hilip]. He understands and welcomes all that serve for the intellect, education, literature ... He seems to have nothing at heart but what has reference to intellectual work.[11]

Dalgairns thought of leaving the Oratory for the Dominicans but was persuaded against it. He then wrote to Faber about returning to London. Faber consulted Hutchison and Stanton who were in Rome. "As regards the Prodigal Son", Hutchison wrote,

> F. R[ichard] and I both think that considering the way he was taken from us, considering too that he was formed as an Oratorian along with us in London and that he finds himself as he says so thoroughly out of place and out of harmony with the others at Birmingham, and lastly considering that ever since leaving us he has still been entirely in sympathy with us and there has never been any breach between us and him it would be unjust to refuse to receive him again supposing he frees himself from his present obligations to the Birm. House and asks us to readmit him. I think he might count on a most affectionate and unanimous welcome from all of us, and, looking on the past three years as a sort of holiday which he has taken, we should at once reinstate him in his former position of seniority.
>
> But I think we must ask him to fight the battle with the P[adre] himself. This is a little penance for his making the mistake of leaving us so easily. We cannot prudently afford just now to enter another "terrific combat". But let our old bellwether clear the fences which now enclose him and we shall I imagine readily open the door to him. . . . There is one little thing I am anxious about. Tho' F. Nn. would not believe it you have all along I think been disposed to be more generous towards him than the rest of us, and I am afraid of his reopening the correspondence with you and of your treating him better than either he deserves or we desire. I do hope you will only show him bare civility if he writes to you. If we have Dalgairns again how strangely things will have come round. This present row I have no doubt sprung from his taking Dalgairns into his house and away from us ... You are put in rather a difficult position by this correspondence. We mustn't give

F. N. a handle for making out that we are conspiring against him . . .[12]

On 19th August Dalgairns wrote to Faber:

On Friday and on Saturday morning I had been praying very hard that my transfer might be effected without a breach of charity and that Mary would direct me how to manage. On that very Saturday I was enabled to speak to the Padre. A general Congregation was announced at breakfast. I thought it only had relation to money matters but to my astonishment the P. produced some papers which he had read to us some months ago on the spirit of the Oratory. He required that we should vote that in substance we agreed with them. I instantly felt that as an honest man I could not do this. I requested to be allowed to speak to him before it was put to the vote. He instantly adjourned the meeting and in fear and trembling I went to him.

I told him at once that I should not be honest if I did not say that I had a settled intellectual conviction that the idea of the London House was more like the historical Philippine idea than was that of B. House. I then proceeded to state that it was a serious matter to me because I was seriously thinking that, holding such views, it was impossible for me to remain with him. I then told him how matters stood and read him M. Lorain's letter [whom Dalgairns had consulted in the matter]. I ended with putting the question point blank to him; "Do you consider that I have the spirit of the Birmingham house?" He showed a most amusing respect for an "intellectual conviction" and asked me once or twice if it really was intellectual, and then said I had a right to hold it. He at last said that he was not unprepared with an answer to my question and would soon come and tell me what he thought.

After three hours of anxious suspense he came. I cannot tell you how kind he was. Do you remember an expression in Callista about "eyes blue as the sapphires of the Eternal City". His eyes looked then just like a saint's and he spoke and acted like one, so disinterestedly, so gently. He said how much he loved me, he then said he felt quite sure he had no resentful feelings against the L. house, and lastly he said that since I asked him the question he could not but answer that I had not

the spirit of the B. house. Then he added that he felt sure that
I wanted quiet, and he advised me to go to Stone [to the Con-
vent] and to remain there for a few days. He then gave me his
hand which I kissed. I could not go on Sunday so I went early
on Monday, and here I am. I feel sure that he wishes me to go
back [to London] because he is sorry for having taken me away
from you and is also anxious to show that he has no unloving
feeling towards you. How very small I feel beside him.[13]

Dalgairns does not seem to have remained of this opinion, for
not long afterwards Faber was writing:

The whole house (at Birmingham), Bernard says, is extremely
united in condemning us, in great spirits, not regretting the
row, and considering themselves a very successful house, and
all that they could wish. He describes their feeling against us
as something awful. The Gen[eral] Cong[regation] was allowed
no vote and had no knowledge. The Cong[regation of] Dep
[uties] did all. Only from time to time the Padre transmitted
from Dublin bitter papers which Ambrose was ordered to
read at a Gen. Cong. One of these papers lashed them to a
perfect phrensy. One passage about our house was as follows:
"I have to tell you, my dear Fathers, that you are despised,
that you are voted slow, and looked down upon. And what is
more I also am despised." B. said it seemed as if his object was
simply to inflame their passions . . .[14]

Newman may be given the last word on the unhappy dispute.
He made out a Memorandum on 11th August 1863.

It now seems as Stanislas [Flanagan] from the first always
maintained that they went to Rome in *order* by that act to show
their independence of me—and their doing it at the end of the
three years was not, as I thought up to now, an accidental
coincidence, but a purpose . . . I do not defend the *mode* in
which I made [the application for Dalgairns in 1853]; it was
imprudent extremely; and I now suppose that it set up the
Londoners' backs, and, in spite of granting my desire, they
never forgave it.*

Chapter XIV

THE WRITER

I

FABER is more attractive as a letter writer than as a writer on spiritual matters. There is indeed a surprising difference of style. The one is straightforward, racy, full of humour, the other rhetorical and flowery. For this reason he is often dismissed on the strength of a prosy paragraph as extravagant, Italianate, Victorian. Yet with all his faults he is an important spiritual writer. His knowledge of mystical authors and hagiography alone deserve more than the condescending attention he receives today.

But he is a difficult author for the modern reader. He can be repetitive and sentimental to an extraordinary extent. He has a *penchant* for private revelations and is at times simply silly. He wrote his spiritual works when he was ill, almost as a means of relaxation, without any literary conscience. He openly delighted in purple patches. There are great slabs of passages, sometimes chapters at a time, which glow with ethereal light but have little content. Hypnotized by his own fluency Faber flows on and on, melodious and tedious. At other times he is as ridiculously down to earth. There are *seven* causes for the greatness of the Blessed Sacrament, *eight* fruits of devotion to it, etc. And then again he pleads too well, till the mind revolts, or he overpleads till the mind disbelieves. There are awful lapses of taste. In fact Faber has almost every fault. It is a formidable undertaking to sift the gold from the rubbish. But gold there is, pure gold.

Some, perhaps many, will never be able to enjoy Faber as he stands. For them he must be read in extract—they have not the stomach for the complete thing—the florid period piece. A paragraph in *The Precious Blood* which is the quintessence of Faber's style may be taken as a test passage. It is not to every taste.

It was upon the sea-shore, and my heart filled with love it

knew not why. Its happiness went out over the wide waters and upon the unfettered wind, and swelled up into the free dome of blue sky until it filled it. The dawn lighted up the faces of the ivory cliffs, which the sun and sea had been blanching for centuries of God's unchanging love. The miles of noiseless sands seemed vast, as if they were the floor of eternity. Somehow the daybreak was like eternity. The idea came over me of that feeling of acceptance which so entrances the soul just judged and just admitted into heaven. *To be saved!* I said to myself, *To be saved!* Then the thoughts of all the things implied in salvation came in one thought upon me; and I said, This is the one grand joy of life; and I clapped my hands like a child, and spoke to God aloud. But then there came many thoughts all in one thought, about the nature and manner of our salvation. *To be saved with such a salvation!* This was a grander joy, the second grand joy of life: and I tried to say some lines of a hymn; but the words were choked in my throat. The ebb was sucking the sea down over the sand quite silently; and the cliffs were whiter, and more daylike. Then there came many more thoughts all in one thought; and I stood still without intending it. *To be saved by such a Saviour!* This was the grandest joy of all, the third grand joy of life; and it swallowed up the other joys; and after it there could be on earth no higher joy. I said nothing; but I looked at the sinking sea as it reddened in the morning. Its great heart was throbbing in the calm; and methought I saw the Precious Blood of Jesus in heaven, throbbing that hour with real human love of me.[1]

His work is in a *genre* of its own. It is not pure theology, nor mere devotion (even when it most appears to be so), not explanatory apologetic, but a very individual mixture of the three. It undoubtedly owes a lot to the popularization of science which had already begun during his lifetime. He hoped to make intelligible to English readers the truths of dogma in the same way as the truths of science were being made intelligible. But Faber's aim was not simply to write textbooks of theology in a popular spirit. He wanted to harmonize theology and the natural sciences, to make clear what was luminously clear to himself— that theology alone could give meaning to natural science. If

God was the creator of the universe then the discoveries of science could not be other than a revelation of God. The growth of scientific knowledge was as romantic to Faber as it was to his agnostic contemporaries. "We see", he wrote,

> how all things are theology and how in it all other sciences regain themselves rather than melt away . . . We seek for men or if so be a man who shall wed all the sciences with theology, who shall reconcile faith and reason in one large lucid philosophy and who shall teach the nations how the church can dilate herself to the size of all the social questions which so vex humanity.[2]

This was Faber's ideal of himself as a writer—to see all things and to see them as the creatures of God. Whether he is discussing the possibility of other beings peopling other worlds or describing the beauty of an Italian landscape, or the knowledge of angels or the habits of animals—his vision is single. There is one simple explanation to all things, "one large lucid philosophy"—God.

In a passage at the beginning of *The Creator and the Creature* he describes London in the '50s.

> Beneath us is that beautiful rolling plain with its dark masses of summer foliage sleeping in the sun for miles and miles away, in the varying shades of blue and green according to the distance or the clouds. There at our feet, on the other side, is the gigantic city, gleaming with an ivory whiteness beneath its uplifted but perpetual canopy of smoke. The villa-spotted hills beyond it, its almost countless spires, its one huge many steepled palace, and its solemn presiding dome, its old bleached tower, and its squares of crowded shipping—it all lies below us in the peculiar sunshine of its own misty magnificence. There, in every variety of joy and misery, of elevation and depression, three million souls are working out their complicated destinies. Close around us the air is filled with the songs of rejoicing birds, or the pleased hum of the insects that are drinking the sunbeams, and blowing their tiny trumpets as they weave and unweave their mazy dance. The flowers breathe sweetly, and the leaves of the glossy shrubs are spotted with bright creatures in painted surcoats or gilded panoply, while the blue dome above seems both taller and bluer than common,

and is ringing with the loud peals of the unseen larks as the steeples of the city ring for the nation's victory [at the conclusion of the Crimean war]. Far off from the river flat comes the booming of the cannon, and here, all unstartled round and round the pond, a fleet of young perch are sailing in the sun, slowly and undisturbedly as if they had a very grave enjoyment of their little lives. What a mingled scene it is of God and man! And all so bright, so beautiful, so diversified, so calm, opening out such fountains of deep reflection, and simple-hearted gratitude to our Heavenly Father.[3]

In all his books Faber delights to return again and again to "the mingled scene" of God, man and creation.

All created life must in its measure imitate the Uncreated Life out of which it sprung. The very habits of animals, and the blind evolutions of matter, are in some sense imitations of God. The fern, that is for every trembling in the breath of the waterfall, in its growing follows some pattern in the mind of God.[4]

All the inferior animals, with their families, shapes, colours, cries, manners and peculiarities, represent ideas in the divine mind and are partial disclosures of the beauty of God, like the foliage of trees, the gleaming of metals, the play of light in clouds, the multifarious odours of wood and field and the manifold sound of waters.[5]

Or more daringly:

When the first cry of the Infant Jesus sounded in the cave, the melancholy splashing of those far western waters was mingled with the imitated howls of beasts in that strange typical festival of heathenism.[6]

It all comes back to God, but God revealed by Jesus Christ— the God of love. Love is the beginning, the middle, the end of Faber's work. It is the key to morality, to creation, to theology.

We cannot look at Him as simply external to ourselves. Things have passed between us; secret relationships are established; fond ties are knitted; thrilling endearments have been exchanged; there are memories of forgivenesses full of tenderness ...[7]

O how often in the fluent course of prayer does not this simple fact, that God is loving us, turn round and face us.[8]

Pain or ease, sorrow or joy, failure or success, the wrongs of my fellow creatures or their praise—what should they all be to me but matters of indifference? God loves me.[9]

He chose us when as yet we lay in the bosom of the great void ... He had a special love for something we by grace might be, and which others could not or would not be.[10]

St John states it, no one can explain it; earth would be hell without it; purgatory is paradise because of it; we shall live upon it in Heaven yet never learn all that is in it—God is love.[11]

I cannot tell how men endure life who do not profess this faith in the Creator's special love.[12]

Surely God cannot have been to others as He has been to us; they cannot have had such boyhoods, such minute secret buildings up of mind and soul; we have a feeling that about our own lives there has all along been a marked purpose, a divine speciality. Yet in truth how many millions of such tender and equally special biographies is the most dear and blessed God living in men's souls throughout all years and all generations! We are not singular among men; it is God's love which is singular in each of us.[13]

But love lies deeper still.

Creation is simply an act of divine love and cannot be accounted for on any other supposition than that of immense and eternal love.[14]

Creation is His love of Himself strongly and sweetly attaining its end through His love of His creatures and their love of Him. Perhaps all the works of God have this mark of His Triune Majesty upon them, this perpetual forthshadowing of the Generation of the Son and the Procession of the Spirit, which have been and are the life of God from all eternity.[15]

Why then does God love us? We must answer, Because He created us. This then would make mercy the reason of His love. But why did God create us? Because he loved us. We are entangled in this circle and do not see how to escape from it.[16]

Because God is God creation must needs swim in joy ... Even
now how joyous it all is with gladness almost divinely rebelling
against its penal destiny of grief ... From the joy therefore of
the highest seraphim to the blythe play of the Christian child
on the village green all joy is from Him ... The joys in the
bright eyes and inarticulate thanksgivings of animals are from
Him.[17]

Faber saw with characteristic clarity where this philosophy
led him. He realized its implications in his theology and especially
its effect on his approach to the spiritual life.

If this account of creative love be true, if God redeemed us
because He persisted in desiring, even after our fall, to have us
with Him as participators in His own eternal beatitude, salvation ought to be easy, even to fallen nature. If it is easy, then it
might appear to some to follow that at least the majority of
believers would be saved.[18]

Faber addressed himself to this "majority of believers". He
called them "invalid souls" or the middle class of the spiritual
world or more explicitly his "poor Belgravians". He hoped to
clarify their faith and thus raise them up to God. He did not write
of the higher paths of sanctity, he hardly mentions dark nights
of the soul. He believed it was this sort of person St Philip Neri
set himself to sanctify in Rome and to whom his sons were called
by God.

At bottom a severely practical man Faber set out in his books
to remedy a lack which was painfully obvious to him. His
"poor Belgravians" wished to live spiritual lives, their vocation
was in the world—and what spiritual food were they given?
Books written for enclosed religious, "dry books" as he called
them, very well for those to whom they were addressed but
hopeless for the poor Belgravians. What was meat to the one
might be poison to the other. Spiritual books designed for those
called to a high vocation when read by those living in the world
could be the cause of deception, pride and more often than not of
despair. Faber's books attempt to beguile his readers from the
world, to attract them to God, almost, one might say, tempt

them to religion. For this purpose the old spiritual books were useless.

> Spiritual books tell us that if we indulge, for instance, our sense of smell in some fragrance it is a huge immortification; yet St Mary Magdalene of Pazzi runs into the garden, plucks a flower, inhales the fragrance with delight and cries out, "O good, most good God! who from all eternity destined this flower to give me a sinner this enjoyment!"[19]

Of course Faber's approach had its disadvantages. Salvation can appear too easy and religion unreal. This never happened in Faber's mind. If his books are read carefully a structure of hard common sense and well-mastered theology is seen below even his most saccharine effusions. But it is true that out of their context or read by a hostile eye there are passages which seem to dissolve away the realities of the spiritual life. Religion seems to have gone, to be replaced by emotion. Similarly, his critics asked, what if the candles at Benediction cease to be merely an attraction to religion and become a substitute for it?

That is the crux of the argument of those who reject Faber's way of attraction. But in doing so it is hard to see (except on aesthetic grounds) how St Francis de Sales, and St Philip Neri would not have to be rejected also. Faber had his own answer.

> We hear people condemning unlucky devotees because they are fond of functions and Benedictions, of warm devotions and of pictures of the Madonna, of feasts and foreign practices ... Now does it follow that because persons are fond of these things they have nothing else in their piety? Because they have one characteristic of good Catholics are they *therefore* destitute of the others? Because they like flowers do they reject fruit? Oh, but mortification is the thing ... Souls are gravely warned, without regard to time or place or person or condition, to be detached from the gifts of God and to eschew sweet feelings and gushing fervours, when the danger is rather in their attachment to their carriages and horses, their carpets and their old china, the parks and the opera, and the dear bright world ... Better far to flutter like a moth round the candles of a gay Benediction, than to live without love in the proprieties of

sensual ease and worldly comfort, which seem, but perhaps are not, without actual sin.[20]

The argument comes round again. If we can love God, even a very little, then we shall be saved. And does it really matter that we have loved Him, even the small amount we do, because of a row of candles, an altar of flowers or even because of a purple patch in a spiritual book?

Faber's attitude is well illustrated by the story of St Giacinta Mariscotti which he tells at the beginning of *All for Jesus*. This Italian saint

> would occupy herself with nothing but the foolish frivolities of the world. All her girlhood passed away in dissipation . . .

Her sister made a good match and she was filled with spite and envy. In the end without a vocation she became a nun. "The first thing our saint did," Faber continues,

> was, out of her own money to build a grand room for herself. She furnished it in first rate style, and decorated it, her biographer says, quite sumptuously . . . She became more and more eaten up with vanity and thought of nothing but herself all day long. Queer training for a saint! In this way she lived nearly ten years. God then sent her a severe illness. She called for the Franciscan monk [*sic*] who was the confessor of the convent; but when he beheld the magnificent furniture of her room he refused to hear her confession, and told her paradise was never meant for such as she was. "What!" she cried, "and shall I not be saved?" He told her the only chance was to beg pardon of God, to repair the scandal she had given and to begin a new life.

This she did.

> Yet for all this no great change or, at least no heroic change, took place. She did not give up her fine things to the Superioress; but she gradually, quite gradually improved in her way of life. Again and again it was necessary for God to send her illnesses . . . and she became a Saint.

Faber points the moral.

> We think it is out of all question our becoming saints. But the
> story of St Giacinta gives us quite a different view; years of
> lukewarmness, venial sin, and unworthy vanity are succeeded
> by a half-and-half conversion, followed up by some little
> other conversions afterwards, just as it may have been with
> so many of us.[21]

Yes, it is easy to be saved because we are loved by God. He
only demands love in return. And what is easier, one might say
more natural, than to love God?

> Is it hard to find our joy in God? Rather is it not hard to find
> our joy in anything else?[22]

> Our hearts bound upwards because God is above. We cannot
> help ourselves. The very purling of our blood in our veins is
> joyous because life is a gift direct from God.[23]

> To serve God because you love him is so easy . . .[24]

> Only to serve Jesus out of love . . .[25]

starts a well-known passage.

> *You must love. You must love. You must love.* There is no other
> way. There is no help for it. Love will teach you everything.[26]

Love will make everything easy.

Faber was a startling phenomenon in mid-19th century London.
What was this man, preaching his embarrassing message of love,
couched in a Baroque idiom, doing in the world of Dickens, of
steam engines and progress? He does not seem to belong. Yet
Faber did belong. The intellectual history of the 19th century is a
series of reactions against Utilitarianism or what Chesterton called
"atheist industrialism". Cobbett, Dickens, Carlyle, Ruskin,
Arnold were as much in reaction against their age as was Faber.
Yet we regard these men as of the very bone of Victorian England.
Faber's reaction, if it can be called such, was a very different
thing to theirs. But then the Oxford Movement differed from the
Pre-Raphaelite Brotherhood.

Looked at in this way Faber is most nearly akin to Dickens.
The reaction of Dickens was the emotional reaction of the natural

man, Faber's was the emotional reaction of the spiritual man. Is it fantastic to say that what Christmas was to Dickens, Marian devotions were to Faber? It was the attempt in both cases to redress the balance, to bring back into life what had been driven out by Bentham—in the one case human brotherhood in the other the religion of love. The one was no less of his age than the other. Faber shows himself to be a Victorian in a hundred different ways. He is betrayed by his style, by his optimism, by his sugary taste, by his sentimentality. We don't like his referring to Our Lady as Mamma. ("Won't Mamma be pleased!" he exclaimed after a crowded procession with the Neapolitan Madonna.) But, then, we also don't like Little Nell.

Faber knew well enough the gulf which existed between his message and his readers. Could he have failed to do so? A less promising age for preaching the gospel of love could hardly be imagined. "We live", he wrote,

> as if we would petulantly say: . . . "You devout people in reality stand in the way of religion. It is hard for us to define enthusiasm; but you surely are enthusiasts. What we mean is, You are all heart and no head . . . All this incarnation of a God, this romance of a gospel, these unnecessary sufferings, this prodigal blood shedding, this exuberance of humiliations, this service of love, this condolence of amorous sorrow; to say the truth it is irksome to us: we are not at home in it at all; the thing might have been otherwise . . . Might we not put this tremendous mythology of Christian love, with all possible respect, a little on one side, and go to heaven by a plain, beaten, sober, moderate path, more accordant to our character as men, and to our dignity as British subjects? If the Anglo-Saxon race really fell in Adam why obviously we must take the consequences. Still, let the mistake be repaired in that quiet, orderly way, and with that proper exhibition of sound sense which are so dear to Englishmen." Well! If it must be so, I can only think of those bold words of St Mary Magdalene of Pazzi: "O Jesus! Thou hast made a fool of Thyself through love!"[26]

That was Faber's apology to his age—and to us. But does this really meet the case? Is it fair that Faber should shield his extravagances in this way? It is no good making preposterous statements and then calling them Christianity. That in effect was Pusey's charge made in the *Eirenikon*—which Newman tacitly endorsed. But *was* Faber's theology extravagant? It is true there are exuberant phrases and occasional verbal exaggerations, especially in his sermons and early writings. But no unbiased reader can fail to see that his theology was carefully thought out. As to his Mariology which Pusey found so scandalous here is his view of Our Lady's position in the scheme of salvation:

1. Our Blessed Lord is the sole Redeemer of the world in the true and proper sense of the word, and in this sense no creature whatsoever shares the honour with Him, neither can it be said of Him without impiety that He is Co-Redeemer with Mary.
2. In a secondary dependent sense and by participation, all the elect co-operate with Our Lord in the redemption of the world.
3. In the same sense, but in a degree to which no others approach, Our Blessed Lady co-operated with Him in the redemption of the world.[27]

There is nothing in Faber's writings which deviates from this position. He did translate Grignion de Montfort's *True devotion to the Blessed Virgin*, apparently none too accurately, and he did say in the preface: "What is the remedy indicated by God Himself? If we may rely on the disclosures of the Saints, it is an immense increase of devotion to Our Blessed Lady; but, remember, nothing short of an immense one . . . Thousands of souls perish because Mary is withheld from them." He expressly does not teach the presence of Our Lady in the Blessed Sacrament. Nor does he teach the presence of the Blessed Sacrament in heaven at the end of time but mentions the belief only to leave it in the uncertainty of a devout opinion.[28]

Many an Anglo-Catholic would not find his a very terrible teaching.

On the subject of Hell Faber is more at fault. It is pardonable that in order not to be misunderstood he emphasizes that Hell really exists. Given his doctrine of the easiness of salvation it is permissible to stiffen, as it were, his theological mixture. But he goes further. He delights in making his readers' skin creep.

> Nay do not start—what you see is indeed the white light of earth's sun; fear not; that sound,—it is the wind that waves the branches of the wood; be assured; your eyes do not deceive you, those are the village spires that are sleeping in the misty quiet landscape; all is right so far. We are here, and we are free: but we ought to have been,—there, and slaves![29]

It is perhaps only a bit of drama in the preacher's repertoire. But it leaves a nasty impression especially when he gives elsewhere a truly horrifying picture of the pain of loss.

> Up and down its burning cage the many-facultied and mightily-intelligenced spirit wastes its excruciating immortality in varying and ever-varying still, always beginning and monotonously completing, like a caged beast upon its iron tether, a threefold movement . . . In rage it would fain get at God to seize Him, dethrone Him, murder Him and destroy Him; in agony it would fain suffocate its own interior thirst for God . . . and in fury it would fain break its tight fetters of gnawing fire . . .[30]

"There are some now," he writes,

> in the green fields, or in the busy towns, on comfortable beds or on the sunshiny seas who in another hour perhaps will have gone there. This is a dreadfully real truth.[31]

There is a note of satisfaction in the tone—perhaps only satisfactorily explained by the streak of harshness, almost amounting to cruelty which ran like a fault through Faber's nature.

Faber scarcely mentions the theological problems connected with suffering—to the modern mind an inexplicable omission. Yet surely in this he is right and we are wrong. He lets the crucifix speak for itself. He takes suffering so much for granted that he describes it as the golden coin in which we are repaid by God for our love.

Faber's spiritual works were written within seven years, at the end of his life, and they form an unusually coherent whole. They were the fruit of long thought and experience gathered when at long last he had the leisure to write. By 1853, the date of *All for Jesus*, his theological opinions and style were fully formed. There is no sign of development in the eight books written in the seven years. They might all be volumes of one large work. It was apparently in this way that Faber thought of them.

All for Jesus (1853) is the best known of Faber's books and the most characteristic. When people think of Faber they think of *All for Jesus*. Its sub-title "Easy ways of divine love" shows its purpose. It is full of stories of the saints to illustrate the way "people living in the world" can "sanctify themselves in ordinary vocations". He wrote it round the sermons and addresses he had given to his Confraternity of the Precious Blood and he intended it to be a sort of spiritual manual for members of the Confraternity. As an introduction to the spiritual life and to the practice of Catholic devotions it was extremely popular. It has remained so up to quite recently.

It is full of good things. There is for instance the delightful story of St Paphnutius who wanted to know to whom on earth he was equal in sanctity. (God revealed to the holy man's surprise that he was equal to a certain piper in an Egyptian village.) But it must be admitted that there is also a great deal that is irritating. As in all his work, but especially in *All for Jesus*, there is an unwelcome mixture of the parochial and trivial with the great and universal. It is also marred by an aggressively Italianizing spirit and a *penchant* for private revelations. The love of God is often debased into mere sentimentality.

> His spirit steals into you and sets up a little throne, etc . . .[33]

> Oh look, children of God, look! etc . . .[34]

There is, too, the famous purple passage:

> Only serve Jesus out of love, and while your eyes are yet unclosed, before the whiteness of death is yet settled on your face, or those around you are sure that that last gentle breathing was indeed your last, what an unspeakable surprise will you have had at the judgment-seat of your dearest love, while the songs of heaven are breaking on your ears, and the glory of God is dawning on your eyes, to fade away no more for ever![35]

He does not always manage to make Catholicism attractive:

> What wonder His servants should yearn for those over whom Jesus yearned Himself! Thus it is they are always alert about missions, schools, religious orders, retreats indulgencies, and jubilees. They are full of plans, or if not of plans, at least of prayers.[36]

> It is so difficult to speak strongly against cheap excursions ... To pray for rain on such days sounds ill-natured and perhaps is so, yet it may hinder multitudes of sins.[37]

This priggishness, so obvious in him as a young man, here makes its last appearance. His later books are mercifully almost without it.

It is a baffling book—so much good and so much bad. It is like a Catholic chapel in the worst taste—the real thing but not a little repellent. Even so when all is said and done the book is a success. Even if you dislike Faber's style (and his religion for the matter of that) you cannot put the book down the same man who took it up—that is if you read it through. In spite of your distaste he has infected you with something of his spirit. He has made you see that love is the key to spiritual progress, that there is no approach to God without love and that God approaches us only in love. As likely as not the old magic, after these hundred years, has worked.

All for Jesus was begun at King William Street in January 1853 and continued at St Mary's, Sydenham. Working with his usual feverish activity, sometimes as long as sixteen hours a day, he finished the book in July and it was published in that month. No book on the spiritual life could be written at that speed *ex nihilo* and in fact the books were germinating in his mind for years. It was his custom to make notes for sermons or conferences, revise them before delivery, revise them again after delivery, and then put them aside for a while. He would then take them up again and write them out. He not only had the scheme of each book in his mind but to a quite unusual extent he had planned in advance the series of books he would write. He read with great rapidity at every available opportunity except during particularly severe bouts of illness. He noted in pencil at the end of the volumes what promised to be of use and thus accumulated a great store of information and apt illustrations.

1500 copies of *All for Jesus* were sold in 30 days, which, considering the fewness of English Catholics, was an extraordinary achievement. The fourth edition was out before a year was up, there were three French translations with seven editions in one year, translations into German, Polish, Italian, Spanish and many other languages. There was also a large sale in America. In 1869 it was estimated that 100,000 copies had been sold. It was of course praised by Wiseman and Manning but it was also praised by Ullathorne and other old Catholics, and from Rome by Father Cardella, S.J. But it was by no means universally accepted. A passage in the second edition on converts was very unpopular with nuns. An English Jesuit, Father Waterworth (somewhat to the embarrassment of his fellow Jesuits), and Bishop Browne both complained to Rome that it contained heresy. It seems, however, that no specific charges were made. As Hutchison said, it was probably the tone which was disliked—and it was difficult to define an heretical tone. The tone indeed might be Evangelical but the content when examined was found to be carefully orthodox. In the years following 1853, however, Faber was an object of some suspicion. He wrote anxiously to Talbot that he would withdraw anything which was not rigidly orthodox.

The opposition was silenced by Pius IX who created Faber a Doctor of Divinity in July 1854. As the century advanced so Faber's popularity increased. The distribution of his books coincided with the triumph of Ultramontanism until it almost seemed as if the Church of the late 19th century had been created by his spirit. It was a strange apotheosis for a convert English clergyman.

Growth in Holiness (1854) is a very different book. It almost entirely lacks the rhetoric of Faber's usual style. The sub-title "The Progress of the Spiritual Life" describes its content.

First there comes the region of beginnings, a wonderful time, so wonderful that nobody realizes how wonderful it is, till they are out of it, and can look back on it. Then stretches a vast extent of wilderness, full of temptation, struggle and fatigue, a place of work and suffering, with angels good and bad, winging their way in every direction, the roads hard to find and slippery under foot, and Jesus with the Cross meeting us at every turn. This is four or five times the length of the first region. Then comes a region of beautiful wooded, watered, yet rocky mountains, lovely yet savage too, liable to terrific tempests and to those sudden overcastings of bright nature, which characterize mountainous districts. This last is the land of high prayer . . . As the great body of devout men die while they are crossing the central wilderness it is of this wilderness which I wish to speak.[38]

It was to have been the middle of three books, the first "on the region of beginnings" and the third "on the regions of wooded, watered yet rocky mountains". They were never written.

It is rather a manual than a book—sane, erudite and shrewd. Faber appears as a man dealing in workmanlike manner with a subject he knows and understands. What he describes he has experienced—fervours, distractions, mortifications. He has trodden the road along which he leads his reader. *Growth in Holiness* is an entirely practical book and the least touched by time.

The Blessed Sacrament (1855) is unfortunately full of high-flown language which can distract the reader from its originality. Books 1 and 2, "The Blessed Sacrament as the greatest work of God" and "as the devotion of Catholics", have striking passages as does Book 4, the "Blessed Sacrament as a picture of Jesus". But these are long and often tedious. Book 3, "The Blessed Sacrament as a picture of God", however, is a bold and almost daring piece of apologetics.

It is remarkable that Faber never passed through a period of scepticism except in his schooldays. Yet *The Blessed Sacrament* reads like the apology of a converted sceptic. Newman's intuition noted this and no doubt also noted the analogy between Faber's mind and the working of his own. Perhaps that is why he derided it. It is not that there is any distrust in Faber's argument. His faith shines through very clearly. Nor is there any hysterical

fideism. But Faber argues with a shadow, and the argument goes
like this: either this amazing thing is true or else there is—Nothing.
It was the wrestling of Blanco White with a different outcome.

Faber begins from the premise that the arguments against the
Blessed Sacrament are no better than those against the Incarnation. And these in their turn are no better than the arguments
against Creation. If it is difficult to think of God under the form
of bread and wine it is also difficult to think of God as a baby.
And if you cannot conceive of an Infant God what is there to
shew you God in Creation itself? Faber answers that there is
nothing. There is precisely nothing for the good reason that God
does not wish to show Himself.

> All manifestations of God, like the Blessed Sacrament, are
> concealments also ... everywhere in this world to believe is
> to see and seeing is not believing.[39]

The very difficulties against faith Faber turns into arguments for it.

> It is then the good will and pleasure of God that He is so in
> His own creation that He will only be found by those who seek
> Him.[40]

But Faber's arguments need to be given in his own words.

> I wish to show you that it [the Blessed Sacrament] is the
> exemplar and the type of all God's operations, the model of
> all the ways in which the Creator vouchsafes to be, to work,
> to hide Himself and to manifest Himself in His own Creation.[41]

> He exists in nature as a hidden God, our reason finds Him out
> as a hidden God. Revelation discloses Him as a hidden God.[42]

> His [Jesus's] very first instinct was an impulse to hide Himself
> and even to fly when He was sought ... He came for the
> express purpose of manifesting Himself, and He did nothing
> but hide Himself.[43]

God hides Himself as revealed in the Bible.

> He hid Himself with one family of patriarchs, and then with
> one people, anything but remarkable for goodness, greatness
> or attractiveness.[44]

He is as much hidden in nature as in the Blessed Sacrament.

> Its laws are as the sacramental accidents; they hide Him ...
> No one is obliged to see Him who will not see Him. No one
> can see Him at all without a moral preparation of heart. The
> very difficulties of nature are used as weapons against God,
> just as the difficulties of the Blessed Sacrament are grounds on
> which many reject the doctrine.[45]

He continues by showing how God is hidden in metaphysics,
in the Church, even in the conscience.

> It seems as if failure were a characteristic of the divine works...
> The creation of the angels was a failure ... Paradise was a
> failure ... The patriarchal system failed ... The law was a
> failure ... When Our Lord appeared what was left of the
> spiritual Israel, but Simeon, Anna and the like? ... In the
> Church particular Churches die out as in Africa, or fall away
> as in Greece or are inundated by heresy as in some of the petty
> German states or are devastated by unbelief as France in the
> eighteenth century ...[46]

> The appearance of things is as if everywhere the Flight into
> Egypt were being enacted, and God was a fugitive before the
> face of His own pursuing creatures ... Apparent defeat, the
> semblance of frustration lies like an intense mist over the ground
> of God's holiest operations. Were it not for simple, joyous,
> child-like faith, the clearest eye might quail, the stoutest heart
> tremble before this astounding spectacle of a defeated God. All
> nature and all grace, all angels and all men, all creation and all
> redemption gathered into one point and so disclosed to men,
> and lo! that one point is a skull-strewn Calvary with the Dead
> Christ upon the Cross.[47]

"Thus," he concludes his argument,

> secrecy, littleness, helplessness, ignominy and being at the mercy
> of creatures are the five laws of the Divine Interference in
> the world; and assisted by grace, we can almost get a habit of
> seeing God everywhere by the application of these laws. They
> form partly a theological and partly a spiritual instinct. What
> it concerns us particularly now to remark is, that these five

laws include nearly all the infidel and heretical objections to the Blessed Sacrament, that the Blessed Sacrament does not stand alone in being open to them, that the Blessed Sacrament is exactly the same kind of manifestation of God, and the same sort of Presence, as He vouchsafes in matter, mind, morals, theology, history, and the Church, and finally that the Blessed Sacrament exhibits these laws in the most vivid and peculiar manner, and thus concentrates upon itself all the light, and divine beauty, and heavenly secrecy that is anywhere in the world, and that it is the exemplar and most finished and intensely godlike height, of Creation and Redemption, of Nature and Grace.[48]

Yes, it comes to this,—that God vouchsafing to dwell in the Blessed Sacrament, it must needs be His greatest work of love. What was Palestine to this? . . . See! out of viewless and im-palpable Nothing that first instantaneous intellectual Creation, angels streaming forth in endless processions of diversified intelligence; and then those material orbs, in countless kinds, some strewn like gold dust over sidereal space in fair white galaxies, some hung like clearly swinging lamps along the streets and squares of the vast ethereal city! He who made them all, and could multiply the work again and again unnumbered times, He, the music of whose speechless voice evoked this splendour and this beauty and this intelligence, who brooded on the deeps of Chaos, who planted Eden, who fashioned Adam, and who in that day was young yet everlasting, in the Same, His whole, undivided, everblessed self who is now in the tabernacle, taken captive by His own insatiable love of the creatures whom His mercy made![49]

The Creator and the Creature or *The Wonders of Divine Love* (1858) is *All for Jesus* with a theological bias. Faber himself wrote that

it stands to the Author's other works in the relation of source and origin.[50]

Not much need be said of it as a great deal has already been quoted. It contains the essential Faber and Faber at his least parochial. It breathes the confidence of a man to whose faith nothing is alien. It is in this book that he formulates most fully his conception of creation as an act of divine love. Faber, a poet by instinct if not in fact, delights to stress over and over again the goodness and beauty of creation.

> Creation is in a sort of a son of God, a mighty family of sons, expressing more or less partially His image, representing His various perfections and all with sufficient clearness to enable the Apostle to say that we are without excuse if we do not perceive the Invisible by the things that are seen.[51]

But he goes further.

> As the image of God's perfection, Creation was the faint shadow of that most gladdening mystery, the eternal generation of the Son ... As the communication of His love, and the love of His own glory, Creation also dimly pictured that unspeakable necessity of the divine life, the eternal procession of the Spirit. We have already seen that Creation was only and altogether love. As the Son is produced by the inward uncreated knowledge which God has of Himself, so is Creation the outward and created knowledge of Himself; and as the Holy Spirit is produced by the inward uncreated love of God, so is Creation His outward and created love. Creation is a mirror of his perfections to Himself as well as to His creatures.[52]

From these heights he returns often enough, as befitted a practical man, to the individual soul.

> It is the grand crisis in everybody's life, an era to date from, when the knowledge that the Creator loves him passes into a sensible conviction.[53]

The Foot of the Cross, also 1858, but sketched out ten years before, is a much less satisfactory book. Its sub-title is "The Sorrow of Mary" and it is really a devotional work based on the seven dolours of Our Lady. It has a prefatory chapter and an epilogue but it remains essentially Faber's highly wrought, often moving but extremely long meditations on these mysteries. He squeezes so much devotion from each dolour that the reader is stunned and perhaps discouraged.

Spiritual Conferences, 1859, contains some good things with much that is obvious and tedious. Faber, however, displays a masterly understanding of the human heart. The first conference is on kindness, a virtue not very congenial to Faber and whose lack in his own life he was to deplore on his deathbed. It is noticeable that it was suggested and inspired by Ward. There is one sentence that sticks in the mind:

> Common states of prayer look uncommon to the man who is always reading books of mystical theology.[54]

The Precious Blood, or *The Price of our Salvation*, 1860, is the work of a tired man. His subject is the Redemption. It is long, often mechanical, and lacks the verve of the earlier works.

Bethlehem, 1860, recaptures his early spirit. There are passages as good as any he ever wrote. But he broke no fresh ground although the theme—the Incarnation—was new. The message of love is the same as before with Jesus at the centre.

> It seems as if He must go out of Himself and summon creatures up from nothing and fall upon their neck and overwhelm them with His love, and so find rest.[55]

> Each single human life in the world amounts to nothing less than a private revelation of God, a revelation which would be enough for the whole world, if an inspired pen recorded it.[56]

As might be expected, he returns again and again to the wonders of creation, comparing them to the wonders of the Incarnation.

> As the Word, He is the utterance of the Father, the expression of Him, the image of Him. Creation is in a finite and created way what He is infinitely and uncreatedly.[57]

> He was as it were necessitated to speak one Word, and that Word, because necessary could not be otherwise than coeternal and consubstantial with Himself. In His love he freely spoke a second Word, which was creation, and that Word, because free, was finite and temporary. It was by His first Word that He spoke His second Word. For creation is more than an echo of the eternal generation of the Son, in the reality of that created nature which the Son has stooped to wear.[58]

We therefore see the position of Jesus in creation.

"Thus", he says,

the predestined created nature of the Word lay everlastingly
in the vast bosom of the Father. It was a human nature eternally
chosen with a distinct and significant predilection. It was the
first creature. It is He who in His assumed nature we call Jesus.
All angels, man, animals, and matter were made because of
Him and for Him simply. He is the sole reason of the existence
of every created thing, the sole interpretation of them all, the
sole rule and measure of every external work of God.[59]

But Faber's theology was not without its moral. Jesus

is the son of God by nature, and rational creatures were to be
the sons of God by adoption through their justification. It was
the end of their creation that they were to be admitted to share
in His filiation. The communication of His sonship was to be
their way into glory. As God appeared as if He entered into
creation through the Person of the Son, so through the same
person does creation find its way to rest in God.[60]

To be sons of God, brothers of Jesus, was the reason for our
creation, why we exist.

It is easy then for us to discern the spirit of devotion to the
Eternal Father . . . It is in itself the most abundant and the
most unalloyed communication of the spirit of Jesus. It is the
ultimate devotion . . . It is in human things a sort of reverential
imitation of the love of the Word and the Holy Ghost for the
coequal Father in divine things. Nay, we must dare yet again,
it is also an imitation of the Father Himself, eternally generating
the Son by the knowledge of Himself, and with the Son eternally breathing out the Holy Ghost as their mutual love; for it
is in the knowledge and love of Him, and in union with His
Son, and with the utterance of the Spirit's voice, that this devotion consists.[61]

The touch, the taste, the glory of the living God, is notoriously
difficult to communicate. Even the humdrum daily experience
of the Christian soul in a state of grace, barely conscious of the
indefinable, almost unnoticed hand that guides it—how can this

be communicated? In terms of earthly love? St John of the Cross dared to do it. Patmore dared as well. Crashaw tried it. They were all, on occasion, great poets. The lay sister, with perhaps far greater experience of God's life within her, makes do with a defective poetic equipment, often little better than that of Wilhelmina Stitch. There is in reality no proper medium of communication. Faber's spiritual works should be judged bearing in mind this enormous difficulty. For he saw the world alight with God's glory. In the last resort the philosophy and the theology, impressive though they may be, are simply props to the main theme. Can there be anything new in the cosmology of love? It is the vision not the message which is important. Faber, too, was trying to communicate the incommunicable—the fire of love he saw everywhere, in the life of the ordinary worldly Catholic, in the life of the saint, in the Blessed Sacrament, in the life of Our Lady, in Our Lord's life, in creation. He is at times repetitive, vulgar, silly. He wholly lacked the reticence of the prose stylist. But every now and again we see what he saw. That is his achievement. A lot can be forgiven and forgotten because of it.

II

Faber is popularly remembered as a writer of bad hymns. Only a few still sung enhance his memory. Those unsung have been consigned to oblivion. But if there were an Oxford Book of English bad verse they would certainly retain a dubious immortality.

O happy Pyx! O happy Pyx!
Where Jesus doth His dwelling fix.

(Holy Communion.)

No Bibles and no books of God were in that Eastern land,
No Pope, no blessed Pope, had they to guide them with his hand;
No Holy Roman Church was there, with its clear and strong
      sunshine,
With its voice of truth, its arm of powers, its sacraments divine.

(The three Kings.)

Yet the hearts of children
Hold what worlds cannot,
And the God of wonders
Loves the lowly spot.
>   (Thanksgiving after Communion.)

The month of May with a grace a day
Shines bright with Our blessed Mother;
    The Angels on high
    In the glorious sky,
Oh they know not such another,
Nay, they know not such another!
>   (Oh! Balmy and bright.)

Faber has been dismissed as an entirely mediocre hymn writer
and was, indeed, so dismissed at the time of his death by many
good critics. And yet and yet . . . Is it, after all, a fair estimate?

The day is done; its hours have run;
    And Thou hast taken count of all,
The scanty triumphs grace hath won,
    The broken vow, the frequent fall.
>   (Evening hymn at the Oratory.)

How apt those "scanty triumphs"! A mediocre poet could not
have written:

Timeless, spaceless, single, lonely,
    Yet sublimely Three,
Thou art grandly, always, only
    God in unity!
Lone in grandeur, lone in glory,
Who shall tell Thy wondrous story,
    Awful Trinity?

>   (Majesty divine.)

Faber never lost the sense of the moral imperative learnt from
Mr Cunningham and the Evangelicals. Indeed it is perhaps a
sense which *cannot* be lost. He revised and polished his theological
works because the impulse behind them was religious. Only the
best satisfied his conscience. But poetry had been the great

snare at the beginning of his career. The poet had nearly defeated the priest. Therefore poetry had to go. As Wordsworth saw, he had not the ruthless egoism of the true poet. However much he might love poetry, whatever delight the writing of it might give him, "duty to himself and others", in Wordsworth's words, had to come first. Poetry, he found after long struggles, was hollow at the centre. Beauty was not enough. God demanded goodness. The hymns were a compromise—poetry and religion, Christianity in charge of his poetic talent, as it were. The attempt was perhaps inevitably doomed, but it was not by any means wholly unsuccessful. In some ways the hymns are a notable achievement. Yet they are marred throughout by what can only be called an atrocious carelessness. He had no pretensions as to their merit and therefore took far less trouble than he should have done. He wrote them at odd times on odd scraps of paper. During a holiday in Yorkshire he wrote the well known "Mother of Mercy" and "The Blessed Sacrament". "Faith of our fathers" was written at Cotton. "Pilgrims of the night" is said to have been inspired by the bells of Elton.

The first little book of hymns was published at King William Street in 1849 and contained twenty-two hymns. A second part brought the number up to 66. All the time a process of revision was going on. Some hymns were found unsuitable and were dropped. Faber wrote others to take their place. By the time the Oratory was established at Brompton in 1854 a new edition was published. This contained 49 hymns not in the earlier compilation and 36 of the earlier hymns were omitted. A supplement of 10 hymns was then added. In the next edition of 1867, after Faber's death, twelve more hymns were omitted and nineteen new ones added. Changes continued to be made in subsequent editions. It is an interesting fact that, like Swinburne, Faber was ignorant of music. The popularity of Faber's hymns has declined but almost every hymn book, Protestant and Catholic, contains a few. During the second world war "Faith of our fathers" was sung by prisoners of all denominations in a Japanese prison camp to keep up the prisoners' morale.

Faber's object in making his collection of hymns was, as in all else he undertook, ambitious, not to say grandiose. He did not merely set out to write hymns to be sung in Catholic churches, badly as such hymns were needed. He set out to write a book of poetical meditations as well. "Everyone", he wrote in his preface,

> who has had experience among the English poor, knows the influence of Wesley's hymns and the Olney collection. Less than moderate literary excellence, a very tame versification, indeed often the simple recurrence of a rhyme is sufficient: the spell seems to lie in that ... It seemed then in every way desirable that Catholics should have a hymn book *for reading* which should contain the mysteries of the faith in easy verse or different states of heart and conscience depicted with the same unadorned simplicity as the "O for a closer walk with God" of the Olney hymns; and that the metres should be of the simplest and least intricate sort, so as not to stand in the way of the understanding or enjoyment of the poor.

Judged by Faber's own standard the collection is a failure. It is not read now and has seldom been read as a devotional work. Moreover Faber lacked a quality taken almost for granted in a poet. Whatever his musical powers his poetic imagination was visually weak. This was not so in his prose and letters but his poetry produces the effect of short-sightedness, of light without sight. It is this which irritates the reader and makes him endorse the early criticism of "Faber's unreality". The same quality of visual diffuseness is to be found in Swinburne. Like Swinburne, Faber relies on the evocative rather than the visual connotation of words. This is not such a defect in a hymn writer as it is in a writer of lyric poetry. Nevertheless it *is* a defect as a comparison between a hymn by Faber and one of the Olney hymns will quickly show.

A short selection from the hymns, necessarily incomplete and omitting much that is well known, may indicate some of the book's better qualities. For when Faber's carelessness is admitted and his visual deficiency understood there is something to enjoy.

> At last I stopped to listen,
>> His voice could not deceive me;
> I saw His kind eyes glisten,
>> So anxious to relieve me:

And I thought I heard Him say,
As He came along His way,
O silly soul! come near Me;
My sheep should never fear me;
I am the Shepherd true.

(True Shepherd.)

Rest comes at length; though life be long and dreary,
    The day must dawn, and darksome night be past;
All journeys end in welcomes to the weary,
    And Heaven, the heart's true home, will come at last.
        Angels of Jesus,
        Angels of light,
        Singing to welcome
        The pilgrims of the night!

(Pilgrims of the night.)

The Church, the Sacraments, the Faith,
    Their uphill journey take,
Lose here what there they gain, and, if
    We lean upon them, break.

(The right must win.)

For goodness all ignoble seems,
    Ungenerous and small,
And the holy are so wearisome,
    Their very virtues pall . . .

The bright examples round me seem
    My dazzled eyes to hurt;
Thy beauty, which they should reflect,
    They dwindle and invert.

(Peevishness.)

He stirred—and yet we know not how
    Nor wherefore He should move.
In our poor human words, it was
    An overflow of love.

It was the first outspoken word
   That broke that peace sublime,
An outflow of eternal love
   Into the lap of time.

He stirred; and beauty all at once
   Forth from His Being broke;
Spirit and strength and living life,
   Created things, awoke.
                (Creation of the Angels.)

There is no little skill in "The Eternal years":

How shalt thou bear the Cross that now
   So dread a weight appears?
Keep quietly to God and think
   Upon the Eternal years.

Its sixteen stanzas all end with "the Eternal years"; a stiff test of versification.

Faber's poetic "blindness", compensated for by a heightened aural and tactile awareness, accounts for his successes in sacred poetry if not in hymnology. It enables him in a unique way to describe the mysterious, the unusual, the almost indescribable.

The space of one swift lightning's flash
   Was the Majesty outspread;
Then angels' songs the silence broke
   And the glorious darkness fled.
                (Light in darkness.)

I see but indistinctly yet
   Forms growing like to what I knew
One sun is rising, one is set,
   But which of these two suns is true?

Within my soul there hath been strife;
   I hear retreating voices rave;
This stirring in me must be life,
   But life on which side of the grave?

Blue sky, green earth, my well-known room!
  I waken up to all the past;
But what a look of cheerless gloom
  That inward light o'er all hath cast!

O Lord! What hast Thou done to me?
  What marks are these my spirit bears?
Why didst Thou come so frighteningly,
  Why take me, Lord! so unawares?

I felt Thy touch; self died,—alas!
  Only a momentary death;
Ah me! how quickly Thou didst pass—
  Within the breathing of a breath!

(Divine favours.)

Faber was at his best when writing of death.

O sorrow! 'tis thy law to feed
  On what should be relief;
O time! of all things surely thou
  Art cruelest to grief . . .

Old grief is worse than new; its pain
  Is deeper in the heart;
The dull blind ache is worse to bear
  Than blow, or wound or smart . . .

Oh that they would not comfort me!
  Deep grief cannot be reached;
Wisdom, to cure a broken heart,
  Must not be wisdom preached . . .

Deep grief is not a past event,
  It is a life, a state,
Which habit makes more terrible
  And age more desolate.

(Deep grief.)

I thought it was less hard to die,
   A straighter road to Thee,
With at least twilight in the sky
   And one narrow arm of sea.

Saviour! what means this breadth of death,
   This space before me lying,
These deeps where life so lingereth,
   This difficulty of dying?

So many turns, abrupt and rude,
   Such ever-shifting grounds,
Such strangely peopled solitude,
   Such strangely silent sounds?

Another hour! What change of pain
   In this last act doth lie!
Surely to live life o'er again
   Were less prolix than to die.

How carefully Thou walkest, Lord!
   Canst Thou have cause to fear?
Who is that Spirit with the sword?
   Art Thou not Master here?

Whom are we trying to avoid?
   From whom, Lord! must we hide?
Oh can the dying be decoyed,
   With his Saviour by his side?

Deeper!—dark! dark! But yet I follow;
   Tighten, dear Lord! Thy clasp!
How suddenly earth seems to hollow,
   There is nothing left to grasp! . . .

Loose sand—and all things sinking! Hark,
   The murmur of a sea!
Saviour! it is intensely dark;
   Is it near Eternity?

Can I fall from Thee even now?
  Both hands, dear Lord! both hands!
Why dost Thou lie so deep, so low,
  Thou shore of the Happy Lands?

Ah! death is very, very wide,
  A land terrible and dry;
If Thou, Sweet Saviour! hadst not died,
  Who would have dared to die?

Another fall!—Surely we steal
  On towards Eternity:—
Lord! is this death?—I only feel
  Down in some sea with Thee.
                    (The length of death.)

CHAPTER XV

LAST YEARS

FABER was now much of an invalid and only part of the week was spent in Brompton. But life was not always dull. There was an exciting episode at Sydenham.

The normal disappearance of gold from the offertory dishes awakened in Chad the genius of a detective. He remained 5 hours in the plate cupboard and then had the melancholy satisfaction of seeing a pious gentleman with St Philip's habit on, to whom the collecting of the offertory was entrusted open the bags and help himself.

The brother had

in his character as a monk given a supper party to the ticket porters of the Forest Hill and Sydenham stations under the vigilant superiorship of Bernard while I was at Ardencaple [The Duchess of Argyll's house].[1]

Then there had been the dramatic death of Mr Plater, the father of the "ewe lamb". "Mr Plater," Faber wrote,

came to see F. Louis [Plater], and after 10 minutes very kind conversation in the recreation room dropped down dead, fighting with his hands and groaning for about one minute, Louis raving violently, but before any could reach the room all was over ...

"The inquest is over, thank God," he wrote later:

They did all they could to annoy us. Poor Louis' examination was most harrowing, his conversion, his quarrel with his father, altercation, etc., etc. I don't know what would have happened if the coroner had not interposed. It was all brutal. They say in the first place that we kidnapped the son and killed the father. One juror declared some red spots on the body were signs of violence. The dissection was very shocking, blood and brains on the coconut matting of the recreation room, and the stench intolerable. The body is now removed, by coroner's warrant, partly dressed in my clothes and partly in F. Alban's.[2]

When the new parish at Brompton was inaugurated the Fathers preached what they called the Mission of St Eutropius. The occasion chosen was the translation to the church of the relics of a martyr which had been in the possession of the Congregation for some years. Owing to the lack of altars the relics had never been exposed before. "The concourse of people was very great," Faber wrote:

> Indeed it appears that our vicars so vigorously carried out the Evangelical precept of compelling the many to enter, that more than once we were forced to compel some of them to go out again in order to allow the procession to go round the church ...

The chapel at King William Street had been too small for processions to Faber's disappointment but at Brompton there was plenty of space. "The processions", he reported with satisfaction,

> were particularly popular, and thanks to our prefects of ceremonies, music and sacristy, there was a good deal of variety in them. There were processions of St Philip, processions of Penance, and of the Precious Blood with the stations.

"The great procession last Sunday night", the letter continues in the hand of another Father,

> was anticipated by a panic and an insurrection of the *coté droite* benches which was extremely alarming but was most providentially calmed down by the Father [Faber]. We had notice that something would be attempted by the Protestants, in retaliation for the disturbance caused by some unknown individuals at a professedly anti-Catholic meeting held in a neighbouring riding school by Dr Butler. When the service began on Sunday night the place was crammed to solidity and for some time the Cardinal could not commence his sermon in consequence of the buzzing and humming that was going on in the lower part of the church. He had hardly finished the first sentence when the catastrophe took place. A child fainted and its mother cried for help. This was taken as a sign

by an urchin on the other side of the church, who let off a squib and cried "Fire!" Most providentially the other conspirators with squibs had not been able to gain admittance through the crowd, and so they were compelled to let off theirs on the other side of the road. The commotion in the church, however, was quite bad enough. One lady got past even the Father into the sanctuary and through the sacristy into the large corridor of the house; upon which the Father gave up individuals and came back to the agitated sea. As the Cardinal was sitting in the pulpit the Father went a little way down the church and rose up on a bench in his white cotta over the mass of confusion, and with a few words descended, leaving the whole assembly in perfect peace ... All went well after that.[3]

Towards the end of 1857 the Dowager Duchess of Argyll, a great friend of the Oratory, offered to buy the Fathers a new organ. John Bowden wrote that it would be the largest in London.

The organ is 25 feet high so the roof will have to be opened to let the sound in. It will have endless stops.

"The swell organ alone", his brother Charles wrote,

will be three times as large as our present organ. Mr Pitts [one of the runaway boys, son of the organ maker near Elton] is nearly off his head with delight.[4]

The organ necessitated extensive alterations in the temporary church and these were carried out during the next few years. The roof was raised 13 feet, large chapels were built on either side of the organ chamber, the sanctuary was enlarged, and a baldacchino was placed over the high altar. Faber, who of course delighted in all these alterations and improvements, raised money for and built a large chapel to St Joseph. He was too ill to see the bulk of the alterations in 1858 carried out but wrote happy letters about the new plans.

We shall look odd enough *outside*, but, like the king's daughter, all our glory will be within.[5]

The Duchess also founded a choir school.

Faber's last years were saddened by many deaths severing

links with the past. Alban Wells, whose mother's home had been Elton Hall and who had been one of the first Wilfridians, died in the Autumn of 1858 of consumption. He had frequently been ill and Faber had written of him some few months before that he had been living simply on the excitement of the Duchess's choral school. This was the first death since that of Stanislas Besant at St Wilfrid's in 1848 though there had been in the meantime no less than three in Birmingham. Lord Arundel and Surrey who had succeeded his father as 14th Duke of Norfolk in 1856 died at Arundel in 1860. Faber loved him deeply and faithfully attended him through two long months of illness. He was thus able to repay the Duke's many kindnesses to the Oratory. His poems on death were probably written at this time. Brother Chad, twice in revolt against Faber, died in 1862—the only one of the little sheaf of Eltonians to die in the Oratorian habit. He had latterly been porter and was seized with his fatal illness in the porter's lodge. "I *forced* the Sacraments on him last night," Faber wrote with typical honesty:

> Fearful temptations against the faith: but I hope all is well and I think it is.[6]

During these last years Faber's friendship with W. G. Ward ripened into intimacy. They had of course known each other since Balliol days but Ward had looked on "Faber of Univ." as little more than a pleasing dilettante. He held that his conversion had revealed unexpected depths of character. From 1853 Faber was Ward's spiritual director. "Contrasted as the two men were in some ways," Wilfrid Ward wrote,

> one gifted with high poetical imagination and the other before all things logical and even mathematical in his cast of mind, there was a strong common element in that realization of the whole realm of the world beyond the veil which lively faith gives to many who are not poets. The present writer has before him the picture of their intercourse in his early youth, the eager and rapid conversation, the impression that the two men were on fire with the importance of the views and plans which they discussed, the tremendous exaggerations of language—fully

conscious perhaps on the side of the Oratorian, while with
Ward they were partly due to the vision of logical consequences which made bad lead at once to worst and good to
best; Faber's glowing and handsome face, and Ward, whose
habitual expression was recently described by Mr Mozley as
"of one who is overflowing with some grand idea or fount of
ideas . . ."

"The Oratorian Fathers who remember that time," Wilfrid
Ward continues,

recall Ward's presence during the recreation hour after dinner
when the two men, eager talkers alike, both of "mighty
presence", with immense vocabularies, with equal positiveness
of logic and superlativeness of rhetoric, sat opposite each
other capping epigrams and anecdotes, while the other Fathers
were gathered round in a ring . . . On one occasion a discussion is in full course on Grace and Predestination, Faber favour-
ing the stringent Thomistic view, Ward the less vigorous
opinion advocated by St Alfonso Liguori. Definitions, citations.
from the great scholastics, are quoted with exact memory and
knowledge of men whose lives are absorbed in the study of
such authorities. Ward, with the intensity of expression which
his friends remember on such occasions, noticing nothing around
him, is proving his view, throwing his arguments into syllog-
isms, illustrating them by sayings of the Saints. As he sways
from side to side, all unnoticed by him a pamphlet falls from
his pocket. One of the Fathers picks it up, intending to restore
it to him when the heat of the contest shall give breathing time.
In the meantime he mechanically opens it at the first page,
thinking perhaps, to see the title "De Actibus humanis" or
"On grace and free will". But it is not so. "Benefit of Mr.
Buckstone. The celebrated comedian will appear in his original
character of Box in *Box and Cox*, the part of Cox being under-
taken by Mr. Compton," are the words which meet his eye.
The argument on Predestination is still going on, but the
audience becomes less attentive. The play bill circulates and
finds its way gradually back to its owner, and the general
laughter, which by this time has become audible, is explained
to him . . .

There was often a humorous *arrière pensée* to the conception

of the English Protestant world as to the untruthful Jesuitism
to which the two converts had surrendered, and sentences
were so turned as to shock its imaginary representative and
confirm his worst fears. A controversial point once arose about
some priest's action, in which the facts had been misinterpreted
in the newspapers but nevertheless the general course pursued
had gone on a recognized and defensible Catholic principle.
Ward was to write to the papers in his defence. He discussed
with Faber the line which he should take in his letter. Both
grounds seemed strong. But the Protestant would have read
truly Jesuitical unscrupulousness into the question he called
upstairs to Faber as he was leaving: "Which shall I do then,
Faber: deny the facts or defend the principle? . . .

Ward in the course of his visits to the theatres found his
way to the old Oratory. "Last night", he remarked to Faber,
"I went to see an excellent piece at the King William Street
Theatre. Between the acts two thoughts came into my head.
The first was, Last time I was in this building I heard Faber
preach. The second was, How much more I am enjoying myself
tonight than I did the last time I was here."

Faber's great breadth of sympathy and his reaction from the
old conventional moderation of Puseyism were points of contact with Ward. "Keble used to say", Ward remarked, "that
the chief characteristic of the English church is *sobriety*; the
Catholic church on the contrary tells you to be 'inebriated' with
the love of God"; and certainly nothing could be less like
Keble's ideal than the religious discussions of Ward and Faber.
They seldom met without some electric shock occurring in the
course of conversation. "Shall I go into retreat?" Ward asked
one day when he felt that the absorbing interest of his intellectual work needed some counteracting spiritual influence. "A
retreat!" exclaimed Faber. "It would be enough to send you to
Hell. Go to the play as often as you can, but don't dream of a
retreat."[7]

Ward disliked all sermons and for that reason disliked Faber's.
But Faber was a notable preacher. Fluent and eloquent he obviously was, but in addition he had a beautiful voice, flexible and
sensitive. He had grown grossly fat but the beauty of his expression
and especially of his eyes is often mentioned.

> Such a holy witch
> That he enchants societies unto him:
> Half all men's hearts are his

were the words from *Cymbeline* Frank put on the title page of the short memoir of his brother. Faber was indeed as much an enchanter in the pulpit as in conversation. He could, however, be disconcerting. He made a point of not altering or toning down his sermons when Protestants or unbelievers were present. The result was sometimes shocking. His references to "Mamma" for "Our Lady" were not easily forgotten and created an erroneous impression of the quality of his mind. As a corollary to this attitude soon after his conversion he abandoned all controversy. An ultramontane sermon on the Papacy caused a flutter but delighted Pius IX. It was significantly called *Devotion to the Pope*. He began a course of lectures on the Immaculate Heart of Mary at King William Street but after the first received letters objecting to the views expressed. When the time came for the second he went into the pulpit, announced he had received the complaints, and told the congregation the course would be discontinued

> because I trust I know what is due to my Lady's honour better than to cast her pearls before swine.[8]

Baron von Hügel related that after preaching with much eloquence for an hour the panegyric on St Ignatius he ended:

> This then, my dear brothers, is St Ignatius's way to heaven; and, thank God, it is not the only way.[9]

He is said to have become exasperated by an unresponsive Irish congregation and exclaimed that having prayed to Jesus and to Mary in vain he would now pray *to them*. At which he knelt in the pulpit, and the congregation followed suit and were soon in tears. In spite of his eloquence he made elaborate notes before he spoke. He was once asked to say a few words to a party of children who were paying a visit to the crib. He did so, but it was discovered afterwards that he had spent the whole afternoon in preparation of the address.

"He was a very early riser," Bowden wrote of these years,

and had usually said his Mass in the private chapel of the house before the rest of the community were stirring. He would then take a cup of tea, and after making his meditation, write steadily until breakfast. The morning was principally spent in conversation and discussion with different Fathers, who reported to him the works entrusted to their care, and received from him the necessary directions for their management. Most of their undertakings, beyond as well as within the walls of the Oratory, were due to his suggestion for their beginning, and to his encouragement and advice for much of their success. The difficulties encountered and the questions arising in their prosecution were promptly and confidently referred to him for solution. At all hours his room was the frequent resort of the Fathers; there were few who would not have felt a blank in the day if they had not paid a visit to what seemed to renew amidst themselves the "School of Christian mirth" of St Philip's room at the Chiesa Nuova.[10]

Faber was of course fully in control of the house. The finances were in a difficult position and he had to exercise the greatest economy—which went very much against the grain. The private resources of individual Fathers had been drained by the new foundation and by Oratorian custom receipts from the church could not contribute in any way to the support of the house. As a matter of fact the public did not contribute enough to maintain even the church services and the deficiency came out of the Fathers' pockets. This financial trouble worried Faber who had never been able to keep a penny of his own, even at Elton. Bowden put down many of his attacks of illness to anxiety over money. In addition to his work as Superior, after 1856 Faber was novice master as well. This, his favourite occupation—he always maintained he was fitted to be novice master but not Superior—took up a lot of his time. Then there were countless letters of spiritual advice he had to write after his books became famous. From year to year the numbers increased. One of the Fathers finding a large heap for the post expressed envy of his talent for letter-writing. "Talent," Faber replied, "it's the fear of

God." St Mary's, Sydenham, was his great recreation. He still spent his time on improvements, planting trees and making vistas. "I went down to St Mary's the other day," Hutchison wrote,

> and I thought the place was looking very nice. The Father, of course, was cutting down trees right and left. At present he is operating in the locality of the acacia walk; it is lucky he is coming back to London soon, or there would be nothing left, though I must own that the cutting down so far has certainly been an improvement.[11]

With all his charm, which did not diminish as he grew older, he was still as hard a Superior as he had been. When a convert clergyman, a widower, came to the Oratory he made him destroy a photograph of his wife. Another Father having just been ordained was not allowed to say his first Mass for a week. A Father who felt himself lacking in humility was made to wash the stairs. Having done so the poor Father still felt himself deficient in humility and had to set to work again. Dalgairns' charge that he went from room to room stirring up opposition to any Father who disagreed with him seems to have been true. Stanton, no mean judge, was however of the opinion that Faber became a better Superior every year. "Of course," he told Newman on 26th February 1855, "his bad health is a disadvantage to the community; but ... I do not see how we could do without him—for instance money matters which he always rides through triumphantly."* The other Fathers seem to have thought Faber a bad manager in financial matters. Faber was still comparatively young at the time of his death. It is likely that he would have mellowed with age.

"On points connected with the ceremonial of the church," Bowden noticed,

> he was inflexibly strict with himself and with others: he observed the slightest faulty detail of individual demeanour, and was especially severe upon any who allowed their private devotion to interfere with their attention to the ceremonies. This was a matter on which he felt so strongly that his manner in the correction of such faults was almost an exception to his usual gentleness. A Father, himself scrupulously exact and well

informed in rubrical matters, once told him that in a function he "trembled in knowing that his eye was upon him".[12]

In the Summer of 1855 he was seized with a severe attack of illness while on a visit to Dublin. "I fear", he wrote,

> I am not to look for a cure. It must stick to me now; and though I shrink from the prospect, yet at present the necessity of daily opium is the worst feature, as I fear I shall write no more books."

On his return to London he wrote:

> I have been examined twice by Sir B. Brodie. He took me by the hand and said, "it is no use concealing matters from you; I fear you are only at the beginning of a very bad business, and in its present stage I can do very little for you. You must go through great suffering and long". Well it is something to know the worst! I *can't* get well except through excruciating torture. It may come soon, it may be delayed for months. Science can't help it on; all it can do is to diminish the interior production of some peculiar acid with a hard name . . . And as far as my *will* goes, I am quite ready for the suffering, and don't doubt it is an immense love which makes God think it worth His while to take so much pains with me. What I fear is my patience, temper and the proper degree of unselfishness.

"The golden coin" of suffering was now to be his to the end. In 1857 he was writing:

> I am but a wreck of a man—my brain quite wrought out with lecturing and writing and constant pain and lameness.

"Since 15th of October," he wrote to Hutchison in 1858,

> up to the Epiphany no use of leg, horrid pain, consultation of Wilson and Tegart in my room, never in the refectory since St Wilfrid's day. Nevertheless thankful. Now mending—can walk. Now look here, it was *five* years last Sunday fortnight since I began, after the High Mass, S.S. Nomini Jesu *All for Jesus*. Since then 1. *All for Jesus*. 2. *Growth in holiness*. 3. *Blessed Sacrament*. 4. *Creator and Creature*. 5. Edition of poems with three thousand new lines. 6. *Sir Lancelot* immensely changed.

7. *Foot of the Cross.* 8. New hymns besides the thirty new ones. 9. *Bethlehem.* 10. *Conferences.* 11. *Ethel's book.* 12. Innumerable preachings. 13. Three books partially prepared, viz. *Precious Blood*, Holy Ghost and second volume of Conferences. 14. Confessing and directing. 15. Business as Superior. 16. Correspondence. 17. A certain amount of intercourse with God. 18. The bearing of pain when I could do nothing else. It is plain that life can't be lived at this rate. But my mind is like a locomotive that has started with neither driver nor stoker.

In May 1859 he wrote to Bowden:

Quite crippled and grievously tormented with some sciatica, or something of the kind. Mr Tegart has just ordered me into hot bath. My patience is nearly worn out. My only comfort is *Filios quos recipit, flagellat.*

"I have three punctual hours of great neuralgia in the head and nausea in the morning," he was writing next year.

I am breaking under my load . . . I am very unwell from sleepless nights, neuralgia in the head, and fits of sickness. I have come to the end of my tether . . . I have done nothing but pray these ten weeks, and I am quite *cowed*.[13]

By 1861 ill health had silenced him. He now could no longer write or preach. That Summer he became the prey to depression and despondency. He had "a loathing" for the community. He was suffering from rupture made more painful by diarrhoea and what he called stone and gravel. But he was not too downcast to write on his holiday of the smell of guano spread on the fields at Filey. "The first morning I rushed to Antony thinking the W.C. had burst." At the end of the year he went to Arundel to the deathbed of Canon Tierney and having contracted bronchitis he fell so ill that his life for a time was despaired of. But as he told Watts Russell, "it has pleased God to raise me from the bed of death in a very wonderful manner". In July 1862 he was writing to Bowden "I had one of the King William Street bilious attacks" and in August "the pain is now almost incessant and the tedium of life almost more than I can bear . . . At worst you can but drop under a burden you can no longer bear". And a few weeks later: "I seem to get on for three days and then back. The thought is growing upon me that I have an *undiscovered disease*."

He had once again been elected Superior and novice master. He made an heroic effort to resume normal community life. "Of late", he wrote,

> I hated to go [to the refectory and recreation] because I had that special chair yet could not use another [because of his size, probably]; now I think I can, still I cannot be what I used to be. You see both Antony and I have lived our lives too quick, and are now getting shelved.[14]

But "the dryness and desolation" was almost unbearable. In one letter he says, "Blessed be God for this piecemeal martyrdom". During Lent of 1863 he was permitted by the doctor to preach again. He preached four times. The penultimate sermon concluded with these words:

> The devil's worst and most fatal preparation for the coming of Anti-Christ is the weakening of men's belief in eternal punishment. *Were they the last words I might ever say to you* nothing should I wish to say to you with more emphasis than this, that next to the thought of the Precious Blood, there is no thought in all your faith more precious or more needful for you than the thought of eternal punishment.[15]

These were not in fact his last words. He preached once more on "Our Blessed Lord bowing His head upon the Cross".

Physical pain was not the only burden he had to bear. Hutchison, who was nearer to him than any other human being, had first broken down in health in 1855. In 1857 he had been forced abroad in an attempt to recover. He travelled to the Holy Land which inspired his book *Loreto and Nazareth* but on his return he was still unable to resume work. In 1860 he was so ill at Sydenham that he was not expected to live. In spite of his own weakness Faber nursed him but it tried his strength. "I am so worn out and broken in nerves and spirits," he wrote at this time,

> from constant nursing, from things going wrong, from want of change, from usual *disagremens* with externs ... I feel so sick and heartless ...[16]

He had to tell Hutchison that he might at any moment die "from effusion on the brain". "Oh, my God," he wrote, "may I never have to do these things again." There was a lot of hard physical work, he even had to do some of the cooking, and above all he had to "keep him up" as he called it. "He has ceased to walk and is pushed about in a bath chair, a piteous sight to see"— Hutchison was still in his thirties. "Here is fifteen years", Faber wrote,

> of intense friendship ending, and the elder is helping the younger to die. It is all right, and though very bitter, very peaceful. *In pace mea amaritudo amarissima*. I had a good quiet secret cry yesterday and am better for it.[17]

The crisis passed and Hutchison was able to resume his life in the community as a semi-invalid for a few more years. But all the time the illness was gaining on him.

After Easter 1863 Faber became rapidly worse. He said Mass for the last time on 26th April. The doctors now pronounced that he had the incurable Bright's disease. He was thought to be dying on 16th June and received the last Sacraments sitting in an armchair dressed in his habit; they were brought to him by Dalgairns followed by all the members of the community. Before the anointing he was asked various questions in the ritual and answered with several additions. To the question: "Do you from your heart ask pardon of every one whom you have offended by word or deed?" he answered: "I do: especially of every member of the community. I have been proud, uncharitable, unobservant, and I ask pardon of all." At the end of the questions he added: "I have been unkind and uncharitable; I wish I had been more kind." 28th June was his 49th birthday and it was thought he would die on that day. He saw the community one by one and gave each a parting present. To one of the Fathers he said with frequent pauses:

> God has been so good and arranged it all so well—I should like to have it settled today. This is my birthday, and the doctor says I am going fast—probably without pain; no, not without pain, for that is impossible, but with as little pain as possible . . .

I wish to die stripped of everything—one thing we must all
go on doing—pray that I may save my soul. He that per-
severes to the end . . ."

But death was still some way away and he struggled on. He exaggerated in his old vein. He disconcertingly told a priest who
proposed settling in Oxford that if he did so he would lose his
soul.[18]

On 11th July Hutchison said his office, revised the proofs
of his book on Loreto and was taken into the garden in a bath
chair. But towards evening he became worse. "He was quite
conscious when we put him to bed," Philip Gordon wrote,

> and he asked what the feast was tomorrow (that is today)
> and when I told him St John Gualbert he was quite satisfied.
> He always had a special devotion to that Saint, and we used
> to laugh at him about a famous sermon on his feast which he
> repeated several times. As the night went on it was plain that
> he was dying, and we gave him absolution and the last blessing;
> he had been to Holy Communion in the morning. He died
> while we were commending his soul. It all seems like a dream;
> we did not tell the Father till I went to him this morning, but
> he was not surprised . . .[19]

He was buried in the graveyard Faber had created at Sydenham—
aged 40.

On 14th July Wiseman, whose death was also not far off, called
at Brompton. "There are many things," he wrote after the
visit,

> which I desired to say to you this afternoon but which I did
> not say; so I must write some of them. I cannot but think how
> consoled and fortified you must now feel, by your having
> from the moment of your joining the Church, so entirely
> devoted your time and abilities to the particular and almost
> exclusive work of promoting and extending in it the spirit of
> holiness and of true piety. And your exertions have been emin-
> ently blessed not only in England but in every country as the
> Holy Father himself declared to me . . . If one has for years
> been endeavouring to cleave to the cross, and to cling to the
> hem of Mary's garment, it is the office of hope to plead these

affectionate occupations of a life in favour of mercy, grace and confidence at the approach of death. I only wish that I could look forward to similar motives and rights, when, in the same crisis, the sense of such heavy responsibilities, so little answered, will weigh on me. I will not dwell on the great work which you have founded, and which will remain, not long, but for ever, to perpetuate the good you have done while living. It is not the mere edifice, however great of the Oratory, which will do this but the Spirit of St Philip which you have brought into London . . ."

Faber was childishly delighted with the letter and sent it round to his friends. When he was well enough he wrote farewell letters to old friends such as Manners and Hope, some of whom came to say goodbye in person. He was delighted to have the Pope's special blessing conveyed through Monsignor Talbot.[20]

But of course it was Newman whom Faber, above all, wanted to see. There had been one or two hopeful letters on Faber's side with chilly replies from Newman. Faber had written in 1860:

Hope tells me you have sent me your affectionate regards. I wish you knew how I feel them and value them—and how *very* dear they are to me. Your affectionate and unworthy son in St Philip.[21]

The answer, if answer there was, does not exist but a year later Faber seems to have written again for Newman wrote to Dalgairns:

Pray thank him [Faber] for his affectionate letter. I do not know what I have to say in return except to assure him that I have no knowledge of such disobedience and wilfulnesses as he fears have occurred on his part during the time when he belonged to our Oratory, and that he may make himself quite easy as to any of us having in our minds any such recollections of him at all. Let him be sure that we all of us thank God for the good work which the London Oratory has done and is doing which is even more than we could have hoped, much as we reasonably expected from those who were its first members.[22]

When Newman came to London in 1861 he did not call at the Oratory but he saw the two Bowdens in Portland Place. Afterwards he wrote to Faber that he had hoped to have called at Brompton and had been disappointed not to see other London Fathers. Faber replied that "there was an impression that you wished to be undisturbed," and ended: "your affectionate and grateful son in St Philip".

During July 1863 Newman made polite enquiries through Dalgairns and, when the end was certain, came to Brompton. "Father Newman has been here this morning," Faber said in a dictated letter,

> he spent full 20 minutes with me. We went into everything. No woman could be tenderer than he was—the whole interview was one effusion of more than kindness, of downright love—all is right and righter than right. We held each other's hand the whole while and talked about our old friendship and went through the breach. He begged me to pray for him when I was before God. You would have been strangely moved had you seen his face when he rose to leave and looked down upon me and said in a voice of the most consummate sweetness, "St Philip be with you, Father". I said smiling, "He will be if you tell him to be and now, Padre, give your blessing" which he did in silence but with great solemnity. F. Philip says tears were in his eyes when he left the room.[23]

Newman's description of the interview which he made in a memorandum on 11th August 1863 was rather different.

> He was nearly the sole speaker for he seemed to wish to disburden his mind. I was with him a quarter of an hour. The physicians, it was said, forbad longer.
> He said he had loved me the best of anyone in the world, next to the late duke of Norfolk. He said that a sermon of mine at St Mary's had been the turning point of his life, for it gave him the first notion he had of supernatural grace. He said he did not forget how I had defended him formally against the priests who, he knew not, were against him—and how I had taken his part about the *Lives of the Saints* against Dr Ullathorne. He said it had pained him much to think that he and his were adding to my many trials. He knew, for instance, how

badly I had been used in the matter of the Translation of scripture.

He said that when, at the end of the three years, his congregation determined on going to Rome without consulting me, he was in a minority of one. He wanted me consulted, and only gave in, when they said that, though I proved to be against the particular application which they proposed to make to Rome, still they would make it. To consult with such a previous determination would be, he felt, a mockery. He said that then unluckily Propaganda, on their application, instead of consulting me, consulted Dr Ullathorne. [See Chapter XIII, p. 270.]

He said that other persons had spoken against me, and that it had been imputed to him; that Ward, for instance, came to him and said: "Is it not remarkable that Father Newman succeeds in none of his undertakings?" and then went away and said that he (Faber) had said so. He said the London Oratory had been out of favour with the Cardinal for several years.

Remarks.

My own view of Faber, poor fellow, is not much changed by the above. It is quite certain that he has from time to time spoken against me. I have at various times taken down the evidence of it. One instance of this. Hope Scott, trying to plead for him, said: "I never heard him say anything against you *except* that your School was against your Rule." This is not only an "exception" but a very huge one—considering what such an assertion implies and how it bears upon our status. But I need not pursue this subject.

Again when he says that *Ward* observed that I did not succeed in my undertakings he does not say he took my part—to say the least he did not set Ward down, tell him it was ungenerous, etc., but he so leaves the matter that Ward goes away with the impression that he (Faber) and not himself had suggested the remark.

But all through, poor fellow (when I saw him July 20) he was, as it were arguing with himself that he had not been so unkind to me; rather than boldly saying he had ever been a hearty friend. How different e.g. would have Ambrose had to speak, if he were at the last! He might reproach himself, as we *all* do, after doing our best, of not doing all he wished to do, but he would know he was always loyal and true to me. Dear Faber has not been so, and feels it.[24]

Still Faber did not die. There were periods of recovery and relapse. He dictated frequent letters to Herbert Harrison, a novice who had been head boy of Westminster School.

It *is* more than I can bear, and yet it is of faith, it is as sure as sure that God is God, that it is *not* more than I can bear, and so it is to be borne.

Death is coming more sensibly but very slowly. The dropsy seems to be gradually draining away and the skeleton of a man appearing in its stead ... I have ordered the chasuble to be [brought] in today. When there came the question of the beautiful lace of my own alb I think I relieved dear F. Richard's mind by reminding him that lace could not be worn with violet. He is getting everything ready as I believe it is important that I should be vested before I am quite cold. The fact is the great fat man whom you left the other day has gone somewhere or other and there is only a little skeleton in the corner of the green chair—and who can say when that is to go ... I doubt if any period of this life I have been more happy than today—but there is still Satan and the dark hours ...[25]

The dropsy, however, returned and there were periods of great pain. "I have collapsed," he wrote to Bowden,

and am more ill than I have ever been before. I regret to say that yesterday I made the announcement that I neither would nor could bear the pain God was putting upon me. I hope I am in a somewhat better disposition today but I hope death is not far absent now. My legs have never been so bad.[26]

Whenever he gave way to impatience he sent for one of the Fathers to give him absolution. He frequently had prayers read to him, especially the prayers of St Gertrude.

He lasted in this condition between life and death during August. In September periods of delirium commenced but even then he rallied. After Communion on the 11th he prayed aloud:

"O Lord, bless my dear community. Oh, how I have loved all the Fathers! How I wish all the Fathers were at home!" "A considerable change", Bowden wrote,

> was perceptible on the 25th. He became quite still, and his attendants were able to put him into bed which had not been done since the month of June. Here he lay supported by pillows, not speaking but gazing steadily at a large white crucifix before him and moving his eyes sometimes from one of the Five Wounds to another. As evening came on it was clear that his end was approaching, and his confessor, Father Dalgairns, determined to watch with him through the night. When he was told that his death was near he only repeated fervently his favourite exclamation, "God be praised!" Shortly after midnight the community was summoned to assist at his last moments, and the commendation of his soul was made, but the crisis passed over, and the Fathers again retired . . .
>
> At six o'clock on the morning of the 26th it was plain that he was not likely to live more than an hour. The time passed in silence; the dying Father was lying on his bed breathing heavily, with his eyes closed, or when open, still fixed upon the crucifix. About half past six Father Rowe said he would go and say Mass for him and an intelligent look showed that his intention was appreciated. Just after seven a sudden change came over the Father; his head turned a little to the right, his breathing seemed to stop; a few spasmodic gasps followed, and his spirit passed away. In those last moments his eyes opened, clear, bright, intelligent as ever, in spite of the look of agony on his face, but opened to the sight of nothing earthly, with a touching expression, half of sweetness and half of surprise.[27]

The body was dressed in the vestments he had prepared and was taken down to the little Oratory. It was laid on a plain mattress and several of the Fathers were continually occupied for the next two days in touching the hands with rosaries and medals as the people filed past. On the 28th, owing to the dropsy, the body was placed in the coffin and sealed. On the 30th at half past nine the Solemn Dirge began. "The coffin was placed before the High Altar," a Catholic paper reported, and the whole of the upper part, as well as the sanctuary, was filled by the clergy who had come from all parts to pay their last tribute to Father Faber. Fr Newman and Fr St John were there from the Birmingham Oratory, Provost Manning with the Chapter of Westminster (the Cardinal was too ill to attend), religious from all orders, and secular clergy from all parts, even from France and Belgium. The whole church was so full that those who came late could not obtain admission at all.[28]

His brother Frank felt too ill to attend and no other members of the Faber family came, which caused a good deal of comment. "A church crowded with the aristocracy in deepest mourning," Oakeley wrote next day,

> bespoke the respect of one class, the tears and sobbing of the poor Irish betokened *their* love of him, and many poor children were there ... There was evidence of deep sorrow, and this was not silent either, for often, when the solemn music paused, and no sound fell for a time upon the ear, the stillness was broken by the sobs of those whose hearts mourned for him who had been their pastor, teacher and friend.[29]

There was a vast crowd outside the church and many others followed the coffin to St Mary's, Sydenham. "It was a fine autumnal day," Bowden wrote,

> and the sun shone brightly as Father Faber's body passed slowly down the walks which he had so often trodden, and was laid in a quiet little burial ground which he had himself marked out and planted round. His grave had been prepared at the foot of the cross of its consecration, and there, with the conviction that they would never look upon his like again, his sorrowing children left him.[30]

The following day Monsignor Manning spoke of Faber in the church of St Mary of the Angels, Bayswater.

> Yesterday a great servant of God was taken from us; we all knew him, some have listened to his words, some have been his penitents, all have known him by his writings, but I think I may venture to say that no one knew him so long or so intimately as myself. I knew him as a boy; we were at the Uni-

versity together, and even then I was astonished at the wonderful gifts which we have all seen developed since. I will not speak of his natural gifts, although for the gift of intellect, for beauty of mind, and eloquence of speech, he stands almost unequalled. These gifts are small compared to the supernatural gifts bestowed on him. He was a great priest; he was the means of bringing multitudes into the one Fold, and he died as a priest should die, amid the prayers and tears of his flock. Though he lived in the world I never saw any one so detached from the world ... In all his writings, in all his teachings there is the same strain throughout—All for Jesus ... I repeat it again, a great servant of God has been taken from us.[31]

In spite of its exaggeration of Faber's intimacy with him Manning's comment was appropriate enough. Henceforth Faber's name was to be coupled with Manning and Ward, those Catholics who were opposed during the next decades to liberal Catholicism —and by implication to Newman. Newman had written on 27th September:

His long sufferings are over, and bring him so much nearer, if not close to his *refrigerium* and reward ... We are having a solemn requiem and various of our boys gave their communions this morning.[32]

Faber's posthumous reputation was decided by various remarks Newman let fall from time to time. *The Blessed Sacrament*, which came out just before the quarrel, was dedicated by Faber

to my most dear Father John Henry Newman to whom in the mercy of God I owe the faith of the Church, the grace of the Sacraments and the habit of St Philip with much more that love knows and feeds upon though it cannot tell in words but which the last day will show.

Yet the book is remembered by two remarks of Newman—that it would promote the growth of scepticism and that Faber believed the Blessed Sacrament would be in heaven at the end of time. The first opinion was tenable enough—Ullathorne may have shared it, certainly there were some who did. But the second was unfair because it misrepresented Faber's words.

When Pusey published his *Eirenikon* he singled out Faber as an example of the extravagance he found in the Roman Church. Newman replied publicly. "You say of the one [Faber]," he wrote,

> that he was "a popular writer"; but is there not a sufficient reason for this in the fact of his remarkable gifts, of his poetical fancy, his engaging frankness, his playful wit, his affectionateness, his sensitive piety, without supposing that the wide diffusion of his works arises out of his particular sentiments about the Blessed Virgin.[33]

The argument was a little dubious and there was a backhand cut at Faber's reputation. If his popularity was caused by his sensitive poetical nature what was the value of his books as theology? Newman wrote privately to Pusey rather differently,

> I believe that Judicious people think [Faber's writings] crude and young, perhaps extravagant. He was a poet.

More shortly he wrote: "As to Faber I never read his books," which, unless the verb is in the present tense, was untrue.[34]

Faber became more and more identified in Newman's mind with the opposition he had to contend with. In his journal he wrote:

> And then when I came home [from Rome] at once Faber was upon me, to bully me, humbug me, and make use of me ... First, in 1853, came my mistake in asking for Dalgairns from the London House, then my going to Ireland, in order to impinge upon Dr Cullen, while Dalgairns intrigued at home in my absence. Then the great plot of him, Faber etc.—and my going to Rome—and the treatment I met at Propaganda. Then the thousand whisperings against me at the London Oratory which have succeeded in prejudicing the Catholic body to a great extent against me ... I must say that the converts have behaved to *me* much worse than the old Catholics when they might have had a little gratitude, to say the least ... And the *Saturday Review*, writing apropos of my letter to the *Globe* of last summer, said that I had disappointed friends and enemies since I had been a Catholic by doing nothing. The reason is conveyed

in the remark of Marshall of Brighton to Fr Ambrose last week: "Why, he has made no converts, as Manning and Faber have."

But on 22nd February 1865 he felt less despondent.

Every year I feel less and less anxiety to please Propaganda, from a feeling that they cannot understand *England*. Next, the two chief persons whom I felt to be unjust to me are gone— the Cardinal [Wiseman] and Faber. Their place has been taken by Manning and Ward; but somehow, from my never having been brought closely into contact with either of them, as with the Cardinal and Faber, I have not that sense of their cruelty which I felt so much as regards the two last mentioned.[35]

One further recorded mention of Faber in Newman's long life may be given.

In 1889 [Newman] had been very ill, and when recovering said to a Father: "Father Faber wrote the hymn called the 'Eternal years'. I have always had the greatest affection for it—in connection with Father Faber, and I always used to think that when I came to die I should like to have it sung to me; and I want you to play it for me."
"Would a harmonium do?"
"Yes, a harmonium would be just the thing; perhaps one could be spared me."
So when evening had set in a harmonium was put in the passage between his two rooms, a Father knelt at his side reciting each verse, while two others played and sang "the Eternal years". "Some people", he then said, "have liked my 'Lead, Kindly light' and it is the voice of one in darkness asking for help from Our Lord. But this (the 'Eternal years') is quite different. This is one with full light, rejoicing in suffering with our Lord, so that mine compares unfavourably with it. This is what those who like 'Lead, Kindly light' have got to come to—they have to learn it!" Then they played and sang it over again. And he said at the end, "I thank you with all my heart. God bless you. I pray that when you go to heaven you may hear the angels singing with the genius that God has endowed them with. God bless you."[36]

It seems that at long last the quarrel had been forgotten. But it is significant that Newman refused to attend the opening of the present Oratory church.

The world in the shape of the *Saturday Review* said of Faber at his death:

> He was not a hero. He had not in him the makings of a saint . . . The older and more wary members of his adopted Church evidently have their misgivings . . . He was not at all the man for bluff, outspoken chaffy and ungammonable undergraduate Oxford; but he was entirely the man for pretty little chorister-boys, feminine or semi-feminine confessions and the imaginative or imaginary Paradise with which he eventually surrounded himself. He was very amiable; he was decidedly ornamental; he had a world of good qualities about him, if only he would have let them alone. A hundred years ago he would have been John Wesley's right hand man; any day he might have made his fortune as a pocket-handkerchief preacher at a proprietary chapel; but if Cardinal Wiseman ever said (as has been reported) that he would gladly give back to the Anglicans all his converts save one we very gravely doubt whether Father Faber was the exception.[37]

Bowden said of him that his life was from first to last *religious* and he ended his biography with these words:

> Words cannot reproduce the gracious presence, the musical voice, the captivating smile—cannot give back to earthly life the charm of person or the fascination of manner any more than the fire of genius or the nobility of soul—and cannot therefore satisfy those whose labours were cheered and sorrows comforted, whose interior lives were formed and directed to God, whose brightest, happiest hours were blessed by the wisdom, holiness and love of Frederick William Faber.[38]

And in conclusion what can be said? Does the truth lie between the opinion of the writer in the *Saturday Review* and the opinion of his friends? At Oxford much of what was levelled against him was true. The writer in the *Saturday Review* evidently knew him at Oxford but not later. He was at Oxford priggish, self-conscious, and indulgently imaginative. He came to this conclusion himself. His charm made these faults, once seen, the more irritating—to some exasperating. As a young convert he was annoyingly pugnacious. Yet Hutchison, who was no fool, maintained that the day he met Faber changed his life. He was not the only one to say the same. Hutchison later described Faber in comparison to the other Fathers in London—no make-weights by any standard—as a ship of the line among frigates. Newman himself, perhaps reluctantly, saw heroic qualities in Faber. What is the explanation? Was he a butterfly or a man of true depth?

The truth is he changed. As a young man the mettle of his character was obscured by his very real worldly graces. But when the storm of difficulty and suffering came upon him the irrelevant was washed away. His granite-like qualities lay bare. The frail poet was seen to be a pugnacious Yorkshireman with a courage equal to his tenacity. Men, like Ward, who had known him at Oxford could hardly believe he was the same man. The facility— what some would have called his perverse facility—was seen to be intelligence. His mind was not shallow because it was dextrous, his eloquence was not a substitute for real thought.

But the deepening of Faber's character was a religious process. He was by nature religious in the sense that he naturally understood religion, just as he naturally understood the intimations of God in nature. Some men are permitted to talk of religion, to preach religion, even to play with religion—and not to live it. This was not allowed to Faber. It was his boast that he had never played at being a Catholic while he was a Puseyite. Perhaps it was Mr Cunningham's Evengelicalism, perhaps it was the pervasive seriousness of the age—whatever it was, he felt it a blasphemy to talk and not to act. Who can say when the break came? When he decided to take Elton? Or was it on his journey to Rome when he read Chiabrera's haunting and accusatory epitaph? That perhaps was the moment of change. From that time the epitaph was his—the epitaph on his past life. Parnassus was abandoned for the little mound of Calvary. The shadow of the cross fell, the "golden coin of suffering" was paid out, little by little he was transformed. "Faber of Univ.," "Water-lily Faber," "Faber of the Lakes" founded a religious order, abandoned it, put himself under obedience, successfully brought the Oratory to London. Changes were steps forward. Bowden was right when he said that Faber's life was from the beginning to end religious. But it was more than that. It was a life of religious growth. Grace, the life of Christ in the soul, does not destroy nature or natural qualities. The grossly fat man of Brompton, pathetically hurt at not being his old self at recreation and having to sit in a special chair, was the man who fled, almost mortally wounded, from Oxford. The qualities in the one may be disliked in the other. As a child he maintained that *any* man is better than the best of women. Half way through his life he outraged his Anglican friends by comparing their Church to Sodom and Gomorrah. On his deathbed he warned the priest going to Oxford he would lose his soul. The boy was as imprudent as the priest who overtaxed his strength Lent after Lent. It is all of a piece.

A man's character is judged by posterity on his accidental remains. It may be on the recorded words of a friend. The words of an enemy may have been lost or forgotten. It may be the other way about. There may be letters, documents, writings. Our knowledge is partial. Posterity has judged Faber on his spiritual writings. But without the life and letters the spiritual writings present a very imperfect picture. Faber and his admirers supposed that eloquence and rhetoric, so effective in the pulpit, adorned his thought. But eloquence and rhetoric can also disguise thought. They can even disguise the man. Who would guess the drive, the humour and the courage of the man from the spiritual writings? Even so, inevitably, the man evades us. There remains the enigma of contrasting qualities: in his character—of love with harshness, wisdom with lack of balance: in his writing—of sublimity with bathos, intellectuality with sentimental fervour: in his manner—of seriousness with flippancy, penetrating spiritual understanding with disconcerting worldliness. Were these contrasts the secret of his charm? That great woman, Mother Margaret Mary Hallahan, after saying goodbye, stood looking back at him. "Oh what a man you are!" She kept repeating, "What a man you are!" Although we cannot experience, as she did, "the gracious presence, the musical voice, the captivating smile", perhaps, after all, hers is the best comment.

Faber's monument is the Oratory at Brompton. The controversial *Lives of the saints*, the hymns, the spiritual works, the sermons, the illiturgical devotions, some, perhaps many, of them mistaken, are of secondary importance. For the Oratory is not simply a beautiful Catholic church. The Oratory stands for the spirit of St Philip Neri which Faber brought into the hard dark London of the 1850s. That was his great achievement—to bring light and tender devotion into the darkness. He set out to do just that and did it.

APPENDIX 1

"IN no long time we became acquainted with the further fact that the nuns of Stone had known what was going on from at least the 20th of August, and so lively was their interest in the news, that while they did not disclose to us what was apparently a secret, one of them in writing to me could not help letting out in the fullness of her heart, what, when the fact came to light, first led me to suspect their previous acquaintance with it. Here there was a combined action, however unintentional, forcing the Birmingham Oratory by means of Propaganda into a line of missionary work which it held to be un-Oratorian ..." This sentence had been toned down by the Birmingham Fathers— of course with Newman's consent. As written by Newman it read: "Here then was a conspiracy, material, if not formal, unintentional, I am willing to grant, but still really a conspiracy in its operation upon us, a conspiracy to force the Birmingham Oratory etc ..."

He wrote of his journey to Rome: "I was most paternally received by the Holy Father as I have put on record elsewhere and I obtained from him more than all I asked; but I cannot forget that I had prepossessions to overcome, in him and at Propaganda and at Chiesa Nuova, which had been inspired by the Fathers at Brompton. I saw papers in the Pope's hand injurious to one who had done them no harm, whose blessing they now ask. Hardly indeed had I begun to explain that I came merely to secure the independence of Oratories generally and our own community in particular from attacks from without than he said, "Capisco il tutto" and the papers disappeared. ... I could not remove the scandal they had caused by publishing in Rome and elsewhere the fact of a quarrel which had been so carefully concealed both by myself and my Congregation. ... These are the facts, but what does St Philip mean by them? He means, I think, to remind us, that it is a necessity of his Oratory that its Congregations should see little of each other. . . . As to our particular quarrel with the Fathers of London we leave it to St Philip; it is enough for us to see its moral and that moral is this:—Be kind to them individually; pray for the welfare of their Congregation; but keep clear of them."

Why was Newman pleased by what had happened at Rome? What had he in fact obtained? The letter in the Pope's hand was evidently one to Barnabò and refers simply to the misunderstanding with regret. It was not a denunciation, though, of course, it does mention Newman's name several times. It was in Stanton's handwriting. A longer description of the interview was given by Newman in a letter to Caswall dated St Paul's conversion 1856 immediately after the event. "The Pope nodded his head & said: *Adesso capisco tutto* or very much that. He went on to allude to what he had done to the London House & said in a serious confidential tone: 'I will tell you my mind about nuns. It is not my wish that you should have them' . . ." (Birmingham Archives).

APPENDIX 2

An account of the Journey to Rome

HUTCHISON and Stanton were in charge of the Roman expedition, Balston and Charles Bowden accompanying them. On arrival they called on George Talbot, the friend of the Pope, who throughout his life had a great influence on the Church in England. Talbot told them "that certainly N[ewman] was crotchetty. There was no doubt of this, in the Achilli case he had been very crotchetty and dissatisfied with him (Talbot) though he had done all in his power for him . . . He asked if we had told N. [about the proposed Brief] and on our saying 'No', he answered: 'Won't this be a regular declaration of war, hadn't you better tell him?' We tried to explain that N. had suspended relations with us and so on and then he said, 'Hadn't you better make it come from Barnabò? You go and consult him and he suggests or advises you to ask for a Brief. Then it is his act not yours! Of course this is just the line we meant to take but I tell you Talbot's words because it shows, I think, his sympathy with and wish to help us . . . (20.7.56).

They were well received by Barnabò. He played down the quarrel but later it appeared he disliked Newman and privately mimicked him. He referred to Newman as '*il Babbo*', 'the Daddy', i.e. the Father of both Oratories. Talbot and the Pope did the same. He told them that a separate Brief for each house was unnecessary as he had already told Newman—who had asked the selfsame thing. When they insisted he told them to enquire at Chiesa Nuova. Chiesa Nuova was of the opinion that a separate brief *was* necessary. The two Fathers were inexplicably surprised at Newman's request for a brief but they immediately saw the advantage to the London house. "His [Newman's] having asked at Propaganda that each house might have its own brief is curious," Hutchison wrote to Faber. "I believe it was his usual round the corner way of shooting and that it was a tentative effort to ascertain the extent and value of his own Brief. But one has no right to assume this and *the fact that F. Newman himself made this proposition to Mgr Barnabò is of great assistance to us as it destroys any appearance of hostility towards him on our part in making this application."* (22.7.56).

There were long and tedious negotiations. While they waited the Fathers called on Mary Giberne a friend and convert of Newman. "Babbo [Newman]", Hutchison wrote, "told Giberne all about the row when he was here, and I have told her our story and Giberne says it is just like him and that when he was young he always had a shocking bad temper. She is also in a row with him. He picked a quarrel with her, or Ambrose did, for him when here in the spring and he has not written to her since" (4.8.56). A few days later he wrote: "Miss Giberne is greatly put about at F. Newman's conduct to us and thinks him utterly in the wrong. From what she has told me Fr St John and Il Babbo must have been in a most excited state when they were in Rome" (9.8.56). Newman had, indeed, made himself unpopular. Talbot who had been away when Newman called on his journey to Rome with St John, was openly hostile. He wrote to Birmingham to say that he had supported the London brief since he believed this was Newman's wish. He regarded this as "a good joke" (4.9.56). Miss Giberne went so far (according to Hutchison) as to write to St John suggesting that he ask Faber to pray for Birmingham novices. This was also presumably thought a good joke. The Fathers received the Brief in Rome on 24th September and the next day left for England.

BIBLIOGRAPHY

A. Letters at London Oratory in bound volumes:
- (i) Vol. 17: Letters by Faber to J. B. Morris, 1833–63.
- (ii) Vol. 21: Various Letters and documents by Faber.
- (iii) Vol. 22: Letters (various) by Faber.
- (iv) Vols. 1–3: Copies of letters in Birmingham Oratory, from Faber to Newman.
- (v) Vols. 8 and 9: Newman's letters to Faber.
- (vi) Vol. 19: Faber to the Fathers of the London Oratory, 1846–63.
- (vii) Vol. 16: Letters from abroad by Faber, 1846 and 1851.
- (viii) Vol. 20: Letters to Bowden from Faber, 1843–63.
- (ix) MS. marked "B" by Fr R. Stanton containing all documents relating to the setting up of the London Oratory. With additions by Fr R. Kerr. Also unnumbered volume: Letters from Rome, 1856.
- (x) Oratory notes, 1845–1910. Typescript about the various Fathers.
- (xi) Letters of Faber from Arundel during the Duke of Norfolk's illness.
- (xii) Vol. 26: Letters of Fathers Knox and Hutchison.
- (xiii) Vols. 4, 6, 7: Copies of letters in Birmingham Oratory from Hutchison, Dalgairns, Knox and others to Newman.

B. Annotated copy by Fr Ralph Kerr of "The Oratory in London" which appeared in the parish magazine. This is an invaluable compilation which supplements Bowden and then in turn is greatly supplemented by Fr Kerr's notes from the letters. One caution is necessary. The letters are not always quoted verbatim though the sense is always correct.

C. *The Life and Letters of Frederick William Faber* by John Edward Bowden, first published six years after Faber's death. I have quoted from the 4th ed. as this contains additional information. Some of the letters printed in it have been lost. It is an accurate picture by a friend who loved Faber but of course, being written so near the time of Faber's death, is noticeably reticent. There is, of course, no mention of the quarrel with Birmingham. It is not a very readable book as it was compiled too quickly. One hundred and thirty-nine letters are printed in it.

D. Archives at Birmingham Oratory.

NOTES

CHAPTER I

1. Memoir of Rev. G. S. Faber, B.D., in *The many mansions in the house of the father* by G. S. Faber, 2nd ed., 1854, p. x.
2. As in J. E. Bowden, *Life and letters of Frederick William Faber, D.D.*, 4th ed. This edition is fuller than the first and it is quoted throughout.
3. *Gentleman's Magazine*, May 1854.
4. Memoir of G. S. Faber, p. xix.
5. *Brief sketch of the early life of the late F. W. Faber*, by his only surviving brother, 10, 11.
6. Quoted by Sir Timothy Eden in *Durham* (County Books), Vol. 2, pp. 538–9.
7. Letter to Frank Faber 1843 in possession of Sir Geoffrey Faber.
8. Bowden, 3.
9. Ibid., 4.
10. *Bethlehem*, 281.
11. T. A. Trollope, *What I remember*, Vol. 1, pp. 89 ff.
12. *Cautions to continental travellers*, 1818, pp. 72–4.

CHAPTER II

1. I am indebted to Mr E. V. Quinn of Balliol College library for this information. Faber matriculated on 29th November 1832.
2. Roundell Palmer, Earl of Selborne, *Memorials, family and personal*, I, pp. 136–8.
3. Letters to J. B. Morris, Vol. 17; date Monday 8.6.33 but postmark July.
4. In a letter Faber claims to have written a great part of the periodical. Bowden mentions only four articles. As the articles are unsigned it is difficult to know.
5. J.B.M., 1.1.34.
6. Ibid., 4.1.34.
7. Ibid., 4.8.34.
8. Augustus Otway Fitzgerald, Balliol undergraduate.
9. Bowden, 11–13.
10. Ibid., 14, 15. Omissions restored.
11. R. E. Prothero, *Life and letters of Dean Stanley*, I, 124–33.
12. Bowden, 17–19. To Palmer.
13. J.B.M., 5.8.35.
14. Bowden, Chapter 2.
15. Ibid., 40–2.
16. J.B.M., 22.5.36.

17. Bowden, 39.
18. Ibid., 47
19. J.B.M., 27.9.36.
20. Bowden, 50.
21. Ibid., 50, 51.
22. Ibid., 52–3.
23. Ibid., 53–4.
24. J.B.M., 31.1.37.
25. Ibid., Ash Wednesday.

CHAPTER III

1. *Saturday Review*, XVI, 1863, 488. Part of Faber's obituary. It is unsigned. The writer may have been Mark Pattison who missed the fellowship at Faber's election.
2. Bowden, 62.
3. J.B.M., 17.4.37.
4. Ibid., 20.6.37. *Scriptural Views of Holy Baptism* (tracts 67–9) by E.B. Pusey.
5. Ibid., 26.6.37.
6. Ibid., 24.7.38.
7. Prothero, I, 218–19.
8. J.B.M., 25.8.39.
9. Bowden, 70–1.
10. J.B.M., 19.6.37.
11. Ibid., 26.6.37.
12. Ibid., 31.8.37.
13. From the notebook of Jessie Harden. Quoted by permission of A. S. Clay.
14. He had met Faber in Cambridge in 1836.
15. C. Whibley, *Lord John Manners and his friends*, 1925, I, 63.
16. Sir W. H. Gregory, *An Autobiography*, 88, 89.
17. Letter to Smythe, Vol. 21, 115, 8.5.39.
18. G. S. Smythe, *Historic fancies*, 102.
19. E. B. de Fonblanque, *Lives of the Lords of Strangford*, 216.
20. Gregory, *op. cit.*, 88, 89.
21. *The Cherwell Water-lily and other poems*, XLI.
22. Ibid., XLVIII.
23. Letter in possession of Sir G. Faber.
24. *The Cherwell Water-lily*, LXXVIII, First Love.
25. Whibley, *op. cit.*, 64–5.
26. Ibid., 66–8.
27. Ibid., 68–9.
28. Ibid., 70.

Chapter IV

1. Bowden, 66–7.
2. Ibid., 68.
3. Ibid.
4. Frederick Oakeley, *Historical notes on the Tractarian Movement: 1833–45* (1865), 74.
5. This and following quotations from *Sights and thoughts in foreign Churches*, 1842.
6. Bowden, 99, 100.
7. Ibid., 126.
8. Ibid., 76.
9. Letters to Morris, 31.1.42.
10. G. D. Campbell, 8th Duke of Argyll, *Autobiography and memoirs*, I, 182.
11. Letters to Morris, 21.7.42.
12. *Sights and thoughts in foreign Churches*, 473.
13. An epistle to a young M.P. from *The Styrian Lake and other poems*, 1842.
14. *Blackwoods*, CVI, Dec. 1869, 696.
15. Roundell Palmer, *op. cit.*, I, 347.
16. *H. C. Robinson on books and their writers*, ed. by E. J. Morley, 605.
17. *Correspondence of H. C. Robinson with the Worsdworth circle 1806–66*, ed. by E. H. Morley, 468. Letter to M.W., 27.8.42.
18. Ibid., 472. To T.R.
19. *Diary reminiscences and correspondence of H. C. Robinson*, ed. by T. Sadler, 206.
20. Ibid., 208.
21. Ibid., 211–2.
22. *H. C. Robinson on books and their writers*, *op. cit.*, 628.
23. *Letters of William and Dorothy Wordsworth, the later years*, ed. by E. De Selincourt, 1230. To Isabella Fenwick, 5.10.44.
24. J.B.M., 27.9.42.
25. Faber wrote "subduing of the poet to the priest", surely wrong.
26. J.B.M., 16.12.42. Dr Travers Twiss, dean and bursar. The master was Dr F. C. Plumptre.
27. Ibid., 31.1.43.
28. He had got to know Wiseman through *Sights and thoughts in foreign Churches*.

Chapter V

1. Bowden, 146–7.
2. Ibid., 147–8
3. Ibid., 152.
4. Ibid., 153.
5. Ibid., 154–5.
6. Ibid., 159–60.
7. Ibid., 157–9.
8. Ibid., 160.

9. Ibid., 161–2.

10. Ibid., 165–6.

11. Ibid., 166–7. But Bowden left out Newman's vision.

12. Ibid., 169–71.

13. Ibid., 169.

14. *Diary reminiscences and correspondence of H. C. Robinson, op. cit.*, 221. Quillinan was a liberal Catholic.

15. To J.B.M., 11.8.43.

16. N. to F., 2.9.43.

17. To J.B.M., 30.9.43.

18. F. to N., 30.9.43.

Chapter VI

1. Tom Godwin's Narrative in "Oratory notes", 1845–1910.

2. Ibid.

3. Bowden, 179.

4. Ibid., 181.

5. F. to N., 6.11.43.

6. To J.B.M., 22.3.44.

7. F. to N., 27.3.44.

8. Tom Godwin, *art. cit.*

9. To J.B.M., 17.7.44.

10. Ibid., 9.8.44.

11. F. to N., 12.8.44.

12. To J.B.M., 9.8.44.

13. F. to N., 28.9.44.

14. N. to F., Advent Sunday '44.

15. F. to N., 3.12.44.

16. Ibid., 12.12.44.

17. *Life of St Wilfrid*, 4.

18. Ibid., 84.

19. To J.B.M., 29.1.45.

20. Ibid., 3.12.44.

21. Ibid., 10.2.45.

22. Ibid. 11.3.45. Also Bowden, 194.

23. Ibid., 25.6.45.

24. Ibid., 13.8.45.

25. F. to N., 5.10.45.

26. Tom Godwin's Narrative, *art. cit.*

27. N. to F., 8.10.45.

28. Tom Godwin's Narrative, *art. cit.*

29. F. to N., 11.10.45.

30. Ibid., 24.10.45.

31. Tom Godwin, *art. cit.*

32. All these circumstances were in Father Hutchison's "Notes", the greater part of which have disappeared. I have had simply to draw on Bowden. The friend was probably Beresford Hope.

33. Bowden may have thought the earlier visit took place immediately before his conversion.

34. To J.B.M., 21.10.45.

35. Ibid., 24.10.45.

36. F. to N., 28.10.45.

37. N. to F., 30.10.45.

38. F. to N., 10.11.45.

39. Ibid., 11.11.45.

40. Tom Godwin, *art. cit.*

41. F. to N., 15.11.45.

42. Tom Godwin, *art. cit.* It is noticeable that this description is less dramatic than Bowden's.

43. Ibid.

44. To J.B.M., 17.11.45.

CHAPTER VII

1. Bowden, 197.

2. Various Letters, Vol. 22, No. 149, 25.11.45.

3. *Letters and Verses of Arthur Penrhyn Stanley D.D. between the years* 1829 *and* 1881, ed. by R. E. Prothero, 93–4.

4. F. to N., 19.11.45.

5. N. to F., 22.11.45.

6. F. to N., 23.11.45.

7. Ibid., 4.12.45.

8. Ibid., 10.12.45.

9. Ibid., 12.12.45.

10. N. to F., 15.12.45.

11. F. to N., 16.12.45.

12. Bowden, 206–7.

13. F. to N., 19.12.45.

14. Tom Godwin, *art. cit.*

15. F. to N., Jan. '46.

16. Bowden, 217, Oratory notes.

17. To J.B.M., 5.12.45.

18. Ibid., 3/4.1.46.

19. Ibid., 21.6.50.

20. Letter to Hutchison, 21.1.46; Vol. 19. No. 2.

21. *Grounds for remaining in the Anglican Communion*, 8, 9.

22. Ibid., 12.

23. Ibid., 19.

24. Ibid., 23.

25. Ibid., 25.

26. Ibid., 39.

27. Ibid., 63.

28. Ibid., 67.

29. Ibid., 68.

30. N. to St J., 18.2.46.

31. F. to J.B.M., 18.3.46.
32. F. to N., 18.3.46.
33. F. to J.B.M., between May and July '46; Letter No. 108.
34. F. to N., 29.1.46.
35. N. to F., 1.2.46.
36. Bowden, 220, 221.
37. Ibid., 233.
38. To Strickson, 27.2.46; Vol. 16, No. 5.
39. *Frances Trollope, her life and literary work*, by F. E. Trollope, II, 62.
40. To B., Annunciation, '46; Vol. 21, No. 69.
41. Bowden, 219–20.
42. Bowden, 236.
43. To J.B.M., Easter Tuesday '46.
44. Bowden, 242–3.
45. To B., 6.4.46; Vol. 21, No. 70.
46. Bowden, 245–6.
47. To W.R., Thursday in Holy Week '46; Vol. 21, No. 1.
48. Bowden, 247.

Chapter VIII

1. Various letters and documents, Vol. 21, No. 127.
2. Ibid., p. 7.
3. Oratory notes, 17–19.
4. Bowden, 250 and 257.
5. To J.B.M., 5.8.46.
6. Ibid.
7. Vol. 21, No. 74. Uncertain date: 21.8.46 difficult.
8. Bowden changes the sense by several alterations to this sentence.
9. Vol. 21, to W.R., 23.7.46, Letter No. 2.
10. Ibid., 2.8.46; Letter No. 3. Allezo is what Faber wrote. It is uncertain what he meant.
11. To J.B.M., 5.7.46
12. Vol. 21, to W.R., 5.10.46; Letter No. 4.
13. Ibid.
14. Ibid., undated; Letter No. 5.
15. Ibid., 1.11.46; Letter No. 6.
16. Ibid., 13.11.46; Letter No. 7.
17. Ibid.
18. Bowden, 274, 5.
19. To B., 22.9.46; Vol. 21, Letter No. 74.
20. Bowden, 256.
21. Letter to Lord Shrewsbury, 24.1.47; Vol. 21, Letter No. 21.
22. Ibid., Ash Wednesday; Letter No. 23 out of order.
23. Ibid., Septuagesima Sunday; Letter No. 22.
24. Ibid., Ash Wednesday; Letter 23.
25. Ibid., 15.3.47; Letter No. 24.
26. Ibid., 18.3.47; Letter No. 25.

27. F. to N. S. Gabriel, 1847.

28. Ibid., Easter Monday 1847. A Requiem is not allowed on Sunday let alone Easter Sunday. Ignorance or slackness?

29. Bowden, 276.

30. Bowden, 278.

31. Bowden, 279.

32. To W.R. 11.12.47; Vol. 21, Letter No. 10.

33. N. to F., 31.12.47.

34. F. to N., 1.1.48.

35. To W.R., 11.2.48; Letter No. 11.

CHAPTER IX

1. F. to N., 2.1.48.

2. Ibid., 27.1.48.

3. Ibid., 30.1.48.

4. N. to F., 6.3.48.

5. Ibid., 27.3.48.

6. F. to N., 29.3.48.

7. Ibid., 30.3.48.

8. Ibid., 1.4.48.

9. Ibid., Monday afternoon (end of April 1848).

10. H. to N., no date; p. 23.

11. Ibid., p. 24.

12. F. to N., end of April 1848?; p. 95.

13. Ibid., 22.5.48.

14. Ibid., 12.5.48.

15. Ibid., May '48. Undated Letter 101A. Mr Gubbins was priest at Cheadle.

16. Ibid., 28.5.48.

17. Birmingham Oratory Letters, V, No. 67, 29th May 1848.

18. E. C. Purcell, *Life and letters of Ambrose Phillipps de Lisle*, II, 204.

19. Birmingham Oratory letters, V, No. 69.

20. Purcell, *op. cit.*, II, 205.

21. F. to N., 5.6.48.

22. Ibid., 12.6.48.

23. Ibid., Easter Monday 1847.

24. To W.R., 13.11.46; Vol. 21, No. 7.

25. Vol. 21, No. 76; St Edward's day 1847.

26. To W.R., 23.9.47; No. 9.

27. Ibid., 11.12.47; No. 10.

28. Ibid., 11.2.48; No. 11.

29. Bowden, 292–4. *Dolman's Magazine*, Sept. 1848.

30. F. to N., 6.10.48.

31. Life of Newman, *op. cit.*, I, 208, 9; 22.10.48.

32. F. to N., 25.10.48.

33. N. to F., 27.10.48.

34. Ward's *Life of Wiseman*, II, 223.

35. Ibid., 224.

36. B. Ward. *Sequel to Catholic Emancipation*, II, 250–1.

37. Ibid., II, 249.

38. Cuthbert Butler, *Bishop Ullathorne*, I, 155–6 (and Ward's *Newman*, I, 212).

39. Butler, *op. cit.*, I, 156–7.

40. Ward's *Newman*, I, 213.

41. *Sequel to Catholic Emancipation*, II, 252.

42. Letter to Rev. E. B. Pusey; p. 374 in 4th ed. of *Difficulties felt by Anglicans in Catholic teachings*.

CHAPTER X

1. F. to N., 24.7.48.

2. Ibid., undated Letter, p. 150.

3. Ward's *Newman*, I, 202–4.

4. N. to F., 4.2.49.

5. F. to N., 5.2.49.

6. Ward's *Newman*.

7. F. to N., 31.1.49.

8. N. to F., 10.2.49.

9. F. to N., 10.2.49.

10. N. to F., 11.2.49.

11. F. to N., 11 and 12.2.49.

12. N. to F., 20.2.49.

13. F. to N., 21.2.49.

14. Ward's *Newman*, I, 217.

15. F. to N., 1.4.49.

16. F. to N., 6.4.49.

17. *Sequel to Catholic Emancipation*, II, 254; no date.

CHAPTER XI

1. F. to N., 16.4.49.

2. Ibid., 18.4.49.

3. Ibid., 21.4.49.

4. Ibid., 24.4.49.

5. Ibid., 25.4.49.

6. Ibid., 26.4.49.

7. Ibid., 27.4.49.

8. Ibid., 29.4.49.

9. Ibid., 16.5.49.

10. N. to H., but with Faber letters, p. 90.

11. Quoted in "The Oratory in London", Brompton Oratory magazine.

12. H. to N., 16.5.49.

13. "Oratory in London."

14. N. to F., 12.5.49.

15. Ibid., 15.5.49.

16. F. to N., before 18.5.49.
17. N. to F., 17.5.49.
18. F. to N., 18.5.49.
19. N. to F., 22.5.49.
20. F. to N., 25.5.49.
21. Ibid.
22. Ibid., 28.5.49.
23. Quoted in "The Oratory in London" in The Oratory Parish magazine. The quotations are not always verbally accurate. It is by Father R. Kerr.
24. F. to N., 4.6.49.
25. Ibid., 6.6.49.
26. Ibid., 8.6.49.
27. Ibid.
28. Ibid., 19 and 26.6.49.
29. Ibid., 27.6.49.
30. Ibid., end of June '49.
31. Ibid., 5.7.49.
32. Ibid., 6.7.49.
33. B. Ferrey, *Recollections of A. N. Welby Pugin*, 127.
34. F. to N., 18.10.49.
35. Ibid., 13.11.49.
36. Bowden, 316–7; 21.11.49.
37. F. to N., 31.10.49.
38. F. to N., 9.7.49.
39. Ibid., *c.* July 49.
40. Ibid., 14.8.49.
41. Ibid., 15.8.49.
42. F. to N., 6.9.49.
43. "Oratory in London."
44. F. to N., in July; p. 90. It does not seem possible to decide what hymn is referred to.
45. Bowden, 318. Newman to John Bowden, 27.2.50.
46. F. to N., 4.12.49.
47. Ibid., 4.11.50.
48. Ibid., 6.11.50.
49. Ibid., 10.11.50.
50. F. to Watts Russell, 15.11.50.
51. F. to N., 5.5.51.

Chapter XII

1. F. to N., 29.12.49.
2. D. to N., 31.12.49.
3. Ibid., 19.6.49.
4. N. to F., 20.6.49.
5. Ibid., 22.6.49.
6. F. to N., 23.6.49.
7. N. to F., 22.7.50.

8. F. to N., 23.6.49.
9. Ibid., 10.9.49.
10. Ibid.
11. D. to N., marked as *c.* 4th Oct. 1850, but clearly it is before 1.10.50.
12. Note to "The Oratory in London", p. 120–1; 1.10.50.
13. Ibid., no date.
14. N. to F., 8.5.51.
15. F. to N., 27.5.51.
16. Ibid., 14.10.51.
17. N. to F., 15.10.51.
18. Vol. 16, *Archiv. Cong. Orat. Lond.*, Letters from abroad, All Saints 1851.
19. Bowden, 330.
20. D. to N., St Thomas '51.
21. Ibid., 27.12.51.
22. D. to N., no conclusive date; p. 114.
23. H. to N., 29.12.51.
24. Note to "The Oratory in London" (pp. 135–6).
25. D. to N., *c.* 28.12.51, probably later.
26. N. to F., 30.12.51.
27. F. to N., 31.12.51.
28. N. to H., Cong. Orat. Lond., 118; no date.
29. F. to N., 10.1.52.
30. H. to N., 23.1.52.
31. F. to B., 22.1.52.
32. "The Oratory in London" (p. 140).
33. F. to N., 22.9.52.
34. F. to B. 17.2.60.
35. Note to "The Oratory in London" (p. 169).
36. "The Oratory in London" (pp. 169–70).
37. Ibid., Note p. 169.
38. *Southwark Record*, Nov. 1924.
39. "The Oratory in London" (p. 177).
40. Ibid., Annotations, 179.

CHAPTER XIII

1. F. to H. Simply marked H[ither G[reen] Saturday; Vol. 19, No. 8.
2. N. to F., 28.9.53.
3. F. to N., 29.9.53.
4. D. to N., 29 or 30.9.53.
5. F. to N., 3.10.53.
6. N. to F., 4.10.53.
7. F. to N., 5.10.53. 2nd sentence altered to make sense.
8. N. to F., 4 and 5.10.53.
9. N. to H., undated 5.10.53.
10. H. to St J., 3.10.53.

The rest of the letters in this chapter are to be found in MS B. by Father R. Stanton with additions by Fathers Kerr and Bellasis. I have also used Father

Kerr's annotations in "The Oratory in London" and letters in the archives of the Birmingham Oratory. These last are marked with an asterisk.

11. This paper is quoted by F. Kerr in his notes to "The Oratory in London".
12. Letters from Rome, No. 8, 23.8.56.
13. As note 11.
14. As note 11.

Chapter XIV

1. *Precious Blood*, 212–3.
2. *Bethlehem*, 323.
3. *The Creator and the Creature*, 2nd ed., 46–7.
4. *Bethlehem*, 281.
5. Ibid., 139.
6. Ibid., 125.
7. *The Creator and the Creature*, 2nd ed., 88–9.
8. Ibid., 165.
9. Ibid., 173.
10. Ibid., 218.
11. Ibid., 295.
12. *Spiritual Conferences*, 2nd ed., 400.
13. *Bethlehem*, 281.
14. *The Creator and the Creature*, 2nd ed., X.
15. Ibid., 170.
16. Ibid., 196.
17. *Bethlehem*, 449–50.
18. *The Creator and the Creature*, X.
19. *All for Jesus*, 16th ed., 173–4.
20. Ibid., 194–6.
21. Ibid., 31–3.
22. *Precious Blood*, 217.
23. *Bethlehem*, 425.
24. *All for Jesus*, 16th ed., 52.
25. Ibid., 53.
26. Ibid., 202.
27. Ibid., 90, 1.
28. *Foot of the Cross*, 449.
29. *Blessed Sacrament*, 3rd ed., 506.
30. *All for Jesus*, 16th ed., 340.
31. *Blessed Sacrament*, 414.
32. *All for Jesus*, 16th ed., 339.
33. Ibid., 53.
34. Ibid., 206.
35. Ibid., 53.
36. Ibid., 40.
37. Ibid., 85.
38. *Growth in Holiness*, 27, 28.
39. *Blessed Sacrament*, 3rd ed., 344.

40. Ibid., 327.
41. Ibid., 267.
42. Ibid., 301.
43. Ibid., 305.
44. Ibid., 322.
45. Ibid., 353–4.
46. Ibid., 395–6.
47. Ibid., 397–8.
48. Ibid., 402.
49. Ibid., 418–9.
50. *The Creator and the Creature*, 2nd ed., 11.
51. Ibid., 169.
52. Ibid., 170.
53. Ibid., 442.
54. *Spiritual Conferences*, 177.
55. *Bethlehem*, 58.
56. Ibid., 245.
57. Ibid., 22.
58. Ibid., 23.
59. Ibid., 29.
60. Ibid., 23–4.
61. Ibid., 524–5.

CHAPTER XV

1. To Hutchison, 23.9.57. Book 19, No. 10.
2. F. to N., Purification and 6.2.54.
3. F. to Lady G. Fullerton, 21, No. 123.
4. "The Oratory in London."
5. Ibid.
6. To Bowden, 29.1.62.
7. W. Ward, *W. G. Ward and the Catholic revival*, reissue 1912, 61–6.
8. Bowden, 407.
9. *Essays and addresses*, 2nd ser., 232.
10. Bowden, 349–50.
11. "The Oratory in London."
12. Bowden, 355.
13. Ibid., 357–61.
14. "The Oratory in London."
15. Bowden, 426–32.
16. To J. Bowden, 1.9.60.
17. "The Oratory in London."
18. Bowden, 434–40.
19. "The Oratory in London."
20. Bowden, 437–9.
21. F. to N., 29.11.60.
22. Notes to "Oratory in London", 245.
23. Letter to F. Herbert Harrison, Book 19, No. 99; no date.

24. Birmingham Archives.
25. Book 19. Various.
26. To Bowden, 3.8.63.
27. Bowden, 442–3.
28. "The Oratory in London."
29. Ibid.
30. Bowden, 445.
31. Ibid., 445–6.
32. Notes to "Oratory in London". Letter to Dalgairns, 27.9.63.
33. *Difficulties felt by Anglicans*, II, 4th ed., 375.
34. Ward's *Newman*, 2nd impr., II, 91, 100.
35. *Ecrits autobiographiques*, II, 388–400.
36. E. Bellasis in the *Month*, Sept. 1891. Cardinal Newman as a musician.
37. *Saturday Review*, XVI, 1863, 488.
38. Bowden, 447.

INDEX